Student Study Guide

for use with

Psychology
An Introduction

Eighth Edition

Benjamin B. Lahey
University of Chicago

Prepared by
Steven A. Schneider
Pima Community College

Boston   Burr Ridge, IL   Dubuque, IA   Madison, WI   New York   San Francisco   St. Louis
Bangkok   Bogotá   Caracas   Kuala Lumpur   Lisbon   London   Madrid   Mexico City
Milan   Montreal   New Delhi   Santiago   Seoul   Singapore   Sydney   Taipei   Toronto

The **McGraw·Hill** Companies

Student Study Guide for use with
PSYCHOLOGY: AN INTRODUCTION
Benjamin B. Lahey

Published by McGraw-Hill, an imprint of The McGraw-Hill Companies, Inc., 1221 Avenue of the Americas, New York, NY 10020. Copyright © 2004, 2001, 1998 by The McGraw-Hill Companies, Inc. All rights reserved.

1 2 3 4 5 6 7 8 9 0 QPD/QPD 0 9 8 7 6 5 4 3

ISBN 0-07-256315-X

www.mhhe.com

Contents

Tips for Successful Studying

Some students take an introductory psychology course because they are considering psychology as a major; others take it because it is a required course for another major; still others take psychology out of a general interest and curiosity about their fellow human beings. Whatever the reason, whatever your major, you are certain to find some topics in this course to be most interesting. Biology/pre-med students will find the chapters dealing with biological psychology and sensation and perception to be particularly interesting. Education majors, parents, and future parents will find the developmental psychology chapter applicable and interesting. Are you interested in health, diet, and exercise? If so, you will find the health psychology chapter to be intriguing. You don't have to be a social scientist to wonder whether intelligence tests are valid, how the human memory system works, what causes mental disorders, or what attracts people to each other. These issues and many others will be explored in your introductory psychology course.

I have taught thousands of introductory psychology students over the past 20 years, and I would like to share some observations about students who succeed in the course and those who fail to live up to their (and my) expectations in the course.

1. Successful students are well organized. Some of my most successful students have been some of my busiest students—those with part-time or full-time jobs, parents with many familial obligations, and students carrying heavy course loads. Their ability to organize their lives and to manage their time, however, allowed them to accomplish their tasks efficiently and effectively. To be well organized, you should use a semester calendar that clearly indicates deadlines for papers, exam dates, and other important dates. Keep your course outlines in a safe place so that you can refer to them during the semester. Be certain that you know the office hours and office phone numbers of your instructors. Make and adhere to a weekly schedule for yourself that builds in all the important activities, including class time, work time, study time, *and* relaxation time.

2. Successful students come to class. As you begin college, one difference you may note from your previous educational experiences is that your instructor may not take attendance. That doesn't signify a lack of concern on the part of your instructor—after all, it's *your* tuition and textbook money. What it does mean is that you are responsible for the decision to come to class or not. Both casual observation and the results of research studies show that students who attend class do better than those who don't attend.

3. Read the material before going to class. My most successful students over the years generally read the text before coming to class. They had a pretty good idea what the lecture was going to be about. This also helped them organize their note taking while in class.

4. Take good notes and review them. In your efforts to be a good learner, it is usually a mistake to try to take down everything that is said in class. Instead, try to outline the lecture, using Roman numerals and letters for the major and minor points. This technique can be particularly effective if the instructor lectures from an outline. Review your notes as soon after class as possible. It is somewhat dismaying while studying for an exam to see class notes in your handwriting that you don't even remember writing.

5. Focus on key terms and concepts. A large and important part of most introductory courses consists of learning the language of the field you are studying. This is necessary in order to communicate with and to think like the professionals in the field. When you study, therefore, you need to learn the language of psychology. You are likely to be tested on the terminology and, even if you are not tested directly on the terms, you will almost certainly be expected to know and understand them.

6. Consider using the SQ3R method for studying. The SQ3R method of studying is a tried and tested technique. Research conducted with students who use this technique indicates significantly greater comprehension of text material. This is how it works:

Survey: Although the temptation when you begin studying is to open the text and begin reading, this technique suggests that you should first get an overview of the material. Read the chapter outline (found in the text) and the chapter overview (found in this study guide). Skim through the text, noting the major headings as well as the charts and pictures. This activity will allow you to get a feel for the chapter, as well as to see how the chapter is organized.

Question: As you survey the chapter, begin noting questions about the material. You may use the Learning Objectives section in this study guide to help you formulate questions about the text. The questions that you formulate will help you pick out the most important parts of the text as you read.

Read: When you have formulated questions, reading the text now becomes purposeful; that is, you are reading in order to answer the questions. As you find the material that answers your questions, consider highlighting it or marking an *X* in the margin. Consider taking notes on the major points as you read the text.

Recite: After you have finished a section of the text, stop and state the answers to the questions in your own words (not the author's). This will help give you practice pronouncing some difficult terminology and will test whether the material you have just learned makes sense to you. Recitation is also a very efficient system; material that has been recited is generally remembered longer than material not recited.

Review: Virtually everyone who sees a movie for the second time comments that the experience was much different from the first viewing. People often say they "got something completely different" from seeing the movie a second time. A similar situation exists when reading a chapter of your text. Review the material soon after reading it. You may test yourself by working through the guided review for each chapter that is included in this study guide. Try to answer the multiple-choice questions in the study guide. These are keyed to the learning objectives found at the beginning of each study guide chapter.

7. Prepare for exams. The most widespread method used by instructors to assess what you have learned is to give an exam. Whereas some students welcome the challenge, for many it provides an exercise in terror. Test anxiety is widely recognized to be a major problem for many students. Some hints for preparing for and taking exams can help. Find out as much as you can about the exam beforehand (remaining, of course, within the bounds of the student code of conduct!). What material will be covered? Will it be multiple-choice, essay, fill-in, or matching? How much time will be allotted? How much weight will be given to various topics? The answers to these questions should help guide your preparation for the exam. Try to always study in the same place and on a regular basis. Your study area should be quiet, well-lit and should contain minimal distractions. Use your study area only for studying. Generally speaking, you study most efficiently when you study alone. Take breaks when you study. Studying is a fatiguing activity, and most students can benefit from a short break every 20 minutes or so. It is certainly time to take a break when you reach the end of a page and then realize you haven't retained a word on the page. Take a break instead of fighting it. The type of test for which you are preparing should dictate how you prepare—for example, study for an essay exam by asking yourself essay questions and writing out good answers. Prepare for a multiple-choice exam by answering multiple-choice questions (be sure to review those in the study guide). Solid preparation, a good night's sleep the night before an exam, and relaxing instead of cramming just prior to the exam should help minimize test anxiety. If your anxiety is severe, seek the advice of a counselor. Many colleges offer courses designed to help deal with test anxiety.

The Harrisburg Area Community College (PA) Student Advisory Board performed a thorough review of the previous edition's *Student Study Guide* material, and contributed toward the improvements you will find in this edition. I hope that you find this *Student Study Guide* to be a helpful resource. I welcome your comments, opinions, and further suggestions for improvements. My address is Steve Schneider, c/o Psychology Department, Pima Community College, 2202 W. Anklam Rd., Tucson, AZ 85709. My e-mail address is steve.schneider@pima.edu.

To the Student: Before You Begin

This *Student Study Guide* has been written to assist you as you read the Eighth edition of *Psychology: An Introduction* by Benjamin B. Lahey. This guide will help you to learn the essential concepts, facts, and theories that are covered in the text; please remember, however, that it is not intended to be used as a substitute for the textbook. This study guide should be used to help you identify essential information, to help you review, to indicate the gaps in your learning, to stimulate your thinking about the ideas in the text, and to test what you have learned. Each chapter of the *Student Study Guide* is divided into the following sections:

Learning Objectives

You can use the learning objectives in two different ways. First, examine the objectives *before* you read the chapter to get an overview of the major topics that will be covered in the text. Pay attention to the terms, concepts, and names mentioned in the objectives. Second, after you have completed reading the chapter, return to the objectives; you should now be able to perform the activities listed in the objectives. You may write your responses to the objectives in the space provided. If you find an objective that seems unclear to you, return to the text and reread that section. The page numbers following each objective refer to the location of the material in the text.

Chapter Overview

The chapter overview is a relatively brief survey of the material in the chapter. It should be read before and after you read the text. The first reading will help to prepare you for the topics covered in the textbook. The second reading will help you to see how the information you have just read in the chapter fits together.

Key Terms Exercise and Who Am I?

The key terms exercise is intended to test your understanding of the key terms that are listed at the beginning of each chapter in the textbook. These matching exercises are grouped according to topic; therefore, some exercises contain only a few terms while others contain more. For your convenience, the key terms are page-referenced to the textbook, and the correct answers immediately follow each exercise. To get the maximum benefit from this activity, keep the answers covered until you have completed all the answers.

Some chapters contain the names of a large number of psychologists. The "Who Am I?" exercise will test your ability to match the names of the psychologists with their contributions to the field. As with the key terms exercise, page references to the text follow the names of the psychologists, and the correct answers immediately follow each exercise (remember to keep the answers covered while you do the exercise).

Review At A Glance

The review at a glance is designed to be a challenging and comprehensive fill-in-the-blanks exercise. The answers are found in the Answer Section that appears later in the chapter. This exercise will help point out the terms or sections of the text you need to review. When all of the blanks have been correctly filled in, you will have a thorough summary of the chapter for future reference and review.

Concept Checks

These fill-in exercises are designed to allow you to check your understanding of several important concepts from each chapter.

Extending the Chapter

This section contains questions from the "Application of Psychology" section of the text and other questions that relate the text material to personal issues, societal issues, and so on. Please note that many of these questions are asking for your opinion about issues; hence, there are no right or wrong answers.

Practice Quiz

The practice quiz consists of three sections:

1) *Short answer questions*, with sample answers provided in the Answer section.

2) *Multiple-choice questions*, with expanded answers provided in the Answer section. One important note: The multiple-choice questions correspond to the learning objectives found at the beginning of every Study Guide chapter. If you miss a multiple-choice question, you might want to review the corresponding learning objective.

3) *True-False questions*, with answers provided at the end of the Answer section.

Part I   Introduction

Chapter 1   What Is Psychology?

Learning Objectives

1. Describe Aristotle's role in the history of psychology and understand the definition of psychology. (p. 4)

2. Identify and define the four goals of psychology. (p. 5)

3. Identify and compare early views of psychology that focused on the elements of conscious experience, including those of Wundt, Titchener, Alston, and Gestalt psychology. (p. 7)

4. Identify and compare views in psychology that focused on the functions of the conscious mind, including those of James, Ebbinghaus, Calkins, and Binet. Also, explain functionalism's influence on contemporary cognitive psychology. (p. 9)

5. Describe the origins of behaviorism and social learning theory. (p. 11)

6. Identify the early views of psychology that focused on the nature of the unconscious mind. (p. 13)

7. Describe the neuroscience, sociocultural, and evolutionary perspectives and explain their influence on contemporary psychology. (p. 15)

8.   Identify and define the terms associated with the sociocultural perspective. (p. 17)

9. Describe how sociocultural factors influenced the history of psychology. (p. 19)

10. Describe the differences between basic and applied areas of psychology; list and describe examples of both areas. (p. 22)

11. Describe the relationship between psychology and psychiatry. (p. 24)

12. Identify the beliefs commonly shared by psychologists about human nature and behavior. (p. 26)

Chapter Overview

Psychology is defined as the science of behavior and mental processes. Psychology is considered to be a science because psychologists acquire knowledge through systematic observation. The four main goals of psychology are to describe, predict, understand, and influence behavior and mental processes.

The influential early psychologists and their areas of interest include Wilhelm Wundt, Edward Titchener and J. Henry Alston (structuralism); Max Wertheimer (Gestalt psychology); William James (functionalism); Hermann Ebbinghaus and Mary Whiton Calkins (human memory); Alfred Binet (measurement of intelligence); Ivan Pavlov, John B. Watson, and Margaret Floy Washburn (behaviorism); and Sigmund Freud (psychoanalysis). Humanistic psychologists believe that humans determine their own fates through the decisions they make.

Although some contemporary behaviorists continue to rule out the study of mental processes, other behaviorists, like Bandura, stress the importance of cognition. Contemporary psychoanalysts continue to emphasize unconscious conflicts, but suggest that motives other than sex and aggression are important.

A contemporary approach, the neuroscience perspective, studies the relationship between the nervous system, heredity, hormones, and behavior. A contemporary perspective that emphasizes culture, gender, and ethnic factors is the sociocultural perspective. Another contemporary perspective that emphasizes the role of natural selection in behavior is the evolutionary perspective. Although the number of women and ethnic minorities in psychology has grown dramatically in recent years, prejudice still plays a negative role in psychology as in all scientific and professional fields.

Modern psychologists work in basic or applied fields. Psychologists who work in basic areas conduct basic research, whereas applied psychologists put psychological knowledge to work helping people in a variety of settings.

Most psychologists would agree with the following statements:

1. Human beings are biological creatures.
2. Each person is unique, yet the same.
3. People can be understood only by taking into account their culture, ethnic identity, and gender identity.
4. Human lives are in a continual process of change.
5. Behavior is motivated, not random or aimless.
6. Humans are social animals working together in groups.
7. People play an active part in choosing their experiences and constructing perceptions.
8. Behavior can be either adaptive or maladaptive.

Key Terms Exercise

For each of the following exercises, match the key terms on the left with the correct definitions on the right. Page references to the text follow the terms so that you may refer to the text for any items you answer incorrectly or do not understand completely. You may check your responses immediately by referring to the answers that follow each exercise.

Psyche and Science Psychology

_____ 1. psychology (p. 5)
_____ 2. behavior (p. 5)
_____ 3. mental processes (p. 5)
_____ 4. theory (p. 5)
_____ 5. introspection (p. 7)

a. private thoughts, emotions, feelings, and motives that others cannot directly observe
b. looking inward at one's own consciousness
c. observable and measurable human action
d. a tentative explanation of facts and relationships in science
e. the science of behavior and mental processes

ANSWERS

1. e	4. d
2. c	5. b
3. a	

The Many Viewpoints in Psychology and Their Origins

_____ 1. structuralism (p. 8)
_____ 2. Gestalt psychology (p. 8)
_____ 3. functionalism (p. 9)
_____ 4. cognition (p. 11)
_____ 5. cognitive psychology (p. 11)
_____ 6. psychometrics (p. 11)
_____ 7. behaviorism (p. 12)
_____ 8. social learning theory (p. 12)
_____ 9. psychoanalysis (p. 13)
_____ 10. humanistic psychology (p. 14)

a. the approach that believes people control their own fates
b. the school of psychology that emphasized the functions of consciousness
c. an approach that emphasizes learning and the measurement of behavior
d. an approach that emphasizes the whole is different than the sum of its parts
e. techniques based on Sigmund Freud's theory of the unconscious
f. the school of psychology that used introspection to determine the structure of the mind
g. intellectual processes of perceiving, believing, thinking, and so on
h. states that most of our behaviors are learned from others in society
i. viewpoint that emphasizes such cognitive processes as perception, memory, and thinking
j. the perspective focusing on the measurement of mental functions

ANSWERS

1. f	6. j
2. d	7. c
3. b	8. h
4. g	9. e
5. i	10. a

Contemporary Perspectives

_____ 1. neuroscience perspective (p. 16)
_____ 2. sociocultural perspective (p. 17)
_____ 3. culture (p. 17)
_____ 4. ethnic group (p. 17)
_____ 5. ethnic identity (p. 17)
_____ 6. gender identity (p. 17)
_____ 7. cultural relativity (p. 18)
_____ 8. evolutionary psychology (p. 20)
_____ 9. applied psychologist (p. 22)

a. a group of persons who are descendants from a common group of ancestors
b. an approach that emphasizes one's culture, ethnic identity, and gender identity
c. thinking about other cultures in relative terms rather than in judgmental terms
d. patterns of behavior, beliefs, and values shared by a group of people
e. a person's sense of belonging to a particular ethnic group
f. one's view of oneself as male or female
g. a psychologist who uses psychological knowledge to prevent and to solve human problems
h. the viewpoint that emphasizes the nervous system in explaining behavior and mental disorders
i. this viewpoint, based on the work of Charles Darwin, emphasizes the role of natural selection

ANSWERS

1. h	6. f
2. b	7. c
3. d	8. i
4. a	9. g
5. e	

Who Am I?

Match the psychologists on the left with their contributions to the field of psychology on the right. Page references to the text follow the names of the psychologists so that you may refer to the text for further review of these psychologists and their contributions. You may check your responses immediately by referring to the answers that follow each exercise.

Part I

_____ 1. Aristotle (p. 4)
_____ 2. J. Henry Alston (p. 8)
_____ 3. William James (p. 9)
_____ 4. Alfred Binet (p. 11)
_____ 5. John B. Watson (p. 12)
_____ 6. Albert Bandura (p. 12)

a. I taught the first course on psychology and founded the functionalist approach to psychology.
b. I was a philosopher who believed in the importance of observation.
c. I am a cognitive behaviorist who believes mental processes can't be ignored.
d. At the request of the Paris Ministry of Education, I developed the first tests to measure intelligence.
e. I believed that only outward behavior can be studied, and I founded the behaviorist approach to psychology.
f. I am best known for my research on heat and cold sensations and for being the first African-American to publish research in an APA journal.

ANSWERS

1. b	4. d
2. f	5. e
3. a	6. c

Part II

_____ 1. Wilhelm Wundt (p. 7)
_____ 2. Max Wertheimer (p. 8)
_____ 3. Hermann Ebbinghaus (p. 10)
_____ 4. Mary Whiton Calkins (p. 10)
_____ 5. Ivan Pavlov (p. 11)
_____ 6. B. F. Skinner (p. 12)
_____ 7. Sigmund Freud (p. 13)

a. I studied perception and helped found the Gestalt approach to psychology.
b. As a behaviorist, I believed that learning shapes our behavior.
c. I opened the Laboratory of Psychology in Leipzig, Germany, in 1879 and used a technique called introspection.
d. I developed a method to study memory called the paired associates method.
e. My techniques of psychoanalysis helped patients to explore their unconscious minds.
f. My work with salivating dogs led to the discovery of classical conditioning.
g. I did a series of important experiments on human memory.

ANSWERS

1. c	5. f
2. a	6. b
3. g	7. e
4. d	

Review At A Glance
(Answers to this section are found on page 15)

Psyche and Science = Psychology: Definition of Psychology

The ancient Greek philosopher Aristótle used the term ___(1)___ to refer to the essence of life. Aristotle believed that psyche escaped as a person took his last dying ___(2)___.

Psychology is defined as the science of ___(3)___ and ___(4)___ processes. Modern psychology uses careful, controlled observation and therefore is considered to be a ___(5)___. Psychologists study the overt actions of people who can be directly observed; these actions are referred to as ___(6)___. Psychologists also study thoughts, feelings, and motives that cannot be directly observed; these are referred to as mental ___(7)___.

Goals of Psychology

The goals of psychology are to ___(8)___, ___(9)___, ___(10)___, and ___(11)___ behavior and mental processes. Although psychology is a science, current explanations are always subject to revision. These tentative explanations of facts and relationships are known as ___(12)___.

The Many Viewpoints in Psychology and Their Origins

Psychology, like other sciences, emerged from the general field of ___(13)___. In 1879, Wilhelm ___(14)___ founded a psychological laboratory in Leipzig, Germany. Wundt and his student, Edward ___(15)___ studied consciousness using a method of looking inward at one's own experiences; this technique is called ___(16)___. Wundt and his followers were interested in the elements and structures of the mind; they were thus called ___(17)___. An early structuralist named J. Henry Alston studied the sensations of ___(18)___ and ___(19)___. Alston is the first African-American researcher to ___(20)___ an article in a journal of the APA.

In Germany, Max Wertheimer and his associates popularized a different approach to the study of consciousness, called ___(21)___ psychology. They believed that the mind could not be broken down into raw elements because the ___(22)___ is different than the sum of its parts. Gestalt psychologists demonstrated their approach with examples of apparent movement, called the ___(23)___ phenomenon.

The first course on psychology was taught in 1875 by William ___(24)___. He believed that the process of consciousness helps the human species to ___(25)___. His approach, which emphasized the purposes or functions of consciousness, is called ___(26)___.

In Germany, Hermann Ebbinghaus applied the scientific method to the study of human ___(27)___. Ebbinghaus's research involved the use of ___(28)___ syllables. In the United States, Mary Whiton Calkins developed the ___(29)___ method to study memory. The influence of functionalism is seen today in the study of ___(30)___ psychology.

In France during the 1890s, Albert Binet and others sought to measure the mind's ___(31)___ capacities. Binet's approach is known as ___(32)___.

In the 1890s, Russian physiologist Ivan Pavlov identified a simple form of learning called ____(33)____. Pavlov's ideas were popularized in the United States by John B. Watson and Margaret Floy Washburn, who believed that only ___(34)___ behavior could be scientifically understood. The school of psychology based on the ideas of Pavlov, Watson, and Washburn is called ____(35)____. Most contemporary behavioral psychologists integrate the study of behavior with the study of ____(36)____. Albert Bandura is associated with this viewpoint, also called _____(37)_____ theory.

Sigmund Freud was an influential founder of psychology who believed that conscious experiences were not as important as the ____(38)____ mind. He believed the roots of psychological problems involved ____(39)____ and ____(40)____ motives. The process Freud formulated to help people with psychological problems is called ____(41)____. Modern psychoanalysts still believe that unconscious ____(42)____ are the chief source of psychological problems; however, many psychoanalysts also stress the importance of other motives as well.

Abraham Maslow and Carl Rogers have popularized the ____(43)____ approach, which holds that humans determine their own fates through the decisions they make.

Contemporary Perspectives in Psychology

Psychologists who are interested in the role played by the brain in such areas as emotion, reasoning, and speaking are approaching psychology from the ____(44)____ perspective. A contemporary perspective that emphasizes cultural, gender, and ethnic factors is called the ____(45)____ perspective. The patterns of behavior, beliefs, and values shared by a group of people is referred to as ____(46)____. A group of people who descended from a common group of ancestors is called an ____(47)____ group. A person's sense of belonging to a particular ethnic group is referred to as ethnic ____(48)____. A person's view of himself or herself as male or female is called ____(49)____. The sociocultural perspective encourages the view of other cultures as being different rather than inferior; this view is called cultural ____(50)____. The sociocultural perspective also emphasizes ____(51)____ differences among members of different ethnic groups, cultures, and genders.

For many years the field of psychology was dominated by ____(52)_____. Until recently, the contributions of women and ____(53)_____ were ignored in most textbooks. Although the number of women and ethnic minorities in psychology has grown in recent years, ____(54)____ continues to play a negative role in psychology.

A contemporary perspective that emphasizes the role of natural selection in behavior is called the____(55)____ perspective. According to this perspective, differing evolutionary pressures on females and males account for many of our ____(56)____ differences.

Martin Seligman used his influence as president of the American Psychological Association to urge psychologists to focus on ____(57)____ psychology.

Specialty Areas of Modern Psychology

Psychologists who work in ____(58)____ areas conduct research. Psychologists who use basic knowledge to solve and prevent human problems are called ____(59)____ psychologists.

The largest specialties within experimental psychology are (1) ___(60)___ psychology, which studies the nervous system and its relationship to behavior; (2) ___(61)___ and ___(62)___, which studies how the sense organs operate and how we interpret information; (3) ___(63)___ and ___(64)___, which focuses on the ways in which we acquire and remember information; (4) ___(65)___, which studies intelligent action; (5) ___(66)___ psychology, which focuses on changes during the lifespan; (6) ___(67)___ and ___(68)___, which studies needs and states that activate behavior, as well as feelings and moods; (7) ___(69)___, the field that focuses on our consistent ways of behaving; (8) ___(70)___ psychology, the area that studies the influence of others on our behavior, and (9) the area that focuses on ethnic, cultural, and gender issues, ___(71)___ psychology.

The majority of psychologists are ___(72)___ psychologists. The major specialties within applied psychology are (1) ___(73)___ psychology, the field concerned with personal problems and abnormal behavior; (2) ___(74)___ psychology, which focuses on personal or school problems and career choices; (3) ___(75)___ - _____ psychology, which deals with work-related psychological issues; (4) ___(76)___ and school psychology, which focuses on learning and other school-related issues; and (5) ___(77)___ psychology, which studies the relationship between psychology and health.

A ___(78)___ has completed an M.D., whereas a psychologist has been trained in psychology and allied fields but has not attended medical school. The specialty within psychology that is most similar to psychiatry is ___(79)___ psychology. Although most states regulate the practice of ___(80)___ _____, psychiatry, and social work, other helping professions are generally not regulated.

What We Know About Human Behavior: Some Starting Places

Although psychology is a diverse field, most contemporary psychologists would agree with the following basic ideas:

1. People are influenced to a large extent by factors such as heredity and the nervous system; that is, humans are ___(81)___ creatures.

2. Although every human is unique, we have similar capacities to think, feel, etc. Therefore, every person is ___(82)___, yet much the ___(83)___.

3. As the sociocultural perspective implies, people can be fully understood only in the context of their culture, ___(84)___ identity, and ___(85)___ identity.

4. Our constant developmental changes and life experiences mean that human lives are in a continual process of ___(86)___.

5. People do things for reasons; that is, behavior is ___(87)___.

6. People need to have contact with each other; we are ___(88)___ animals.

7. People are not passive; we play an ___(89)___ role in creating our experiences.

8. Although we are usually able to adjust to the challenges of life, sometimes we act in harmful ways; behavior can be either ___(90)___ or ___(91)___.

Concept Checks

Fill in the missing components of the following concept boxes. The correct answers are located in the "Answers" section at the end of the chapter.

Early Approaches to Psychology

Approach	Focus	Key Names
structuralism		Wundt, Titchener, Alston
	human consciousness cannot be broken down into its elements; the phi phenomenon illustrates the "whole is different than the sum of its parts"	
functionalism		William James
	measurement of mental functions such as intelligence, personality, and others	
behaviorism		Pavlov, Watson, Washburn

Contemporary Perspectives

Perspective	Focus
social learning theory	
	emphasizes the importance of culture, ethnic identity, and gender identity
humanistic perspective	
	emphasizes the relationship between the nervous system, hormonal and genetic factors, and behavior
evolutionary perspective	
	conflicts in the unconscious mind are the main source of psychological problems
cognitive perspective	

Extending the Chapter: Psychology, Societal Issues, and Human Diversity

These questions may be assigned to you. Whether or not they are assigned, they are designed to be challenging questions to encourage you to think independently about the material in the chapter. Many of the questions have no right or wrong answers.

1. Which contemporary approach to psychology makes the most sense to you? Why?

2. A high-school freshman takes her first puff on a cigarette. How might the following perspectives view this behavior: social learning theory, humanistic theory, the neuroscience perspective, and the sociocultural perspective?

3. Describe the advantages and disadvantages of being a member of an individualistic culture. (You may substitute collectivist culture, if you are more familiar with a collectivist culture.)

4. How do the various perspectives view the issue of responsibility for one's own behavior?

Practice Quiz

The practice quiz consists of three sections: 1) Short answer questions, 2) Multiple-choice questions, and 3) True-False questions. At the end of the chapter you will find suggested answers to the short answer questions, answers and explanations for the multiple-choice questions, and answers to the true-false questions.

Short Answer Questions

1. List and describe the goals of psychology.

   _____

   _____

   _____

2. Explain the concept of cultural relativity.

   _____

   _____

   _____

3. Explain the difference between basic and applied areas of modern psychology; give two examples of each.

   _____

   _____

   _____

Multiple-Choice Questions

1. The author defines psychology as the science of behavior and
   a. mental processes.
   b. overt actions.
   c. phenomena.
   d. observation.
   LO 1

2. Psychology is considered to be a science because psychologists
   a. use logic to develop their theories.
   b. use careful and controlled observation.
   c. can be completely objective in their study of human behavior.
   d. have developed techniques to let them understand private thoughts and emotions.
   LO 1

3. Research that is conducted to find out under what circumstances bystanders will help in a crisis is part of which goal of psychology?
   a. describe
   b. predict
   c. understand
   d. influence
   LO 2

4. Which of the four goals of psychology is achieved when we can explain behavior?
   a. describe
   b. predict
   c. understand
   d. influence
   LO 2

5. Surveys are conducted in order to achieve which of the following goals of psychology?
   a. describe
   b. predict
   c. understand
   d. explain
   LO 2

6. The technique of introspection was essential to which group of psychologists?
   a. Gestalt psychologists
   b. behaviorists
   c. functionalists
   d. structuralists
   LO 3

7. If a man wearing a fake beard and a black academic robe asks you to describe the sensations of biting into an apple,
   a. leave the area immediately.
   b. he's probably a behaviorist trying to condition you.
   c. he's probably a psychoanalyst looking into your unconscious.
   d. he might be a structuralist asking you to do introspection.
   LO 3

8. The phi phenomenon illustrates an important principle for
   a. behaviorists.
   b. Gestalt psychology.
   c. structuralists.
   d. functionalists.
   LO 3

9. What was the focus of structuralism?
   a. mental processes
   b. observable events
   c. unconscious thought
   d. mental elements
   LO 3

10. According to William James, psychology should emphasize
    a. what the mind can do.
    b. the basic structure of the mind.
    c. the factors that have aided our evolution.
    d. both *a* and *c*.
    LO 4

11. Which of the following psychologists developed nonsense syllables to study human memory?
    a. Pavlov
    b. Wertheimer
    c. Ebbinghaus
    d. Watson
    LO 4

12. Psychometrics, a perspective popularized by Binet, focuses on
    a. the measurement of mental functions.
    b. unconscious mental activity.
    c. looking inward at one's own consciousness.
    d. the freedom to determine one's life by the decisions one makes.
    LO 4

13. When Pavlov discovered that his dogs associated the sound of the bell with food, he called this
    a. functionalism.
    b. conditioning.
    c. introspection.
    d. the phi phenomenon,
       LO 5

14. Social learning theory has attempted to integrate the ideas of behaviorism with the study of
    a. the unconscious.
    b. Gestalt psychology.
    c. humanistic psychology.
    d. cognition.
       LO 5

15. Watson's belief that psychology should focus only on overt behavior became the foundation of which perspective?
    a. psychoanalysis
    b. Gestalt psychology
    c. social learning theory
    d. behaviorism
       LO 5

16. Which of the following ideas is most likely to be associated with humanistic psychology?
    a. self-concept
    b. cultural relativism
    c. the phi phenomenon
    d. introspection
       LO 6

17. Unconscious motives are the roots of psychological problems according to
    a. psychoanalysts.
    b. behaviorists.
    c. Gestalt psychologists.
    d. humanistic psychologists.
       LO 6

18. According to Freud, two innate motives that are at the root of psychological problems are sex and
    a. social needs.
    b. physical needs.
    c. guilt.
    d. aggression.
       LO 6

19. In the early 1900s, Ramon y Cajal first identified
    a. the structure of the unconscious.
    b. neurons.
    c. hormones.
    d. the basic principles of heredity.
       LO 7

20. Which of the following is (are) studied in the neuroscience perspective?
    a. the influence of heredity on behavior
    b. the influence of hormones on behavior
    c. the areas of the brain that affect behavior
    d. all of the above
       LO 7

21. In order to fully understand people, it is necessary to understand the beliefs and values of their culture according to
    a. functionalism.
    b. structuralism.
    c. the sociocultural perspective.
    d. the neuroscience perspective.
       LO 7

22. The process of natural selection is central to which of the following perspectives?
    a. sociocultural
    b. evolutionary
    c. neuroscience
    d. social learning
       LO 7

23. Gender identity and ethnic identity are topics that are of most importance to
    a. biological psychologists.
    b. sociocultural psychologists.
    c. humanistic psychologists.
    d. Gestalt psychologists.
       LO 8

24. According to the sociocultural perspective, which of the following refers to a person's sense of belonging to a particular ethnic group?
    a. cultural relativity
    b. ethnic identity
    c. gender identity
    d. racial identity
       LO 8

25. Cultural relativity promotes the idea that
    a. some cultures are more advanced than others.
    b. some cultures operate on a higher moral plane than others.
    c. it is useful to think about different cultures in judgmental terms.
    d. cultures should be thought of as being different rather than superior or inferior.
    LO 8

26. Who completed a doctorate in psychology at Johns Hopkins but was never awarded a degree?
    a. Sigmund Freud
    b. J. Henry Alston
    c. Elizabeth Scarborough
    d. Christine Ladd-Franklin
    LO 9

27. Mamie Phipps Clark and Kenneth Clark were African-American psychologists who conducted research that
    a. influenced a decision by the Supreme Court.
    b. supported the ideas of the structuralists.
    c. discouraged the use of hypnosis.
    d. led to the discovery of the neuron.
    LO 9

28. Research on the self-concept of African-American children, which helped guide the Supreme Court in the *Brown v. Board of Education* ruling, was conducted by
    a. Inez Prosser.
    b. Mamie and Kenneth Clark.
    c. George Sanchez.
    d. Elizabeth Scarborough.
    LO 9

29. According to the text, all of the following are examples of applied psychology *except*
    a. clinical psychology.
    b. developmental psychology.
    c. industrial psychology.
    d. educational psychology.
    LO 10

30. Which of the following is *not* considered a basic area of psychology?
    a. sensation and perception
    b. cognition
    c. counseling psychology
    d. personality
    LO 10

31. A basic area of psychology that studies ways in which our behavior is influenced by other people is called
    a. personality.
    b. motivation and emotion.
    c. social psychology.
    d. developmental psychology.
    LO 10

32. What is the difference between a psychologist and a psychiatrist?
    a. about $25 an hour
    b. A psychiatrist has completed medical school.
    c. A psychologist has completed graduate school in psychology
    d. both *b* and *c*
    LO 11

33. Which of the following has completed medical school and has obtained an M.D. degree?
    a. psychologist
    b. psychiatrist
    c. social worker
    d. clinical psychologist
    LO 11

34. Psychologists generally agree with all of the following statements *except*
    a. human beings are biological creatures.
    b. all behavior is predictable.
    c. every person is different, yet the same.
    d. behavior is motivated.
    LO 12

35. What do we know to be true about human behavior?
    a. Humans are social animals.
    b. People do not have free wills.
    c. It can only be understood by psychologists.
    d. Most human traits are innate.
    LO 12

True-False Questions

_____1. Psychology is defined as the science of behavior and mental processes.

_____2. According to the text, one of the goals of psychology is to control behavior.

_____3. William James was an influential early structuralist.

_____4. Psychometrics focuses on the measurement of mental functions.

_____5. Watson's approach to behaviorism emphasized the importance of cognition.

_____6. Humanistic psychologists believe each person can control his/her own destiny.

_____7. The sociocultural perspective is not as influential as it once was.

_____8. Cognition is an important basic area of psychology.

_____9. There is no real difference in the training of psychologists and psychiatrists.

_____10. Humans play an active role in creating their own experiences.

ANSWERS SECTION

Concept Checks

Early Approaches to Psychology

Approach	Focus	Key Names
structuralism	sought to determine the structure of the mind through introspection	Wundt, Titchener, Alston
Gestalt psychology	human consciousness cannot be broken down into its elements; the phi phenomenon illustrates the "whole is different than the sum of its parts"	Wertheimer
functionalism	emphasized the _functions_ of consciousness, rather than the structure	William James
psychometrics	measurement of mental functions such as intelligence, personality, and others	Binet
behaviorism	psychology should study only overt, measurable behavior	Pavlov, Watson, Washburn

Contemporary Perspectives

Perspective	Focus
social learning theory	behavior is learned from others in society
sociocultural perspective	emphasizes the importance of culture, ethnic identity, and gender identity
humanistic perspective	humans determine their own fates through the decisions they make
neuroscience perspective	emphasizes the relationship between the nervous system, hormonal and genetic factors, and behavior
evolutionary perspective	emphasizes the role of natural selection in explaining and understanding behavior
psychoanalysis	conflicts in the unconscious mind are the main source of psychological problems
cognitive perspective	this perspective emphasizes the processes involving perceiving, believing, thinking, knowing, and so on

Answers to Review At A Glance

1. psyche
2. breath
3. behavior
4. mental
5. science
6. behavior
7. processes
8. describe
9. predict
10. understand
11. influence
12. theories
13. philosophy
14. Wundt
15. Titchener
16. introspection
17. structuralists
18. heat
19. cold
20. publish
21. Gestalt
22. whole
23. phi
24. James
25. survive
26. functionalism
27. memory
28. nonsense
29. paired associates
30. cognitive
31. intellectual

32. psychometrics
33. conditioning
34. outward
35. behaviorism
36. cognition
37. social learning
38. unconscious
39. sexual
40. aggressive
41. psychoanalysis
42. conflicts
43. humanistic
44. biological
45. sociocultural
46. culture
47. ethnic
48. identity
49. gender identity
50. relativity
51. individual
52. white males
53. ethnic minorities
54. prejudice
55. evolutionary
56. gender
57. positive
58. basic
59. applied
60. biological
61. sensation
62. perception

63. learning
64. memory
65. cognition
66. developmental
67. motivation
68. emotion
69. personality
70. social
71. sociocultural
72. applied
73. clinical
74. counseling
75. industrial-organizational
76. educational
77. health
78. psychiatrist
79. clinical
80. clinical psychology
81. biological
82. different
83. same
84. ethnic
85. gender
86. change
87. motivated
88. social
89. active
90. adaptive
91. maladaptive

Sample Answers for Short Answer Questions

1. **List and describe the goals of psychology.**

   The goals of psychology are: 1) to describe psychological phenomena more accurately and completely; 2) to predict future behavior; 3) to understand behavior and mental processes well enough to explain them; and 4) to influence behavior in beneficial ways.

2. **Explain the concept of cultural relativity.**

   The sociocultural perspective emphasizes the concept of cultural relativity. This notion encourages thinking about cultures in relative terms rather than in judgmental terms. It suggests that different cultures, ethnic groups, and genders are different rather than superior or inferior when compared with another.

3. **Explain the difference between basic and applied areas of modern psychology; give two examples of each.**

   Psychologists who work in basic areas generally are involved in research on various psychological processes. These psychologists may spend a good portion of their time in the laboratory and may be interested in confirming or modifying psychological theories. Examples of basic areas include sensation and perception, learning and memory, cognition, and developmental psychology. Applied psychologists seek to use information acquired by basic psychologists to solve and prevent human problems. Applied psychologists also may engage in applied research. Applied areas include clinical psychology, counseling psychology, and industrial-organizational psychology.

Multiple-Choice Answers

1. The answer is *A*. Overt actions are of special interest to behavioral psychologists, and all scientists are interested in the observation of phenomena.
2. The answer is *B*. Logic alone doesn't make for science. Choices C and D are very much debatable.
3. The answer is *B* because the research is attempting to predict behavior. Description of behavior is often accomplished through the use of questionnaires and surveys; understanding behavior implies an explanation of the behavior, while influencing behavior implies that people's behavior is changed in desirable ways.
4. The answer is *C*. We understand behavior when we can *explain* our knowledge of facts and relationships in psychology, in addition to describing and predicting.
5. The answer is *A*. Surveys don't try to influence behavior; they try to take a sort of snapshot of behavior, that is, they try to describe behavior.
6. The answer is *D*. The structuralists tried to understand the elements of consciousness by looking inward, a process called introspection.
7. The answer is *D*. The beard and robe are meant to conjure up the image of Edward Titchener, an influential structuralist. Introspection was the technique that structuralists used to look inward in an effort to isolate the basic elements of the mind.
8. The answer is *B*. The phi phenomenon occurs when individuals perceive movement between two stationary stimuli. This shows that the whole (that is, the perception of movement) is different than the sum of the parts (two stationary objects). Gestalt psychologists believed the mind could not be broken down into raw elements.
9. The answer is *D*. Structuralists like Wundt and Titchener used introspection in an effort to understand the elements of the mind. Unconscious thought was a topic of great import to the psychoanalysts, and observable events were important to the behaviorists.
10. The answer is *D*. James was interested in studying the functions of the mind, rather than the individual structures of the mind. He was also interested in topics he considered to be evolutionarily important.
11. The answer is *C*. Ebbinghaus conducted important early research on human memory. Pavlov and Watson were behaviorists, and Wertheimer was a Gestalt psychologist. For more practice in associating the names of psychologists with their fields, try the "Who Am I?" matching exercise that follows the key terms exercise.
12. The answer is *A*. Psychometrists use instruments to measure personality, intelligence, job aptitude, and so on. *B* refers to psychoanalysis, C refers to introspection, and *D* refers to humanistic psychology.
13. The answer is *B*. Functionalism was a school of thought popularized by William James; the phi phenomenon is a Gestalt psychology term dealing with the perception of movement.

14. The answer is *D*. Social learning theory has its roots in behaviorism, but has attempted to broaden the perspective by also emphasizing the importance of cognition.

15. The answer is *D*. Watson, Pavlov, and Margaret Floy Washburn are considered to be influential early behaviorists.

16. The answer is *A*. Humanistic psychologists have emphasized that humans determine their fates through the decisions they make. According to their view, society often makes it difficult to have an accurate self-concept.

17. The answer is *A*. Behaviorists tend to focus on observable behavior, Gestalt psychologists focus on perceptual experiences, and humanistic psychologists focus on the capacity of humans to exercise their free will.

18. The answer is *D*. Although Freud emphasized these two motives, later psychoanalysts emphasized other motives, such as the need to feel adequate in social relationships.

19. The answer is *B*. This research was instrumental in the development of the neuroscience perspective.

20. The answer is *D*. The neuroscience perspective still faces great challenges in unraveling the relationships between the brain, hormones, heredity, and behavior.

21. The answer is *C*. As the world continues to shrink in the 21st century, this perspective is likely to increase in importance.

22. The answer is *B*. The process of natural selection, also known as "survival of the fittest," is used by evolutionary psychologists to explain a wide range of behavior.

23. The answer is *B*. Although these topics are of increasing importance to many fields within psychology, they are studied in great detail by sociocultural psychologists.

24. The answer is *B*. Cultural relativity is the idea that cultures are best thought of in relative rather than judgmental terms. Gender and racial identity refer to one's sense of belonging to a gender or racial group.

25. The answer is *D*. This notion emphasizes viewing other cultures in *relative* rather than in judgmental terms.

26. The answer is *D*. Gender discrimination accounted for the failure of Johns Hopkins to award the degree. Mary Whiton Calkins experienced the same type of discrimination at Harvard University.

27. The answer is *A*. The historic Supreme Court decision, *Brown v. The Board of Education*, ruled that segregated schools could no longer be considered "separate but equal."

28. The answer is *B*. Kenneth Clark was later to be elected president of the American Psychological Association.

29. The answer is *B*. Applied psychologists apply knowledge acquired by experimental psychologists. Developmental psychology is considered to be a basic field of modern psychology.

30. The answer is *C*. Basic areas of psychology emphasize research and adding to the knowledge base of psychology. Counseling psychology is considered to be an applied field of psychology.

31. The answer is *C*. All of the other choices are also areas of basic or experimental psychology.

32. The answer is *D*. The other choice is an old comedy one-liner (sorry!).

33. The answer is *B*. Psychologists, on the other hand, have completed their training in a graduate school in psychology.

34. The answer is *B*. While most psychologists would probably agree that behavior is *largely* predictable, few would suggest that *all* behavior is predictable.

35. The answer is *A*. Psychologists would agree about this statement. The other statements are opinions, or are not widely held beliefs.

Answers to True-False Questions

1. T	6. T
2. F	7. F
3. F	8. T
4. T	9. F
5. F	10. T

Chapter 2 — Research Methods in Psychology

Learning Objectives

1. Identify the requirements of using the scientific method in psychology. (p. 34)

2. Distinguish between theories and hypotheses, and discuss the importance of using representative samples in research. (p. 34)

3. Identify three descriptive research methods used in psychology, and discuss how they are used. (p. 36)

4. Describe the correlational method and distinguish between positive and negative correlation. (p. 38)

5. Explain the statement: "Correlation does not necessarily mean causation." (p. 41)

6. Identify formal experiments, and describe when they are appropriately used. (p. 41)

7. Distinguish between a dependent and an independent variable; distinguish between a control group and an experimental group. (p. 44)

8. Discuss the importance of the placebo effect, blind experiments, and manipulation checks. (p. 45)

9. List and define the five major ethical principles of research with human participants. (p. 47)

10. Discuss the use of nonhuman animals in research and describe the ethical principles associated with these studies. (p. 49)

11. (From the Applications of Psychology section) Describe the challenges involved in designing a formal experiment. (p. 51)

Chapter Overview

When psychologists conduct research, they work with empirical evidence. P[...]ts use operational definitions to describe their empirical evidence. The scientific method involves using car[...]rvation, developing theories, forming hypotheses, and testing these hypotheses. Research psychologists mu[...]re their samples are representative and the results of their studies are replicated. Psychologists use[...]e major scientific methods: (1) descriptive methods, which help to describe behavior and that include the [...] of surveys, naturalistic observation, and clinical methods; (2) correlational studies, which help to predict behavior by studying the relationship between variables; and (3) formal experiments, which study the cause-and-effect relationships between variables and help psychologists to understand and influence behavior.

     Formal experiments usually involve an experimental group, which receives the independent variable, and a control group. Differences in the dependent variable between the groups are believed to be caused by the independent variable. Important considerations in conducting formal research include placebo control, blind experiments, and manipulation checks.

     Psychologists adhere to ethical principles of research, which protects the rights of human participants by avoiding coercion, uninformed participation, and unnecessary deception, by offering participants the results of the studies in which they participate, and by ensuring confidentiality. In conducting research with animals, psychologists are guided by the principles of necessity, health, and humane treatment.

Key Terms Exercise

For each of the following exercises, match the key terms on the left with the correct definitions on the right. Page references to the text follow the terms so that you may refer to the text for any items you answer incorrectly or do not understand completely. You may check your responses immediately by referring to the answers that follow each exercise.

Basic Concepts of Research/Research Methods

_____ 1. empirical evidence (p. 34)
_____ 2. operational definition (p. 34)
_____ 3. replication (p. 35)
_____ 4. survey method (p. 36)
_____ 5. naturalistic observation (p. 37)
_____ 6. clinical method (p. 37)
_____ 7. correlational method (p. 38)
_____ 8. coefficient of correlation (p. 39)

a. the method of observing people while they receive psychological help from a mental health professional

b. a research method using interviews and questionnaires

c. a research method that records behavior in natural life settings

d. a numerical expression of the strength of a relationship between two variables

e. a research method that measures the strength of relationship between variables

f. the process in which a study is repeated until reasonable confidence in the results is achieved

g. evidence based on observations of publicly observable phenomena that can be confirmed by others

h. definitions based on the procedures used to measure a scientific phenomenon

ANSWERS

1. g	5. c
2. h	6. a
3. f	7. e
4. b	8. d

Formal Experiments I

_____ 1. formal experiment (p. 41)
_____ 2. independent variable (p. 44)
_____ 3. dependent variable (p. 44)
_____ 4. experimental group (p. 44)
_____ 5. control group (p. 44)

a. the group that receives none of the independent variable
b. the variable whose value can be controlled by the experimenter
c. the group that receives the independent variable
d. the variable whose value depends on the independent variable
e. a method that allows the researcher to manipulate the independent variable to study its effect on the dependent variable

ANSWERS
1. e
2. b
3. d
4. c
5. a

Formal Experiments II

_____ 1. random assignment (p. 44)
_____ 2. experimental control (p. 44)
_____ 3. placebo effect (p. 45)
_____ 4. blind experiments (p. 45)
_____ 5. experimenter bias (p. 45)

a. formal experiments in which the researcher does not know which participants are in the experimental or control group
b. potential influences on the dependent variable caused by experimenters interacting differently with participants in the experimental and control groups
c. requirement that participants be assigned to experimental groups randomly rather than in some systematic way
d. requirement that all explanations for differences in the dependent variable are controlled in formal experiments, except for differences in the independent variable
e. changes in behavior produced by a condition thought to be inert or inactive

Answers

1. c
2. d
3. e
4. a
5. b

Review At A Glance
(Answers to this section are found on page 31)

Basic Concepts of Research

The use of systematic observations and following the rules of evidence form the bases for the ____(1)____ _____ . Psychologists work with evidence from observations of publicly observable behaviors; this evidence is called ____(2)____ evidence. The evidence is described in terms of the operations of measurement, or ____(3)____ definitions. Tentative explanations of facts and relationships in sciences are referred to as ____(4)____. A theory is tested by making predictions based on the theory; these predictions are called ____(5)____. The relatively small number of participants studied to learn about every human being or every animal is called a ____(6)____. Researchers must ensure that their samples are typical; that is, the samples must be ____(7)____. In order to accept research results, these results must be confirmed by more than one study; this is referred to as ____(8)____.

Scientific Methods: How We Learn About Behavior and Mental Processes

The simplest of the scientific methods involves ____(9)____. An example of this method involves asking people questions directly; this is the ____(10)____ method. The primary advantage of this technique is the ability to gather much information in a short amount of time; the main disadvantage involves the questionable ____(11)____ of the data. Another descriptive approach, called ____(12)____ observation, involves observing and recording behavior in real-life settings. A third technique, observing people who are receiving help from a psychologist, is the ____(13)____ method.

To understand the relationship between variables, psychologists use a technique called the ____(14)____ method. When psychologists observe factors whose numerical values can vary, they are studying ____(15)____. The main difference between naturalistic observation and correlational studies is that correlational studies use ____(16)____. Researchers interested in studying the relationship between two variables, such as intelligence and job performance, would use a statistic called the ____(17)____ of correlation. If two variables have a positive correlation, then participants who have low scores on one variable also have low scores on a ____(18)____ variable. If participants with lower scores on one variable have *higher* scores on a second variable, then the variables are said to have a ____(19)____ correlation. A coefficient of correlation of +1.00 is referred to as a ____(20)____ positive correlation, whereas a coefficient of correlation of −1.00 reflects a perfect ____(21)____ correlation. It's important to remember that, when two variables correlate, it does not necessarily mean that one variable ____(22)____ the other.

An approach that allows the researcher to deliberately arrange the variables and to draw conclusions about cause-and-effect is ____(23)____ experiments. Formal experiments compare quantitative measures of behavior under ____(24)____ _____. In formal experiments, the factor that is controlled by the researcher is called the ____(25)____ variable. The factor that depends on the effects of the independent variable is the ____(26)____ variable. In a study designed to test the effects of caffeine on job performance, caffeine is considered the ____(27)____ variable, whereas job performance is the ____(28)____ variable. For simple experiments, two groups of participants are used. The group that receives the independent variable is called the ____(29)____ group, whereas the group that does not is called the ____(30)____ group. In order for the results of formal experiments to be considered valid, two important conditions must be met. First, the participants must have been assigned ____(31)____ to the experimental or control group. Second, all alternative explanations for the findings must be ruled out through experimental ____(32)____. One type of experimental control produces changes in behavior produced by a condition in a formal experiment thought to be inert or inactive; this is referred to as the ____(33)____ effect. In formal experiments, when the researchers recording the data do not know which participants have received which condition of the independent variable, it is called a ___(34)___ experiment. Blind experiments help to keep researchers from recording the data in a way that would support their ____(35)____. Blind experiments also rule out the possibility of ____(36)____ bias. If neither the researchers nor the participants know who is in the experimental group or who is in the control group, the experiment is called a ____(37)____ _____ experiment. Procedures to see if the arrangement of the independent variable accomplishes what the researcher has intended are called ____(38)____ checks.

Ethical Principles of Research

The following issues are important ethical principles for psychological research with human participants. Individuals should not be pressured into participating in research; that is, there should be freedom from ____(39)____. When a full description of the experiment is made available to potential participants, the principle being followed is ___(40)___ _____. Except under certain circumstances, it is not considered ethical to misrepresent the true purpose of a study. Such misrepresentation is called limited ____(41)____. When participants are provided with the results of the study, this is termed ____(42)____. Participants must be assured of their anonymity; that is, their ____(43)____ must be protected.

Psychologists conduct research with animals for several reasons. In many cases, for example with brain research, it would be unethical to do the research with ____(44)____. Also, using animals allows psychologists to conduct experiments that are more precisely ____(45)____. Psychologists have also learned much by comparing the behavior of animals of different ____(46)____. Finally, psychologists are interested in learning about other animal species. Animal research is considered ethical only when all of the following conditions are met: ____(47)____, health, and ____(48)____ treatment.

Concept Checks

Fill in the missing components of the following concept boxes. The correct answers are located in the "Answers" section at the end of the chapter.

Basic Concepts of Research

Concept	Definition
theory	
	a prediction based on a theory that is tested in a study
	a relatively small number of participants studied to learn about every human being or animal
representative	

Research Methods

Method	Explanation	Advantage/Disadvantage
survey method	a descriptive approach that uses interviews and questionnaires	
	a descriptive approach in which behavior is recorded in natural settings	**adv:** allows observation of behavior in its natural context; **disadv:** observers may influence "natural" settings
clinical method		**adv:** in-depth study of a person's behaviors, thoughts and so on; **disadv:** very small sample size
correlational studies		**adv:** allows researchers to understand strength of relationship between variables; **disadv:** correlation does not prove causation
formal experiment	researchers study the effect of the independent variable on the dependent variable	

Extending the Chapter: Psychology, Societal Issues, and Human Diversity

These questions may be assigned to you. Whether or not they are assigned, they are designed to be challenging questions to encourage you to think independently about the material in the chapter. Many of the questions have no right or wrong answers.

I. From the "Applications of Psychology" Section

Describe the challenges in designing a formal research study to investigate whether expressing negative emotions improves a person's physical health over the next 6 months.

II. Psychology, Societal Issues, and Human Diversity

1. Most Western research psychologists would agree that the scientific method is the only certain way to acquire valid information about psychology. What other approaches do different cultures use to acquire credible information about behavior and mental processes? (Hint: palm reading, astrology, reading tea leaves, and others)

2. Explain the arguments both favoring and opposing the use of animals in research. What is your opinion? Why?

3. Are psychologists able to study behavior and mental processes with the same degree of objectivity with which other scientists (for example, geologists) approach their disciplines? Defend your answer.

Practice Quiz

The practice quiz consists of three sections: 1) Short answer questions, 2) Multiple-choice questions, and 3) True-False questions. At the end of the chapter, you will find suggested answers to the short answer questions, answers and explanations for the multiple-choice questions, and answers to the true-false questions.

Short Answer Questions

1. List and describe ethical issues involved in conducting research with humans.

_____

_____

2. List three conditions that must be met in order for research with nonhuman animals to be considered ethical.

_____

_____

3. Explain the difference between a positive correlation and a negative correlation.

_____

_____

Multiple-Choice Questions

1. Each of the following is a key component of the scientific method *except*
   a. testing hypotheses.
   b. following rules of evidence.
   c. believing that your theory is correct even if the evidence suggests otherwise.
   d. systematic observation.
   LO 1

2. In order for human behavior to be studied by science, psychologists must believe that human behavior is
   a. hypothetical.
   b. random.
   c. predictable.
   d. universal.
   LO 1

3. According to the text, in order to be valid, a sample must be
   a. replicated.
   b. representative.
   c. theoretical.
   d. large.
   LO 2

4. Each of the following is true *except*
   a. a theory is used to test an hypothesis.
   b. a hypothesis is used to test a theory.
   c. in order to be valid, a sample must be representative.
   d. theories are tentative explanations.
   LO 2

5. In order to be accepted, research results must be
   a. descriptive.
   b. representative.
   c. hypothetical.
   d. replicated.
   LO 2

6. Of the research methods described in the text, which are described as the simplest methods?
   a. correlational
   b. descriptive
   c. quantitative
   d. experimental
   LO 3

7. Each of the following research methods is a type of descriptive study *except*
   a. correlational studies.
   b. the survey method.
   c. naturalistic observation.
   d. the clinical method.
   LO 3

8. A psychology student wishes to find out more about test anxiety. She constructs a "Test Anxiety Questionnaire" and gives it to other students. Which technique is she using?
   a. survey method
   b. correlational method
   c. clinical method
   d. formal experiment
   LO 3

9. If you were interested in describing "Happy Hour" behavior among college students, which technique would be most likely to yield accurate data?
   a. survey method
   b. formal experiment
   c. naturalistic observation
   d. clinical method
   LO 3

10. In a research study, participants recorded the number of cigarettes smoked per day. "Number of cigarettes smoked per day" is referred to as a
    a. sample.
    b. variable.
    c. coefficient.
    d. hypothesis.
    LO 4

11. Psychologists seeking to establish a relationship between family income and years of formal education would use which research method?
    a. the clinical method
    b. naturalistic observation
    c. formal experiments
    d. correlational methods
    LO 4

12. In a correlational study, variable A is found to generally increase in value as variable B increases. The two variables have a
    a. perfect positive correlation.
    b. perfect negative correlation.
    c. positive correlation.
    d. negative correlation.
    LO 4

13. If researchers find a correlation coefficient of zero, it means
    a. as one variable increases, the other decreases.
    b. as one variable increases, the other also increases.
    c. there is no relationship between the variables.
    d. one variable is the cause of the other variable.
    LO 4

14. If two variables have a perfect positive correlation,
    a. it proves that one variable causes the other.
    b. then one variable can be perfectly predicted if you know the value of the second variable.
    c. as one variable increases in value, the other decreases in value.
    d. as one variable increases in value, the other variable may increase or decrease in value.
    LO 5

15. If criminal activity were found to increase as temperatures increase, researchers could conclude that
    a. warm weather causes crime.
    b. crime causes warm weather.
    c. crime and temperature are positively correlated.
    d. crime and temperature have a correlation coefficient of zero.
    LO 5

16. The goal of correlational research is to
    a. prove cause-and-effect relationships.
    b. show the degree of relationship between two variables.
    c. manipulate the independent variable.
    d. observe behavior in its natural environment.
    LO 5

17. Which of the following is an advantage of using formal experimental methods?
    a. Only these methods can establish whether there is any relationship between two variables.
    b. Only these methods allow behavior to be observed as it naturally occurs.
    c. Only these methods allow researchers to determine people's opinions about various issues.
    d. Only these methods allow scientists to determine cause-and-effect relationships.
    LO 6

18. In which of the following scientific methods are quantitative measures compared in different conditions created by researchers?
    a. survey method
    b. naturalistic observation
    c correlational method
    d. formal experiment
    LO 6

19. If a researcher wished to determine whether one variable was the cause of another variable, which research method would she use?
    a. correlational study
    b. formal experiment
    c. survey
    d. naturalistic observation
    LO 6

20. The members of which group receive the independent variable?
    a. the experimental group
    b. the control group
    c. the independent group
    d. Depending on the research, any of the above might receive the independent variable.
    LO 7

21. A psychologist is studying the effects that different noise levels have on stress. In the experiment, noise levels are the
    a. correlation.
    b. dependent variable.
    c. independent variable.
    d. control group.
    LO 7

22. A psychologist studied the effect of blood alcohol on driving behavior. In this study the driving behavior was the _____ variable.
    a. control
    b. independent
    c. dependent
    d. manipulated
    LO 7

23. The purpose of the control group is to
    a. control the outcome of the study.
    b. control the behavior of the participants.
    c. have a group that receives none of the independent variable.
    d. have a group that receives none of the dependent variable.
    LO 7

24. Researchers who behave differently toward participants in the experimental and control groups are engaging in
    a. a double-blind experiment.
    b. a manipulation check.
    c. experimenter bias.
    d. the placebo effect.
    LO 8

25. One way to minimize experimenter bias in formal research studies is to use
    a. placebos.
    b. manipulation checks.
    c. correlational data.
    d. blind experiments.
    LO 8

26. A participant in a study is not certain whether he is receiving the medication with the active ingredients or just a sugar pill. In this study, the sugar pill is
    a. the independent variable.
    b. the dependent variable.
    c. a placebo.
    d. part of the experimental group.
    LO 8

27. In a double-blind experiment, which of the following is true?
    a. Researchers do not know which participants are in the experimental or control group.
    b. Participants don't know if they are in the experimental or control group.
    c. Researchers and participants perform manipulation checks.
    d. both *a* and *b*
    LO 8

28. When a researcher provides the results of her study to all the participants, she is following the ethical principle of
    a. freedom from coercion.
    b. informed consent.
    c. debriefing.
    d. deception.
    LO 9

29. Before participating in research, potential participants must receive a full description of the experiment. This is the ethical principle of
    a. limited deception.
    b. confidentiality.
    c. debriefing.
    d. informed consent.
    LO 9

30. Sandra participates in a research study. When she is finished with her participation, she receives a copy of the complete results of the study. The researchers are practicing the principle of
    a. informed consent.
    b. adequate debriefing.
    c. confidentiality.
    d. freedom from coercion.
    LO 9

31. If a student is *required* to participate in a research study in order to pass a course, this is a violation of the ethical principle of
    a. confidentiality.
    b. freedom from coercion.
    c. informed consent.
    d. debriefing.
    LO 9

32. To be considered ethical, which of the following conditions must be met by researchers using animals?
    a. necessity
    b. health
    c. humane treatment
    d. all of the above
    LO 10

33. Which of the following represents an advantage of using nonhuman animals in research?
    a. more precisely controlled research
    b. unethical to do research with humans
    c. learn about other species
    d. all of the above
    LO 10

34. In designing your own formal study, which of the following issues must be decided?
    a. the dependent variable
    b. assignment of participants to experimental or control groups
    c. the independent variable
    d. all of the above
    LO 11

35. If your hypothesis is that "expressing negative emotions improves physical health," what is the dependent variable?
    a. mental health
    b. positive emotions
    c. negative emotions
    d. physical health
    LO 11

True-False Questions

_____ 1. A hypothesis is a prediction based on a theory.

_____ 2. Correlational studies are the simplest type of research method.

_____ 3. Surveys can yield information about the cause and effect of behavior.

_____ 4. A negative correlation means there is no relationship between the two variables.

_____ 5. If two variables have a strong positive correlation, it proves that one variable causes the other.

_____ 6. In formal research, the group that receives the independent variable is called the experimental group.

_____ 7. One reason to conduct a blind experiment is to eliminate experimenter bias.

_____ 8. In double-blind experiments, neither the researchers nor the participants know who is in the experimental group.

_____ 9. Requiring students to participate in research violates the ethical principle of freedom from coercion.

_____ 10. Nonhuman animals are rarely used in research any more.

ANSWERS SECTION

Concept Checks

Basic Concepts of Research

Concept	Definition
theory	a tentative explanation of facts and relationships in science
hypothesis	a prediction based on a theory that is tested in a study
sample	a relatively small number of participants studied to learn about every human being or animal
representative	a sample that is typical of the entire group being studied

Research Methods

Method	Explanation	Advantage/Disadvantage
survey method	a descriptive approach that uses interviews and questionnaires	**adv:** can collect a great deal of information in a short amount of time; **disadv:** accuracy of information is questionable
naturalistic observation	a descriptive approach in which behavior is recorded in natural settings	**adv:** allows observation of behavior in its natural context; **disadv:** observers may influence "natural" settings
clinical method	a descriptive approach that studies people while they receive help from a psychologist	**adv:** in-depth study of a person's behaviors, thoughts and so on; **disadv:** very small sample size
correlational studies	measures the strength of relationship between 2 variables	**adv:** allows researchers to understand strength of relationship between variables; **disadv:** correlation does not prove causation
formal experiment	researchers study the effect of the independent variable on the dependent variable	**adv:** allows researchers to understand cause-and-effect relationship; **disadv:** may require "artificial" setting, for example, a laboratory

Answers to Review At A Glance

1. scientific method
2. empirical
3. operational
4. theories
5. hypotheses
6. sample
7. representative
8. replication
9. description
10. survey
11. accuracy
12. naturalistic
13. clinical
14. correlation
15. variables
16. quantifiable data

17. coefficient
18. second
19. negative
20. perfect
21. negative
22. causes
23. formal
24. different conditions
25. independent
26. dependent
27. independent
28. dependent
29. experimental
30. control
31. randomly
32. control

33. placebo
34. blind
35. hypothesis
36. experimenter
37. double blind
38. manipulation
39. coercion
40. informed consent
41. deception
42. debriefing
43. confidentiality
44. humans
45. controlled
46. species
47. necessity
48. humane

Sample Answers for Short Answer Questions

1. **List and describe ethical issues involved in conducting research with humans.**

    The text lists five ethical issues: 1) freedom from coercion, which means individuals should not be pressured into participating in research; 2) informed consent, which generally obligates a researcher to fully describe the purpose of the study before individuals are asked to participate; 3) limited deception, which spells out the conditions under which participants might be deceived about their participation; 4) adequate debriefing, which gives participants the right to know the results of the study; and 5) confidentiality, which obligates researchers to keep confidential everything they learn about a participant.

2. **List three conditions that must be met in order for research with nonhuman animals to be considered ethical.**

    The three conditions are necessity (the study must be necessary to significantly advance psychology), health (all animals must be well cared for), and humane treatment (efforts must be made to minimize discomfort to animals).

3. **Explain the difference between a positive correlation and a negative correlation.**

    Correlational studies measure the strength of the relationship between two variables. Positive correlation refers to the idea that scores on one variable move in the same direction as the scores of the second variable. If income and educational levels were positively correlated, it would mean that as income increased, so did educational levels. Likewise, as income decreased, so did educational levels. Negative correlation means that the scores on one variable move in the opposite direction as the scores on the second variable, so that as one variable increased in value, the other variable decreased in value.

Answers to Multiple Choice Questions

1. The answer is *C*. The scientific method urges its practitioners to remain open to alternative explanations and approaches.
2. The answer is *C*. Psychologists are engaged in figuring out the rules that govern behavior and mental processes. If behavior were not predictable, there would be no rules to figure out.
3. The answer is *B*. Many samples use a relatively small number of participants; therefore, it is important that the sample be representative of the larger group being studied. Research studies (not samples) should be replicated, and samples don't need to be large to be valid.
4. The answer is *A*. A theory is a tentative explanation; a hypothesis is a prediction based on a theory that is tested in a research study.
5. The answer is *D*. Replication means researchers have found the same results in different experiments. This is an essential principle of science. The other choices are not requirements for acceptance of research results.
6. The answer is *B*. Descriptive methods seek only to describe what exists. These methods are not looking for relationships between variables or seeking to explain the causes of behavior.
7. The answer is *A*. The correlational method, which quantifies the relationship between variables, is not considered a descriptive study.
8. The answer is *A*. The correlational method is used to discover the relationship between variables. The clinical method involves observing people who are receiving help for psychological problems. Formal experiments involve manipulation of the independent variable to study its effect on the dependent variable.
9. The answer is *C*. Naturalistic observation allows the researcher to observe behavior as it naturally occurs. Presumably, this approach would allow a researcher more accurate information than merely surveying college students. Formal experiments are not intended to be descriptive, and the clinical method involves observing people while they receive help for psychological problems.
10. The answer is *B*. Since the number of cigarettes smoked per day varies from person to person and from day to day for the same person, it is a variable. A correlational study might seek to relate this variable to another variable.

11. The answer is *D*. Correlational methods are used to discover the degree of relationship between variables, such as income and education.

12. The answer is *C*. When two variables have a positive correlation, their values tend to move in the same direction. A negative correlation occurs when the value of two variables move in opposite directions. Perfect correlations (either positive or negative) allow researchers to predict with perfect accuracy the score on one variable if the score of the second variable is known.

13. The answer is *C*. A correlation of zero means that if you know the value of one of the variables, you can't tell *anything* about the value of the second variable.

14. The answer is *B*. Perfect correlations (either positive or negative) allow researchers to predict with perfect accuracy the score on one variable, if the score of the second variable is known. It is important to remember that correlational studies do not prove that one variable is the cause of the other.

15. The answer is *C*. This is a reminder that, just because two variables have a positive correlation, it doesn't prove that one variable causes the other.

16. The answer is *B*. Answers *A* and *C* refer to formal research, whereas answer *D* refers to naturalistic observation.

17. The answer is *D*. Correlational techniques can only suggest that a relationship between variables exists; formal experimental methods can determine whether one variable is the cause of the other. Answer *B* refers to naturalistic observation, whereas answer *C* refers to survey methods.

18. The answer is *D*. Formal experiments are the only method in which the researcher manipulates conditions. Surveys and naturalistic observation are descriptive methods, and the correlational method compares the relationship between two variables.

19. The answer is *B*. Formal experiments are the only type of research that allow researchers to make conclusions about cause and effect.

20. The answer is *A*. In conducting formal research, the experimental group receives the independent variable; the control group does not.

21. The answer is *C*. In formal experiments, the variable that is controlled by the experimenter is the independent variable. The variable whose value depends on the independent variable is called the dependent variable. Thus, in this experiment, the amount of stress is the dependent variable.

22. The answer is *C*. Since driving behavior depends upon the blood alcohol level of the driver, it is considered the dependent variable. In this experiment, blood alcohol level is the independent variable.

23. The answer is *C*. None of the other answers make any sense!

24. The answer is *C*. Experimenter bias is subtle, but it can have dramatic effects. One reason for blind research is to minimize the possibility of experimenter bias.

25. The answer is *D*. Placebos refer to changes in behavior produced by a condition believed to be inert or inactive. Manipulation checks help to determine if the arrangement of the independent variable accomplished what the researcher intended. Correlational data refers to data that measures the relationship between two variables.

26. The answer is *C*. Participants occasionally report dramatic effects from placebo pills.

27. The answer is *D*. It is referred to as double blind because both the researchers and participants are kept blind.

28. The answer is *C*. The results should be provided to participants as soon as possible and in language they can understand.

29. The answer is *D*. Informed consent also implies that participants must be told that they are free to withdraw from the experiment without penalty.

30. The answer is *B*. Each of the other choices also refers to ethical principles of research.

31. The answer is *B*. Forcing anyone to participate in research is a definite no-no!

32. The answer is *D*. Necessity implies the study must be necessary to significantly advance psychology. Health refers to the requirement that all animals must be well cared for, and humane treatment means efforts must be made to minimize discomfort to animals.

33. The answer is *D*. Other advantages include learning how to protect endangered species.

34. The answer is *D*. It is, indeed, challenging to design (let alone actually carry out) formal research.

35. The answer is *D*. Since physical health depends upon whether or not one expresses negative emotions, it is the dependent variable. In this experiment, "expressing negative emotions" is the independent variable.

Answers to True-False Questions

1.	T	6.	T
2.	F	7.	T
3.	F	8.	T
4.	F	9.	T
5.	F	10.	F

Chapter 3   Biological Foundations of Behavior

Learning Objectives

1. Understand the importance of the neuron, and differentiate among the neuron's cell body, dendrite, and axon. (p. 58)

2. Describe the processes of neural transmission and synaptic transmission. (p. 60)

3. Distinguish between the central nervous system and the peripheral nervous system and explain the differences among afferent neurons, efferent neurons, and interneurons. (p. 65)

4. List the functions of the somatic and autonomic nervous systems, and describe the roles of the sympathetic and parasympathetic divisions of the autonomic nervous system. (p. 66)

5. Describe the techniques that provide images of the brain and brain functions. (p. 70)

6. List the three major divisions of the brain, and know their subcomponents. (p. 72)

7. Explain the basic functions of the hindbrain and midbrain. (p. 72)

8. Discuss the functions of the regions of the forebrain, including the thalamus, hypothalamus, limbic system, and the cerebral cortex. (p. 72)

9. Identify the location and functions of the four cortical lobes and the association areas of the cerebral cortex. (p. 75)

10. Explain how the two cerebral hemispheres communicate, and describe the changes that occur if the corpus callosum is severed. (p. 80)

11. Discuss the role of the cerebral cortex in processing intellectual and emotional information. (p. 81)

12. Identify examples of the brain acting as a developing system and an interacting system, and explain the differences between parallel and serial processing. (p. 84)

13. Identify the endocrine glands, and understand how the endocrine system communicates and how it regulates body processes. (p. 86)

14. Identify the hormones related to each endocrine gland, and understand their functions. (p. 87)

15. Discuss the relationship between genes and chromosomes, and explain how dominant and recessive genes affect physical and behavioral traits. (p. 91)

16. Summarize the role of twin studies and adoption studies in genetic research. (p. 95)

17. Discuss the influence of both heredity and experience on behavior. (p. 96)

18. (From the Application section) Describe the relationship between the brain and mental disorders such as schizophrenia and Alzheimer's disease. (p. 99)

Chapter Overview

The human nervous system is a complex network of neural cells that carries messages and regulates bodily functions and personal behavior. The individual cells of the nervous system are called neurons. The parts of a neuron include the cell body, dendrites, and axons. Neurons are separated from each other by a tiny synaptic gap. Chemical substances called neurotransmitters transmit electrical messages across the synapse.

The central nervous system is composed of the brain and the spinal cord. The peripheral nervous system carries messages to and from the rest of the body. It is composed of both the somatic and autonomic nervous systems. The autonomic nervous system consists of the sympathetic division, which prepares the body for stress, and the parasympathetic division, which plays its primary role under peaceful conditions.

Scientists have developed exciting brain-imaging techniques that can create images of the activities of the living brain. These techniques include the EEG, the PET scan, and the MRI.

The brain has three major parts. The first of these, the hindbrain, contains a) the medulla, which controls breathing and a variety of reflexes; b) the pons, which is concerned with balance, hearing, and some parasympathetic functions; and c) the cerebellum, which is chiefly responsible for maintaining muscle tone and coordinating muscular movements. A second part of the brain, the midbrain, is a center for reflexes related to vision and hearing.

The forebrain, the third major part of the brain, includes two distinct areas. The first area contains the thalamus, a switching station that routes sensory information to the appropriate areas of the brain, the hypothalamus, which is involved with our motives and emotions, and most of the limbic system. The second area contains the cerebral cortex, which controls conscious experience, intellectual activities, the senses, and voluntary actions. The cortex contains two cerebral hemispheres connected by the corpus callosum. Each hemisphere of the cortex contains four lobes: the frontal lobe is involved with speaking and voluntary movement; the parietal lobe is involved with the sense of touch; the temporal lobe is involved with hearing and understanding language; and the occipital lobe is involved with vision. The cerebral cortex is also important in processing emotions. The brain is viewed as a developing system. Each part of the brain interacts with the entire nervous system, and the parts work together in intellectual, physical, and emotional functions.

The endocrine system contains glands that secrete hormones. This system influences emotional arousal, metabolism, sexual functioning, and other bodily processes. The pituitary gland is referred to as the master gland, since its hormones help to regulate the activity of the other glands. The adrenal glands secrete epinephrine and norepinephrine, which are involved in emotional arousal and affect the metabolic rate and sexual arousal. The islets of Langerhans secrete glucagon and insulin, which control blood sugar and energy levels. The gonads produce sex cells for human reproduction and also estrogen and testosterone, which are important to sexual functioning and the development of secondary sex characteristics. The thyroid gland secretes thyroxin, which helps control the metabolic rate. The parathyroid glands secrete parathormone, which controls the level of nervous activity. The pineal gland, attached to the top of the thalamus, secretes melatonin.

Human characteristics and behaviors are influenced by genetic inheritance. The cells contain structures called chromosomes, which consist of strands of DNA. Genes are made up of varying sequences of adenine, thymine, guanine, and cystine; genes are the basic units of inheritance. Most normal human cells contain 46 chromosomes arranged in 23 pairs. The sex cells, however, each contain only 23 chromosomes and are capable of combining into a new zygote with a unique set of chromosomes.

Researchers interested in hereditary influences on behavior have used twin studies and adoption studies. Although inheritance plays a significant role in influencing human behavior, environmental and other personal factors also play important roles. Research into disorders such as schizophrenia and Alzheimer's disease underscores the influence of the brain in both normal and disturbed behavior.

Key Terms Exercise

For each of the following exercises, match the key terms on the left with the correct definitions on the right. Page references to the text follow the terms so that you may refer to the text for any items you answer incorrectly or do not understand completely. You may check your responses immediately by referring to the answers that follow each exercise.

The Nervous System (I)

_____ 1. brain (p. 58)
_____ 2. spinal cord (p. 58)
_____ 3. neuron (p. 58)
_____ 4. cell body (p. 58)
_____ 5. dendrites (p. 59)
_____ 6. axons (p. 59)
_____ 7. nerve (p. 59)

a. a thick bundle of long neurons running outside the brain and spinal cord
b. the mass of neural cells and related cells encased in the skull
c. the nerve fibers in the spinal column
d. neuron endings that transmit messages to other neurons
e. extensions of the cell body that usually receive messages from other neurons
f. an individual nerve cell
g. the central part of the nerve cell, containing the nucleus

ANSWERS
1. b   5. e
2. c   6. d
3. f   7. a
4. g

The Nervous System (II)

_____ 1. ions (p. 60)
_____ 2. myelin sheath (p. 61)
_____ 3. synapse (p. 62)
_____ 4. neurotransmitters (p. 62)
_____ 5. neuropeptides (p. 64)
_____ 6. central nervous system (p. 65)
_____ 7. peripheral nervous system (p. 65)

a. the junction between neurons
b. the brain and the spinal cord
c. electrically charged particles
d. chemical substances that help carry messages across synapses
e. nerves that branch off from the brain and spinal cord to all parts of the body
f. a fatty coating that insulates many axons and speeds neural transmission
g. a group of neurotransmitters that influence the action of other neurotransmitters

ANSWERS

1. c	5. g
2. f	6. b
3. a	7. e
4. d	

The Nervous System (III)

_____ 1. afferent neurons (p. 65)
_____ 2. efferent neurons (p. 65)
_____ 3. interneurons (p. 65)
_____ 4. somatic nervous system (p. 66)
_____ 5. autonomic nervous system (p. 67)
_____ 6. sympathetic division (p. 67)
_____ 7. parasympathetic division (p. 69)

a. carries messages from the sense organs to the central nervous system.
b. helps process simple reflexes in the brain and spinal cord
c. the division of the autonomic nervous system that prepares the body for stress
d. the division of the autonomic nervous system that promotes body maintenance and energy conservation under non-stressful conditions
e. the division of the peripheral nervous system that regulates the actions of the internal body organs
f. the division of the peripheral nervous system carrying messages from the sense organs to the central nervous system and from the central nervous system to the skeletal muscles
g. carries messages from the central nervous system to the organs and muscles

ANSWERS

1. a	5. e
2. g	6. c
3. b	7. d
4. f	

Structures and Functions of the Brain (I)

_____ 1. hindbrain (p. 72)
_____ 2. medulla (p. 72)
_____ 3. pons (p. 72)
_____ 4. cerebellum (p. 72)
_____ 5. midbrain (p. 72)
_____ 6. forebrain (p. 72)
_____ 7. thalamus (p. 74)

a. a forebrain structure routing sensory messages to the brain

b. involved in balance, hearing, and some parasympathetic functions

c. two structures that coordinate muscle movements, learning, and memory

d. the swelling just above the spinal cord, responsible for breathing and a variety of reflexes

e. a small area at the top of the hindbrain that mainly serves as a reflex center for orienting the eyes and ears

f. lowest part of the brain, primarily responsible for "housekeeping" functions

g. part of the brain that contains the thalamus, hypothalamus, most of the limbic system and the cerebral cortex

ANSWERS

1. f	5. e
2. d	6. g
3. b	7. a
4. c	

Structures and Functions of the Brain (II)

_____ 1. hypothalamus (p. 74)
_____ 2. limbic system (p. 74)
_____ 3. cerebral cortex (p. 74)
_____ 4. frontal lobes (p. 76)
_____ 5. parietal lobes (p. 78)
_____ 6. temporal lobes (p.78)
_____ 7. occipital lobes (p. 79)

a. the largest structure of the forebrain, controlling conscious experience and intelligence

b. involved in motivation, emotion, and the functions of the autonomic nervous system

c. a neural system composed of the amygdala, the hippocampus, the septal area, and the cingulate cortex

d. contains the somatosensory area

e. contains the visual area

f. involved in planning, organization, voluntary motor movements, and speech

g. contains areas involved in hearing and understanding language

ANSWERS

1. b	5. d
2. c	6. g
3. a	7. e
4. f	

Endocrine System and Genetic Influences (I)

_____ 1. endocrine system (p. 86)
_____ 2. hormones (p. 87)
_____ 3. pituitary gland (p. 87)
_____ 4. adrenal glands (p. 88)
_____ 5. islets of Langerhans (p. 88)
_____ 6. gonads (p. 89)

a. chemical substances that influence internal organs
b. the system of glands that produces hormones
c. play an important role in physical and emotional arousal
d. embedded in the pancreas and helps regulate blood sugar levels
e. produce the sex cells and secrete hormones important in sexual arousal
f. the body's "master gland"

ANSWERS

1. b	4. c
2. a	5. d
3. f	6. e

Endocrine System and Genetic Influences (II)

_____ 1. thyroid gland (p. 89)
_____ 2. parathyroid glands (p. 90)
_____ 3. pineal gland (p. 90)
_____ 4. chromosomes (p. 92)
_____ 5. genes (p. 93)

a. secrete parathormone, which is important in nervous system functioning
b. segments of chromosomes made up of base pairs of adenine, thymine, guanine, and cystine
c. strands of DNA in cells
d. secretes thyroxin, which helps regulate metabolism
e. secretes melatonin, important in the regulation of biological rhythms

ANSWERS

1. d	4. c
2. a	5. b
3. e	

Review At A Glance
(The answers to this section begin on page 53)

Nervous System: The Biological Control Center

The complex mass of nerve cells encased in the skull is the ___(1)___. The brain is connected to a bundle of long nerves running through the spine called the ___(2)___ ___(3)___. The most important unit of the nervous system is the individual nerve cell, or ___(4)___. The central part of the neuron is called the ___(5)___ _____; it contains the cell's control center, or ___(6)___. The small branches extending out from the cell body receive messages from other neurons and are called ___(7)___. The small branches at the other end of the nerve cell transmit messages to other neurons; these are ___(8)___. The nervous system contains about ___(9)___ _____ neurons. Each neuron can receive messages from or transmit messages to ___(10)___ to ___(11)___ other neural cells. A bundle of long neurons outside the brain and spinal cord is a ___(12)___.

Neurons, the "wires" of the nervous system, also contain built-in supplies of ___(13)___ power. The fluids inside and outside the neuron contain electrically charged ___(14)___. In its resting state, the overall ion charge within the cell membrane is ___(15)___, whereas the fluid outside the cell membrane, which contains sodium ions, is ___(16)___. The cell membrane allows some chemicals to pass through, but not others; it is ___(17)___.

In its normal resting state, with mostly negative ions inside and mostly positive ions outside, the neuron is electrically ___(18)___. When the membrane is stimulated and positively charged sodium ions enter the neuron, the process is termed ___(19)___. Neural transmission operates according to the ___(20)___ -_____-_____principle. If sufficient depolarization occurs, the axon conducts a neural impulse, known as an ___(21)___ _____. The action potential travels the length of the ___(22)___. A drug that interrupts the flow of depolarization is ___(23)___. Axons are insulated by a fatty covering called a ___(24)___ _____. The myelin sheath grows thicker in late ___(25)___. A disease that destroys the myelin sheath of many neurons is ___(26)___ _____.

Although neurons are linked together, there is a small gap between them called the ___(27)___. Neural messages are carried across the synaptic gap by chemicals called ___(28)___. Neurotransmitters are stored in synaptic vessicles located in the synaptic ___(29)___. Neurotransmitters float across the gap and fit into receptor sites on the adjacent ___(30)___; this causes an ___(31)___ _____ that allows the neural message to continue. The chemical structure of some drugs is similar enough to a neurotransmitter to fit the receptor sites of the receiving ___(32)___. Other drugs block receptor sites; drugs such as Prozac reduce the reabsorption of a ___(33)___.

Divisions of the Nervous System

The nervous system consists of two major divisions: (1) the brain and spinal cord, collectively called the ___(34)___ _____ _____, and (2) the nerves that branch off the brain and spinal cord to the rest of the body, called the ___(35)___ _____ _____. Messages that come from the body into the central nervous system are carried by ___(36)___ neurons. Messages going out from the central nervous system are carried by ___(37)___ neurons. Simple reflexes are processed in the brain and spinal cord by ___(38)___.

The peripheral nervous system consists of two divisions. The first is called the ____(39)____ nervous system; it carries messages from the central nervous system to the skeletal muscles and receives messages from the sense organs, muscles, joints, and skin and transmits them to the _____(40)_____ nervous system. The second, the ____(41)____ nervous system, carries messages to and from the glands and visceral organs; it automatically controls many essential functions of the body, regulates emotion, and helps to control our ____(42)____. The autonomic nervous system itself is composed of the sympathetic and _____(43)_____ nervous systems. The sympathetic system prepares the body to respond to ____(44)____. In some cases the sympathetic system activates organs; in other cases, the sympathetic system ____(45)____ organs that are not essential in times of stress. The parasympathetic system plays its primary role under more ____(46)____ conditions. When stress levels are low, the parasympathetic system stimulates maintenance activities, as well as energy ____(47)____ and storage.

Structures and Functions of the Brain

One brain-image technique that records the brain's electrical activity is called the ____(48)____, or ____(49)____. A second technique uses a computer interpretation of brain activity; this technique is called ____(50)____ _____ _____, or PET scan. A third technique detects and interprets activity from the nuclei of atoms in living cells; this approach is called ____(51)____ _____ _____, or ____(52)____. A type of MRI that measures brain activity by measuring the oxygen use of groups of neurons is called a ____(53)____ MRI.

The lowest part of the brain, responsible for routine functions, is the ____(54)____. The hindbrain has three main structures: (1) a part responsible for controlling breathing and a variety of reflexes, called the ____(55)____; (2) a structure involved in balance, hearing, and some parasympathetic functions, called the ____(56)____; and (3) a part that is mainly responsible for maintaining muscle tone and muscular coordination, called the ____(57)____. Networks of neurons which span the medulla and pons and which play roles in wakefulness, arousal level, and attention are called the ____(58)____ _____.

The small area at the top of the hindbrain that serves primarily as a reflex center for orienting the eyes and ears is the ____(59)____. The forebrain consists of two main areas. The first area contains a structure that primarily routes messages from sense organs to the appropriate parts of the brain called the ____(60)____ and the ____(61)____, a tiny structure involved with motives, emotions, and the functions of the autonomic nervous system; the hypothalamus apparently contains ____(62)____ centers.

The hypothalamus influences emotional arousal by working with a complex brain system called the ____(63)____ system. A part of the limbic system involved in aggression and that processes information about emotional stimuli is the ____(64)____. A limbic structure that is believed to tie together memories stored in different parts of the cerebral cortex is the ____(65)____. Other limbic structures that process cognitive information in emotions are the ____(66)____ area and the ____(67)____ cortex.

Cerebral Cortex: Sensory, Cognitive, and Motor Functions

The largest structure in the forebrain, called the cerebral cortex, is involved in ____(68)____ experience, language, and ____(69)____. The cortex is frequently called the ____(70)____ matter of the brain, while the cerebrum is the ____(71)____ matter.

Each hemisphere contains four lobes, and each lobe performs different cognitive functions. The ____(72)____ lobes play an important role in organizing behavior and in predicting the consequence of behavior. The left hemisphere contains ____(73)____ area, which is involved in our ability to speak language. Broca's research on stroke victims who developed expressive ____(74)____ found that the strokes had occurred in this area of the brain. Another area of the frontal lobe, which is involved in the control of voluntary motor movement, is called the ____(75)____ area. The unfortunate case of Phineas Gage demonstrated the role of the ____(76)____ lobes in the inhibition of socially inappropriate behavior. A more recent case, that of "J.Z.," further demonstrated the role of the frontal lobes in controlling ____(77)____ aspects of our behavior. The ____(78)____ lobes contain the somatosensory area, which is involved in the sense of ____(79)____ and other body senses. The temporal lobes, extending backward from the temples, are involved with the sense of ____(80)____. In the left temporal lobe, ____(81)____ area plays an important role in understanding spoken language. Damage to this area causes Wernicke's ____(82)____, which leaves victims unable to understand language spoken to them by others. The ____(83)____ lobes contain the visual area and play an essential role in processing sensory information from the eyes. Association areas are sometimes called the ____(84)____ _____ of the cortex. The cerebral cortex consists of two cerebral hemispheres joined by the ____(85)____. The corpus callosum allows ____(86)____ between the two hemispheres. The left hemisphere tends to handle ____(87)____ information, and the right side tends to handle visual and ____(88)____ information.

Patients who have had the corpus callosum surgically severed are referred to as ____(89)____-_____ patients. Research with these patients has revealed the localization of language expression abilities in the ____(90)____.

The results of a variety of studies suggest that the two cerebral hemispheres process different aspects of ____(91)____. The right hemisphere plays an important role in expressing emotions and in ____(92)____ the emotions expressed by others. Research suggests that positive emotions are processed more in the ____(93)____ hemisphere and negative emotions are processed more in the ____(94)____ hemisphere.

If the cortex is damaged, other areas can take over the functions of the damaged area; this is referred to as ____(95)____. The brain continues to change in structure well into the ____(96)____ decade of life. A process that decreases gray matter from childhood through middle adulthood is called selective neural ____(97)____. Research suggests new neurons can grow in the cortex and hippocampus of some mammals, a process called ____(98)____. The brain is an interacting system that often uses ____(99)____ processing.

Endocrine System: Chemical Messengers of the Body

Another system that plays a role in communication and regulation of bodily processes is the ___(100)___ system. This system consists of ___(101)___ that secrete neuropeptides and hormones into the bloodstream. Neuropeptides help provide coordination and ___(102)___ among the endocrine glands. In addition, some neuropeptides influence ___(103)___ activity. The hormones are regulated by the brain, particularly by the ___(104)___. Some hormones are chemically identical to some of the ___(105)___. Hormones aid the ability of the ___(106)___ _____ to control the body. The following glands are the most important from a psychological standpoint:

1. Located near the bottom of the brain and largely controlled by the hypothalamus is the ___(107)___ gland. This gland secretes hormones that help regulate the other glands and is frequently referred to as the ___(108)___ _____. The pituitary regulates the body's reactions to ___(109)___ and resistance to ___(110)___.

2. The glands that sit atop the kidneys and play an important role in emotional arousal are the ___(111)___ glands. These glands secrete two hormones that help the body prepare for stress: ___(112)___ and ___(113)___.

3. The glands that are embedded in the pancreas and regulate the blood sugar level are the ___(114)___. These glands secrete ___(115)___ and ___(116)___.

4. The glands responsible for sex cell production are the ___(117)___. In females, the glands are the ___(118)___, whereas in males they are the ___(119)___. The most important sex hormones are ___(120)___ in females and ___(121)___ in males.

5. The gland that helps regulate metabolism is the ___(122)___ gland. This gland secretes the hormone ___(123)___, which is necessary for mental development in children and for control of weight and level of activity in adults. A deficiency of thyroxin can cause a type of mental retardation called ___(124)___.

6. Embedded in the thyroid are four glands called the ___(125)___ glands. These secrete a hormone called ___(126)___, which is important in the functioning of the nervous system.

7. Attached to the top of the thalamus is the ___(127)___ gland, which secretes ___(128)___.

Genetic Influences on Behavior

In a seabird called the tern, knowing how to build a nest is part of the bird's ___(129)___ inheritance. Among human beings, inheritance seems to ___(130)___ broad dimensions of our behavior.

The cells of our body contain structures called ___(131)___. Chromosomes consist of long strands of deoxyribonucleic acid, also called ___(132)___. DNA usually forms a type of curved ladder called a double ___(133)___. The backbones of DNA create a structure connected by base pairs of four substances: adenine, thymine, ___(134)___, and cystine. Sequences of these pairs that influence a body structure or function are called ___(135)___; thus, genes are the basic building blocks of ___(136)___. All human cells except sex cells have ___(137)___ chromosomes, arranged in 23 pairs, and each chromosome carries ___(138)___ of genes. Sex cells are called ___(139)___ and contain ___(140)___ unpaired chromosomes. A sperm unites with an ovum through the process of ___(141)___; in this process, a new cell, called a ___(142)___, is formed. Zygotes contain 23 ___(143)___ of chromosomes, with the mother and father each contributing half. On the average, brothers and sisters will have about ____(144)____ percent of their genes in common; the exception is ____(145)____ twins, who are formed from a single zygote and share all their genes.

When the gene contributed by one parent conflicts with the gene contributed by the other parent for the same characteristic, the ____(146)____ gene will normally reveal its trait. Some traits are revealed only when the same gene has been contributed by both parents; these are ____(147)____ genes. The presence of an additional 21st chromosome can result in ____(148)____ syndrome.

Genes influence the synthesis of ____(149)____ in our cells. The nature of our neurons is influenced by our genes; our experiences in the ____(150)____ can also influence our neurons.

Although researchers have studied genetic influences on animals, selective breeding experiments cannot be carried out with humans for ____(151)____ reasons. Instead, researchers have used two descriptive research methods. The first method involves comparing the characteristics of identical or ____(152)____ twins with dizygotic twins, formed from the fertilization of two ova by two sperm cells. The second method compares the characteristics of ___(153)___ children with those of both their biological parents and their adoptive parents.

Research strongly suggests that much of our behavior, both normal and abnormal, is influenced by both ____(154)____ factors and by our experiences.

Applications of Psychology: Madness and the Brain

The central feature of schizophrenia is a marked abnormality of ____(155)____ _____. Brain-imaging techniques reveal a shrunken cerebral cortex and enlarged ____(156)____ in persons with schizophrenia. Recent findings indicate that the ____(157)____ may not function normally in individuals with schizophrenia. Brain abnormalities are also reflected in abnormal levels of the neurotransmitter ____(158)____. Evidence also exists that ____(159)____ can cause persons who are genetically predisposed to have episodes of schizophrenia. According to Mednick's "double strike" theory, schizophrenia is most likely to occur in those who (1) have a ____(160)____ _____ and (2) who suffered some health complication before or during ____(161)____. Another disease characterized by brain deterioration and that has an apparent genetic predisposition is ___(162)___ disease.

Concept Checks

Fill in the missing components of the following concept boxes. The correct answers are located in the "Answers" section at the end of the chapter.

Structure of a Neuron/Neural Transmission

Structure	Function
cell body	
	usually receives neural messages from other neurons
axons	
	the resting state of a neuron, in which negative ions are generally inside the cell membrane and positive ions are generally outside
depolarization	
	triggered by depolarization, a neural message travels the length of the axon
	a protective fatty coating that covers and protects many axons

Structures and Functions of the Brain

Structure	Function
hindbrain	
	the part of the forebrain involved in motivation and emotion; it also helps regulate body temperature, endocrine activity, immune system functioning, aggression, and even pleasure
limbic system	
	the largest forebrain structure and is involved in conscious experience, voluntary action, language, and intelligence
lobes of the cerebral cortex	
	helps maintain muscle tone and cardiac reflexes as well as influencing wakefulness, arousal level, and attention

Endocrine Glands and Functions

Name of Gland	Function
pituitary gland	
	involved in physical and emotional arousal
islets of Langerhans	
	produce sex cells and hormones important in sexual arousal
thyroid gland	
	important in functioning of the nervous system
	largely responsible for regulating biological rhythms such as sleep and wakefulness and menstrual cycles in females

Extending the Chapter: Psychology, Societal Issues, and Human Diversity

These questions may be assigned to you. Whether or not they are assigned, they are designed to be challenging questions to encourage you to think independently about the material in the chapter. Many of the questions have no right or wrong answers.

I. From the "Applications of Psychology" section

1. Discuss the results of brain imaging research on persons with schizophrenia.

2. Describe the neurotransmitters that are implicated in schizophrenia.

3   Summarize the research on the causes of schizophrenia.

4. Discuss the areas of the brain that are involved in Alzheimer's disease.

II. Psychology, Societal Issues, and Human Diversity

1. As researchers unlock the genetic factors that influence behavior, how might this affect the way society views individual responsibility for behavior?

2. Research topic: Researchers are beginning to appreciate how a child's early environment can influence the physical development of the brain.

Practice Quiz

The practice quiz consists of three sections: 1) Short answer questions, 2) Multiple-choice questions, and 3) True-False questions. At the end of the chapter you will find suggested answers to the short answer questions, answers and explanations for the multiple-choice questions, and answers to the true-false questions.

Short Answer Questions

1. Explain the relationship between inheritance, genes, DNA, and chromosomes.

   _____

   _____

2. Distinguish between dominant and recessive traits.

   _____

   _____

3. Describe the research methods used to help sort out the influences of nature and nurture in humans.

   _____

   _____

Multiple-Choice Questions

1. The part of the neuron that usually receives messages from other neurons is called the
   a. dendrite.
   b. axon.
   c. cell body.
   d. synapse.
      LO 1

2. The part of the neuron responsible for transmitting messages to the next neuron is the
   a. dendrite.
   b. myelin sheath.
   c. cell body.
   d. axon.
      LO 1

3. When positively charged ions enter the neuron, the process is called
   a. polarization.
   b. depolarization.
   c. semipermeability.
   d. synaptical transmission.
      LO 2

4. A flowing storm of ions characterizes
   a. synaptic transmission.
   b. an action potential.
   c. neurotransmitters.
   d. none of the above.
      LO 2

5. Which of the following makes it difficult for messages to be transmitted across synapses?
   a. excitatory neurotransmitters
   b. inhibitory neurotransmitters
   c. myelin sheath
   d. action potential
      LO 2

6. Which of the following transmit messages from the body into the central nervous system?
   a. afferent neurons
   b. efferent neurons
   c. association neurons
   d. transmittal neurons
      LO 3

7. The central nervous system is the primary
   location of
   a. efferent neurons.
   b. afferent neurons.
   c. interneurons.
   d. nerves.
      LO 3

8. Which division of the nervous system is
   composed of all the nerves that branch from the
   brain and spinal cord?
   a. peripheral nervous system
   b. afferent nervous system
   c. central nervous system
   d. somatic nervous system
      LO 3

9. All of the following are functions of the
   autonomic nervous system *except*
   a. breathing.
   b. voluntary movements.
   c. sweating.
   d. sexual arousal.
      LO 4

10. Which of the following generally helps prepare
    our bodies to respond to stress?
    a. sympathetic nervous system
    b. parasympathetic nervous system
    c. somatic nervous system
    d. Broca's area
       LO 4

11. For what purpose are PET scans and MRIs
    used?
    a. observing the process of polarization
    b. observing images of the brain
    c. measuring the responsiveness of the
       autonomic nervous system
    d. measuring the sensitivity of the skin's pain
       receptors
       LO 5

12. The hindbrain structure responsible for
    maintaining muscle tone and coordination of
    muscle movements is the
    a. medulla
    b. pons
    c. cerebellum
    d. thalamus
       LO 6

13. The hypothalamus is located within the
    a. midbrain.
    b. thalamus.
    c. medulla.
    d. forebrain.
       LO 6

14. A small area at the top of the hindbrain that
    helps regulate sensory reflexes is called the
    a. medulla.
    b. pons.
    c. forebrain.
    d. midbrain.
       LO 7

15. If a person's cerebellum was damaged in an
    accident, you would expect the person to have a
    problem with
    a. breathing and heart rate.
    b. seeing and hearing.
    c. talking and understanding.
    d. balance and muscle coordination.
       LO 7

16. The hypothalamus plays a role in each of the
    following *except*
    a. motives and emotions.
    b. regulating body temperature.
    c. many autonomic functions.
    d. routing sensory messages to the brain.
       LO 8

17. Which of the following is a component of the
    limbic system helping to process information
    about aggression and emotional stimuli?
    a. hippocampus
    b. cingulate cortex
    c. amygdala
    d. septal area
       LO 8

18. People who experience Wernicke's aphasia
    have had damage to the
    a. frontal lobe.
    b. somatosensory area.
    c. temporal lobe.
    d. occipital lobe.
       LO 9

19. The processing of sensory information from the eyes is carried out in which lobe of the cerebral cortex?
    a. frontal
    b. parietal
    c. temporal
    d. occipital
    LO 9

20. The structure that allows communication between the two cerebral hemispheres is called the
    a. corpus callosum
    b. cingulate cortex
    c. reticular formation
    d. association area
    LO 10

21. Research with split-brain patients has revealed the localization of which types of abilities in the left hemisphere?
    a. emotional expression
    b. recognition of stimuli
    c. abstract thinking
    d. language expression
    LO 10

22. Research suggests that positive emotions are more likely to be processed in the
    a. corpus callosum.
    b. left hemisphere.
    c. right hemisphere.
    d. amygdala.
    LO 11

23. Which of the following computer terms is analogous to the brain's interacting system?
    a. serial processing
    b. parallel processing
    c. multiple processing
    d. binary processing
    LO 12

24. The gland that is often considered to be the master gland is the
    a. adrenal.
    b. pituitary.
    c. gonads.
    d. thyroid.
    LO 13

25. How are hormones different from neurotransmitters?
    a. Hormones are chemical messengers.
    b. Hormones are carried in the bloodstream.
    c. Hormones are not regulated by the brain.
    d. Hormones are by-products of neurotransmitters.
    LO 13

26. The gland(s) that produce(s) male and female sex hormones is (are) the
    a. pituitary gland.
    b. thyroid gland.
    c. adrenal glands.
    d. gonads.
    LO 14

27. Which of the following statements is *not* correct?
    a. Chromosomes consist of DNA.
    b. A normal human cell contains 46 chromosomes.
    c. A normal gamete contains 23 chromosomes.
    d. Adenine is the most important substance carrying the genetic code.
    LO 15

28. How is it possible for two brown-eyed parents to have a blue-eyed child?
    a. If both parents contribute a recessive gene.
    b. If both parents contribute a dominant gene.
    c. If one parent contributes a recessive gene and one parent contributes a dominant gene.
    d. It's impossible for two brown-eyed parents to have a blue-eyed child unless they adopt.
    LO 15

29. Down syndrome
    a. is caused by the presence of an additional 21st chromosome.
    b. can cause mental retardation.
    c. causes obvious physical irregularities.
    d. all of the above
    LO 15

30. Which of the following characterizes dizygotic twins?
    a. They are formed when two different eggs are fertilized by different sperm cells.
    b. They are formed by a single fertilized egg.
    c. They are identical in appearance.
    d. They are identical in genetic structure.
    LO 16

31. To determine the influence of inheritance on behavior, psychologists have used what type of research?
    a. adoption studies
    b. twin studies
    c. formal experiments
    d. both a and b
    LO 16

32. Which of the following is characteristic of monozygotic twins?
    a. They are referred to as identical twins.
    b. They are formed from a single ovum.
    c. They are virtually identical in genetic structure.
    d. all of the above
    LO 16

33. Research on the role of inheritance in personality and abnormal behavior suggests that
    a. personality is inherited.
    b. abnormal behavior is inherited.
    c. personality and abnormal behavior may be influenced in part by inheritance.
    d. none of the above
    LO 17

34. Each of the following has been demonstrated in the brains of schizophrenics *except*
    a. greatly enlarged ventricles.
    b. a smaller hippocampus.
    c. abnormal levels of acetylcholine.
    d. abnormal levels of dopamine.
    LO 18

35. According to Mednick, schizophrenia is likely in persons who
    a. have a genetic predisposition.
    b. suffer a health complication before or during birth.
    c. live with a schizophrenic parent.
    d. both *a* and *b*
    LO 18

True-False Questions

_____ 1. In the neuron, the axon transmits messages to other neurons.

_____ 2. Messages are carried across the synapse by neurotransmitters.

_____ 3. The parasympathetic nervous system generally prepares the body to respond to stress.

_____ 4. The midbrain contains three essential structures: the medulla, the pons and the cerebellum.

_____ 5. The occipital lobes process sensory information from the eyes.

_____ 6. Generally, the left hemisphere plays a greater role in the expression of emotions.

_____ 7. Some hormones are chemically identical to neurotransmitters.

_____ 8. The thyroid gland is referred to as the master gland.

_____ 9. Monozygotic twins are referred to as identical twins.

_____10. The IQs of adopted children are more similar to their adoptive parents than to their biological parents.

ANSWERS SECTION

Concept Checks

Structure of a Neuron/Neural Transmission

Structure	Function
cell body	contains the nucleus
dendrite	usually receives neural messages from other neurons
axon	transmits messages to other neurons
polarized state	the resting state of a neuron, in which negative ions are generally inside the cell membrane and positive ions are generally outside
depolarization	process during which positively charged ions flow into the neuron
action potential	triggered by depolarization, a neural message travels the length of the axon
myelin sheath	a protective fatty coating that covers and protects many axons

Structures and Functions of the Brain

Structure	Function
hindbrain	its main responsibility is in general "housekeeping" functions; the medulla controls breathing and other reflexes; the pons helps control balance and hearing; the cerebellum helps maintain muscle tone and coordinates muscular movements
hypothalamus	the part of the forebrain involved in motivation and emotion; it also helps regulate body temperature, endocrine activity, immune system functioning, aggression and even pleasure
limbic system	a neural system composed of the amygdala, hippocampus, septal area, and cingulate cortex; also involved in emotional behavior (both arousal and cognitive aspects)
cerebral cortex	the largest forebrain structure and is involved in conscious experience, voluntary action, language, and intelligence
lobes of the cerebral cortex	frontal lobes help us to organize and predict the consequences of our behavior and are involved in our ability to speak; the parietal lobes contain the somatosensory and motor areas; the temporal lobes are involved in hearing and understanding language; the occipital lobes are involved in vision
reticular formation	helps maintain muscle tone and cardiac reflexes as well as influencing wakefulness, arousal level, and attention

Endocrine Glands and Their Functions

Name of Gland	Function
pituitary gland	the body's master gland; regulates the activity of the other endocrine glands
adrenal glands	involved in physical and emotional arousal
islets of Langerhans	helps regulate the level of sugar in the blood
gonads	produce sex cells and hormones important in sexual arousal
thyroid gland	helps to regulate metabolism
parathyroid glands	important in functioning of the nervous system
pineal gland	largely responsible for regulating biological rhythms such as sleep and wakefulness and menstrual cycles in females

Answers to Review At A Glance

1. brain
2. spinal
3. cord
4. neuron
5. cell body
6. nucleus
7. dendrites
8. axons
9. 100 billion
10. 1,000
11. 10,000
12. nerve
13. electrical
14. ions
15. negative
16. positive
17. semipermeable
18. polarized
19. depolarization
20. all-or-none
21. action potential
22. axon
23. Novocain
24. myelin sheath
25. adulthood
26. multiple sclerosis
27. synapse
28. neurotransmitters
29. knob
30. dendrite
31. action potential
32. dendrite
33. neurotransmitter
34. central nervous system
35. peripheral nervous system
36. afferent
37. efferent
38. interneurons
39. somatic
40. central
41. autonomic
42. motivations
43. parasympathetic
44. stress
45. inhibits
46. peaceful
47. conservation
48. electroencephalogram
49. EEG
50. positron emission tomography
51. magnetic resonance imaging
52. MRI
53. functional
54. hindbrain
55. medulla
56. pons
57. cerebellum
58. reticular formation
59. midbrain
60. thalamus
61. hypothalamus
62. pleasure
63. limbic
64. amygdala
65. hippocampus
66. septal
67. cingulate
68. conscious
69. intelligence
70. gray
71. white
72. frontal
73. Broca's
74. aphasia
75. motor
76. frontal
77. complex
78. parietal
79. touch
80. hearing
81. Wernicke's
82. aphasia
83. occipital
84. silent areas
85. corpus callosum
86. communication
87. verbal
88. spatial
89. split-brain
90. left hemisphere
91. emotion
92. understanding
93. left
94. right
95. plasticity
96. fifth
97. pruning

98. neurogenesis
99. parallel
100. endocrine
101. glands
102. communication
103. brain
104. hypothalamus
105. neurotransmitters
106. nervous system
107. pituitary
108. master gland
109. stress
110. disease
111. adrenal
112. epinephrine
113. norepinephrine
114. islets of Langerhans
115. glucagon
116. insulin
117. gonads
118. ovaries
119. testes

120. estrogen
121. testosterone
122. thyroid
123. thyroxin
124. cretinism
125. parathyroid
126. parathormone
127. pineal
128. melatonin
129. genetic
130. influence
131. chromosomes
132. DNA
133. helix
134. guanine
135. genes
136. inheritance
137. 46
138. thousands
139. gametes
140. 23
141. fertilization

142. zygote
143. pairs
144. 50
145. identical (monozygotic)
146. dominant
147. recessive
148. Down
149. proteins
150. environment
151. ethical
152. monozygotic
153. adopted
154. genetic
155. thought processes
156. ventricles
157. thalamus
158. dopamine
159. stress
160. genetic predisposition
161. birth
162. Alzheimer's

Sample Answers for Short Answer Questions

1. **Explain the relationship between inheritance, genes, DNA, and chromosomes.**

   The cells of the body contain chromosomes. Chromosomes are long strands of DNA. DNA usually forms a double helix. The backbones of these structures are connected at intervals by base pairs of four substances: adenine, thymine, guanine and cystine. Sequences of bases pairs that contain the information needed to influence some aspect of a structure or function of the body are called genes. Genes are therefore the basic biological units of inheritance.

2. **Distinguish between dominant and recessive traits.**

   A dominant gene will reveal its trait whenever the gene is present, whereas a recessive gene will reveal its trait only when the same recessive gene has been inherited from both parents.

3. **Describe the research methods used to help sort out the influences of nature and nurture in humans.**

   Researchers have relied on two descriptive methods. One method involves comparing traits of monozygotic (identical) twins with those of dizygotic (fraternal) twins. A second technique compares the traits of adopted children with the traits of both their biological and adoptive parents.

Multiple-Choice Answers

1. The answer is *A*. Dendrites usually receive messages, whereas axons help transmit messages to other neurons. The cell body of the neuron contains the nucleus, whereas the synapse is the area between neurons.
2. The answer is *D*. Remember that the axon acts on the next cell.
3. The answer is *B*. The polarized state is the resting state of the neuron, when negative ions are mostly inside and positive ions are mostly outside the cell membrane. Semipermeability refers to the fact that some, but not all, ions can pass through the membrane. When electrical charges reach the synapse, transmission across the gap occurs.
4. The answer is *B*. The process of depolarization along the membrane of a neuron allows for the massive influx of sodium ions.
5. The answer is *B*. Excitatory neurotransmitters increase the likelihood of messages crossing the synapse. The myelin sheath is a fatty coating encasing many axons; it insulates the axon and helps increase the speed at which it conducts neural impulses. The action potential refers to the chain of events that allow for the transmission of neural messages.
6. The answer is *A*. Efferent neurons transmit messages from the central nervous system to the organs and muscles of the body, while association neurons are the neurons in the brain and spinal cord that process the information. Transmittal neurons do not, as far as I know, exist.
7. The answer is *C*. Afferent neurons carry messages from the sense organs to the central nervous system, whereas efferent neurons carry messages from the central nervous system to the organs and muscles of the body. Neurons that are neither afferent nor efferent are interneurons.
8. The answer is *A*. The central nervous system consists of the brain and the spinal cord. All other nerves are part of the peripheral nervous system.
9. The answer is *B*. Voluntary movements are higher-order functions and are not processed by the autonomic nervous system.
10. The answer is *A*. The sympathetic nervous system generally helps prepare us for stress, whereas the parasympathetic system generally plays its role under more peaceful conditions.
11. The answer is *B*. PET stands for positron emission topography and MRI stands for magnetic resonance imaging.
12. The answer is *C*. The medulla controls breathing and a variety of reflexes. The pons helps regulate balance, hearing, and some parasympathetic functions. The thalamus helps to route messages to the appropriate parts of the brain.
13. The answer is *D*. Other parts of the forebrain include the thalamus, the limbic system, and the lobes of the cerebral cortex.
14. The answer is *D*. The medulla and pons are both part of the hindbrain. The forebrain is the structure that contains the cerebral cortex.
15. The answer is *D*. The cerebellum consists of two rounded structures located in the hindbrain behind the pons. The cerebellum also plays a role in learning and memory that involve coordinated sequences of information.
16. The answer is *D*. The routing function is carried out by the thalamus.
17. The answer is *C*. The amygdala plays a key role in the formation of memories about emotionally charged events.
18. The answer is *C*. Wernicke's aphasia is characterized by an inability to understand language spoken by others. Wernicke's area is located in the left hemisphere.
19. The answer is *D*. Damage to the visual area of the occipital lobe can result in partial or even total blindness.
20. The answer is *A*. Severing the corpus callosum results in some unusual behavior, discussed in the section on split brains.
21. The answer is *D*. When information is presented to the left visual field of each eye, the information reaches the right hemisphere, which has no area controlling verbal expression. As a result, the patient is unable to identify the information. Note that the language functions of the cerebral hemispheres are often reversed in left-handed persons.
22. The answer is *B*. Conversely, the right hemisphere is more likely to process negative emotions.
23. The answer is *B*. The ability of the brain to process several types of information at the same time makes it similar to parallel processing in computers. Serial processing refers to handling one type of information at a time.
24. The answer is *B*. The hormones of the pituitary gland help to regulate the activities of the other glands in the endocrine system.

25. The answer is *B*. Neurotransmitters are the chemicals found in the brain.
26. The answer is *D*. The adrenals are involved in emotional arousal. The thyroid gland helps to regulate metabolism. The pituitary gland is often called the master gland because it helps to regulate the other glands in the endocrine system.
27. The answer is *D*. Four substances in differing sequences carry the genetic code. The four substances are adenine, thymine, guanine, and cystine.
28. The answer is *A*. If both brown-eyed parents possess a recessive gene for blue eyes, and if both contribute this gene to their offspring, their child will have blue eyes.
29. The answer is *D*. Down syndrome is one of a variety of chromosomal abnormalities that results in mental retardation.
30. The answer is *A*. Dizygotic twins are no more alike genetically than siblings born at different times; monozygotic twins, however, develop from a single fertilized egg cell and are also called identical twins.
31. The answer is *D*. Both twin studies and adoption studies have allowed psychologists to begin to understand the influence of heredity on behavior. These studies are correlational in nature, however, and not based on formal experiments as described in Chapter 2.
32. The answer is *D*. Dizygotic twins, by contrast, are formed from two separate ova and two sperm. Genetically, they are no more alike than siblings born at different times.
33. The answer is *C*. Although research has shown that genetic factors clearly influence behavior and mental processes, they do not explain all of the differences between people.
34. The answer is *C*. MRI images have revealed many of the dramatic differences between a normal brain and the brains of people diagnosed with schizophrenia.
35. The answer is *D*. This hypothesis is referred to as the "double-strike" theory of schizophrenia.

Answers to True-False Questions

1. T	6. F
2. T	7. T
3. F	8. F
4. F	9. T
5. T	10. F

Part II Awareness

Chapter 4 Sensation and Perception

Learning Objectives

1. Distinguish between sensation and perception, and define sense organ, sensory receptor, and stimulus. (p. 114)

2. Define transduction. (p. 114)

3. Compare and contrast the absolute threshold and the difference threshold. (p. 115)

4. Understand sensory adaptation. (p. 115)

5. Define psychophysics and understand Weber's law. (p. 115)

6. Understand the nature of light. (p. 118)

7. Describe how the different parts of the eye work together to produce vision. (p. 119)

8. Describe the roles played by the rods and cones in both dark adaptation and light adaptation. (p. 120)

9. Compare and contrast the trichromatic theory and the opponent-process theory of color vision, describing the evidence for each. (p. 122)

10. Understand the nature of sound. (p. 126)

11. Explain how different parts of the ear work together to produce audition (the sense of hearing). (p. 128)

12. Describe the roles played by the vestibular organ and the kinesthetic receptors in providing information about orientation and movement. (p. 132)

13. List the four different general types of skin receptors, and describe the three types of stimuli that can be detected by the skin. (p. 133)

14. Explain the gate control theory of pain, and describe the role played by endorphins in runner's high, acupuncture, and placebos. (p. 135)

15. Define phantom limb pain, and identify its possible causes. (p. 137)

16. List the basic taste sensations, and identify other factors that influence our perception of taste. (p. 140)

17. List the seven primary qualities of odors, and explain the role of pheromones in regulating behavior. (p. 141)

18. Name and describe the five Gestalt principles of perceptual organization. (p. 144)

19. Describe the four kinds of perceptual constancy. (p. 145)

20. Identify the monocular cues and binocular cues of depth perception. (p. 146)

21. Distinguish between the visual illusions, and describe how they are produced. (p. 149)

22. Identify how individual and cultural factors influence perception. (p. 152)

23. (From the Application section) Discuss the relationship among visual perception, illusion, and art. (p. 154)

Chapter Overview

Sensation refers to the ability of the sense organs to receive messages from the outside world, while perception refers to the ability to organize and interpret these messages.

We receive external stimuli through specialized sensory receptor cells. First, sense organs receive stimuli. Next, they transduce this sensory energy into neural impulses. The neural impulses are then sent to the brain to be interpreted. The field that studies the relationships between physical stimuli and psychological sensations is called psychophysics.

The sense of sight functions by detecting light energy. The intensity of a light wave determines its brightness, while the wavelength largely determines color. The eye, which works much like a camera, is the primary sense organ for seeing. Light enters the eye through the cornea and lens and then enters the retina. Rods and cones transduce light waves into neural impulses for transportation to the brain. The 100 million rods are located throughout the retina but are not found in the fovea. Although they are active in peripheral vision and vision in dim light, they do not play a role in color vision. The 6 million cones, clustered mainly near the fovea, are involved in color vision. Two theories that explain color vision are trichromatic theory and opponent-process theory.

The sense of hearing functions by detecting sound waves. The frequency of sound waves determines pitch, while their intensity determines loudness. The outer ear collects sound waves, which vibrate the eardrum. The eardrum is connected to a series of movable bones in the middle ear. The inner ear, which contains the cochlea and the organ of Corti, transduces the sound waves' energy into neural impulses. These impulses are transported to the brain.

The sensory system also receives information about internal stimuli. For example, the vestibular organ provides information about body orientation, and the kinesthetic sense reports body position and movement. The various skin senses can detect pressure, temperature, and pain.

Humans also possess chemical senses, such as taste and smell. These senses respond to chemicals in the environment rather than to energy.

The interpretation of sensory neural impulses that have been transmitted to the brain is called perception. Perception is an active mental process. Gestalt principles explain many of the ways in which humans tend to organize sensory information. Individual factors, such as motivation and prior learning, also affect perception.

Key Terms Exercise

For each of the following exercises, match the key terms on the left with the correct definitions on the right. Page references to the text follow the terms so that you may refer to the text for any items you answer incorrectly or do not understand completely. You may check your responses immediately by referring to the answers that follow each exercise.

Sensation (I)

_____ 1. sense organs (p. 114)
_____ 2. sensory receptor cells (p. 114)
_____ 3. sensation (p. 114)
_____ 4. perception (p. 114)
_____ 5. stimulus (p. 114)

a. cells that translate messages into neural impulses
b. organs that receive stimuli
c. the process of organizing and interpreting information
d. any aspect of the outside world that influences our behavior.
e. the process of receiving, translating, and transmitting messages from the outside world to the brain

ANSWERS
1. b   4. c
2. a   5. d
3. e

Sensation (II)

_____ 1. transduction (p. 114)
_____ 2. absolute threshold (p. 115)
_____ 3. difference threshold (p. 115)
_____ 4. sensory adaptation (p. 115)
_____ 5. psychophysics (p. 115)
_____ 6. Weber's law (p. 116)

a. a weakened sensation resulting from prolonged presentation of the stimulus
b. the smallest magnitude of a stimulus that can be detected half of the time
c. a specialty field that studies sensory limits, sensory adaption, etc.
d. the translation of energy from one form into another
e. the amount of change in a stimulus needed to detect a difference is in direct proportion to the intensity of the stimulus
f. the smallest difference between two stimuli that can be detected half of the time

ANSWERS

1. d   4. a
2. b   5. c
3. f   6. e

Vision (I)

_____ 1. retina (p. 119)
_____ 2. rods (p. 119)
_____ 3. cones (p. 119)
_____ 4. fovea (p. 120)

a. the central spot of the retina
b. cells located in the center of the retina that code information about light, dark, and color
c. the area that contains the rods and cones
d. cells located outside the center of the retina that code information about light and dark

ANSWERS

1. c   3. b
2. d   4. a

Vision (II)

_____ 1. optic nerve (p. 120)
_____ 2. blind spot (p. 120)
_____ 3. dark and light adaptation (p. 121)
_____ 4. trichromatic theory (p. 122)
_____ 5. opponent-process theory (p. 124)

a. a theory of color vision that suggests the eye has two kinds of color processors
b. changed sensitivity of the eye in response to a change in overall illumination
c. the nerve that carries messages about vision to the brain
d. a theory of color vision that suggests that the eye has three kinds of cones
e. the area where the optic nerve attaches to the retina

ANSWERS

1. c   4. d
2. e   5. a
3. b

Hearing

_____ 1. audition (p. 126)
_____ 2. eardrum (p. 128)
_____ 3. hammer, anvil, and stirrup (p. 128)
_____ 4. cochlea (p. 128)
_____ 5. basilar membrane (p. 130)
_____ 6. organ of Corti (p. 130)

a. the sense of hearing
b. a membrane in the middle ear
c. a structure of the inner ear that is filled with fluid
d. contains receptor cells that transduce sound waves into neural impulses
e. tiny bones of the middle ear
f. the organ of Corti rests upon this

ANSWERS
1. a   4. c
2. b   5. f
3. e   6. d

Body Senses, Chemical Senses, and Perception

_____ 1. vestibular organ (p. 132)
_____ 2. kinesthetic receptors (p. 132)
_____ 3. semicircular canals (p. 132)
_____ 4. gustation (p. 140)
_____ 5. olfaction (p. 140)
_____ 6. stereochemical theory (p. 142)
_____ 7. perceptual constancy (p. 146)
_____ 8. monocular and binocular cues (p. 146)

a. the theory that odor receptors are stimulated by specific molecules
b. the sense of taste
c. receptors that provide information about movement, posture, and orientation
d. structures in the inner ear that provide the brain with information about balance and movement
e. three tubes in the vestibular organ that inform the brain about tilts of the head and body
f. the sense of smell
g. visual cues that permit us to perceive depth
h. the tendency to perceive objects as being relatively unchanging

ANSWERS
1. d   5. f
2. c   6. a
3. e   7. h
4. b   8. g

Review At A Glance
(Answers to this section are found on page 73)

Sensation: Receiving Messages about the World

Humans receive messages through their sense organs. Sense organs operate through ___(1)___ _____ _____.
These cells allow us to receive, translate, and transmit messages to the brain, a process called ___(2)___. We
interpret this information through a process called ___(3)___. Any aspect of the outside world that directly
influences our behavior is a ___(4)___. Stimuli are translated from one form of energy to another through a process
called ___(5)___. Sensory receptor cells transduce sensory energy into ___(6)___ _____.

Not all sensory messages can be detected. The smallest magnitude of a stimulus that can be detected half the
time is the ___(7)___ _____; the smallest difference between two stimuli that can be detected half the time is

called the ___(8)_____. Stimuli that are presented for prolonged periods may cause weaker sensations due to ___(9)_____. The field that studies sensory limits and sensory adaptation is ___(10)___. The law stating that the amount of change in a stimulus needed to detect a difference is proportional to the intensity of the original stimulus is called ___(11)_____.

Vision: Your Human Camera

Visible light is part of a form of energy called ___(12)_____, which includes electricity and radio waves. Light is composed of waves that have both ___(13)___ and ___(14)___. The intensity of the light determines the ___(15)___, while the ___(16)___ determines the hue we see.

In the eye, light first passes through a clear protective coating called the ___(17)___. The colored part of the eye, the ___(18)___, regulates the light passing through the pupil into the ___(19)___. The lens is held in place by ligaments that are attached to the ___(20)_____. This muscle regulates the image that falls on the light-sensitive ___(21)___. Two types of receptor cells in the retina are the ___(22)___ and ___(23)___. Each eye has about ___(24)_____ cones and about ___(25)_____ rods. The greatest concentration of cones is in the ___(26)___. In good light, ___(27)_____ is best for images focused directly on the fovea. The rods are located throughout the retina except in the center. There are four differences between rods and cones: (1) rods are largely responsible for ___(28)___ vision; (2) rods are much more sensitive to ___(29)___ than the cones; (3) rods produce images that are perceived with less ___(30)_____; and (4) only cones code information about ___(31)___. An area near the center of the retina contains no rods or cones and is called the ___(32)_____. Information in the optic nerve crosses over at the ___(33)_____.

The processes by which the eyes change their sensitivity to darkness or light are referred to as dark and light ___(34)___. Color is the conscious experience that results as the eye and nervous system process ___(35)___ energy. The theory that there are three kinds of cones in the retina, responding to either the red, green, or blue range of wavelength, is referred to as ___(36)___ theory. Trichromatic theory cannot explain three phenomena: ___(37)___ colors, color ___(38)___ and partial color ___(39)___.

The opponent-process theory states that the three kinds of cones stimulate two kinds of ___(40)___-_____ mechanisms. One is the ___(41)___-_____ processing mechanism, while the other is the ___(42)___-_____ processing mechanism. The trichromatic theory accurately describes events at the ___(43)___, while the opponent-process theory best describes the activities of ___(44)___ in the rest of the visual system.

Hearing: Sensing Sound Waves

The sense of hearing is called ___(45)___. Audition occurs when there are vibratory changes in the air known as ___(46)_____. The rate of vibration of sound waves is termed the ___(47)___ of cycles; its unit of measurement is called ___(48)___. Our experience of these sound vibrations is called ___(49)___. The loudness of a sound is determined by its ___(50)___. Intensity is measured in units called ___(51)___. The complexity of a sound wave determines the ___(52)___ of a sound.

The external part of the ear, which helps to collect and localize sound, is the ___(53)___. The pinna is connected to the middle ear by the ___(54)___ auditory canal. The first structure of the middle ear is the ___(55)___. Sound waves vibrate the eardrum; this sets into movement the three bones of the middle ear, called the ___(56)___, ___(57)___, and ___(58)___. In the inner ear, a membrane called the ___(59)___ ___ is set into motion. The vibration of the oval window creates waves in the fluid-filled ___(60)___. The pressure of these waves is relieved by the ___(61)___ ___. The ear's sensory receptors, located in the organ of ___(62)___, are stimulated by a membrane in the cochlea called the ___(63)___ ___. The organ of Corti then codes the messages to the brain, based on the ___(64)___ and the ___(65)___ of the sound waves. Not all sounds are transmitted from the outer ear to the cochlea; for example, we hear ourselves speak largely through bone ___(66)___ hearing. The existence of two ears helps us to ___(67)___ the origin of sounds.

Body Senses: Messages from Myself

Messages about the orientation and movement of the body come from two kinds of sense organs. The first, located in the inner ear, is the ___(68)___ ___. This organ is composed of (1) fluid-filled sacs called the ___(69)___ and ___(70)___, which tell the brain about the body's orientation, and (2) three nearly circular tubes that inform the brain about tilts of the head and body, called the ___(71)___ ___. The sensory receptors of each canal are located in the ___(72)___.

The ___(73)___ sense consists of individual receptors located in the skin, muscles, joints, and tendons. The skin can detect ___(74)___, ___(75)___, and ___(76)___. It contains four types of receptors: ___(77)___ nerve endings, ___(78)___ cells, tactile ___(79)___, and specialized ___(80)___ bulbs. Apparently, all four types play a role in detecting ___(81)___, while the free nerve endings are also the primary receptors for temperature and ___(82)___.

The sensitivity of the skin differs from one region to the next. The most sensitive regions are the ___(83)___, the ___(84)___, and the ___(85)___. With regard to temperature, one set of spots on the skin detects ___(86)___ and one set detects ___(87)___, but the sensation of intense ___(88)___ is created by both warm and cold spots.

Free nerve endings throughout the body serve as ___(89)___. These are receptors for stimuli that are experienced as ___(90)___ in the brain. We often experience first and second pain due to the existence of ___(91)___ and ___(92)___ neural pathways. No direct relationship exists between the pain stimulus and the amount of pain a person experiences. Sometimes circumstances can block pain. One theory that explains these phenomena is called the ___(93)___ ___ theory of pain. This theory proposes that messages from ___(94)___ are allowed in or blocked from the brain by neural "gates." Pain gates allow more slow-pain neural transmission to the ___(95)___ system in two ways. First, pain messages ___(96)___ the pain gates and make them transmit slow pain messages more readily due to the action of substance P. Second, messages from the midbrain make it more likely that slow pain impulses will be carried to the ___(97)___ system.

The pain gates appear to be operated by specialized neurons called ___(98)___ neurons. These neurons inhibit the pain neurons by using substances called ___(99)___. Women have a second pain-gate mechanism, based on the hormone ___(100)___. The opiate morphine duplicates the effects of ___(101)___. Additionally, runner's high appears to be the result of the release of high levels of ___(102)___. Research also suggests that the pain-reducing effects of ___(103)___ and placebo medications may be due to stimulating the body's endorphins. Endorphins may have a negative effect on the body's ___(104)___ system. After receiving a cut, inflammation leads to the sensitization of ___(105)___ near the cut. This occurs because nocioreceptors become increasingly sensitive and because substance P can turn nerve endings usually involved in the sense of ___(106)___ into nocioreceptors. Research conducted on phantom limb pain has found that when sensory and pain neurons are cut, the corresponding ___(107)___ cortex becomes sensitive to input that activates nearby portions of the somatosensory cortex.

Chemical Senses: The Flavors and Aromas of Life

The sense of taste, called ___(108)___, and the sense of smell, called ___(109)___, respond to chemicals. There are approximately ___(110)___ taste buds on the tongue, each containing approximately a dozen sensory receptors called ___(111)___. The taste buds are clustered together in bumps called ___(112)___. All of our sensations of taste result from the following basic sensations: ___(113)___, sourness, ___(114)___, bitterness, and ___(115)___. We lose taste buds as we ___(116)___.

Olfactory receptor cells are located in the nasal cavity in a mucous-coated sheet called the ___(117)___. One system of classifying odors suggests that all of the complex odors and aromas of life are combinations of ___(118)___ primary qualities. Professionals who create perfumes and other aromas, however, distinguish ___(119)___ different types of odors. Nearly all of the odors that humans can detect are ___(120)___ compounds. The theory that odor receptors can only be stimulated by molecules of a specific size and shape is called the ___(121)___ theory.

In many animals, the vomeronasal organ, located behind the olfactory epithelium, contains receptors for ___(122)___. Pheromones are released in the sweat and urine of animals and are detected by the ___(123)___ organ of other animals. This process helps stimulate the release of sexual hormones, ovulation, sexual behavior, and ___(124)___ toward other animals. In humans, pheromones influence female ___(125)___ cycles.

Perception: Interpreting Sensory Messages

The process of organizing and interpreting neural energy is ___(126)___. Gestalt psychologists have described the following ways in which we organize our visual perception: (1) the center of attention and the background, called ___(127)___-___, can be reversed; (2) we tend to perceive ___(128)___ in lines and patterns; (3) things that are close together are perceived as belonging together, according to the principle of ___(129)___; (4) similar things tend to be perceived together, according to the principle of ___(130)___; and (5) incomplete figures are perceived as wholes, according to the concept of ___(131)___.

Although raw sensations are constantly changing, we tend to perceive objects as being fairly constant and unchanging. This tendency is called ___(132)___ and relates to the brightness, color, size, and shape of objects.

We are able to perceive a three-dimensional world with a two-dimensional retina because we use ___(133)___ in depth perception. Those cues that can be seen by one eye are ___(134)___ cues, while those that are perceived by both eyes are called ___(135)___ cues. The monocular cues are texture ___(136)___, linear ___(137)___, superposition, shadowing, speed of ___(138)___, aerial ___(139)___, accommodation and ___(140)___ position. The binocular cues are convergence and retinal ___(141)___.

Intentional manipulations of cues to create a perception of something that is not real are referred to as ___(142)___. An illusion that is viewed in everyday life is the ___(143)___ illusion.

There is evidence that ___(144)___ and ___(145)___ factors play an important role in perception.

Painters often use ___(146)___ cues of depth perception to create the illusion of a ___(147)___ -dimensional object.

Concept Checks
Fill in the missing components of the following concept boxes. The correct answers are located in the "Answers" section at the end of the chapter.

Structures and Functions of Body Senses and Chemical Senses

Structure	Function
	inner ear structures that provide the brain with information about movement; structures are the semicircular canals, the saccule and utricle
nocioreceptors	
gate control theory of pain	
	taste buds on the tongue that are sensitive to sweetness, sourness, saltiness, bitterness, and fattiness
olfactory epithelium	
	organ in the nasal cavity of many animals that contains receptors to detect pheromones

Structures and Functions of the Eyes and Ears

Structure	Function
	opens and closes to control the amount of light that passes through the pupil into the lens
retina	
	located throughout the retina except in the fovea; they are largely responsible for peripheral vision and are highly sensitive to light; they cannot code information about color
cones	
	carries neural messages to the brain
pinna	
	a thin membrane in the middle ear that vibrates in response to sound waves
	a long, curled structure, filled with fluid; it is set into motion by the oval window
organ of Corti	

Extending the Chapter: Psychology, Societal Issues, and Human Diversity

These questions may be assigned to you. Whether or not they are assigned, they are designed to be challenging questions to encourage you to think independently about the material in the chapter. Many of the questions have no right or wrong answers.

I. From the "Applications of Psychology" section

1. Describe the ways in which successful painters use Gestalt principles of perception.

2. Discuss Leonardo da Vinci's advice for painters; how does this relate to Gestalt principles of visual perception?

II. Psychology, Societal Issues, and Human Diversity

1. From the Human Diversity section of the text: describe the perception and management of pain in your culture. How did your parents and/or other caregivers respond when you were experiencing pain? Were there differing expectations based on gender or on age?

2. If future research supports human sensitivity and reactivity to pheromones, how should the production of these pheromones be regulated?

3. The perception of different foods as being tasty or disgusting is largely dependent upon one's cultural background. Describe some foods that you enjoy that others find unappetizing; likewise, what foods do you avoid that others enjoy?

4. The ease with which humans are subject to visual and other types of illusions suggests that, in reality, the world is not always the way we perceive it. What is your reaction to this statement?

Practice Quiz

The practice quiz consists of three sections: 1) Short answer questions, 2) Multiple-choice questions, and 3) True-False questions. At the end of the chapter you will find suggested answers to the short answer questions, answers and explanations for the multiple-choice questions, and answers to the true-false questions.

Short Answer Questions

1. List and explain five Gestalt principles of perceptual organization.

_____

_____

2. List and describe four examples of perceptual constancy.

_____

_____

3. Distinguish between monocular cues and binocular cues of depth perception. Give two examples of each.

_____

_____

Multiple-Choice Questions

1. Each of the following is part of the process of sensation *except*
   a. receiving messages.
   b. translating messages.
   c. transmitting messages.
   d. interpreting messages.
   LO 1

2. Which of the following describes the process of transduction?
   a. when a friend plays the radio below your absolute threshold
   b. when light waves are converted to neural impulses
   c. when stimuli occur that are not attended to
   d. none of the above
   LO 2

3. After repeatedly asking your roommate to turn down the stereo so that you can study your psychology, you lose your temper. You rush into the living room, where your roommate indicates that the stereo *was* turned down! The amount by which the stereo was turned down was below your
   a. difference threshold.
   b. absolute threshold.
   c. sensory adaption level.
   d. in-between threshold.
   LO 3

4. The smallest magnitude of a stimulus that can be detected is called the
   a. absolute threshold.
   b. difference threshold.
   c. minimum threshold.
   d. transduction threshold.
   LO 3

5. An architect is designing apartments and wants them to be soundproof. She asks a psychologist what the smallest amount of sound is that can be heard. Her question is most related to the
   a. absolute threshold.
   b. difference threshold.
   c. Weber's law.
   d. sensory receptors.
   LO 3

6. Joe was upset when he started his car because the radio blared out loudly. Then he realized that he was the one who last played the car radio. "I didn't think I had the volume turned up so high," he thought. What phenomenon might have occurred when Joe played the car radio previously?
   a. the absolute threshold
   b. the difference threshold
   c. sensory adaptation
   d. transduction
   LO 4

7. Weber's law
   a. refers to the ability to detect changes in the intensity of various stimuli.
   b. helps to explain the process of sensory adaptation.
   c. is useful in predicting the absolute threshold.
   d. both *a* and *b*
   LO 5

8. The brightness of a visual sensation is determined by the
   a. intensity of the light wave.
   b. frequency of the light wave.
   c. saturation of the light wave.
   d. radiation of the light wave.
   LO 6

9. In the eye, light waves are transduced into neural impulses by
   a. the cornea and the iris.
   b. the pupil and the lens.
   c. the rods and the cones.
   d. none of the above
   LO 7

10. The amount of light entering the eye is controlled by the
   a. pupil.
   b. lens.
   c. iris.
   d. fovea.
   LO 7

11. When compared with cones, rods
   a. are responsible for peripheral vision.
   b. are less sensitive to light.
   c. produce images perceived with good visual acuity.
   d. can code information about color.
   LO 8

12. Rods and cones stop firing almost completely during the process of
   a. dark adaptation.
   b. light adaptation.
   c. color vision.
   d. monochromacy.
   LO 8

13. Which of the following events is explained by the opponent-process theory of color vision?
   a. complementary colors
   b. color afterimages
   c. neuron responses
   d. all of the above
   LO 9

14. The frequency of sound waves is measured in
   a. hertz.
   b. decibels.
   c. timbre.
   d. none of the above.
   LO 10

15. The loudness of a sound depends primarily on its
   a. intensity.
   b. timbre.
   c. complexity.
   d. noise level.
   LO 10

16. The eardrum, hammer, anvil, and stirrup are located in the
   a. inner ear.
   b. middle ear.
   c. outer ear.
   d. external auditory canal.
   LO 11

17. The organ of Corti codes neural messages for the brain based on
   a. the intensity of a sound wave.
   b. the frequency of a sound wave.
   c. the pitch of a sound wave.
   d. both *a* and *b*
   LO 11

18. In the ear, sound waves are transduced into neural messages by receptors located in the
   a. organ of Corti.
   b. hammer, anvil, and stirrup.
   c. middle ear.
   d. pinna.
   LO 11

19. Where are the sensory receptors of the vestibular organ located?
   a. cerebral cortex
   b. muscles and joints
   c. skin
   d. inner ear
   LO 12

20. Information about the location and movement of skin, muscles, joints, and tendons is provided by
   a. basket cells.
   b. kinesthetic receptors.
   c. tactile discs.
   d. specialized end bulbs.
   LO 12

21. Nocioreceptors are free nerve endings that transmit information to the brain about
   a. temperature.
   b. pressure.
   c. olfaction.
   d. pain.
   LO 13

22. Which skin receptors are the primary receptors for detecting temperature?
    a. free nerve endings
    b. specialized end bulbs
    c. tactile discs
    d. tactile epithelium
    LO 13

23. Each of the following phenomena may be explained by endorphins *except*
    a. visual acuity.
    b. runner's high.
    c. acupuncture.
    d. placebos.
    LO 14

24. Pain gates appear to involve
    a. endorphins.
    b. estrogen in women.
    c. placebos.
    d. both *a* and *b*
    LO 14

25. Research suggests phantom limb pain involves
    a. the hypothalamus.
    b. endorphins.
    c. the corpus callosum.
    d. the somatosensory cortex.
    LO 15

26. Each of the following is a basic taste sensation *except*
    a. spicy.
    b. sweet.
    c. sour.
    d. bitter.
    LO 16

27. Molecules responsible for each of the primary odors have a specific shape that will fit only one type of receptor, according to the
    a. olfactory-epithelium approach.
    b. opponent-process theory of smell.
    c. integrated-key theory.
    d. stereochemical theory.
    LO 17

28. The tendency to mentally fill in incomplete figures is the Gestalt principle of perception called
    a. figure-ground.
    b. proximity.
    c. dissimilarity.
    d. closure.
    LO 18

29. The perception of items as containing a center and a background is referred to as the Gestalt principle of
    a. proximity.
    b. figure-ground.
    c. continuity.
    d. similarity.
    LO 18

30. We continue to perceive that a penny is round, regardless of the angle from which it is viewed. This is an example of a process called
    a. perceptual constancy.
    b. light adaptation.
    c. figure-grounding.
    d. proximity.
    LO 19

31. Each of the following is a monocular cue *except*
    a. texture gradient.
    b. aerial perspective.
    c. accommodation.
    d. convergence.
    LO 20

32. The Ames room demonstrates
    a. convergence.
    b. retinal disparity.
    c. a visual illusion.
    d. all of the above
    LO 21

33. The moon looks bigger at the horizon than it does higher in the sky because
    a. the beams are passing through denser air, which magnifies them.
    b. it is a different color, which makes it look bigger.
    c. it appears larger in comparison to trees and buildings on the horizon.
    d. the moon's light falls on the fovea when it is low on the horizon.
    LO 21

34. According to the text, research with hungry college students and with sexually aroused males helps to demonstrate
   a. the influence of motivation on perception.
   b. individual influences on perception.
   c. cultural influences on perception.
   d. none of the above
      LO 22

35. According to the text, effective painters, drawers, and sculptors make good use of
   a. depth perception cues.
   b. visual illusions.
   c. perceptual constancy cues.
   d. all of the above
      LO 23

True-False Questions

_____ 1. Each of the sense organs engages in the process of transduction.

_____ 2. In the eyes, the rods are receptor cells that can detect color.

_____ 3. According to the trichromatic theory of color vision, the visual system has two kinds of color processors.

_____ 4. The eardrum is located in the inner ear.

_____ 5. The transduction of sound waves into neural impulses takes place in the organ of Corti.

_____ 6. Nocioreceptors are receptors for stimuli relating to temperature.

_____ 7. Runner's high is most likely due to the effects of endorphins.

_____ 8. One of the basic sensations to which the taste buds are sensitive is bitterness.

_____ 9. Researchers have not yet determined whether human behavior is influenced by pheromones.

_____10. Both monocular and binocular cues are involved in depth perception.

ANSWERS SECTION

Concept Checks

Structures and Functions of Body Senses and Chemical Senses

Structure	Function
vestibular organ	inner ear structures that provide the brain with information about movement; structures are the semicircular canals, the saccule, and utricle
nocioreceptors	receptors for stimuli that are experienced as painful in the brain
gate control theory of pain	neural gates regulate the transmission of impulses from the nocioreceptors to the brain
papillae	taste buds on the tongue that are sensitive to sweetness, sourness, saltiness, bitterness, and fattiness
olfactory epithelium	receptor cells at the top of the nasal cavity responsible for detecting odors
vomeronasal organ	organ in the nasal cavity of many animals that contains receptors to detect pheromones

Structures and Functions of the Eyes and Ears

Structure	Function
iris	opens and closes to control the amount of light that passes through the pupil into the lens
retina	the light-sensitive area at the back of the eye
rods	located throughout the retina except in the fovea; they are largely responsible for peripheral vision and are highly sensitive to light; they cannot code information about color
cones	concentrated in the fovea and code information about light, dark, and color
optic nerve	carries neural messages to the brain
pinna	the outer ear, which is responsible for collecting sound waves
eardrum	a thin membrane in the middle ear that vibrates in response to sound waves
cochlea	a long, curled structure, filled with fluid; it is set into motion by the oval window
organ of Corti	contains the receptor cells that transduce the sound waves of the cochlear fluid into neural impulses

Answers to Review At A Glance

1. sensory receptor cells
2. sensation
3. perception
4. stimulus
5. transduction
6. neural energy
7. absolute threshold
8. difference threshold
9. sensory adaptation
10. psychophysics
11. Weber's law
12. electromagnetic radiation
13. frequency
14. intensity
15. brightness
16. wavelength
17. cornea
18. iris
19. lens
20. ciliary muscle
21. retina
22. rods
23. cones
24. 6 million
25. 125 million
26. fovea
27. visual acuity
28. peripheral
29. light
30. visual acuity
31. color
32. blind spot
33. optic chiasm
34. adaptation
35. light
36. trichromatic
37. complementary
38. afterimages
39. blindness
40. color-processing
41. yellow-blue
42. red-green
43. cones
44. neurons
45. audition
46. sound waves
47. frequency
48. hertz
49. pitch
50. intensity
51. decibels
52. timbre
53. pinna
54. external
55. eardrum
56. hammer
57. anvil
58. stirrup
59. oval window
60. cochlea
61. round window
62. Corti
63. basilar membrane
64. intensity
65. frequency
66. conduction
67. locate
68. vestibular organ
69. saccule
70. utricle
71. semicircular canals
72. cupula
73. kinesthetic
74. pressure
75. temperature
76. pain
77. free
78. basket
79. discs
80. end
81. pressure
82. pain
83. fingertips
84. lips
85. genitals
86. warmth
87. coldness
88. heat
89. nocioreceptors
90. pain
91. rapid
92. slow
93. gate control
94. nocioreceptors
95. limbic
96. sensitize
97. limbic
98. gate
99. endorphins
100. estrogen
101. endorphins
102. endorphins
103. acupuncture
104. immune
105. nocioreceptors
106. touch
107. somatosensory
108. gustation
109. olfaction
110. 10,000
111. taste buds
112. papillae
113. sweetness
114. saltiness
115. fattiness
116. age
117. olfactory epithelium
118. seven
119. 146
120. organic
121. stereochemical
122. pheromones
123. vomeronasal
124. aggression
125. reproductive
126. perception
127. figure-ground
128. continuity
129. proximity
130. similarity
131. closure
132. perceptual constancy
133. cues
134. monocular
135. binocular
136. gradient
137. perspective
138. movement
139. perspective
140. vertical
141. disparity
142. visual illusions
143. moon
144. individual
145. cultural
146. monocular
147. three

Sample Answers to Short Answer Questions

1. **List and explain five Gestalt principles of perceptual organization.**

   The principle of figure-ground means that we organize our visual perceptions into both the center of our attention (the figure) and the indistinct background (the ground). Continuity refers to the tendency to perceive lines or patterns that follow a smooth contour as being part of a single unit. Proximity means that items that are close together are perceived as belonging together. Similarity suggests similar things are perceived as being related. Closure allows us to perceive meaning by mentally filling in missing information in order to create complete perceptions.

2. **List and describe four examples of perceptual constancy.**

   Perceptual constancy refers to our ability to perceive objects as remaining relatively unchanged in spite of changes in raw sensations. Brightness constancy allows us perceive objects as being the same brightness, even if the lighting changes. Likewise, color constancy means that we tend to perceive objects as being the same color even if lighting changes. Size constancy refers to our ability to perceive objects as being the same size, even when we view them from different distances. Shape constancy means we perceive objects as being the same shape even when we look from different angles and distances.

3. **Distinguish between monocular cues and binocular cues of depth perception. Give two examples of each.**

   Monocular cues refers to depth perception as seen by one eye, whereas binocular cues involves depth perception using both eyes. Examples of monocular depth perception include texture gradient, linear perspective, superposition, shadowing, speed of movement, aerial perspective, accommodation, and vertical position. Two binocular cues (which occur when both eyes perceive the same object) are convergence and retinal disparity.

Multiple-Choice Answers

1. The answer is *D.* Alternatives *A, B,* and *C* are all part of the process of sensation, whereas the process of interpreting messages is called perception.
2. The answer is *B.* The process of transduction refers to translating one form of energy to another. Thus, in order for people to see, light waves must be transduced into neural impulses.
3. The answer is *A.* The difference threshold is the smallest difference between two stimuli that can be detected half the time. Your roommate did, in fact, turn down the volume of the stereo, but the difference was so small that you could not detect it. Now, aren't you sorry that you yelled at your roomie?
4. The answer is *A.* The absolute threshold refers to the smallest magnitude of a stimulus that can be detected, whereas the difference threshold is the smallest difference between two stimuli that can be detected half the time.
5. The answer is *A.* The minimal amounts of stimuli that can be detected are referred to as the absolute threshold. The difference threshold refers to detecting differences between two stimuli.
6. The answer is *C.* Sensory adaptation refers to the weakened magnitude of a sensation resulting from prolonged presentation of a stimulus. Other examples include getting used to the cool water in a swimming pool and getting used to loud rock music.
7. The answer is *A.* Weber's law states that the *difference* threshold is in direct proportion to the intensity of the original stimulus. This helps to predict our ability to detect changes in stimuli. The *absolute* threshold refers to the smallest magnitude of a stimulus that can be detected.
8. The answer is *A.* The intensity of a light is related to the brightness of the sensation, whereas the saturation of a color is related to the variety of wavelengths that comprise the color.
9. The answer is *C.* The rods and cones are receptor cells that are found in the retina. The cornea is a protective covering on the eye's surface. The iris regulates the amount of light that enters the eye. The pupil is the opening of the iris, while the lens focuses light on the retina.
10. The answer is *C.* The colored part of the eye, the iris, opens and closes to regulate the amount of light passing through the pupil into the lens.

11. The answer is *A*. Each of the other alternatives is true of cones.
12. The answer is *A*. When we enter a dark room after being in sunlight, the rods and cones are not sensitive enough to be stimulated by the low-intensity light. The receptors thus get to rest before regaining their sensitivity to light. In light adaptation, on the other hand, the rods and cones that have been in the dark for a while are extremely sensitive to light.
13. The answer is *D*. According to the opponent-process theory, there are two kinds of cones in the retina that respond to light in either the red-green or yellow-blue ranges of wavelength.
14. The answer is *A*. The frequency of sound waves is measured in hertz, whereas the intensity is measured in decibels and the complexity is reflected in the timbre of a sound.
15. The answer is *A*. The intensity of a sound is determined by how densely compacted the air molecules are in the sound wave.
16. The answer is *B*. The middle ear transduces sound waves into mechanical energy and passes the energy on to the inner ear.
17. The answer is *D*. The intensity is coded by the number of receptors that fire, while the frequency is coded according to location in the organ of Corti and the firing of volleys of impulses by different groups of neurons.
18. The answer is *A*. The organ of Corti is located in the cochlea of the inner ear. The outer ear, called the pinna, helps to collect sound waves. The middle ear transduces sound waves into mechanical energy. The hammer, anvil, and stirrup are small bones located in the middle ear.
19. The answer is *D*. The vestibular organ of the inner ear is composed of two structures: the semicircular canals and the saccule and utricle.
20. The answer is *B*. Kinesthetic receptors are individual sensory receptors located in the skin, muscles, joints, and tendons. Basket cells, tactile discs, and specialized end bulbs are different receptors found in the skin.
21. The answer is *D*. Nocioreceptors transmit messages along two different pathways, corresponding to first and second pain.
22. The answer is *A*. End bulbs detect skin pressure and skin pleasure, and tactile discs detect pressure.
23. The answer is *A*. Endorphins have been implicated in everything from the gate control theory of pain to the experience of runner's high, the pain-reducing effects of acupuncture, and the effects of placebos.
24. The answer is *D*. Although the effect of endorphins on gate neurons has been known for some time, recent research has pointed to the importance of estrogen in helping block pain for women.
25. The answer is *D*. Research suggests that when sensory and pain neurons from one part of the part have been cut, the corresponding somatosensory cortex becomes sensitive to input from parts of the body that activate nearby portions of the somatosensory cortex.
26. The answer is *A*. The missing basic taste sensations are saltiness and fattiness.
27. The answer is *D*. All of the other choices are flights of whimsy.
28. The answer is *D*. Figure-ground refers to the tendency to focus on figure, while the remainder of a stimulus is indistinct background. The principle of proximity suggests that things that are close together are usually perceived as belonging together. Dissimilarity is not a Gestalt principle.
29. The answer is *B*. The center of our attention is the figure and the rest is background, as demonstrated by the vase figure.
30. The answer is *A*. The principle of perceptual constancy in this particular example is called shape constancy. Other examples of perceptual constancy are brightness constancy, color constancy, and size constancy.
31. The answer is *D*. Both monocular and binocular cues allow us to perceive depth. Monocular cues are those that can be seen using one eye. Binocular cues require both eyes for depth perception. Convergence is an example of a binocular cue.
32. The answer is *C*. Visual illusions are astounding because they intentionally manipulate the perceptual cues we use in order to create a perception of something that is not real.
33. The answer is *C*. When the moon is seen higher in the sky, there are no objects with which to compare it.
34. The answer is *B*. Research suggests hungry college students are more likely to interpret ambiguous pictures as being food; sexually aroused males perceive females as being more physically attractive. Motivation in these studies has influenced the perception of the participants.
35. The answer is *D*. Artists use monocular cues of depth perception to create the illusion of three-dimensional objects.

Answers to True-False Questions

1. T
2. F
3. F
4. F
5. T

6. F
7. T
8. T
9. F
10. T

Chapter 5   States of Consciousness

Learning Objectives

1. Define consciousness, and describe the features of daydreams. (p. 162)

2. Explain Hilgard's concept of divided consciousness. (p. 163)

3. Identify the characteristics of the unconscious mind. (p. 163)

4. List and describe the stages of sleep. (p. 165)

5. Compare and contrast REM sleep and non-REM sleep features. (p. 165)

6. Explain circadian rhythms, and describe the consequences of interrupting circadian rhythms. (p. 168)

7. Describe what is understood about the content and meaning of dreams. (p. 170)

8. Describe the theories that seek to explain why we sleep and dream. (p. 173)

9. Describe the following sleep phenomena: nightmares, night terrors, sleepwalking, and sleeptalking. (p. 174)

10. Distinguish among the following sleep disorders: insomnia, narcolepsy, and sleep apnea. (p. 175)

11. List the characteristics of altered states of consciousness. (p. 177)

12. Describe the meditation process and the controversy regarding the benefits of meditation. (p. 177)

13. Identify the characteristics of the hypnotic state and describe the relationship between mesmerism and hypnosis. (p. 178)

14. Describe depersonalization and astral projection. (p. 180)

15. List the variables that influence individual responses to drugs. (p. 183)

16. Describe the risks associated with drug use. (p. 183)

17. Name the four major categories of psychotropic drugs. (p. 184)

18. Explain the effects of stimulants and compare the effects of amphetamines and cocaine. (p. 184)

19. Identify depressant drugs and compare their various effects. (p. 186)

20. Describe the effects of inhalants, hallucinogens, and marijuana. (p. 187)

21. Differentiate between act-alike and designer drugs. (p. 188)

22. (From the Application section) Discuss the issues regarding legal consciousness-altering drugs. (p. 190)

Chapter Overview

Consciousness is a state of awareness. Daydreams are a period of thinking and feeling not bound by logic. Divided consciousness refers to the splitting off of two conscious activities that occur simultaneously. The unconscious mind processes information without our being consciously aware.

Sleep begins as we enter a semiwakeful hypnagogic state and becomes progressively deeper as we enter dream sleep. We typically enter REM sleep four to six times each night. REM sleep, accompanied by dreams, rapid eye movement, and by an "autonomic storm," is not the only part of the dream cycle that is filled with dreams. The nature of non-REM dreams differs from REM dreams. Sleep cycles follow a pattern called the circadian rhythm. Most of the conscious experience in dreams is visual, and most dreams have some positive or negative emotional content. Much of the content of our dreams is directly related to things going on in our waking lives, a term called day residue. Freud distinguished between the manifest content of dreams and the latent, or symbolic meaning of dreams. Sleeping and dreaming seem essential to physical and physiological health; sleep deprivation brings on fatigue, inefficiency, and irritability. Nightmares, night terrors, sleepwalking, and sleeptalking are fairly common sleep phenomena.

Three types of sleep disorders are insomnia, narcolepsy, and sleep apnea. Altered states of consciousness share several common characteristics, including distortions of perception, intense positive emotions, a sense of unity, and others. Many persons achieve a very relaxed state by a process called meditation. Hypnosis is sometimes used to alter consciousness and to relieve pain. Depersonalization is the experience of one's body or surroundings becoming distorted or unreal in some way.

Consciousness can be altered through the use of various psychotropic drugs. These may be classified as stimulants, depressants, inhalants, and hallucinogens. Although risks differ from drug to drug, all drug users run the risk of abuse, dependence, addiction, and direct or indirect side effects.

Stimulants are drugs that activate the central nervous system. Even mild stimulants like caffeine and nicotine are physiologically addictive. Amphetamines and cocaine are other highly addictive stimulants. Depressants influence conscious activity by depressing parts of the central nervous system. Alcohol, tranquilizers, sedatives, and narcotics are all depressant drugs. Inhalants are usually toxic and often cause brain damage. Hallucinogens alter perceptions, cause hallucinations, and are often associated with bizarre or violent behavior. Psychological dependence is common with hallucinogens. Marijuana is a popular although illegal drug that produces a sense of well-being and sometimes alters perception. Health risks are also associated with the use of legal consciousness-altering drugs, such as caffeine, nicotine, and alcohol.

Key Terms Exercise

For each of the following exercises, match the key terms on the left with the correct definitions on the right. Page references to the text follow the terms so that you may refer to the text for any items you answer incorrectly or do not understand completely. You may check your responses immediately by referring to the answers that follow each exercise.

Wide Awake

_____ 1. consciousness (p. 162)
_____ 2. daydreams (p. 162)
_____ 3. divided consciousness (p. 163)
_____ 4. unconscious mind (p. 163)

a. mental processes that occur without conscious awareness
b. a state of awareness
c. focused thinking about fantasies
d. occurs when two conscious activities that occur simultaneously are split

ANSWERS
1. b   3. d
2. c   4. a

Sleeping and Dreaming

_____ 1. hypnagogic state (p. 165)
_____ 2. myoclonia (p. 165)
_____ 3. REM sleep (p. 167)
_____ 4. day residue (p. 172)
_____ 5. stimulus incorporation (p. 172)
_____ 6. manifest content (p. 173)
_____ 7. latent content (p. 173)
_____ 8. night terror (p. 175)
_____ 9. sleepwalking (p. 175)

a. rapid eye movement sleep, often during dreaming
b. a falling sensation that may occur during the hypnagogic state
c. a twilight state between wakefulness and sleep
d. the literal meaning of a dream
e. the symbolic meaning of a dream
f. walking and carrying on activities during non-REM sleep
g. an upsetting experience that occurs during deep non-REM sleep
h. Freud's term for the fact that the content of dreams is related to events taking place in our lives during the day.
i. occurs when the real-world event included in a dream is actually taking place while we are asleep

ANSWERS

1. c	6. d.
2. b	7. e
3. a	8. g
4. h	9. f
5. i	

Altered States of Consciousness

_____ 1. meditation (p. 177)
_____ 2. transcendental state (p. 178)
_____ 3. hypnosis (p. 178)
_____ 4. depersonalization (p. 180)

a. an altered state of consciousness that transcends normal human experience
b. methods of focusing attention away from thoughts and producing relaxation
c. an altered state in which the individual is susceptible to suggestion
d. the perception that one's body or surroundings are unreal

ANSWERS

1. b	3. c
2. a	4. d

Altering Consciousness with Drugs

_____ 1. psychotropic drugs (p. 181)
_____ 2. stimulants (p. 184)
_____ 3. depressants (p. 186)
_____ 4. opiates (p. 187)
_____ 5. inhalants (p. 187)
_____ 6. hallucinogens (p. 187)

a. drugs that increase the activity of motivational centers in the brain
b. drugs that alter perceptions
c. narcotic drugs derived from the opium poppy
d. drugs that reduce the activity of the central nervous system
e. substances that produce intoxication when inhaled
f. drugs that alter conscious experience

ANSWERS

1. f	4. c
2. a	5. e
3. d	6. b

Review At A Glance

(Answers to this section begin on page 92)

Wide Awake: Normal Waking Consciousness

Consciousness is a state of ____(1)____. Although other states of consciousness exist, we assume that the real consciousness is ___(2)___ consciousness. A period of thinking and feeling not bound by what is logical or likely to happen describes ____(3)____. Freud believed that daydreams reduce the tension left by unfulfilled ___(4)___. Some researchers have found, however, that daydreams may actually ___(5)___ tension.

When our conscious awareness becomes split and we perform two activities that require conscious awareness at the same time, this is called ___(6)___ consciousness.

Today a number of psychologists are attempting to scientifically investigate the unconscious mind. For example, psychologists have studied what happens when we tune out one voice we hear and pay attention to a second voice, an experience called the ___(7)___ _____ phenomenon. Researchers have found that we are able to process words we hear without being ___(8)___ aware of them.

Sleeping and Dreaming: Conscious While Asleep

The sleep cycle contains several stages. After daydreaming, we generally pass into a relaxed twilight state called the ___(9)___ state. Occasionally we experience a sense of falling, and our body experiences a sudden jerk called a ___(10)___. Sleep researchers have distinguished ___(11)___ levels of sleep on the basis of electroencephalogram (EEG) recordings. We pass through these levels, upward and downward, many times during the night. Several times per night the sleeper enters a stage called ___(12)___ sleep. Because of eye movements during dreaming, dream sleep is often called rapid eye movement or ___(13)___ sleep. Other important physical changes also occur during sleep. One researcher has likened dream sleep to an "___(14)___ _____." REM sleep is also characterized by ___(15)___ lubrication and erection of the clitoris in females and ___(16)___ erection in males.

Research suggests the average college student spends about two hours per night in ___(17)___ sleep, divided into four to six separate episodes. The longest REM dream, about an hour, usually occurs during the ___(18)___ part of the sleep cycle. Dreams also occur during ___(19)___ sleep. Non-REM dreams are more likely to consist of ___(20)___ impressions that are less emotional and are less likely to involve visual images. Non-REM dreams are ___(21)___ likely to be spontaneously recalled after waking than are REM dreams. A cycle of waking and sleeping that regulates our pattern of sleep is called the ___(22)___ _____. A part of the hypothalamus as well as a hormone called ___(23)___ appear to be key factors in regulating sleepiness. The body has other circadian rhythms linked to the sleep-awake cycle. For example, the largest amount of growth hormone is secreted by the ___(24)___ _____ during the first two hours of sleep. Two other examples of circadian rhythm linked to the sleep cycle are body temperature and the production of ___(25)___. Participants who were isolated in chambers that were always kept lighted evidenced a ___(26)___-_____ cycle. The disruption of circadian rhythms that results from long airline flights is called ___(27)_____ _____. Similar circadian rhythm disruptions occur with individuals whose work is subject to ___(28)___-_____ rotations.

Most of the conscious experience of dreams is ___(29)___. Only about one-fourth of dream images include

___(30)___ sensations and about twenty percent include bodily sensations. Dreams usually include ___(31)___ intense colors and have mostly blurry backgrounds. The dreamer has an ___(32)___ role in nearly three-fourths of dreams. About ___(33)___ of the other characters in dreams are friends, acquaintances, or family members. Most dreams contain ___(34)___ emotions, but negative dreams late in the sleep cycle are more likely to wake us. Men are slightly more likely to recall positive dreams, and the characters in men's dreams are somewhat more socially ___(35)___. Dreams fascinate us because they can be ___(36)___ and bizarre.

According to Freud, the content of dreams that is directly related to events going on in our daytime lives is called day ___(37)___. When stimuli that occur during sleep are directly incorporated into our dreams, it is called ___(38)_____.

According to Freud, the events we experience in a dream are the ___(39)___ content, while the symbolic meaning of the dream is the ___(40)___ content. When we miss sleep, we apparently create a "___(41)_____" that needs to be made up. In one experiment, no detrimental effects occurred when sleep was gradually reduced from eight to four hours per night. However, irritability and fatigue occurred when the amount of nightly sleep was ___(42)___ reduced. According to Hobson, sleep helps to restore the sleep-___(43)___ system in the brain stem. Research suggests sleep is essential in maintaining good ___(44)___. REM sleep appears to play an important role in the ___(45)___ of newly learned information. According to Webb, sleep serves a ___(46)___ role.

Participants who were awakened whenever they entered REM sleep became irritable and fatigued, and on subsequent nights they showed an increase in ___(47)___ sleep.

The terrifying dreams that occur during REM sleep are called ___(48)___. An experience that occurs during non-REM sleep that leaves the individual in a state of panic is called a ___(49)_____. Walking and carrying on complicated activities during the deepest part of non-REM sleep is called ___(50)___, while talking during any phase of the sleep cycle is ___(51)___.

Sleep Disorders

The troublesome but highly treatable disorders of the sleep process are called sleep ___(52)___. Individuals who sleep less than they wish are experiencing ___(53)___. Individuals who have difficulty falling asleep when they wish are experiencing ___(54)___-_____ insomnia, while those who wake up earlier than they wish experience ___(55)___-_____ insomnia. Although these disorders are found in individuals experiencing no other psychological problems, they are more common in individuals experiencing ___(56)___, anxiety, or ___(57)___. A rare sleep disorder in which individuals fall deeply asleep while at work or even while in conversation with others is called ___(58)___. While asleep, the sudden interruption of breathing lasting longer than 30 seconds is called ___(59)_____.

Altered States of Consciousness

Among the common characteristics of altered states of consciousness are distortions of ___(60)___, intense positive ___(61)___, a sense of ___(62)___, illogical, indescribable, ___(63)___ and self-evident ___(64)___.

Assuming a relaxed position, breathing deeply and slowly, and directing all attention toward breathing describe the process of ___(65)___. In some forms of meditation, the individual silently repeats a word or sound; this is called a ___(66)___. Some experienced meditators achieve an altered state of consciousness called the ___(67)___ state.

The hypnotic state usually has the following qualities: (1) a sense of deep ___(68)___, (2) alterations referred to as ___(69)___ hallucinations, (3) a loss of the sense of touch or pain referred to as hypnotic ___(70)___, (4) a sense of passing back in time called hypnotic ___(71)___ _____, and (5) hypnotic ___(72)___.

A physician practicing in the 1700s who treated patients with "magnetic seances" was Franz Anton ___(73)___. The process of putting people into trances was for many years called ___(74)___. In recent years, some doctors and dentists have found hypnosis to be an effective way to relieve ___(75)___.

An altered state of consciousness in which the body is perceived as being distorted or unreal is called ___(76)___. The illusion that the mind has left the body is called ___(77)___ _____.

Drugs and Altered Consciousness

Drugs that alter conscious experiences are called ___(78)___ drugs. The categories of psychotropic drugs are (1) drugs that increase the activity of the central nervous system, ___(79)___; (2) those that reduce the activity of the central nervous system, ___(80)___; (3) those that produce alterations in perceptual experience, ___(81)___; and (4) those that produce a sense of intoxication when inhaled, ___(82)___.

Some factors that influence an individual's response to a drug include (1) dose and ___(83)___, (2) personal ___(84)___, (3) ___(85)___, (4) the ___(86)___ situation, and (5) ___(87)___. The risks associated with drug use include (1) the potential to cause damage or impair psychological functioning, called ___(88)___ _____; (2) a need to use the drug regularly in order to feel comfortable psychologically, called psychological ___(89)___; (3) a chemical need for the drug, called physiological ___(90)___; (4) powerful and potentially dangerous ___(91)___ side effects; and (5) the risk of infection or other ___(92)___ side effects.

Drugs that increase the activity of motivational centers in the brain are called ___(93)___ (uppers). Among the most widely used stimulants are (1) the drug found in coffee, tea, and cola, ___(94)___; and (2) the drug found in tobacco, ___(95)___. Other stimulants that produce a sense of increased energy and a euphoric high are called ___(96)___. Prolonged excessive use of amphetamines may lead to amphetamine ___(97)___. A widely abused stimulant made from the leaves of the coca plant is ___(98)___. Repeated use of cocaine rapidly leads to ___(99)___. After the prolonged use of cocaine, the user experiences a cocaine crash, marked by ___(100)___, agitation, confusion, and exhaustion. Withdrawal from cocaine addiction is marked by intense depression, ___(101)___, and craving for cocaine.

Drugs that depress parts of the central nervous system are called ___(102)___. A state of relaxation is produced by the highly addictive group of depressants called ___(103)___. A sense of relaxation for a briefer period is provided by ___(104)___. Powerful and highly addictive depressants are called ___(105)___. Narcotics such as morphine and heroin are derived from the opium poppy and are called ___(106)___. Substances, such as glue and paint, that are inhaled to produce a sense of intoxication are called ___(107)___.

Drugs that powerfully alter consciousness, such as LSD and mescaline, are called ___(108)___. One highly dangerous hallucinogen, originally developed as an animal tranquilizer, is ___(109)___. A powerful although illegal drug that generally produces a sense of relaxation and well-being is ___(110)___. Although not physically addictive, regular users experience ___(111)___ symptoms when they stop using marijuana. Two special drug-related concerns involve ___(112)___-_____ and ___(113)___ drugs.

Application of Psychology: The Legal Consciousness-Altering Drugs

Coffee, tea, and cola contain the powerful stimulant ___(114)___. Prolonged use of caffeine, even at moderate levels, can produce physiological ___(115)___. Caffeine also produces marked increases in blood pressure, especially during times of ___(116)___. Most smokers begin during their teenage years, when they are vulnerable to ___(117)___ and the perception of smoking as a forbidden fruit. Most regular smokers become ___(118)___. Nicotine stimulates the pleasure centers in the ___(119)___ system; it also increases alertness by stimulating the ___(120)___ lobes of the cortex. It also soothes the ___(121)___ it creates.

A widely abused addictive depressant drug is ___(122)___. The amount of alcohol consumption that can be harmful depends on the person and the ___(123)___. Also, the potential harmful effects can affect job performance, relationships, and personal ___(124)___. Drinking during pregnancy has been linked to ___(125)___ _____ syndrome in infants. Alcohol can result in psychological ___(126)___ and physiological ___(127)___. Alcohol is not always harmful. Research suggests individuals who drink an average of ___(128)___ drink daily live longer than those who do not drink at all.

Concept Checks

Fill in the missing components of the following concept box. The correct answers are located in the "Answers" section at the end of the chapter.

Sleeping and Dreaming

Concept	Description
hypnagogic state	
	a machine that measures electrical brain activity
REM sleep	
	dreams are brief, less emotional, and less visual
	a Freudian term referring to the large part of dream content related to events taking place in our lives during the day
stimulus incorporation	

Sleep Phenomena

Concept	Description
	terrifying dreams that occur during REM sleep
	individual awakens in a state of panic; occurs during non-REM sleep
sleepwalking	
	two major varieties are sleep-onset and early-awakening
narcolepsy	
sleep apnea	sudden interruption of breathing during sleep

Psychoactive Drugs

Type of Drug	Effect	Examples
stimulants	increase the activity of the motivational centers in the brain	
depressants	depress parts of the CNS	
inhalants		glue, cleaning fluid, and paint
	powerfully alter consciousness by altering perceptual experiences	LSD and mescaline
designer drugs	produce a dreamlike high	

Extending the Chapter: Psychology, Societal Issues, and Human Diversity

These questions may be assigned to you. Whether or not they are assigned, they are designed to be challenging questions to encourage you to think independently about the material in the chapter. Many of the questions have no right or wrong answers.

I. From the "Applications of Psychology" section

1. Discuss the impact of advertising on the use of caffeine, alcohol, and nicotine by young people in the United States. Provide concrete examples from radio, television, and print media. Should these media be further regulated? If not, why not?

2. What justification exists for some dangerous consciousness-altering drugs to be legal, whereas most consciousness-altering drugs are illegal?

II. Psychology, Societal Issues, and Human Diversity

1. Why do humans generally find great attraction to altered states of consciousness?

2. Some altered states of consciousness are associated with religious ceremonies. How can our society continue to celebrate diversity and honor religious freedom while still regulating consciousness-altering drugs?

3. Why do you think hypnosis is not more widely used as a substitute anesthesia in surgical procedures?

4. (From the Human Diversity section of the text) What factors account for the differing rates of drug use among different racial and ethnic groups?

5. What impact do the anti-smoking campaigns have on young would-be smokers? Design a research study to generate answers.

Practice Quiz

The practice quiz consists of three sections: 1) Short answer questions, 2) Multiple-choice questions, and 3) True-False questions. At the end of the chapter you will find suggested answers to the short answer questions, answers and explanations for the multiple-choice questions, and answers to the true-false questions.

Short Answer Questions

1. What are the characteristics of altered states of consciousness?

_____

_____

_____

2. What are the characteristics of hypnosis?

_____

_____

_____

3. List and describe the risks associated with drug use.

_____

_____

_____

Multiple-Choice Questions

1. According to Freud, which state of consciousness helps to reduce the tension of unmet needs and wishes?
   a. depersonalization
   b. divided consciousness
   c. daydreaming
   d. flowing consciousness
   LO 1

2. Driving long distances while thinking about other events is an example of
   a. REM sleep.
   b. the unconscious mind.
   c. myoclonia.
   d. divided consciousness.
   LO 2

3. The ability to focus on one voice and tune out other voices has been labeled
   a. the cocktail party phenomenon.
   b. divided consciousness.
   c. the hypnagogic state.
   d. depersonalization.
   LO 3

4. According to researchers, voices that we tune out may nevertheless be processed
   a. consciously.
   b. unconsciously.
   c. in a hypnagogic state.
   d. in a state of flowing consciousness.
   LO 3

5. Myoclonia is experienced in which stage of sleep?
   a. hypnagogic stage
   b. light sleep
   c. deep sleep
   d. REM sleep
   LO 4

6. How many hours per night does the average college student spend dreaming?
   a. 1
   b. 2
   c. 4
   d. 6
   LO 4

7. Which of the following may occur during REM sleep?
   a. movement of the eyes
   b. increased blood flow to the brain
   c. irregular breathing
   d. all of the above
   LO 5

8. The difference between REM and non-REM dreams is that
   a. non-REM dreams have more imagery.
   b. REM dreams are less frequent.
   c. non-REM dreams have bizarre content.
   d. non-REM dreams are closer to normal thinking.
   LO 5

9. Which of the following appears to be regulated by a circadian rhythm?
   a. the secretion of growth hormone
   b. body temperature
   c. sleep-awake cycles
   d. all of the above
   LO 6

10. If you are a manager of a manufacturing plant where workers are required to work in rotating shifts, which rotation would be least disruptive to the workers?
    a. from day shift to night shift
    b. from swing shift to day shift
    c. from night shift to day shift
    d. from day shift to swing shift
    LO 6

11. According to Freud, the symbolic meaning of dreams is called the
    a. manifest content.
    b. latent content.
    c. hypnagogic content.
    d. reality content.
    LO 7

12. Most dreams contain
    a. positive emotions.
    b. negative emotions.
    c. neutral emotions.
    d. acts of aggression.
    LO 7

13. Research suggests consolidation of newly learned material is enhanced by
    a. myoclonia.
    b. circadian rhythms.
    c. non-REM sleep.
    d. REM sleep.
    LO 8

14. The important missing element when we do not get enough sleep appears to be
    a. the hypnagogic stage.
    b. light sleep.
    c. REM sleep.
    d. all of the above.
    LO 8

15. According to sleep researcher Hobson, the purpose of sleep and dreaming is to
    a. keep us from functioning during nighttime hours, for which we are ill-prepared.
    b. allow the sleep-inhibiting system a chance to rest.
    c. allow the sleep-promoting areas a chance to rest.
    d. both *b* and *c*
    LO 8

16. The upsetting nocturnal experiences that occur during non-REM sleep are
    a. sleepwalking.
    b. nightmares.
    c. night terrors.
    d. sleeptalking.
    LO 9

17. What do night terrors have in common with sleepwalking?
    a. They occur during deep non-REM phases.
    b. They occur during the hypnagogic state.
    c. They both signify abnormal behavior.
    d. They are examples of divided consciousness.
    LO 9

18. A sleep disorder characterized by the sudden interruption of breathing is called
    a. narcolepsy.
    b. sleep apnea.
    c. insomnia.
    d. myoclonia.
    LO 10

19. All of the following characterize altered states of consciousness *except*
    a. distortions of reality.
    b. intense positive emotions.
    c. self-evident reality.
    d. logical experiences.
    LO 11

20. Which of the following is true of meditators?
    a. Mantras are often used when meditating.
    b. Meditation generally produces a relaxed state.
    c. Some meditators reach a transcendental state.
    d. all of the above
    LO 12

21. What did psychologist David Holmes conclude about the physiological effects of meditation?
    a. There are actually no benefits.
    b. The benefits are no more than with other types of relaxation.
    c. It is the best technique for reducing stress and high blood pressure.
    d. Nothing is really known about the benefits.
    LO 12

22. Which of the following is *not* a characteristic of the hypnotic experience?
    a. hypnotic hallucinations
    b. hypnotic analgesia
    c. hypnotic control
    d. hypnotic repression
    LO 13

23. Each of the following is a characteristic of depersonalization *except*
    a. It may occur spontaneously.
    b. It is not unusual among young adults.
    c. It may include astral projection.
    d. It is an indication of insanity.
    LO 14

24. An individual's response to a drug can be affected by
    a. dose and purity of the drug.
    b. the individual's personal characteristics.
    c. the social situation.
    d. all of the above
    LO 15

25. Richard finds that he feels comfortable psychologically only when he can smoke marijuana daily. He shows evidence of
    a. drug abuse.
    b. psychological dependence.
    c. physiological addiction.
    d. severe emotional problems.
    LO 16

26. Painful withdrawal symptoms and increased tolerance for larger and larger doses of a drug are characteristic of
    a. marijuana abuse.
    b. cocaine abuse.
    c. psychological addiction.
    d. physiological addiction.
    LO 16

27. Each of the following is a stimulant *except*
    a. alcohol.
    b. caffeine.
    c. amphetamines.
    d. cocaine.
    LO 17

28. Which of the following is not considered a depressant?
    a. sedatives
    b. nicotine
    c. alcohol
    d. opiates
    LO 18

29. Which of the following generally characterizes withdrawal from cocaine dependence?
    a. chills and sweats
    b. physical pain
    c. depression
    d. changes in heart rate
    LO 18

30. Each of the following is considered to be addictive *except*
    a. sedatives.
    b. tranquilizers.
    c. narcotics.
    d. hallucinogens.
    LO 19

31. Which of the following hallucinogenic drugs was originally developed as an animal tranquilizer?
    a. PCP (angel dust)
    b. LSD
    c. mescaline
    d. psilocybin
    LO 20

32. Each of the following is a potential side effect of prolonged marijuana use *except*
    a. damage to the chromosomes of reproductive cells.
    b. reverse tolerance.
    c. a decrease in the efficiency of cognitive processing.
    d. a decrease in the action of male sex hormones.
    LO 20

33. Drugs such as MDA and MDMA (ecstasy) are considered to be
    a. look-alike drugs.
    b. act-alike drugs.
    c. designer drugs.
    d. depressants.
    LO 21

34. The motivation to smoke cigarettes is related to
    a. peer pressure.
    b. the "forbidden fruit" for teenagers.
    c. the addictive properties of nicotine.
    d. all of the above.
    LO 22

35. Alcohol is considered to be
    a. a depressant, because it frequently leaves drinkers feeling depressed.
    b. a stimulant, because it makes the drinker less inhibited.
    c. a depressant, because it depresses inhibitory mechanisms in the brain.
    d. both a stimulant and a depressant.
    LO 22

True-False Questions

_____ 1. Research supports Freud's idea that the purpose of daydreams is to reduce tension.

_____ 2. The electroencephalogram is a measure of brain activity used in measuring stages of sleep.

_____ 3. When we sleep, dreams occur only when we are in REM.

_____ 4. Body temperature appears to follow a circadian rhythm.

_____ 5. The state of meditation usually produces an increase in sympathetic autonomic arousal.

_____ 6. While under hypnosis, some individuals report hypnotic analgesia.

_____ 7. Unlike most stimulants, cocaine is not an addictive drug.

_____ 8. Withdrawal from cocaine dependence differs considerably from heroin or nicotine addiction.

_____ 9. Morphine, heroin, and codeine are all derived from the opium poppy.

_____10. Hallucinogens are considered highly addictive.

ANSWERS SECTION

Concept Checks

Sleeping and Dreaming

Concept	Description
hypnagogic state	relaxed state between wakefulness and sleep
EEG (electroencephalogram)	a machine that measures electrical brain activity
REM sleep	rapid eye movement sleep, often accompanies dreaming
non-REM sleep	dreams are brief, less emotional and less visual
day residue	a Freudian term referring to the large part of dream content related to events taking place in our lives during the day
stimulus incorporation	stimuli that occur during sleep wind up in our dreams

Sleep Phenomena

Concept	Description
nightmares	terrifying dreams that occur during REM sleep
night terrors	individual awakens in a state of panic; occurs during non-REM sleep
sleepwalking	walking and other complicated activities that occur during non-REM sleep
insomnia	two major varieties are sleep-onset and early-awakening
narcolepsy	a rare disorder in which the individual unexpectedly falls deeply asleep
sleep apnea	sudden interruption of breathing during sleep

Psychoactive Drugs

Type of Drug	Effect	Examples
stimulants	increase the activity of the motivational centers in the brain	amphetamines and cocaine
depressants	depress parts of the CNS	sedatives, tranquilizers, and narcotics
inhalants	a sense of intoxication when inhaled	glue, cleaning fluid, and paint
hallucinogens	powerfully alter consciousness by altering perceptual experiences	LSD and mescaline
designer drugs	produce a dreamlike high	MDA and MDMA (ecstasy)

Answers to Review At A Glance

1. awareness
2. waking
3. daydreams
4. needs
5. create
6. divided
7. cocktail party
8. consciously
9. hypnagogic
10. myoclonia
11. four
12. dream
13. REM
14. autonomic storm
15. vaginal
16. penile
17. REM
18. last

19. non-REM
20. fragmentary
21. less
22. circadian rhythm
23. melatonin
24. pituitary gland
25. cortisol
26. 25-hour
27. jet lag
28. work-shift
29. visual
30. auditory
31. few
32. active
33. half
34. positive
35. restrained
36. creative

37. residue
38. stimulus incorporation
39. manifest
40. latent
41. sleep debt
42. abruptly
43. inhibiting
44. health
45. consolidation
46. protective
47. REM
48. nightmares
49. night terror
50. sleepwalking
51. sleeptalking
52. disorders
53. insomnia
54. sleep-onset

55. early-awakening	80. depressants	105. narcotics
56. stress	81. hallucinogens	106. opiates
57. depression	82. inhalants	107. inhalants
58. narcolepsy	83. purity	108. hallucinogens
59. sleep apnea	84. characteristics	109. phencyclidine (PCP)
60. perception	85. expectations	110. marijuana
61. emotion	86. social	111. withdrawal
62. unity	87. moods	112. act-alike
63. transcendent	88. drug abuse	113. designer
64. reality	89. dependence	114. caffeine
65. meditation	90. addiction	115. addiction
66. mantra	91. direct	116. stress
67. transcendental	92. indirect	117. peer pressure
68. relaxation	93. stimulants	118. addicted
69. hypnotic	94. caffeine	119. limbic
70. analgesia	95. nicotine	120. frontal
71. age regression	96. amphetamines	121. discomfort
72. control	97. psychosis	122. alcohol
73. Mesmer	98. cocaine	123. situation
74. mesmerism	99. addiction	124. health
75. pain	100. depression	125. fetal alcohol
76. depersonalization	101. agitation	126. dependence
77. astral projection	102. depressants	127. addiction
78. psychotropic	103. sedatives	128. one
79. stimulants	104. tranquilizers	

Sample Answers to Short Answer Questions

1. **What are the characteristics of altered states of consciousness?**

   According to the text, there are seven characteristics: 1) distortions of perception; 2) intense positive emotions; 3) a sense of unity with a spiritual force; 4) illogical; 5) indescribable; 6) transcendent, or a sense of "going beyond" normal experience; and 7) self-evident reality.

2. **What are the characteristics of hypnosis?**

   According to the text, the hypnotic state typically has the following characteristics: 1) relaxation; 2) hypnotic hallucinations; 3) hypnotic analgesia; 4) hypnotic age regression; and 5) hypnotic control.

3. **List and describe the risks associated with drug use.**

   According to the text, the risks are: 1) drug abuse; 2) psychological dependence; 3) physiological addiction, tolerance, and withdrawal; 4) direct side effects, ranging from numbness to brain damage; and 5) indirect side effects, such as infection.

Multiple-Choice Answers

1. The answer is *C.* Freud's explanation of daydreaming, however, fails to explain the fact that many daydreams *create* rather than release tension.

2. The answer is *D.* According to Hilgard, our conscious awareness becomes split, and we simultaneously perform two activities requiring conscious awareness.

3. The answer is *A.* The label results from the fact that this phenomenon often occurs at parties.

4. The answer is *B.* Researchers have found that even words that were ignored can be processed without conscious awareness.

5. The answer is *A.* The hypnagogic stage is the relaxed twilight state between wakefulness and sleep. Occasionally, while in this state, we suddenly feel as though we are falling and our body experiences a sudden jerking movement called a myoclonia.

6. The answer is *B.* While the length of the dreams vary, the longest is usually about an hour and typically occurs during the last part of the sleep cycle.

7. The answer is *D.* REM sleep, which occurs while we dream, occurs during an "autonomic storm." Dreams also occur during non-REM sleep.

8. The answer is *D.* Non-REM dreams are more likely to be brief, less emotional, and are less likely to involve visual images.

9. The answer is *D.* The hypothalamus and the hormone melatonin appear to play key roles in regulating the body's internal clock.

10. The answer is *C.* When rotating from the night shift to the day shift, you stay awake longer on the first day of the rotation. This is consistent with the natural tendency to lengthen our circadian rhythms.

11. The answer is *B.* Freud believed that the latent content contained the true meaning of a dream. The manifest content was the obvious, but superficial, meaning of the dream.

12. The answer is *A.* Negative dreams occurring late in the sleep cycle are more likely to wake us up, causing us to forget many of our positive dreams.

13. The answer is *D.* During REM sleep a gene is activated that controls the modification of connections between neurons.

14. The answer is *C.* Researchers have demonstrated that REM-deprived participants are irritable and fatigued, and, on subsequent nights, show an increase in the amount of REM sleep.

15. The answer is *B.* According to Hobson, the sleep-inhibiting system, located in the brain stem, is active when we are awake and needs sleep to replenish itself.

16. The answer is *C.* Night terrors occur in the deepest phases of non-REM sleep and are most common in preschool-age children. Nightmares, on the other hand, occur during REM sleep.

17. The answer is *A.* Often the person experiencing a night terror has no clear recollection of an accompanying dream.

18. The answer is *B.* Sleep apnea is particularly common in older adults who snore. Narcolepsy is a rare sleep disorder in which the person suddenly falls into a deep sleep during the middle of the day. Insomnia refers to a variety of difficulties in which individuals sleep less than they wish.

19. The answer is *D.* In fact, many of the experiences that occur in altered states are illogical.

20. The answer is *D.* Although mantras contain religious meaning, researchers have found that any pleasant sound can produce the same effect.

21. The answer is *B.* The question of whether the benefits of meditation are greater than the benefits from other types of relaxation remains controversial.

22. The answer is *D.* Although hypnotic repression does not exist, hypnotic age regression (in which a subject feels that he is experiencing an earlier time in his life) does exist.

23. The answer is *D.* Although recurrent depersonalization experiences may be an indication of psychological problems, they are not, by themselves, an indication of insanity.

24. The answer is *D.* In addition to the factors listed in the question, the expectations that we have of the drug's effects and the mood at the time of taking the drug can also affect the response to the drug.

25. The answer is *B*. Psychological dependence occurs when the individual needs to use the drug to feel comfortable psychologically. Drug abuse occurs when it causes biological damage or impaired psychological or social functioning. Physiological addiction occurs when the body begins to require the presence of the drug and the user begins to experience withdrawal symptoms in the drug's absence.

26. The answer is *D*. A psychological addiction is referred to as dependence.

27. The answer is *A*. Whereas choices *B*, *C*, and *D*, are stimulants, that is, drugs that activate motivational centers in the brain, alcohol is a depressant.

28. The answer is *B*. Nicotine is a highly addictive stimulant.

29. The answer is *C*. The other alternatives often accompany withdrawal from heroin or tobacco.

30. The answer is *D*. Sedatives, tranquilizers, and narcotics are recognized as highly addictive drugs. Hallucinogens can alter perceptual experiences but are not generally considered to be addictive.

31. The answer is *A*. PCP is generally considered one of the most dangerous drugs on the street.

32. The answer is *A*. Among other problems created by the prolonged use of marijuana are a weakening of the body's immune system and an increased risk of lung cancer.

33. The answer is *C*. Designer drugs are those that have been designed by chemists so recently that they have not yet been classified as illegal. This was the case when ecstasy first appeared.

34. The answer is *D*. For all these reasons, rates of tobacco use remain high, in spite of its proven dangers.

35. The answer is *C*. Although alcohol does make drinkers less inhibited, and it can reduce tension and anxiety, its classification as a depressant refers to its effect on the nervous system.

Answers to True-False Questions

1. F   6. T

2. T   7. F

3. F   8. T

4. T   9. T

5. F   10. F

Part III   Learning and Cognition

Chapter 6   Basic Principles of Learning

Learning Objectives

1. Identify the key features of the definition of learning. (p. 198)

2. Identify the significant elements in Pavlov's study of classical conditioning; for example, association. (p. 199)

3. Define classical conditioning and its terminology, including UCS, UCR, CS, and CR. (p. 201)

4. Identify applications of classical conditioning and their importance. (p. 204)

5. Identify and define the processes involved in operant conditioning as well as its connection to the "law of effect." (p. 206)

6. Explain how positive reinforcement is influenced by timing and consistency. (p. 207)

7. Distinguish between primary reinforcement and secondary reinforcement. (p. 208)

8. Compare and contrast the four schedules of reinforcement: fixed ratio, variable ratio, fixed interval, and variable interval. (p. 208)

9. Describe the process of shaping. (p. 210)

10. Define negative reinforcement, and compare escape conditioning to avoidance conditioning. (p. 212)

11. List the dangers of using punishment, and identify guidelines for the appropriate use of punishment. (p. 213)

12. Distinguish between classical and operant conditioning. (p. 215)

13. Distinguish between stimulus discrimination and stimulus generalization. (p. 216)

14. Identify how extinction occurs. (p. 219)

15. Describe how spontaneous recovery and disinhibition are related to extinction. (p. 220)

16. Compare the cognitive and connectionist interpretations of learning. (p. 222)

17. Describe the characteristics of place learning, latent learning, insight learning, and learning sets. (p. 222)

18. Define modeling, and explain the roles of vicarious reinforcement and vicarious punishment in learning. (p. 226)

19. Explain how biological factors affect learning, including learned taste aversions. (p. 227)

20. (From the Application section) Describe and provide examples of superstitious behavior. (p. 230)

Chapter Overview

Learning refers to any relatively permanent change in behavior brought about through experience. One type of learning is called classical conditioning. In this type of learning, a previously neutral stimulus called a conditioned stimulus (CS) is paired with an unconditioned stimulus (UCS) that elicits an unlearned or unconditioned response (UCR). Eventually, the CS comes to elicit a conditioned response (CR) that is identical or very similar to the UCR. Classical conditioning occurs because of the association in time of a neutral stimulus and a stimulus that already elicits the response. Contemporary research indicates that classical conditioning may play a role in resistance to disease and sexual arousal.

Operant conditioning is a form of learning in which the consequences of behavior lead to changes in the probability of its occurrence. Positive reinforcements increase the probability of a response. Two important issues involving the use of positive reinforcement are the timing and consistency of reinforcements.

Primary reinforcers, such as food and water, are innately reinforcing; secondary reinforcers are learned. There are four different schedules of reinforcement, each resulting in different patterns of behavior. The schedules are fixed ratio, variable ratio, fixed interval, and variable interval. Shaping refers to the process of reinforcing behaviors that are progressively more similar to the target response. Negative reinforcement occurs when the reinforcing consequence is (1) the removal of a negative event, also called escape conditioning, or (2) the avoidance of a negative event, also called avoidance conditioning. Punishment is a negative consequence of a behavior that reduces the frequency of the behavior. Stimulus discrimination occurs when a response is more likely in the presence of a specific stimulus than in the presence of other stimuli. Stimulus generalization has occurred when an individual responds to similar but different stimuli.

When a learned response stops occurring because the aspect of the environment that originally caused the learning has changed, the process is called extinction. Extinction is often slowed because of spontaneous recovery and disinhibition.

Psychologists disagree about whether learning results from neural connections between specific stimuli and specific responses or whether learning is a change in cognition. Research that supports the cognitive view includes Tolman's studies of place learning and latent learning, Köhler's studies of insight learning, and Bandura's work on modeling. The ability of humans to learn from experience is not limitless; it is influenced in a number of ways by biological factors.

Superstitious behavior is learned through flukes in positive reinforcement.

Key Terms Exercise

For each of the following exercises, match the key terms on the left with the correct definitions on the right. Page references to the text follow the terms so that you may refer to the text for any items you answer incorrectly or do not understand completely. You may check your responses immediately by referring to the answers that follow each exercise.

Classical and Operant Conditioning

_____ 1. learning (p. 198)
_____ 2. classical conditioning (p. 202)
_____ 3. operant conditioning (p. 206)
_____ 4. positive reinforcement (p. 206)
_____ 5. fixed ratio schedule (p. 208)
_____ 6. variable ratio schedule (p. 209)
_____ 7. fixed interval schedule (p. 209)
_____ 8. variable interval schedule (p. 210)

a. a schedule in which the reinforcer is given following the first response after a predetermined amount of time

b. learning in which the consequences of behavior lead to changes in the probability of its occurrence

c. a schedule in which the reinforcer is given following the first response after a variable amount of time

d. a schedule in which the reinforcer is given after a varying number of responses have been made

e. any consequence of a behavior that leads to an increase in the probability of its occurrence

f. a relatively permanent change in behavior brought about through experience

g. a schedule in which the reinforcer is given only after a specified number of responses

h. a form of learning in which a previously neutral stimulus is paired with an unconditioned stimulus

ANSWERS
1. f   5. g
2. h   6. d
3. b   7. a
4. e   8. c

Operant Conditioning

_____ 1. shaping (p. 211)
_____ 2. negative reinforcement (p. 212)
_____ 3. punishment (p. 213)
_____ 4. extinction (p. 219)
_____ 5. response prevention (p. 220)

a. when a learned response stops occurring because of the removal of the original source of learning

b. positively reinforcing behaviors that successively become more similar to desired behaviors

c. the prevention of avoidance responses to ensure that the individual sees that the negative consequence does not occur

d. a negative consequence that leads to a reduction in the frequency of the behavior that produced it

e. reinforcement that comes from the removal or avoidance of a negative event as a consequence of a behavior

ANSWERS

1. b   4. a
2. e   5. c
3. d

Spontaneous Recovery, Disinhibition, and Theoretical Interpretations of Learning

_____ 1. spontaneous recovery (p. 220)
_____ 2. disinhibition (p. 220)
_____ 3. cognitive map (p. 222)
_____ 4. learning set (p. 225)
_____ 5. modeling (p. 226)
_____ 6. superstitious behavior (p. 230)

a. a temporary increase in the strength of an extinguished response caused by an intense but unrelated stimulus

b. an inferred mental awareness of the structure of a physical space or related elements

c. learning based on observation of the behavior of another

d. a temporary increase in the strength of a conditioned response that is likely to occur during extinction after the passage of time

e. behavior that is reinforced when a reinforcing stimulus accidentally follows a response

f. improvement in the rate of learning to solve new problems through practice solving similar problems

ANSWERS

1. d   4. f
2. a   5. c
3. b   6. e

Who Am I?

Match the psychologists on the left with their contributions to the field of psychology on the right. Page references to the text follow the names of the psychologists so that you may refer to the text for further review of these psychologists and their contributions. You may check your responses immediately by referring to the answers that follow.

_____ 1. Ivan Pavlov (p. 199)
_____ 2. John B. Watson (p. 204)
_____ 3. B. F. Skinner (p. 2011)
_____ 4. Edward C. Tolman (p. 222)
_____ 5. Wolfgang Köhler (p. 224)
_____ 6. Albert Bandura (p. 226)

a. I believe that modeling is an important aspect of learning.
b. I observed insight learning in my friend Sultan.
c. I was an American behaviorist who taught little Albert to fear white rats.
d. I believed that rats were capable of place learning and latent learning and could form cognitive maps.
e. I was a Russian physiologist who believed that conditioning was a form of learning through association.
f. My name is associated with superstitious reinforcement, schedules of reinforcement, and a learning apparatus.

ANSWERS

1. e   4. d
2. c   5. b
3. f   6. a

Review At A Glance
(Answers to this section are found on page 112)

Definition of Learning

In psychology, any relatively permanent change in behavior brought about by experience is referred to as ___(1)___.

Classical Conditioning: Learning by Association

The scientific study of classical conditioning began around the turn of the century with an accidental discovery made by a Russian physiologist named Ivan ___(2)___. While studying the role of saliva in digestion, Pavlov observed that his laboratory dogs began to ___(3)___ even before an attendant placed food in their mouths. The sight of the attendant had come to elicit the same ___(4)___ to food. Pavlov considered ___(5)___ to be the association in time of a neutral stimulus and a stimulus that elicits the response. The key phrase in classical conditioning is the ___(6)___ in _____ of the two stimuli. The ___(7)___ and the timing of the association are both important.

A stimulus that can elicit a response without any learning is called a ___(8)___, or ___(9)___. An unlearned, inborn reaction to the unconditioned stimulus is referred to as a ___(10)___, or ___(11)___. A stimulus that is originally unable to elicit a response but acquires the ability to do so through classical conditioning is a ___(12)___, or ___(13)___. When the previously unconditioned response can be elicited by the conditioned stimulus, it is called a ___(14)___, or ___(15)___.

Responding to the mere sight of a needle as if you were actually being injected is brought about by ___(16)___. Classical conditioning is defined as a form of learning in which a previously ___(17)___ stimulus (CS) is followed by a stimulus (UCS) that elicits an ___(18)___ response (UCR). As a result, the ___(19)___ stimulus comes to elicit a response, the CR, that is similar to the UCR. Classical conditioning is considered a form of learning because an old behavior can be elicited by a new ___(20)___. Classical conditioning does not depend upon the ___(21)___ of the individual that is being conditioned.

The experiment conducted by ___(22)___ and Rayner on Little Albert demonstrated the classical conditioning of ___(23)___. A method for reversing a classically conditioned response is called ___(24)___. Research suggests that classical conditioning plays a role in the functioning of the body's ___(25)___ system. Other researchers have explored the role of classical conditioning in ___(26)___ _____.

Operant Conditioning: Learning from the Consequences of Your Behavior

People often change the frequency with which they do things based on the ___(27)___ of their actions. Learning from the consequences of behavior is called ___(28)___ _____. When the consequences of a behavior tend to increase its occurrence, this is called ___(29)___ _____. Teachers helped a girl overcome her shyness by praising her only when she played with another child. In this case, the consequence of playing with other children was positive, and the frequency of her behavior ___(30)___. To ensure that positive reinforcement was responsible for the changes in behavior, the teachers stopped reinforcing her for playing with peers in the ___(31)___ phase of the research, and then reinforced her again in the fourth phase.

In operant conditioning, the behavior that becomes more frequent is the ___(32)___ response, and the positive consequence of that response is the positive ___(33)___. There are two important issues in the use of reinforcement: (1) the greater the delay between the response and the reinforcer, the slower the learning; this is called ___(34)___ _____ _____; and (2) for learning to take place, positive reinforcement should be given ___(35)___.

Reinforcers that do not have to be acquired through learning, such as food, water, and physical activity, are called ___(36)___ reinforcers. In contrast, reinforcers that are learned are ___(37)___ reinforcers.

Positive reinforcers may not always follow every response but may occur on a variety of ___(38)___. Two schedules are based on the number of ___(39)___. When a reinforcer is given only after a specified number of responses, it is called a ___(40)___ _____ schedule. If a reinforcer is given after a varying number of responses has been made, it is a ___(41)___ _____ schedule. Two additional schedules are based on the passage of ___(42)___. When a reinforcer follows the first response occurring after a predetermined amount of time, it is termed a ___(43)___ _____ schedule. When reinforcement is given to the first response after a varying amount of time, it is a ___(44)___ _____ schedule.

If the response to be reinforced is not likely to occur, a technique can be used that reinforces responses that are progressively more similar to the desired response. This is called the method of successive ___(45)___, or ___(46)___. Many animal learning laboratories use a special learning apparatus called a ___(47)___ box.

Sometimes the reinforcing consequence removes or avoids a negative event. This situation is called ___(48)___ _____. One form of negative reinforcement occurs when the behavior causes a negative event to stop; this is referred to as ___(49)___ _____. Another form of negative reinforcement occurs when the behavior causes something not to happen when it otherwise would have happened; this is called ___(50)___ _____.

If the consequence of a behavior is negative and, as a result, the frequency of a behavior decreases, the behavior has been ___(51)___. Although punishment can be an effective method of reducing the frequency of the behavior, there are several dangers in using punishment. For example, punishment is often ___(52)___ to the punisher. Punishment also may have a generalized ___(53)___ effect on the individual. Punishment is often painful and may lead the person who is punished to dislike or to act ___(54)___ toward the punisher. Punishers may find an increase in the behavior they are trying to punish, a result known as the ___(55)___ ___. Finally, even when punishment is effective in suppressing inappropriate behavior, it does not teach the individual how to act more ___(56)___ instead.

The following guidelines are suggested for the use of punishment: (1) do not use ___(57)___ punishment; (2) reinforce ___(58)___ behavior to take the place of the inappropriate behavior you are trying to eliminate; (3) do not punish people; punish specific ___(59)___ instead; (4) do not mix punishment with ___(60)___ for the same behavior; (5) once you have begun to punish, do not ___(61)___ ___.

Classical and operant conditioning differ in three primary ways: (1) classical conditioning involves an ___(62)___ between two stimuli, while operant conditioning involves an association between a response and the resulting ___(63)___; (2) classical conditioning usually involves ___(64)___ involuntary behavior, whereas operant conditioning usually involves more complicated ___(65)___ behaviors; and (3) in classical conditioning the individual does not have to do anything for the CS or the UCS to be presented, but in operant conditioning the reinforcement is ___(66)___ on the response.

As part of adapting to the world, most responses are more likely to occur in the presence of some stimuli than in the presence of others; this is called stimulus ___(67)___. The stimulus in which the response is reinforced is referred to as the ___(68)___ ___, whereas the stimulus in which the response is never reinforced is called ___(69)___. The opposite of stimulus discrimination is stimulus ___(70)___, which refers to the fact that similar stimuli tend to elicit the same response.

Extinction: Learning When to Quit

The process by which a learned response stops because of a change in the part of the environment that originally caused the learning is termed ___(71)___. In classical conditioning, a CR will be extinguished if the CS is presented repeatedly, but the ___(72)___ is no longer paired with it. In operant conditioning, extinction results from a change in the ___(73)___ of behavior. The extinction of operantly conditioned behavior is affected by the reinforcement schedule and the type of reinforcement, according to the ___(74)___ ___ effect. Responses learned through ___(75)___ ___ are the most difficult responses to extinguish. Avoidance responses can be extinguished by using ___(76)___ ___.

Extinction often proceeds irregularly. If there is a long time between presentations of the CS, the response being extinguished can undergo ___(77)___ ___. If some intense but unrelated stimulus occurs, the extinguished response may temporarily return; this is termed ___(78)___.

Theoretical Interpretations of Learning

One view of learning suggests that during the learning process ___(79)___ connections are made between specific stimuli and specific responses. Another view holds that learning involves changes in ___(80)___. Edward C. Tolman concluded that laboratory rats who chose to take a shortcut to reach a goal had actually learned a ___(81)___ of the location of the goal. In another experiment, Tolman concluded that a group of unreinforced rats had learned as much about the location of a goal as a reinforced group. This type of unreinforced learning is called ___(82)___. Wolfgang Köhler provided additional evidence for the cognitive view with his research on chimpanzees. When presented with a problem, the chimps would not reach a solution gradually; rather, they developed a sudden cognitive change called ___(83)___. Although connectionist theorists have difficulty explaining insight, according to Harlow, the monkeys were successful at solving problems because they had acquired a ___(84)___. Albert Bandura has demonstrated the importance of learning by observation, referred to as ___(85)___. We are more likely to imitate a model whose behavior we see reinforced; this is called ___(86)___. On the other hand, we are less likely to imitate a model whose behavior we see punished; this is termed ___(87)___.

Biological Factors in Learning

Learning is influenced in a number of ways by ___(88)___ factors. Apparently, people are biologically prepared to learn some kinds of ___(89)___ more readily than others. Also, people seem to be highly prepared to learn to avoid certain kinds of foods; this is called ___(90)___. Researchers have shown learned taste aversion in the foods eaten by cancer patients just prior to undergoing nausea-producing ___(91)___. Researchers have demonstrated that creating a learned ___(92)___ in coyotes makes them less likely to hunt sheep.

Application of Psychology: Learning the Wrong Things

Skinner has suggested that ___(93)___ are learned through flukes in positive reinforcement.

Concept Checks

Fill in the missing components of the following concept boxes. The correct answers are located in the "Answers" section at the end of the chapter.

Classical Conditioning

Term	Definition	Example from Pavlov's Experiment
	stimulus that can elicit the response without any learning	meat powder
unconditioned response (UCR)		salivation
conditioned stimulus (CS)	a stimulus that eventually can elicit responses as a result of being paired with an unconditioned stimulus	
	a response similar or identical to the UCR that is elicited by a conditioned stimulus	salivation (in response to the CS)

Operant Conditioning

Term	Clue	Examples
	innately reinforcing	food, water
	reinforcement learned through classical conditioning	school grades, money
	reinforcers given after a specified number of responses	wages earned by piece work
	reinforcers given after a varying number of responses	gambling, sales commissions
	reinforcers given after a specified period of time	visits by members of Congress to their constituents
	reinforcers given after a varying amount of time	fishing
	successive approximations	learning motor skills, cleaning up bedrooms, and so on
	removal or avoidance of a negative event	causing a negative event to stop or causing something negative not to occur

Extending the Chapter: Psychology, Societal Issues, and Human Diversity

These questions may be assigned to you. Whether or not they are assigned, they are designed to be challenging questions to encourage you to think independently about the material in the chapter. Many of the questions have no right or wrong answers.

I. From the "Application of Psychology" section

1. What examples of superstitious behavior have you personally observed?

2. Why do you suppose many actors and athletes engage in superstitious behavior before a performance?

II. Psychology, Societal Issues, and Human Diversity

1. Culture exerts a tremendous impact on childrearing practices. Discuss attitudes about punishment in your culture. How do these ideas compare with the suggestions found in the text?

2. How might a student develop a variety of classically and operantly conditioned responses to college classes?

3. If you have a pet (or know someone who does), in what ways have you conditioned your pet's behavior? How has your pet conditioned *your* behavior?

4. Research topic: Much research has been conducted on where in the brain memory is stored, processed, retrieved, and so on. Find and evaluate an article on this topic.

Practice Quiz

The practice quiz consists of three sections: 1) Short answer questions, 2) Multiple-choice questions, and 3) True-False questions. At the end of the chapter you will find suggested answers to the short answer questions, answers and explanations for the multiple-choice questions, and answers to the true-false questions.

Short Answer Questions

1. List three ways in which classical and operant conditioning differ.

_____

_____

2. Distinguish among place learning, latent learning, and insight learning.

_____

_____

3. Define modeling, and discuss its importance in human learning.

_____

_____

Multiple-Choice Questions

1. Which of the following is/are part of the definition of learning?
   a. change in behavior
   b. relatively permanent
   c. brought about by experience
   d. all of the above
   LO 1

2. Pavlov's initial interest in classical conditioning was stimulated when he observed his research dogs salivating at the sight of
   a. food.
   b. the attendants.
   c. saliva.
   d. the food dish.
   LO 2

3. In classical conditioning, an unlearned, inborn reaction to an unconditioned stimulus is a(n)
   a. unconditioned stimulus.
   b. conditioned stimulus.
   c. unconditioned response.
   d. conditioned response.
   LO 3

4. In Pavlov's classic experiment, meat powder was the
   a. unconditioned stimulus.
   b. unconditioned response.
   c. conditioned stimulus.
   d. conditioned response.
   LO 3

5. Classical conditioning apparently plays a role in the development of
   a. resistance to disease.
   b. allergic reactions.
   c. sexual arousal.
   d. all of the above.
   LO 4

6. Irrational fears that are thought to be caused by classical conditioning are called
   a. psychosomatic illnesses.
   b. avoidance behaviors.
   c. phobias.
   d. stimulus discrimination.
   LO 4

7. Learning that results from the consequences of behaviors is called
   a. extinguished conditioning.
   b. operant conditioning.
   c. classical conditioning.
   d. positive conditioning.
   LO 5

8. Which of the following best describes the law of effect?
   a. A conditioned stimulus will produce a conditioned response.
   b. The consequence of a response determines whether the response will be repeated.
   c. Reinforcers should be given immediately after a response.
   d. Behaviors will be elicited if the conditioned response is strong.
   LO 5

9. If positive reinforcement is not given within a short time following the response, learning will proceed slowly. This phenomenon is called
   a. delay of reinforcement.
   b. extinction.
   c. conditioned response.
   d. consistency.
   LO 6

10. Jill was trying to operantly condition her dog to roll over. Each time her dog rolled over she immediately said "good dog." However, the dog did not roll over on command. Which of the following may best explain why?
    a. Jill used inconsistent reinforcement.
    b. The CS did not match the CR.
    c. Jill should have delayed reinforcement.
    d. Saying "good dog" was not reinforcing to her dog.
    LO 6

11. Reinforcers that are innately reinforcing, such as food, water, and warmth are called
    a. primary reinforcers.
    b. secondary reinforcers.
    c. extinguished reinforcers.
    d. superstitious reinforcers.
    LO 7

12. If a child is rewarded for appropriate behavior every 15 minutes, what type of schedule is being used?
    a. fixed ratio
    b. variable ratio
    c. fixed interval
    d. variable interval
    LO 8

13. Salespeople who are paid exclusively by commission are reinforced on which type of schedule?
    a. fixed ratio
    b. fixed interval
    c. variable ratio
    d. variable interval
    LO 8

14. If you wanted to teach a chicken to play the piano, you should
    a. wait for a musically inclined chicken to show up.
    b. extinguish piano-playing behavior.
    c. use shaping.
    d. use negative reinforcement.
    LO 9

15. Behavior that is reinforced because it causes a negative event to stop is called
    a. shaping.
    b. punishment.
    c. escape conditioning.
    d. avoidance conditioning.
    LO 10

16. Both escape conditioning and avoidance conditioning are forms of
    a. superstitious behavior.
    b. positive reinforcement.
    c. negative reinforcement.
    d. secondary reinforcement.
    LO 9

17. Which of the following is suggested as a guideline for the use of punishment?
    a. Do not use physical punishment.
    b. Do not give punishment mixed with rewards.
    c. Make it clear to the individual which behavior is being punished.
    d. all of the above
    LO 10

18. If the consequence of a behavior is negative and the frequency of that behavior decreases, the behavior has been
    a. positively reinforced.
    b. negatively reinforced.
    c. disinhibited.
    d. punished.
    LO 11

19. Which of the following is correct?
    a. Classical conditioning usually involves reflexive behavior, while operant conditioning usually involves more complicated, spontaneous behavior.
    b. Classical conditioning usually involves more complicated, spontaneous behavior, while operant conditioning, involves reflexive behavior.
    c. In classical conditioning, the reinforcement is contingent on the behavior of the learner.
    d. In operant conditioning the UCS and CS occur independently of the learner's behavior.
    LO 12

20. John loves to receive mail. Over the years, he has learned to tell the difference between the sound of the mail truck and the other cars and trucks that pass his house. What process is at work here?
    a. stimulus discrimination
    b. stimulus generalization
    c. extinction
    d. negative reinforcement
    LO 13

21. After Little Albert was conditioned to fear a white rat, he also displayed fear responses to a white rabbit and a white coat. This is an example of
    a. stimulus generalization.
    b. stimulus discrimination.
    c. variable interval reinforcement.
    d. superstitious behavior.
    LO 13

22. When Sandy's disruptive classroom behavior stops because the teacher and other students no longer pay attention to the behavior, the process is called
    a. stimulus discrimination.
    b. extinction.
    c. stimulus generalization.
    d. punishment.
    LO 14

23. Behaviors that have been reinforced on a variable schedule are more difficult to extinguish than those that have been continuously reinforced. This is known as
    a. the partial reinforcement effect.
    b. an extinction schedule.
    c. shaping.
    d. avoidance conditioning.
    LO 14

24. The most difficult responses of all to extinguish are those learned through
    a. positive reinforcement.
    b. variable schedules.
    c. escape conditioning.
    d. avoidance conditioning.
    LO 14

25. Behaviors that appear to be extinguished may return when some dramatic, but unrelated, stimulus event occurs. This is called
    a. spontaneous recovery.
    b. stimulus generalization.
    c. stimulus discrimination.
    d. external disinhibition.
    LO 15

26. What do spontaneous recovery and disinhibition have in common?
    a. The UCS becomes neutral.
    b. The UCR is diminished.
    c. An extinguished response returns.
    d. A response is generalized.
    LO 15

27. The neural-connection view of learning is supported by which of the following?
    a. place learning
    b. latent learning
    c. insight learning
    d. none of the above
    LO 16

28. According to Tolman's research, rats are capable of
    a. latent learning.
    b. forming cognitive maps.
    c. insight learning.
    d. both *a* and *b*
    LO 16

29. Köhler's research with Sultan supports which theoretical view of learning?
    a. insight learning
    b. latent learning
    c. place learning
    d. modeling
    LO 17

30. Learning to learn insightfully is a characteristic of
    a. latent learning.
    b. place learning.
    c. learning sets.
    d. modeling.
    LO 17

31. Those who are concerned about the effects that televised aggression has on children are likely to focus on
    a. insight learning
    b. latent learning
    c. place learning
    d. modeling
    LO 18

32. Modeling demonstrates the importance of _____ in learning.
    a. secondary reinforcers
    b. biological factors
    c. preparedness
    d. cognition
    LO 18

33. Learned taste aversion is a form of
    a. operant conditioning.
    b. classical conditioning.
    c. insight learning.
    d. none of the above.
    LO 19

34. Researchers have found which of the following effective in avoiding learned taste aversions as a result of chemotherapy?
    a. fasting before chemotherapy
    b. eating novel and distinctive-tasting food
    c. allowing youngster to play videogames prior to chemotherapy
    d. all of the above
    LO 19

35. Occasionally, behavior is reinforced when the reinforcing stimulus accidentally follows the response. This is referred to as
a. classical conditioning.
b. a primary reinforcer.
c. extinction.
d. superstitious behavior.
    LO 20

True-False Questions

_____ 1. In classical conditioning, a stimulus that comes to elicit responses by being paired with an unconditioned stimulus is called a conditioned stimulus.

_____ 2. The infamous Little Albert experiment demonstrated the power of operant conditioning.

_____ 3. Food and water are examples of secondary reinforcement.

_____ 4. Gambling is a behavior that is typically rewarded on a fixed schedule.

_____ 5. Another term for shaping is "the method of successive approximations."

_____ 6. Escape conditioning and avoidance conditioning are two types of negative reinforcement.

_____ 7. In classical conditioning, the reinforcing consequence is contingent upon the occurrence of the response.

_____ 8. Stimulus discrimination applies more to laboratory animals than to humans.

_____ 9. The ability to form cognitive maps is consistent with the cognitive rather than the connectionist point of view.

_____10. According to Bandura and others, modeling is a powerful type of learning.

ANSWERS SECTION

Concept Checks

Classical Conditioning

Term	Definition	Example from Pavlov's Experiment
unconditioned stimulus (UCS)	stimulus that can elicit the response without any learning	meat powder
unconditioned response (UCR)	an unlearned, inborn reaction to an unconditioned stimulus	salivation
conditioned stimulus (CS)	a stimulus that eventually can elicit responses as a result of being paired with an unconditioned stimulus	metronome
conditioned response (CR)	a response similar or identical to the UCR that is elicited by a conditioned stimulus	salivation (in response to the CS)

Operant Conditioning

Term	Clue	Examples
primary reinforcer	innately reinforcing	food, water
secondary reinforcer	reinforcement learned through classical conditioning	school grades, money
fixed ratio schedule	reinforcers given after a specified number of responses	wages earned by piece work
variable ratio schedule	reinforcers given after a varying number of responses	gambling, sales commissions
fixed interval schedule	reinforcers given after a specified period of time	visits by members of Congress to their constituents
variable interval schedule	reinforcers given after a varying amount of time	fishing
shaping	successive approximations	learning motor skills, cleaning up bedrooms, and so on
negative reinforcement	removal or avoidance of a negative event	causing a negative event to stop or causing something negative not to occur

Answers to Review At A Glance

1. learning
2. Pavlov
3. salivate
4. reflexive response
5. classical conditioning
6. association/time
7. frequency
8. UCS
9. unconditioned stimulus
10. UCR
11. unconditioned response
12. CS
13. conditioned stimulus
14. CR
15. conditioned response
16. classical conditioning
17. neutral
18. unlearned
19. conditioned
20. stimulus
21. behavior
22. Watson
23. fear
24. counterconditioning
25. immune
26. sexual arousal
27. consequences
28. operant conditioning
29. positive reinforcement
30. increased
31. reversal
32. operant
33. reinforcer
34. delay of reinforcement
35. consistently
36. primary
37. secondary
38. schedules
39. responses
40. fixed ratio
41. variable ratio
42. time
43. fixed interval
44. variable interval
45. approximations
46. shaping
47. Skinner
48. negative reinforcement
49. escape conditioning
50. avoidance conditioning
51. punished
52. reinforcing
53. inhibiting
54. aggressively
55. criticism trap
56. appropriately
57. physical
58. appropriate
59. behaviors
60. rewards
61. back out
62. association
63. stimuli
64. reflexive
65. voluntary
66. contingent
67. discrimination
68. discriminative stimulus
69. S^{delta}
70. generalization
71. extinction
72. UCS
73. consequences
74. partial reinforcement
75. avoidance learning
76. response prevention
77. spontaneous recovery
78. disinhibition
79. neural
80. cognition
81. cognitive map
82. latent learning
83. insight
84. learning set
85. modeling
86. vicarious reinforcement
87. vicarious punishment
88. biological
89. fears
90. learned taste aversion
91. chemotherapy
92. taste aversion
93. superstitions

Sample Answers to Short Answer Questions

1. **List three ways in which classical and operant conditioning differ.**

   Three differences are: 1) classical conditioning involves an association between two stimuli, whereas operant conditioning involves an association between a response and the consequence that follows the response; 2) classical conditioning involves reflexive behaviors, whereas operant conditioning usually involves more complicated, voluntary behaviors; and 3) in classical conditioning, the individual doesn't actually have to do anything for the CS or UCS to be presented, whereas in operant conditioning, the reinforcement occurs only if the learner actually makes a response.

2. **Distinguish among place learning, latent learning, and insight learning.**

   Place learning, demonstrated by Tolman's research, occurs as learners form a cognitive map, and supports the cognitive view of learning. Latent learning, also demonstrated by Tolman, is learning that occurs in the absence of any apparent reinforcement, and also supports the cognitive view of learning. Insight learning, demonstrated by Köhler's research, refers to a sudden cognitive change that helps a learner to solve a problem. Insight learning is yet additional support for the cognitive view of learning.

3. **Define modeling and discuss its importance in human learning.**

Modeling is learning based on observation of others. Its significance is that we don't have to directly experience everything in the world in order to become conditioned. For example, a healthy respect for bees can be learned by watching another person receive a bee sting.

Multiple-Choice Answers

1. The answer is *D*. Note that the definition of learning is restricted to *relatively* permanent, as opposed to temporary, changes in behavior.
2. The answer is *B*. The dogs had learned to associate the attendants with the food—the stimulus of the attendant came to elicit the response of salivation.
3. The answer is *C*. In the first phase of classical conditioning, the unconditioned stimulus produces an unconditioned response.
4. The answer is *A*. Since the meat powder is a stimulus that brought about a response (salivation) without any prior conditioning, it is called an unconditioned stimulus.
5. The answer is *D*. Assuming you answered this question correctly, before you proceed be sure that you understand *how* these various responses are classically conditioned.
6. The answer is *C*. Some psychologists believe that phobias are learned when a neutral stimulus is paired with a fear-inducing stimulus.
7. The answer is *B*. The term *operant* is derived from the word *operate*. That is, when our behavior operates on the world, it produces consequences for us. These consequences determine whether or not we will continue the behavior.
8. The answer is *B*. The law of effect, postulated by Thorndike, became the basis for operant conditioning.
9. The answer is *A*. Other important issues in the use of positive reinforcement include the need to be consistent in the delivery of the positive reinforcement and being certain that the positive reinforcer is actually reinforcing.
10. The answer is *D*. Jill's dog underscores the importance of making sure that the reinforcer used to modify behavior must, in fact, be reinforcing to the learner.
11. The answer is *A*. Secondary reinforcers, on the other hand, are learned. They take on their reinforcing value through classical conditioning. As an example, consider the process by which money became a powerful reinforcer for you.
12. The answer is *C*. If the reward is based on the passage of a fixed amount of time, it is a fixed interval schedule.
13. The answer is *C*. Variable versus fixed refers to the predictability of the reinforcer. That is, variable reinforcers reward on an unpredictable schedule. Ratio refers to the number of behaviors, while interval refers to the amount of time. Thus, a variable ratio implies that the rewards are unpredictable and based on the number of behaviors. A fixed interval schedule, on the other hand, produces a predictable reinforcer after a set amount of time.
14. The answer is *C*. Shaping is a technique that can produce complex behavior by reinforcing behaviors that are successively more similar to the desired behavior. Shaping is also called the method of successive approximations.
15. The answer is *C*. Both escape conditioning and avoidance conditioning are examples of negative reinforcement. Avoidance conditioning is reinforcing because it prevents something negative from happening.
16. The answer is *C*. Negative reinforcement occurs when the reinforcing consequence removes or avoids a negative event.
17. The answer is *D*. In addition to the guidelines mentioned in the question, the text discusses dangers in the use of punishment. These include the fact that the punishment is often reinforcing to the punisher, the generalized inhibiting effect on the individual receiving the punishment, and the criticism trap.
18. The answer is *D*. Punishment and negative reinforcement are often confused. Be sure that you understand the differences between them.
19. The answer is *A*. This is an important question, since it requires you to understand the fundamentals of both classical and operant conditioning. If the answer made sense to you, congratulations! If you struggled with the question, you might wish to review the sections on classical and operant conditioning. Many students find that they need to spend some extra time with this material.

20. The answer is *A*. While stimulus discrimination elicits different responses to different stimuli (at a traffic signal we go on green and stop on red), stimulus generalization elicits the same response to similar stimuli (we go on all green lights regardless of where they are located).

21. The answer is *A*. Little Albert's fear response had generalized to other similar objects. Had he *not* reacted fearfully to these stimuli, he would have demonstrated discrimination.

22. The answer is *B*. Extinction refers to the process of unlearning a learned response due to the removal of the original source of learning. In this instance, Sandy's behavior was conditioned and maintained by the teacher and the other members of the class. When they began to ignore the behavior, they effectively removed the original source of learning.

23. The answer is *A*. Think of examples of specific behaviors that have been partially reinforced and that are difficult to extinguish.

24. The answer is *D*. The person making the response never knows whether or not the stimulus has been removed so the individual persists in making the response.

25. The answer is *D*. In contrast to external disinhibition, spontaneous recovery is likely to occur during extinction and doesn't require the occurrence of a dramatic event. When you suddenly spot your former significant other in the mall (the one you thought you were "over") and experience a conditioned emotional response, you have just experienced spontaneous recovery.

26. The answer is *C*. Both spontaneous recovery and disinhibition remind us that the road to extinction is not always smooth.

27. The answer is *D*. Place learning, latent learning, and insight learning are all examples of the cognitive approach to learning.

28. The answer is *D*. At different times, Tolman's research with rats confirmed their abilities to engage in both place learning and latent learning. Both of these experiments support the cognitive view of learning.

29. The answer is *A*. Köhler's research suggested that Sultan learned because of a cognitive change—new insight into the problems he was presented.

30. The answer is *C*. Learning sets suggest that new problems can be solved more quickly when the learner is allowed to practice similar problems.

31. The answer is *D*. Modeling refers to learning based on the observation of another's behavior. In this case, the actors on television may be modeling extremely aggressive behavior.

32. The answer is *D*. Modeling, or learning by observing others, can be an extremely efficient way to learn. Modeling underscores the importance of cognitive factors in learning.

33. The answer is *B*. Learned taste aversion occurs when we develop a negative reaction to a particular taste because it has been associated with nausea or illness.

34. The answer is *D*. The principles of classical conditioning are being used to help improve the quality of life for many who are undergoing chemotherapy.

35. The answer is *D*. Superstitious behavior is often described as being "resistant to extinction." Can you explain why this is so?

Answers to True-False Questions

1. T	6. T
2. F	7. F
3. F	8. F
4. F	9. T
5. T	10. T

Chapter 7 Memory

Learning Objectives

1. Identify the operations involved in the information-processing view of memory and describe the three-stage theory of memory. (p. 236)

2. Discuss the role of the sensory register in the stage theory of memory. (p. 237)

3. Define short-term memory, and describe how its life span and capacity can be influenced. (p. 237)

4. Discuss differences between short-term memory and long-term memory. (p. 240)

5. Distinguish among the three kinds of long-term memory: procedural, episodic, and semantic. (p. 241)

6. Discuss the organization of memory in long-term memory. (p. 242)

7. Identify different ways of measuring the retrieval of information from long-term memory, and explain serial learning and the tip-of-the-tongue phenomenon. (p. 244)

8. Distinguish between deep and shallow processing in the levels of processing model, and describe the role of elaboration. (p. 247)

9. Distinguish among the four major theories of forgetting: decay theory, interference theory, reconstruction (schema) theory, and motivated forgetting. (p. 249)

10. Describe the synaptic theories of memory. (p. 257)

11. Distinguish between anterograde amnesia and retrograde amnesia. (p. 259)

12. (From the Application section) Discuss the results of research relating eyewitness testimony and memory. (p. 263)

Chapter Overview

The stage theory of memory states that human memory consists of three stages: (1) the sensory register, which holds an exact image of each sensory experience for a very brief interval until it can be fully processed; (2) short-term memory, which holds information for approximately 30 seconds (information will fade from short-term memory unless the material is rehearsed; the capacity of short-term memory is 7 ± 2 items, but this can be increased by organizing the material into larger chunks); and (3) long-term memory, which indexes information and stores it primarily in terms of its meaning. Three kinds of long-term memory are procedural, episodic, and semantic. Procedural memory is memory for skills and other procedures. Episodic memory refers to memory for specific experiences that can be defined in terms of time and space, while semantic memory refers to memory for meaning.

The organization of memory in long-term memory has been characterized as an associative network. One network model is called the spreading activation model.

Three ways that psychologists measure memory retrieval are the recall method, the recognition method, and the relearning method.

An alternative to the stage model is the levels of processing model, which views the differences between short-term and long-term memory in terms of degree rather than separate stages.

Psychologists have identified four ways in which forgetting occurs: (1) decay theory, which states that forgetting occurs simply because time passes; (2) interference theory, which states that forgetting occurs because other memories interfere with retrieval (interference may occur from memories that were formed by prior learning, called proactive interference, or from memories that were formed by later learning, called retroactive interference); (3) schema theory, which holds that memory changes over time to become more consistent with our beliefs, knowledge, and expectations; and (4) repression, the process by which memories that are upsetting or threatening may be forgotten.

The biological basis of memory is called the memory trace or engram. A theory that has been proposed to explain the biological nature of memory is synaptic facilitation, which views learning as a change in the synapses.

Amnesia is a major memory disorder. Anterograde amnesia, caused by damage in the hippocampus, is an inability to store and/or retrieve new information. Retrograde amnesia is the inability to retrieve old, long-term memories.

Research suggests that eyewitness testimony and recall may be inaccurate because of biased questioning or the characteristics of the eyewitnesses. A controversial use of hypnosis to recall past memories is called hypnotic age regression.

Much research has been conducted trying to improve the accuracy of eyewitness testimony.

Key Terms Exercise

For each of the following exercises, match the key terms on the left with the correct definitions on the right. Page references to the text follow the terms so that you may refer to the text for any items you answer incorrectly or do not understand completely. You may check your responses immediately by referring to the answers that follow each exercise.

Memory (I)

_____ 1. encode (p. 236)
_____ 2. stage theory of memory (p. 236)
_____ 3. sensory register (p. 236)
_____ 4. short-term memory (STM) (p. 236)
_____ 5. rehearsal (p. 238)
_____ 6. long-term memory (p. 240)

a. the first stage of memory that briefly holds exact images until they can be processed
b. the second stage of memory that can store five to nine bits of information
c. mental repetition in order to retain information in short-term memory
d. a storehouse for information that is kept for long periods of time
e. a theory of memory based on the idea that we store information in three separate but linked memories
f. to represent information in some form in the memory system

ANSWERS

1. f	4. b
2. e	5. c
3. a	6. d

Memory (II)

_____ 1. procedural memory (p. 241)
_____ 2. semantic memory (p. 241)
_____ 3. episodic memory (p. 241)
_____ 4. recall method (p. 244)
_____ 5. recognition method (p. 244)
_____ 6. relearning method (p. 244)
_____ 7. serial position effect (p. 244)
_____ 8. levels of processing model (p. 247)

a. memory for experiences that can be defined in terms of space and time
b. memory for meaning without reference to time and place of learning
c. memory for motor movements and skills
d. a measure of memory based on the ability to retrieve information from long-term memory without cues
e. a measure of memory based on the ability to select correct information from among the options provided
f. immediate recall of a list of items is better for items at the beginning and end of the list than for those in the middle
g. states the distinction between short-term and long-term memory is a matter of degree rather than different kinds of memory
h. a measure of memory based on the time it takes to relearn forgotten material

ANSWERS

1. c	5. e
2. b	6. h
3. a	7. f
4. d	8. g

Forgetting/Biological Basis of Memory

_____ 1. decay theory (p. 249)
_____ 2. interference theory (p. 250)
_____ 3. reconstruction (schema) theory (p. 251)
_____ 4. repression (p. 255)
_____ 5. engram (p. 257)
_____ 6. synaptic facilitation (p. 257)
_____ 7. anterograde amnesia (p. 259)
_____ 8. retrograde amnesia (p. 261)

a. a memory trace that is the biological basis of memory
b. the theory that forgetting occurs when similar memories interfere with storing and retrieving information
c. neural activity causes structural changes in the synapses that lead to more efficient learning and memory
d. Freud's theory that forgetting occurs because the conscious mind pushes unpleasant information into the unconscious
e. the theory that forgetting occurs as the memory trace fades over time
f. a memory disorder characterized by the inability to store new information in long-term memory
g. memory disorder characterized by an inability to retrieve old, long-term memories
h. information stored in LTM sometimes changes over time to become consistent with our beliefs, knowledge, and expectations

ANSWERS

1. e	5. a
2. b	6. c
3. h	7. f
4. d	8. g

Review At A Glance
(Answers to this section are found on page 128)

Three Stages of Memory: An Information-Processing View

Most recent theories of memory borrow a concept used in computer design called ___(1)_____. Raw sensory information is represented, or ___(2)___, in some form in the memory system. Selected information is transferred to a more permanent memory storage by ___(3)___ mechanisms. As information is needed, it is ___(4)___ from memory, although some is lost or becomes irretrievable.

The stage theory assumes that we have a ___(5)___-_____ memory. The first of these stages is the ___(6)_____, which holds images until they can be processed. Visual information is retained for about ___(7)___ second, while auditory information can be retained as an echo for as long as ___(8)___ seconds.

The second stage of memory, called ___(9)___-_____ memory, stores information for less than ___(10)_____ _____ unless it is renewed by mental repetition, also called ___(11)___. Although information in short-term memory can be stored in many forms, humans seem to prefer transforming information into sounds or ___(12)_____. The capacity of short-term memory, as described by George Miller, is ___(13)___ bits of information. Short-term memory also serves as our ___(14)___ memory. Research suggests that it takes us about ___(15)___ of a second to examine each item in our short-term memory. Miller calls the units of memory ___(16)___. The capacity of short-term memory can be expanded by using techniques called ___(17)_____.

Information is stored for long periods of time in ___(18)___-_____ memory. Long-term memory differs from short-term memory in several important ways. Unlike short-term memory, where information can be scanned, the vast amount of information in long-term memory is organized by being ___(19)___, and information is retrieved by using ___(20)___. In contrast to short-term memory, which stores information in terms of physical qualities, information in long-term memory is primarily stored in terms of its meaning, also referred to as ___(21)_____.

Many psychologists believe that information in long-term memory is not just durable, but it is actually ___(22)___. Finally, while STM is primarily stored in the ___(23)___ lobes of the cerebral cortex, information in LTM is first integrated in the ___(24)___ and then permanently stored in the language and perception areas of the ___(25)___.

There appears to be different types of long-term memory. Memory for skills, such as how to ride a bicycle, is called ___(26)___ memory. Memory associated with meaning is called ___(27)___ memory. Information about specific experiences is stored in ___(28)___ memory. Some psychologists include semantic memory and episodic memory under the heading ___(29)___ memory.

Organization in LTM helps facilitate the retrieval of information from the vast amount stored in the LTM. The organization of memory has been characterized as an ___(30)___ network. An influential network model is called the ___(31)_____ model.

Psychologists have identified three ways of measuring memory retrieval. In the ___(32)___ method, participants are asked to recall information with few or no cues. In the ___(33)___ method, participants must recognize the correct information from among alternatives. The ___(34)___ method measures the relearning of previously memorized information. The superior recall for items at the beginning and end of a serial list is called the ___(35)_____ effect. Research on the tip-of-the-tongue phenomenon suggests we are able to recall about ___(36)___ the items within a minute or so.

An alternative approach to the stage model, called the ___(37)___ _____ _____ model, suggests that there is only one memory store beyond the sensory register. This model suggests that information will be kept only briefly if it is processed at a ___(38)___ level, but will be kept longer if processed at a ___(39)___ level. Information can be deeply processed by creating more associations between the new memory and existing memories, a technique called ___(40)___. Research suggests that a good way to promote elaboration is to relate the information to ___(41)___.

Forgetting and Why It Occurs

Forgetting occurs because memories that are not used fade over time, according to the ___(42)___ theory. Although it appears that the passage of time is a cause of forgetting in the sensory register and ___(43)___-_____ memory, the decay theory does not appear to explain forgetting in ___(44)___-_____ memory.

Forgetting in long-term memory occurs because other memories interfere with the retrieval of information, according to the ___(45)___ theory. Interference is most likely to occur when memories are ___(46)___. Interference due to prior learning is ___(47)___ interference, whereas interference created by later learning is ___(48)_____ interference.

A theory that information stored in LTM changes over time to become more consistent with our beliefs, knowledge, and expectations is called ___(49)___ theory. Research suggests distortions occur during the process of ___(50)___. Current versions of schema theory are based on the distinction between ___(51)___ and semantic memory. One type of reconstruction error involves memory for something that did not occur; this is called a ___(52)_____ memory.

Sigmund Freud's explanation for forgetting, that the conscious mind pushes unpleasant information into unconsciousness, is called ___(53)___. More recent research indicates that ___(54)___ emotional arousal can actually lead to better recall than neutral experiences. Our memories for intensely negative events, however, tend to be disorganized and ___(55)___. Vivid memories for emotional events, called ___(56)___ memories, also tend to be distorted over time.

Biological Basis of Memory: The Search for the Engram

The physical change in the nervous system that occurs when we learn something has been referred to as the memory trace or ___(57)___. Hebb's theory, synaptic facilitation, suggests that learning is due to a physical change at the ___(58)___. A classical conditioning study conducted on ___(59)___ has provided support for Hebb's theory. More recent research suggests changes in synapses are based on changes in their proteins for ___(60)___, but not for ___(61)___. Research on Alzheimer's disease has identified ___(62)___ as an important chemical in the formation of memory. Other research indicates that events that create negative emotional arousal tend to stimulate the region of the brain called the ___(63)___, which helps to improve ___(64)___. Negative emotional arousal also inhibits the ___(65)___. Inhibition of the hippocampus appears to result in ___(66)___ for emotionally charged memories.

An inability to consciously retrieve new information from long-term memory is found in the memory disorder called ___(67)___. Anterograde amnesia usually does not affect the ability to acquire ___(68)___ memories, but seems to destroy some ___(69)___ memories. Researchers believe that this condition is caused by damage in the forebrain structure called the ___(70)___. Individuals who are unable to retrieve old, long-term memories are experiencing ___(71)___. Both retrograde and anterograde amnesia are experienced by individuals with ___(72)___. This disorder is caused by the prolonged loss of the vitamin ___(73)___ from the diet of chronic alcoholics. Individuals with Korsakoff's syndrome often engage in ___(74)___.

Application of Psychology: Eyewitness Testimony and Memory

Research suggests that eyewitness testimony and recall may be inaccurate due to biased ___(75)___. Eyewitnesses also are inaccurate when they "look but do not ___(76)___." Allport's research has confirmed that stereotypes and ___(77)___ affect the accuracy of eyewitness testimony. Characteristics of ___(78)___ may also influence the accuracy of recall. With regard to repressed memories of sexual and physical abuse in childhood, a number of studies indicate that some of these memories may be ___(79)___.

The use of hypnosis to recall memories of some past event is called ___(80)___ ___ ___. One study found that memories dredged up during hypnotic age regression are more erroneous than factual. Similar controversy surrounds the use of hypnosis to aid the recall of eyewitnesses to ___(81)___. Research suggests that the accuracy of eyewitness identification in lineups can be improved by establishing good ___(82)___ with the eyewitness, by asking ___(83)___ questions, by using ___(84)___ who are similar to the suspects, and by presenting the persons in the lineup one at a time.

Concept Checks

Fill in the missing components of the following concept boxes. The correct answers are located in the "Answers" section at the end of the chapter.

Stages of Memory

Concept	Characteristics
	first stage of memory; holds images until they can be processed
short-term memory	
	information is indexed and stored primarily in terms of meaning; retrieval assisted by the use of cues
procedural memory	
	memory associated with meaning, such as word knowledge
episodic memory	

Theories of Forgetting

Theory of Forgetting	Explanation
	memories that are not used fade over time
interference theory	
schema theory	
	painful memories are pushed into the unconscious

Extending the Chapter: Psychology, Societal Issues, and Diversity

These questions may be assigned to you. Whether or not they are assigned, they are designed to be challenging questions to encourage you to think independently about the material in the chapter. Many of the questions have no right or wrong answers.

I.   From the "Applications of Psychology" section

1.   Discuss the memory-related factors leading to inaccurate eyewitness testimony.

2.   What have researchers learned about the relationship between stereotypes and eyewitness testimony?

3.   Describe the results of research on the recall of repressed memories of sexual and physical abuse.

4.   What suggestions are made to improve the accuracy of eyewitness testimony?

II.   Psychology, Societal Issues, and Diversity

1.   If you were trying to help another student improve her study skills, what ideas from this chapter would you suggest?

2.   If memory-enhancing and memory-blocking drugs are found to be effective in the future, how should these be regulated?

3.   (From the Human Diversity section of the text) In what ways does culture influence memory? (Hint: Consider the methods used to memorize as well as the content of memory.)

Practice Quiz

The practice quiz consists of three sections: 1) Short answer questions, 2) Multiple-choice questions, and 3) True-False questions. At the end of the chapter you will find suggested answers to the short answer questions, answers and explanations for the multiple-choice questions, and answers to the true-false questions.

Short Answer Questions

1. Identify and describe three different ways of measuring the retrieval of memories.

_____

_____

2. What is the serial position effect?

_____

_____

3. Explain the levels of processing model of memory.

_____

_____

Multiple-Choice Questions

1. Which of the following is *not* a stage in the information-processing model of memory?
   a. short-term memory
   b. long-term memory
   c. episodic memory
   d. sensory register
   LO 1

2. According to the information-processing model, attention serves as a
   a. temporary memory buffer.
   b. control mechanism.
   c. retrieval mechanism.
   d. sensory register.
   LO 1

3. The sensory register has all of the following characteristics *except*
   a. visual information lasts about a quarter of a second
   b. it holds an exact image of each sensory experience
   c. auditory information lasts about 4 seconds
   d. the capacity is 7 ± 2 bits of information
   LO 2

4. Which of the following best describes the memory capacity of the sensory register?
   a. Capacity is limited on the average to 7 chunks of information.
   b. There is the potential for partial recall of everything ever experienced in episodic memory.
   c. It is designed to hold an exact image of the sensory experience.
   d. It depends on the effort put into the process of attention.
   LO 2

5. Suppose that you call the information operator to find a friend's phone number. When you dial your friend's number, you get a busy signal. Later, when you start to dial the number again, you realize you have forgotten it. This experience probably occurred because the phone number was only temporarily stored in your
   a. short-term memory.
   b. long-term memory.
   c. sensory register.
   d. none of the above.
   LO 3

6. One technique to help overcome the limited capacity of STM is called
   a. chunking.
   b. rehearsal.
   c. working memory.
   d. semantic codes.
   LO 3

7. Working memory is a special function of
   a. the sensory register.
   b. short-term memory.
   c. long-term memory.
   d. any of the above.
   LO 3

8. The phone number discussed in question 5 probably could have been remembered for a longer period if you had practiced
   a. chunking.
   b. repression.
   c. rehearsal.
   d. both *a* and *c*.
   LO 3

9. Each of the following is true regarding differences between STM and LTM *except*
   a. information in LTM is indexed.
   b. information in STM is stored in terms of physical qualities.
   c. information in LTM may be permanent.
   d. information in LTM is primarily stored in the frontal lobes of the cortex.
   LO 4

10. Although short-term memory stores information in terms of physical qualities, long-term memory stores information in terms of
   a. acoustic codes.
   b. semantic codes.
   c. attitudes.
   d. all of the above .
   LO 4

11. You remember some specific plays from the football game you watched on television last week. You are most likely using
   a. episodic memory.
   b. procedural memory.
   c. semantic memory.
   d. all of the above.
   LO 5

12. What do episodic and semantic memories have in common?
   a. They are forms of working memory.
   b. They are easily described in words.
   c. They can easily be retrieved.
   d. They are forms of procedural memory.
   LO 5

13. Which characteristic of long-term memory facilitates the retrieval of information?
   a. unlimited capacity
   b. the organization of material
   c. the chunking of information
   d. the ability of long-term memory to store procedural information
   LO 6

14. Which concept states that memories are linked together through experience?
   a. semantic memory
   b. reconstructive memory
   c. associative network
   d. serial forgetting
   LO 6

15. When you get to the grocery store, you realize you left your shopping list at home. According to the serial position effect, the items on the list you are most likely recall are
   a. at the beginning of the list.
   b. in the middle of the list.
   c. at the end of the list.
   d. both *a* and *c*.
   LO 7

16. The tip-of-the-tongue phenomenon appears to be caused by a problem in
   a. retrieval.
   b. engrams.
   c. storage.
   d. repression.
   LO 7

17. The type of remembering necessary to correctly answer this multiple choice question is
   a. recall.
   b. recognition.
   c. relearning.
   d. rehearsal.
   LO 7

18. Which of the following is a way of testing retrieval of long-term memories?
   a. recall
   b. recognition
   c. relearning
   d. all of the above
   LO 7

19. The process of reading material and relating it to previous learning or to your own life is called
   a. rehearsal.
   b. consolidation.
   c. elaboration.
   d. chunking.
   LO 8

20. The levels of processing model states that deep processing involves greater _____ than shallow processing.
   a. rehearsal
   b. engrams
   c. consolidation
   d. elaboration
   LO 8

21. Which theory suggests that forgetting is caused by a fading memory trace?
    a. schema theory
    b. repression
    c. decay theory
    d. interference theory
    LO 9

22. The expression "You can't teach an old dog new tricks" would support which theory of forgetting?
    a. repression
    b. retroactive interference
    c. proactive interference
    d. pass interference
    LO 9

23. After having the same phone number for years, you move and get a different, but similar, phone number. Retroactive interference would be demonstrated by your difficulty to remember
    a. the new phone number.
    b. the old phone number.
    c. either phone number.
    d. your new address.
    LO 9

24. Research on memories that become distorted to fit our schema indicates that this process occurs during
    a. the formation of memories
    b. the process of retrieval
    c. proactive inhibition
    d. repression
    LO 9

25. Mike thinks of himself as a good fisherman. His friends have noticed that every time he tells the story about the "big one" he caught a few years ago, he seems to remember the fish as larger and larger, and the experience as more and more dramatic. Mike's behavior is consistent with which theory of forgetting?
    a. decay
    b. interference
    c. schema
    d. repression
    LO 9

26. The theory of forgetting that suggests the conscious mind pushes information into the unconscious is called
    a. decay.
    b. schema theory.
    c. interference.
    d. repression.
    LO 9

27. The vivid recall of a negative emotional experience is called a
    a. flashbulb memory.
    b. flashback.
    c. reconstructive flash.
    d. none of the above.
    LO 9

28. According to Hebb, the process that creates unique patterns of neural activity that reverberate through neural loops, thus making synapses more efficient, is called
    a. the engram.
    b. anterograde amnesia.
    c. the memory loop.
    d. synaptic facilitation.
    LO 10

29. Simple forms of learning, such as classical conditioning of the gill withdrawal reflex in the sea snail, appear to physically take place
    a. in the creature's hippocampus.
    b. only in creatures without a brain.
    c. at the synaptic level.
    d. outside of the nervous system.
    LO 10

30. Neuroscientists researching the causes of Alzheimer's disease have identified which of the following as playing an important role in the formation of memory?
    a. dopamine
    b. caffeine
    c. acetylcholine
    d. epinephrine
    LO 10

31. An inability to store and/or retrieve new information in long-term memory is characteristic of
    a. RNA.
    b. anterograde amnesia.
    c. retrograde amnesia.
    d. retroactive amnesia.
    LO 11

32. A key brain structure that is often damaged in patients with anterograde amnesia is the
    a. hippocampus.
    b. cerebral cortex.
    c. hypothalamus.
    d. amygdala.
    LO 11

33. Korsakoff's syndrome
    a. is caused by prolonged thiamine deficiency.
    b. is characterized by anterograde and retrograde amnesia.
    c. is characterized by confabulation.
    d. all of the above
    LO 11

34. According to the work of Loftus and others in the area of eyewitness testimony, eyewitnesses
    a. are likely to repress traumatic information.
    b. are strongly influenced by decay theory.
    c. are not easily misled.
    d. can be misled when they are asked misleading questions.
    LO 12

35. According to the U.S. Department of Justice, each of the following is a recommendation to improve eyewitness testimony *except*
    a. establish good rapport with eyewitnesses.
    b. ask open-ended questions.
    c. use "fillers" who are similar in appearance to the suspect.
    d. place all the suspects in the same lineup.
    LO 12

True-False Questions

_____ 1. In the three-stage theory of memory, the first stage is called short-term memory.

_____ 2. One method to improve the capacity of short-term memory is called chunking.

_____ 3. Short-term memory and long-term memory appear to be stored in the same areas of the brain.

_____ 4. One type of declarative memory is called procedural memory.

_____ 5. A multiple-choice question is a measure of recognition.

_____ 6. According to the levels of processing model, creating more associations leads to greater elaboration.

_____ 7. According to schema theory, forgetting occurs when similar memories interfere with the retrieval of information.

_____ 8. Research suggests that even flashbulb memories can become distorted or forgotten.

_____ 9 According to many researchers, changes in the synapses of the brain contain the biological bases of memory.

_____10. A forebrain structure believed to play an important role in long-term memory is the engram.

ANSWERS SECTION

Concept Checks

Stages of Memory

Concept	Characteristics
sensory register	first stage of memory; holds images until they can be processed
short-term memory	also called working memory; can hold 5 to 9 bits of information briefly
long-term memory	information is indexed and stored primarily in terms of meaning; retrieval assisted by the use of cues
procedural memory	memory for skills, such as riding a bicycle
semantic memory	memory associated with meaning, such as word knowledge
episodic memory	memory for specific experiences, such as your first day on campus

Theories of Forgetting

Theory of Forgetting	Explanation
decay theory	memories that are not used fade over time
interference theory	other memories interfere with recall; proactive interference is created by prior learning, and retroactive interference is created by later learning
schema theory	memories become more consistent with our beliefs, knowledge, and expectations over time
motivated forgetting	painful memories are pushed into the unconscious

Answers to Review At A Glance

1. information processing
2. encoded
3. control
4. retrieved
5. three-stage
6. sensory register
7. 1/4
8. 4
9. short-term
10. 30 seconds
11. rehearsal
12. acoustic codes
13. 7 ± 2
14. working
15. .04
16. chunks
17. chunking strategies
18. long-term
19. indexed
20. cues
21. semantic codes
22. permanent
23. frontal
24. hippocampus
25. cerebral cortex
26. procedural
27. semantic
28. episodic
29. declarative
30. associative
31. spreading activation
32. recall
33. recognition
34. relearning
35. serial position
36. half
37. levels of processing
38. shallow
39. deeper
40. elaboration
41. yourself
42. decay
43. short-term
44. long-term
45. interference
46. similar
47. proactive
48. retroactive
49. schema
50. retrieval
51. episodic
52. false
53. repression
54. negative
55. confused
56. flashbulb
57. engram
58. synapse
59. sea snails
60. LTM
61. STM
62. acetylcholine
63. amygdala
64. recall
65. hippocampus
66. disorganization
67. anterograde amnesia
68. procedural
69. declarative
70. hippocampus
71. retrograde amnesia
72. Korsakoff's syndrome
73. thiamine
74. confabulation
75. questioning
76. see
77. prejudices
78. eyewitnesses
79. erroneous
80. hypnotic age regression
81. crimes
82. rapport
83. open-ended
84. fillers

Sample Answers for Short Answer Questions

1.   **Identify and describe three differing ways of measuring the retrieval of memories.**

Psychologists have conducted research on the following three retrieval methods: 1) the recall method, which measures the ability to retrieve information from long-term memory with few or no cues; 2) the recognition method, which measures memory based on the ability to recognize the correct information from a group of alternatives (think multiple-choice exam); and 3) the relearning method, which measures the savings involved in relearning previously memorized information.

2.   **What is the serial position effect?**

This refers to the superior recall of items at the beginning and end of a list of items, compared to those items listed in the middle.

3. **Explain the levels of processing model of memory**.

This model represents an alternative to the 3-stage theory of memory. It assumes there is only one type of memory beyond the sensory register. The durability of this information depends upon how well the information is processed as it is being encoded. Generally, the more deeply information is processed, the longer the memory will be kept. Deep processing involves greater elaboration, which refers to creating more associations between the new memory and existing memories.

Multiple-Choice Answers

1. The answer is *C*. According to the Atkinson-Shriffin stage theory of memory, the three stages of memory are each separate, but linked. Episodic memory refers to memory about specific experiences in life.
2. The answer is *B*. Other control mechanisms are storage and retrieval.
3. The answer is *D*. The capacity mentioned in *D* refers to the capacity for short-term memory.
4. The answer is *C*. The seven chunks of information response is associated with short-term memory.
5. The answer is *A*. Presumably, since the information was not rehearsed, the phone number faded after a short period of time.
6. The answer is *A*. Chunking is the process of putting more than one bit of information into a unit, thereby expanding the capacity of STM.
7. The answer is *B*. This function further limits the already small capacity of short-term memory.
8. The correct answer is *D*. Chunking is a method of putting bits of information together. For example, you might chunk the first three numbers of the phone number. People frequently do this with their social security numbers. Instead of remembering it as nine individual numbers, we tend to remember it as a chunk of three numbers followed by a chunk of two numbers followed by a chunk of four numbers. A second approach for remembering the phone number is to mentally rehearse it. A third technique, not mentioned in the question, is to use a phone with an automatic redial.
9. The answer is *D*. Information in LTM is first held in the hippocampus and then permanently stored in the language and perception areas of the cortex.
10. The correct answer is *B*. Although short-term memory is usually stored in terms of the sights, sounds, and touch of experiences, long-term memory primarily stores information in terms of meaning.
11. The answer is *A*. Episodic memory stores information about specific experiences. Procedural memory is memory for skills, such as riding a bicycle. Semantic memory is memory about the meaning of words.
12. The answer is *B*. Both episodic and semantic memory are considered to be types of declarative memory.
13. The answer is *B*. While LTM appears to have unlimited capacity, this characteristic does not facilitate the retrieval of information. The chunking of information is a process carried about by the short-term memory. Finally, the ability of LTM to store procedural information does not facilitate the retrieval of information.
14. The answer is *C*. According to this view, memories form links that we use to think about information we have stored in memory.
15. The answer is *D*. The serial position effect has important implications for everything from the manner in which evidence is presented in a trial to how you can most effectively prepare for an exam.
16. The correct answer is *A*. The tip-of-the-tongue phenomenon suggests that the information is stored, but for some reason we're not pressing the right mental buttons to retrieve it.
17. The answer is *B*. Multiple choice questions provide more cues for retrieving information than do fill-in questions. The question not only provides the problem; it also provides the correct answer.
18. The answer is *D*. Each method measures a different aspect of long-term memory.
19. The answer is *C*. Elaboration is the process of creating more associations between the new memory and existing memories.
20. The answer is *D*. Elaboration refers to the creation of more associations between a new memory and existing memories. When you tie in the concepts you are reading about in your psychology text to events in your own life, you are elaborating.

21. The answer is *C*. Decay theory suggests that the change in the brain that occurs after something is learned gradually fades unless the material is rehearsed.
22. The answer is *C*. The expression implies that any attempt to teach a dog would be interfered with by the dog's prior learning; proactive interference suggests that prior learning interferes with later learning. Retroactive interference suggests that something learned later interferes with something previously learned.
23. The answer is *B*. Retroactive interference refers to interference created by later learning.
24. The answer is *B*. Distortions of memory most likely occur when we try to remember things; that is, during the process of retrieval.
25. The answer is *C*. Schema theory, unlike decay theory, suggests that, over time, memory changes to become more consistent with our beliefs, knowledge, and expectations. Over time, Mike's memory may become distorted to become consistent with his belief that he is a good fisherman.
26. The answer is *D*. Repression is Freud's theory. It is often used synonymously with the term *motivated forgetting*.
27. The answer is *A*. Although flashbulb memories can be recalled in vivid detail, they are nonetheless subject to the normal processes of forgetting.
28. The answer is *D*. This process implies that some forms of learning may be remembered at the synapse.
29. The answer is *C*. This finding supports Hebb's notion of synaptic facilitation.
30. The answer is *C*. Alzheimer's disease destroys neurons containing acetylcholine. Studies also have shown that drugs that block acetylcholine disrupt the formation of memory.
31. The answer is *B*. Retrograde amnesia is the disorder characterized by an inability to retrieve old, long-term memories. Interestingly, in both anterograde and retrograde amnesia, there is little or no disruption to STM.
32. The answer is *A*. Isn't it interesting that the hippocampus keeps turning up as a key brain structure throughout this chapter?
33. The answer is *D*. Confabulation may be thought of as an exaggerated version of reconstructive distortion.
34. The answer is *D*. Loftus and others have shown that misleading questions presented to eyewitnesses can actually cue the recall of items that were not present.
35. The answer is *D*. Eyewitnesses are more likely to make mistakes if there is more than one suspect in the lineup.

Answers to True-False Questions

1. F   6. T

2. T   7. F

3. F   8. T

4. F   9. T

5. T   10. F

Chapter 8　Cognition, Language, and Intelligence

Learning Objectives

1. Define cognition, and identify its three primary facets. (p. 274)

2. Understand what concepts are, and distinguish between simple and complex concepts. (p. 275)

3. Distinguish between the basic and prototypical characteristics of natural concepts. (p. 275)

4. Define problem solving, and describe the three major cognitive operations involved in problem solving. (p. 279)

5. Distinguish among the following problem-solving strategies: trial-and-error, algorithmic, and heuristic. (p. 280)

6. Discuss the importance of framing and emotional factors in decision making. (p. 281)

7. Define artificial intelligence, and explain how it is used in problem solving. (p. 282)

8. Identify the major characteristics of human experts. (p. 282)

9. Define creativity, and distinguish between convergent thinking and divergent thinking. (p. 283)

10. List and describe the four steps involved in Wallas's description of creative problem solving. (p. 284)

11. Define language, including the meaning of semantic content, the distinction between the surface structure of language and the deep structure of language, and the generative property of language. (p. 285)

12. Distinguish among phonemes, morphemes, and syntax. (p. 286)

13. Identify the Whorfian hypothesis. (p. 287)

14. Discuss the research results regarding the language capabilities of animals. (p. 289)

15. Define intelligence, and compare the position of psychologists who view intelligence as a general ability to those who view it as several specific abilities. (p. 291)

16. List Sternberg's cognitive components of intelligent behavior. (p. 293)

17. Distinguish between fluid intelligence and crystallized intelligence. (p. 294)

18. Identify intelligence tests, and discuss how they are useful. (p. 295)

19. Discuss the concept of intelligence quotient, and distinguish between ratio IQ and deviation IQ. (p. 296)

20. List and describe characteristics of good intelligence tests. (p. 298)

21. Define tacit intelligence, and describe its relationship to general intelligence. (p. 299)

22. Identify the factors that contribute to an individual's intelligence. (p. 300)

23. Describe the importance of intelligence scores in modern society. (p. 301)

24. Discuss possible reasons for the recent rise in intelligence test scores. (p. 302)

25. Identify the race-ethnic differences in intelligence and achievement scores, and describe the controversies and policy implications raised by the publication of *The Bell Curve*. (p. 305)

26. Distinguish between mental retardation and giftedness. (p. 308)

27. (From the Application section) Identify techniques to help improve critical thinking. (p. 311)

Chapter Overview

Cognition refers to the process by which information is obtained through the senses, transformed through the processes of perception and thinking, stored and retrieved through the processes of memory, and used in the processes of problem solving and language.

The basic units of thinking are called concepts. Concepts are categories of things, events, or qualities linked together by some common feature or features. Some concepts are based on a single common feature, while others are more complex. Not all concepts are equally easy to learn; some are more natural than others. Natural concepts are both basic and prototypical.

Problem solving is the use of information to reach a goal that is blocked. Problem solving uses cognitive operations, which include formulating the problem, understanding the elements of the problem, and generating and evaluating alternative solutions. The term *artificial intelligence* describes computers that are programmed to think like humans. Algorithmic and heuristic operations are two types of cognitive strategies used to solve problems. Expert problem solvers generally excel in a limited number of areas, they work quickly, they spend time analyzing a problem, they recognize more patterns, and they use self-monitoring. Creative problem solving requires the ability to think in flexible and unusual ways, called divergent thinking; problem solving that is more logical and conventional is called convergent thinking.

Language is a symbolic code used in human communication. The meaning that is communicated is called the semantic content of language. Human language is highly efficient and generative; an infinite set of utterances can be made using a finite set of elements and rules. These rules are referred to as syntax. Phonemes are the smallest units of sound, while morphemes are the smallest units of meaning in a language.

Psychologists have long been interested in the relationship between language and thought. The Whorfian or linguistic relativity hypothesis states that the structure of language influences thinking. Controversy continues over whether animals are able to understand syntax.

Intelligence refers to the cognitive abilities of an individual to learn from experience, to reason well, and to cope effectively with the demands of daily living. Some psychologists believe that intelligence is a single factor, while others view intelligence as many different kinds of intellectual abilities. Gardner suggests there are seven independent types of intelligence, whereas Sternberg focuses on the cognitive components of intelligence. The intelligence quotient (IQ) is obtained by dividing an individual's mental age by his or her chronological age. This approach to calculating intellectual ability has been replaced by the deviation IQ, which compares individual scores to a normal distribution. Useful IQ tests must be standardized, objective, reliable, valid, and evaluated against proper norms. Some researchers have focused on everyday intelligence, also called tacit intelligence. An individual's level of intelligence is determined both by inherited and environmental factors. Some researchers believe that intelligence scores have risen dramatically over the past several generations. The publication of *The Bell Curve* has sparked controversy concerning the relationship between heredity and intelligence, and the impact of intelligence on economic well-being.

Mental retardation varies in degree, from mild to profound. Retardation can result from a variety of causes, including genetic factors, birth trauma, maternal drug use, or early deprivation. At the other extreme in intelligence, a longitudinal study of gifted children has found these individuals to be functioning well in most aspects of life.

It is possible to improve one's critical thinking skills by increasing one's mental efforts, improving problem formulation and breaking out of mental sets

Key Terms Exercise

For each of the following exercises, match the key terms on the left with the correct definitions on the right. Page references to the text follow the terms so that you may refer to the text for any items you answer incorrectly or do not understand completely. You may check your responses immediately by referring to the answers that follow each exercise.

Concepts and Problem Solving

_____ 1. cognition (p. 274)
_____ 2. concepts (p. 274)
_____ 3. mental set (p. 279)
_____ 4. algorithms (p. 280)
_____ 5. heuristics (p. 280)
_____ 6. artificial intelligence (p. 282)
_____ 7. expert systems (p. 282)
_____ 8. convergent thinking (p. 283)
_____ 9. divergent thinking (p. 283)

a. computer programmed to think like humans
b. categories of objects or events that are linked together by some common feature or features
c. efficient problem-solving strategies that do not guarantee a correct solution
d. intellectual process through which information is obtained, transformed, stored, and used
e. loosely organized, unconventional thinking
f. logical, conventional thinking
g. patterns of reasoning that guarantee finding a correct solution
h. a habitual way of viewing a problem
i. problem-solving computer programs that operate in a narrow area

ANSWERS

1. d	6. a
2. b	7. i
3. h	8. f
4. g	9. e
5. c	

Language

_____ 1. language (p. 285)
_____ 2. semantic content (p. 285)
_____ 3. surface structure (p. 286)
_____ 4. deep structure (p. 286)
_____ 5. phoneme (p. 286)
_____ 6. morpheme (p. 286)
_____ 7. syntax (p. 287)
_____ 8. linguistic relativity hypothesis (p. 287)

a. the underlying structure that contains a statement's meaning
b. the meaning that is communicated in symbols such as language
c. the smallest unit of meaning in a language
d. a symbolic code used in communication
e. the smallest unit of sound in a language
f. the grammatical rules of a language
g. the superficial structure of a statement
h. the idea that the structure of a language influences thinking

ANSWERS

1. d	5. e
2. b	6. c
3. g	7. f
4. a	8. h

Intelligence I

_____ 1. intelligence (p. 291)
_____ 2. fluid intelligence (p. 294)
_____ 3. crystallized intelligence (p. 295)
_____ 4. intelligence quotient (p. 296)
_____ 5. normal distribution (p. 298)
_____ 6. standardization (p. 298)

a. a numerical value of intelligence derived from an intelligence test
b. methods for administering tests in the same way to all individuals
c. the cognitive ability of an individual to learn from experience, to reason well, and to cope with the demands of daily living
d. the ability to learn or invent new strategies to deal with new problems
e. the ability to use previously learned skills to solve familiar problems
f. a symmetrical pattern of scores in which most scores are clustered near the center

ANSWERS
1. c   4. a
2. d   5. f
3. e   6. b

Intelligence II

_____ 1. norms (p. 299)
_____ 2. objectivity (p. 299)
_____ 3. reliability (p. 299)
_____ 4. validity (p. 299)
_____ 5. tacit intelligence (p. 299)

a. the practical knowledge and skills needed to deal with everyday problems
b. similarity in test scores even if the test is administered at different times and/or by different examiners
c. a test's ability to measure what it's supposed to measure
d. scoring a test question so that the same score is produced regardless of who does the scoring
e. standards created by the scores of a large group of individuals used as the basis of comparison for test scores

ANSWERS

1. e
2. d
3. b
4. c
5. a

Who Am I?

Match the psychologists on the left with their contributions to the field of psychology on the right. Page references to the text follow the names of the psychologists so that you may refer to the text for further review of these psychologists and their contributions. You may check your responses immediately by referring to the answers that follow each exercise.

_____ 1. Benjamin Whorf (p. 287)
_____ 2. Sir Francis Galton (p. 291)
_____ 3. Howard Gardner (p. 292)
_____ 4. Robert Sternberg (p. 293)
_____ 5. David Wechsler (p. 295)
_____ 6. Alfred Binet (p. 295)

a. I developed intelligence scales for children and adults.
b. I developed the first useful intelligence test (in France).
c. I believe there are seven independent types of intelligence, including artistic and athletic.
d. It's my belief that language influences thinking.
e. I proposed the cognitive components of intelligent behavior.
f. My writings in the late 1800s helped popularize the concept of intelligence.

ANSWERS
1. d   4. e
2. f   5. a
3. c   6. b

Review At A Glance

(Answers to this section begin on page 147)

Definition of Cognition

The intellectual processes through which information is obtained, transformed, stored, retrieved, and used is ____(1)____. Cognition processes ____(2)____; it is active, and it is ____(3)____.

Concepts: The Basic Units of Thinking

Categories of objects and events linked together by common features are called ____(4)____. These basic units of thought may involve one common feature, or they may be more complex. When two or more common characteristics are simultaneously present, this is a ____(5)____ concept. Concepts that have one or another characteristic, or both of them, are ____(6)____ concepts.

Some concepts are easier to learn than others; these are ____(7)____ concepts. Natural concepts have two primary characteristics: they are ____(8)____ and ____(9)____. Basic concepts have a medium degree of ____(10)____. In contrast, a high degree of inclusiveness is found in ____(11)____ concepts, and a low degree of inclusiveness is found in ____(12)____ concepts. Among the important characteristics of basic concepts are (1) they share many common ____(13)____; (2) they share similar ____(14)____; (3) they often share motor ____(15)____; and (4) they are easily ____(16)____.

The second defining characteristic of natural concepts is that they are good examples, or ____(17)____.

Thinking and Problem Solving: Using Information to Reach Goals

The cognitive process that uses information to reach a goal that is blocked is called ____(18)____ _____. There are three major steps in problem solving: (1) ____(19)____ the problem, (2) understanding and ____(20)____ the elements of the problem, and (3) ____(21)____ and evaluating alternative solutions.

A habitual way of viewing a problem is called a ____(22)____ _____. Three types of cognitive strategies are used in problem solving: (1) trial-and-error, (2) a type in which every possible solution is examined and which guarantees a solution, called an ____(23)____, and (3) a shortcut strategy that increases the probability of finding a correct solution, but doesn't guarantee a correct solution, known as ____(24)____. A heuristic that involves making judgments about the unknown on the assumption that it is similar to what we already know is called the ____(25)____ heuristic. Decision making is also influenced by the way a problem or question is presented; this is called ____(26)____. According to the text, both cognitive and ____(27)____ factors influence our decision making.

The term artificial intelligence describes ____(28)____ that are programmed to think like humans. Problem-solving computer programs, such as MYCIN, that operate in a very narrow area, are called ____(29)____ _____. Generally, computers are best at solving problems when the problem area is ____(30)____-_____. Human experts share the following characteristics: they excel in a ____(31)____ number of areas, they are fast, they spend time ____(32)____ a problem, they recognize more ____(33)____, they use their memory more effectively, they use a ____(34)____ level of analysis, and they are self-____(35)____.

The ability to produce novel and socially valued products or ideas is ____(36)____. Thinking that is logical and conventional is called ____(37)____ thinking, whereas thinking that is loosely organized, only partially directed, and unconventional is called ____(38)____ thinking. Most formal education emphasizes ____(39)____ thinking. Divergent thinking produces answers that must be evaluated ____(40)____. Most researchers believe that creative thinking is separate from general ____(41)____. One explanation of the creative process suggests that it proceeds in four steps: preparation, ____(42)____, illumination, and ____(43)____.

Language: Symbolic Communication

Language is a symbolic code used in communication. The meaning that is communicated is referred to as ____(44)____ _____. Noam Chomsky has distinguished between the superficial structure of a statement, called ____(45)____ _____, and the underlying structure that contains the statement's meaning, called ____(46)____ _____. Human language is a highly ____(47)____ system. Language gives us the ability to create an infinite number of utterances from a fixed set of elements and rules; this is called the ____(48)____ property of language. The smallest unit of sound in a language is a ____(49)____, whereas the smallest unit of meaning in a language is a ____(50)____. The rules of a language are called ____(51)____. Differences exist between rules of syntax and the ____(52)____ rules of grammar. The hypothesis that the structure of a language influences thinking, proposed by Benjamin Whorf, is called the ____(53)____ _____ hypothesis. Linguistic relativity has led us to substitute some ____(54)____ - terms for some terms that were masculine.

Unlike bees, which are able to communicate only in ways that are limited by inheritance, human language is ____(55)____ and must be learned through interactions with ____(56)____ speakers. Human languages can generate an ____(57)____ number of unique and novel utterances. The experiences of a parrot named Alex and chimpanzees named Washoe and Koko suggest animals are able to learn to use a human ____(58)____. Researchers, however, question whether a chimpanzee's use of language exhibits an understanding of ____(59)____.

Intelligence: The Sum Total of Cognition

The ability of an individual to learn from experience, to reason well, and to cope well with daily life is ____(60)____. Sir Francis Galton popularized the notion of intelligence in the late 1800s. He believed intelligence is inherited and is composed of a single ____(61)____ factor. Charles Spearman uses the term ____(62)____ to refer to this general factor, but other psychologists believe intelligence is a collection of many separate abilities. Louis Thurstone, for example, devised a test to measure ____(63)____ different abilities, whereas J. P. Guilford believes intelligence is made up of ____(64)____ different abilities. According to Howard Gardner, there are ____(65)____ independent types of intelligence. Research suggests the brains of people with a higher "g" have more ____(66)____ connections and they can process simple cognitive tasks more ____(67)____.

Robert Sternberg has proposed a theory that specifies the ____(68)____ _____ of intelligence.

Other psychologists distinguish between the ability to learn or invent new strategies to solve a new problem, called ____(69)____ intelligence, and the ability to use previously learned skills to solve familiar problems, called ____(70)____ intelligence. Throughout an adult's working years, there is an improvement in ____(71)____ intelligence, although ___(72)___ intelligence declines after middle age.

Around 1900, Alfred ___(73)___ became the first person to develop a useful measure of intelligence. Binet's test was refined by Lewis ___(74)___ of Stanford University. A similar intelligence test was also developed by David ___(75)___. Intelligence tests are designed to be a ___(76)___ of some of the cognitive abilities that constitute intelligence. They are useful in predicting the performance of individuals in situations that require ___(77)___.

IQ scores are calculated by dividing a person's ___(78)___ age by his ___(79)___ age and multiplying the result by ___(80)___. Binet's approach, which calculates the ___(81)___ IQ, is no longer used in contemporary intelligence tests. A newer approach to measuring intellectual ability, termed the ___(82)___ IQ, assumes that the scores of large numbers of individuals who take an intelligence test will fall in a ___(83)___ distribution. Most scores will be clustered around the ___(84)___, and as scores deviate from the average they become progressively less common. Using this approach, the average intelligence score is set at ___(85)___.

Good intelligence tests, as well as other psychological tests, are characterized by: (1) ___(86)___, so that tests are given the same way to all who take the test; (2) ___(87)___, in which the test is given to a large representative sample of the population; (3) ___(88)___, so that there is little or no ambiguity as to what constitutes a correct answer; (4) ___(89)___, so that the scores obtained would be the same if administered on two different occasions or by two different examiners; and (5) ___(90)___, so that a test measures what it is supposed to measure.

The practical knowledge and skills needed to deal with everyday problems is called ___(91)___ intelligence. Tacit intelligence is related to general intelligence in the following three ways: (1) those who have very low levels of general intelligence usually do not have highly developed ___(92)___ intelligence; (2) it is unlikely that those with limited ___(93)___ intelligence will succeed in highly complex areas of general intelligence; and (3) those with highly developed general intelligence are more likely to have good ___(94)___ knowledge across many different areas.

Research both on twins and on persons adopted at birth confirm the importance of ___(95)___ in determining IQ. Another important factor in intelligence appears to be one's intellectual ___(96)___.

A strong correlation exists between IQ and success in ___(97)___ and in ___(98)___. Intelligence predicts success in occupations because: (1) many occupations require advanced ___(99)___; (2) those with higher intelligence are easier to ___(100)___; and (3) those with higher intelligence tend to perform better in ___(101)___ jobs.

In many countries, evidence suggests that intelligence scores have ___(102)___ dramatically over the past few generations. Among the possible explanations for these findings are: (1) improved health and ___(103)___; (2) increases in levels of ___(104)___; (3) increases in environmental ___(105)___; and (4) in the United States, dramatic changes in the lives of persons of ___(106)___. The last several decades have seen a narrowing of the gap of intellectual and academic scores between ___(107)_____ groups in the United States. The changes have occurred since the end of official ___(108)___ in the United States.

A book about intelligence, called *The Bell Curve*, suggests that North American society is moving toward a

_____(109)_____, in which the environmental contributions to intelligence are equalized and the influence of genetics on intelligence will increase. The book further contends that society is headed toward ___(110)___ decline. Although critics and research dispute many of the book's ideas, the book raises important questions about the role of ___(111)___ merit in our society.

Degrees of mental retardation range from mild to ___(112)___. Retardation can result from genetic disorders, ___(113)___ trauma, maternal infections, maternal use of alcohol or psychoactive ___(114)___, or early sensory or maternal ___(115)___. Approximately 90 percent of the population with retardation is ___(116)___ retarded; thus, the vast majority of people who have mental retardation can lead productive and satisfying lives.

"Gifted" is usually defined in terms of high IQ scores and high levels of ___(117)___. Gifted programs are funded on two assumptions: (1) that the nation needs to enrich the education of its brightest future leaders, and (2) that bright children occasionally need help to avoid having ___(118)___ problems. The results of the ___(119)___ study and others on highly intelligent people indicate that they function very well in every evaluated area of life.

Application of Psychology: Improving Critical Thinking

According to the text, improved critical thinking skills can result from increased ___(120)___ effort, improved ___(121)___ formulation and by breaking out of unproductive ___(122)_____. A type of mental set in which we have difficulty in seeing new uses for objects is called ___(123)_____. Critical thinking can be made more effective by ___(124)___ one's critical thinking. A general strategy for problem solving includes the following steps: (1) formulate the problem; (2) generate all possible ___(125)___; (3) eliminate poor solutions; (4) examine the ___(126)___ of the remaining solutions; (5) generate ways to implement the solution; and (6) ___(127)___ the solution.

Concept Checks

Fill in the missing components of the following concept boxes. The correct answers are located in the "Answers" section at the end of the chapter.

Thinking

Concept	Definition
algorithm	
	making judgments about the unknown on the assumption that it is similar to what is already known
convergent thinking	
	loosely organized, unconventional thinking

Differing Views of Intelligence

Theorist	Concept
Galton, Spearman, Wechsler	
	there are seven independent types of intelligence
Sternberg	
	developed the first useful intelligence test
	working at Stanford, refined the work of Binet

Characteristics of Good Intelligence Tests

Characteristic	Definition
	all individuals are administered the test the same way
	standards used as the basis of comparison for scores on a test
objectivity	
reliability	
validity	

Extending the Chapter: Psychology, Societal Issues, and Human Diversity

These questions may be assigned to you. Whether or not they are assigned, they are designed to be challenging questions to encourage you to think independently about the material in the chapter. Many of the questions have no right or wrong answers.

I.   From the "Application of Psychology" section

1.   Select a problem you recently tried to solve, and demonstrate how using the material in the text might have improved the quality of the solution.

2.   What is the most useful idea regarding critical thinking that you read in this section?

II.   Psychology, Societal Issues, and Human Diversity

1.   Describe the research seeking to understand cultural influences on inferential reasoning. Discuss other ways in which one's culture might impact one's thinking.

2.   Describe the ways in which our society rewards and punishes divergent thinkers.

3.   Does society place too much emphasis on intelligence test scores? In what ways does society overemphasize these scores?

4.   To what extent is racism and sexism a result of racist and sexist language? How can and how should this type of language be regulated?

5.   Inasmuch as intellectually gifted children represent a potentially important resource for our society, how should public policy be designed to nurture such abilities in children?

Practice Quiz

The practice quiz consists of three sections: 1) Short answer questions, 2) Multiple-choice questions, and 3) True-False questions. At the end of the chapter you will find suggested answers to the short answer questions, answers and explanations for the multiple-choice questions, and answers to the true-false questions.

Short Answer Questions

1. Describe the characteristics of basic concepts, according to Rosch.

_____

_____

2. List and describe three characteristics of those with expertise in some field.

_____

_____

3. Distinguish between phonemes and morphemes, and describe the importance of syntax.

_____

_____

Multiple-Choice Questions

1. Which of the following is an important characteristic of cognition?
   a. Cognition processes information.
   b. Cognition is active.
   c. Cognition is functional.
   d. all of the above
      LO 1

2. If a concept has two or more common characteristics present at the same time, it is a
   a. disjunctive concept.
   b. conjunctive concept.
   c. natural concept.
   d. novel concept.
      LO 2

3. According to Eleanor Rosch, basic concepts
   a. are very inclusive.
   b. are difficult to name.
   c. share many common attributes.
   d. rarely share similar shapes.
      LO 3

4. Which of the following represents the proper sequence of cognitive operations involved in problem solving?
   a. generate and evaluate solutions, formulate the problem, understand the elements
   b. understand the elements, generate and evaluate solutions, formulate the problem
   c. formulate the problem, generate and evaluate solutions, understand the elements
   d. formulate the problem, understand the elements, generate and evaluate solutions
      LO 4

5. Amy is trying to solve a problem by using a strategy that guarantees a correct solution. The technique she is using is
   a. algorithms.
   b. representativeness.
   c. heuristics.
   d. availability.
      LO 5

6. Voting for a candidate based on having heard her on TV rather than on having systematically studied the viewpoints of all the candidates is problem solving based on
   a. algorithms.
   b. convergence.
   c. divergence.
   d. heuristics.
   LO 5

7. Framing refers to
   a. the decision to use heuristics or algorithms.
   b. the usefulness of trial-and-error.
   c. artificial intelligence.
   d. the way a question or problem is posed.
   LO 6

8. The MYCIN program
   a. is an example of an expert system.
   b. has replaced the need for physicians to diagnose and treat some diseases.
   c. agreed with medical experts in almost every case .
   d. all of the above
   LO 7

9. When compared with novices, each of the following is true of human experts *except*
   a. experts rely less on self-monitoring.
   b. experts work quickly.
   c. experts excel in a limited number of areas.
   d. experts use their memory more effectively.
   LO 8

10. People who are creative tend to use
    a. convergent thinking.
    b. divergent thinking.
    c. subordinate thinking.
    d. little or no thinking.
    LO 9

11. Each of the following is a step in the creative process *except*
    a. illumination.
    b. creation.
    c. elimination.
    d. verification.
    LO 10

12. According to Wallas, which creative problem solving step involves a period of rest?
    a. preparation
    b. incubation
    c. illumination
    d. verification
    LO 10

13. Bill suddenly realized how to solve a difficult problem. According to Wallas, Bill has just completed the creative process step called
    a. verification.
    b. incubation.
    c. preparation.
    d. illumination.
    LO 10

14. Which of the following contains the underlying meaning in a statement?
    a. deep structure
    b. surface structure
    c. phonemes
    d. syntax
    LO 11

15. When we say that language is generative, we mean that
    a. it is passed down from generation to generation.
    b. novel language utterances generate new thoughts.
    c. there is no limit to what can be said.
    d. dialects change over several generations.
    LO 11

16. Which of the following is the correct sequence used by children in language development?
    a. morphemes, phonemes, and then syntax
    b. syntax, phonemes, and then morphemes
    c. phonemes, morphemes, and then syntax
    d. syntax, morphemes, and then phonemes
    LO 12

17. According to the Whorfian hypothesis
    a. language influences thought.
    b. language is generative.
    c. morpheme use precedes phoneme use.
    d. animals can successfully use syntax.
    LO 13

18. Although apes have been taught American Sign Language (ASL), many researchers contend
    a. they can't communicate with each other.
    b. they rarely express their emotions.
    c. they show little evidence of understanding syntax.
    d. they are unable to teach other apes ASL.
    LO 14

19. Research with Alex the parrot and with Washoe the chimpanzee demonstrated their abilities to learn
    a. several human languages.
    b. to use language.
    c. to solve complex mathematical problems.
    d. to use proper syntax.
    LO 14

20. The term "g" refers to the idea that intelligence
    a. is made of genetically inherited abilities.
    b. may be grouped into subcategories.
    c. has a basic general component.
    d. was developed by Sir Francis Galton.
    LO 15

21. According to Gardner, each of the following is a type of intelligence *except*
    a. linguistic.
    b. spatial.
    c. crystallized.
    d. kinesthetic.
    LO 15

22. Individuals who score high in general intelligence are believed to
    a. have a greater ability to form new neural connections.
    b. be better at learning from experience.
    c. be able to process simple cognitive tasks more quickly.
    d. all of the above
    LO 15

23. According to Sternberg, each of the following is a cognitive component of intelligent behavior *except*
    a. encode.
    b. verify.
    c. apply.
    d. respond.
    LO 16

24. Which type of intelligence improves throughout an adult's working years?
    a. fluid
    b. musical
    c. kinesthetic
    d. crystallized
    LO 17

25. Each of the following is true regarding intelligence tests *except*
    a. the first tests were developed by Binet.
    b. there is widespread agreement concerning the definition of intelligence.
    c. intelligence tests do a good job of predicting success in school.
    d. intelligence tests use a small sample of some of the cognitive abilities that comprise intelligence.
    LO 18

26. Joe has a mental age of 10 and a chronological age of 8. His ratio IQ score is
    a. 80.
    b. 100.
    c. 120.
    d. 125.
    LO 19

27. When a test measures what it claims to measure it is
    a. valid.
    b. reliable.
    c. standardized.
    d. objective.
    LO 20

28. Every time Sally took the SAT tests, her scores were exactly the same. This means the SAT tests have a high degree of _____ for Sally.
    a. standardization
    b. reliability
    c. validity
    d. meaning
    LO 20

29. The ability to solve everyday problems is referred to as
    a. crystallized intelligence.
    b. fluid intelligence.
    c. kinesthetic intelligence.
    d. tacit intelligence.
    LO 21

30. Research conducted with twins as well as with adopted children has tended to support the influence of which factor on intelligence?
    a. environment
    b. learning
    c. heredity
    d. none of the above
    LO 22

31. According to the text, a strong positive correlation exists between IQ and success in
    a. education.
    b. tacit knowledge.
    c. occupations.
    d. both *a* and *c*.
    LO 23

32. Each of following is suggested as a possible reason for the recent increase in intelligence scores *except*
    a. improved health and nutrition.
    b. smaller families.
    c. greater selectivity in marriage partners.
    d. greater environmental complexity.
    LO 24

33. According to the authors of *The Bell Curve*
    a. intelligence will become less important in our society as computers do more and more work.
    b. technology is helping to shrink the gap between rich and poor.
    c. IQ is a poor predictor of success in school.
    d. the future will see a widening gap between those who are intelligent and affluent people and those who are less intelligent and less affluent.
    LO 25

34. The longitudinal study of highly intelligent people initiated by Louis Terman has revealed
    a. that the intellectually gifted have a greater likelihood of experiencing mental disorders.
    b. no significant differences in achievement when compared with a group of normal IQ individuals.
    c. that the gifted group was shorter than average.
    d. higher achievements and lower rates of alcoholism for the intellectually gifted.
    LO 26

35. Each of the following is an effective strategy for improving critical thinking *except*
    a. breaking out of unproductive mental sets.
    b. trying to engage in more functional fixedness.
    c. increasing your mental effort.
    d. trying to formulate the problem in two different ways.
    LO 27

True-False Questions

_____ 1. According to Rosch, natural concepts are good prototypes.

_____ 2. Heuristics are useful since they guarantee a solution to a problem.

_____ 3. The way a question is framed can strongly influence the answer.

_____ 4. One difference between experts and novices is that experts don't need to spend much time analyzing a problem.

_____ 5. The kind of thinking most likely to be rewarded in school is divergent thinking.

_____ 6. The grammatical rules of language are called syntax.

_____ 7. Researchers are in basic agreement that animal language shows syntax.

_____ 8. According to Gardner, there are seven independent types of intelligence.

_____ 9. The ratio IQ is the type most commonly used today.

_____10. Traditional IQ tests do a good job of measuring tacit intelligence.

ANSWERS SECTION

Concept Checks

Thinking

Concept	Definition
algorithm	pattern of reasoning that guarantees a correct solution
representativeness heuristic	making judgments about the unknown on the assumption that it is similar to what is already known
convergent thinking	logical, conventional thinking that focuses on a problem
divergent thinking	loosely organized, unconventional thinking

Differing Views of Intelligence

Theorist	Concept
Galton, Spearman, Wechsler	intelligence is a single factor
Gardner	there are seven independent types of intelligence
Sternberg	researched the cognitive components of intelligent behavior
Binet	developed the first useful intelligence test
Terman	working at Stanford refined the work of Binet

Characteristics of Good Intelligence Tests

Characteristic	Definition
standardization	all individuals are administered the test the same way
norms	standards used as the basis of comparison for scores on a test
objectivity	the same score is achieved regardless of who does the scoring
reliability	test produces similar scores even if it is administered on different occasions or by different examiners
validity	test measures what it is supposed to measure

Answers to Review At A Glance

1. cognition
2. information
3. useful
4. concepts
5. conjunctive
6. disjunctive
7. natural
8. basic
9. prototypical
10. inclusiveness
11. superordinate
12. subordinate
13. attributes
14. shapes
15. movements
16. named
17. prototypes
18. problem solving
19. formulating
20. organizing
21. generating
22. mental set
23. algorithm
24. heuristics
25. representativeness
26. framing
27. emotional
28. computers
29. expert systems
30. well-defined
31. limited
32. analyzing
33. patterns
34. deeper
35. monitoring
36. creativity
37. convergent
38. divergent
39. convergent
40. subjectively
41. intelligence
42. incubation
43. verification
44. semantic content
45. surface structure
46. deep structure
47. efficient
48. generative
49. phoneme
50. morpheme
51. syntax
52. prescriptive
53. linguistic relativity
54. gender-neutral
55. flexible
56. fluent
57. infinite
58. language
59. syntax
60. intelligence
61. general
62. g
63. seven

64. 150
65. seven
66. neural
67. quickly
68. cognitive components
69. fluid
70. crystallized
71. crystallized
72. fluid
73. Binet
74. Terman
75. Wechsler
76. sample
77. intelligence
78. mental
79. chronological
80. 100
81. ratio
82. deviation
83. normal
84. average
85. 100

86. standardization
87. norms
88. objectivity
89. reliability
90. validity
91. tacit
92. tacit
93. general
94. practical
95. heredity
96. environment
97. education
98. occupations
99. education
100. train
101. complex
102. risen
103. nutrition
104. education
105. complexity
106. color
107. race-ethnic

108. segregation
109. meritocracy
110. genetic
111. intellectual
112. profound
113. birth
114. drugs
115. deprivation
116. mildly
117. creativity
118. psychological
119. Terman
120. mental
121. problem
122. mental sets
123. functional fixedness
124. monitoring
125. solutions
126. consequences
127. implement

Sample Answers for Short Answer Questions

1. **Describe the characteristics of basic concepts, according to Rosch.**

   According to Rosch, some concepts are more natural than others. One characteristic of natural concepts is that they are basic. Basic concepts have a medium degree of inclusiveness. They also share many common attributes. Members of basic concepts also share similar shapes; they often share similar movements, and basic concepts are easily named.

2. **List and describe three characteristics of those with expertise in some field.**

   Generally, experts excel in a limited number of areas. Experts work with great speed, they spend sufficient time analyzing a problem, they recognize more patterns than novices, they use their memory more effectively, they use a deeper level of analysis, and they use self-monitoring.

3. **Distinguish between phonemes and morphemes, and describe the importance of syntax.**

   A phoneme is the smallest unit of sound in a language. A morpheme is the smallest unit of meaning in a language. An individual phoneme might not convey meaning unless it is combined with other phonemes. Syntax refers to the grammatical rules of a language. These rules are understood by the speakers of a language and allow an infinite number of utterances to be made.

Multiple-Choice Answers

1. The answer is *D*. Cognition consists of the intellectual processes through which information is obtained, transformed, stored, retrieved, and used.

2. The answer is *B*. Disjunctive concepts, in contrast to conjunctive concepts, are defined by the presence of one common characteristic, *or* a second characteristic, or *both* characteristics.

3. The answer is *C*. Natural concepts are both basic and prototypical. Basic concepts have a medium degree of inclusiveness, share many common attributes, share similar shapes, often share motor movements, and are easily named. The second quality of natural concepts is that they are good prototypes; that is, they are good examples. Generally, natural concepts are easily learned.

4. The answer is *D*. Following this strategy may help you to improve your own problem-solving skills.

5. The answer is *A*. The use of algorithms is a time-consuming strategy, which makes them ideal for computer use.

6. The answer is *D*. Heuristics involve using shortcut strategies to solve problems; basing one's vote on having seen one candidate on TV is an example of a shortcut.

7. The answer is D. Research strongly suggests that the way a question is framed can dramatically impact decision making.

8. The answer is *A*. Although MYCIN is an example of an expert system, it agreed with medical experts 72 percent of the time and is *not* considered a replacement for physicians.

9. The answer is *A*. According to Glaser and Chi, experts actually have a high awareness of their errors and make corrections promptly.

10. The answer is *B*. Convergent thinking is logical, conventional, and focused, whereas divergent thinking is unconventional and loosely organized.

11. The answer is B. The missing second step in the creative process is called incubation, in which the problem is set aside for a while after the initial preparation period.

12. The answer is *B*. According to Wallas, this period involves setting the problem aside while it "incubates."

13. The answer is *D*. According to Wallas, the four steps in the creative process are preparation, incubation, illumination, and verification.

14. The answer is *A*. According to Chomsky, the superficial spoken or written structure of a statement is the surface structure, whereas the underlying meaning of the statement is held by the deep structure.

15. The answer is *C*. The generative property of language gives us the potential for an unlimited number of utterances from a finite set of rules and elements.

16. The answer is *C*. Children first babble in the sounds of their language (phonemes), then progress to morphemes, and finally acquire syntactic rules.

17. The answer is *A*. The Whorfian hypothesis, also called the linguistic relativity hypothesis, states the structure of a language influences the way people think.

18. The answer is *C*. According to some critics, the apes fail to use language to comment on the world and they do not understand syntax.

19. The answer is *B*. Although Alex, Washoe, Koko, and others have been taught to use language to communicate, none have been able to demonstrate any of the other alternatives

20. The answer is *C*. The concept of "g" is Spearman's notion that intelligence is a single broad concept. Other psychologists, from Thurstone to Gardner, view intelligence as a collection of several independent abilities.

21. The answer is *C*. Gardner suggests there are seven independent types of intelligence; in addition to those listed in the question, the others are logical-mathematical, musical, interpersonal, and intrapersonal.

22. The answer is *D*. General intelligence is referred to as "g."

23. The answer is *B*. The sequence is encode, infer, map, apply, compare, and respond.

24. The answer is *D*. Fluid intelligence declines after middle age. Musical intelligence and kinesthetic intelligence are two of Gardner's types of intelligence.

25. The answer is *B*. Although psychologists may agree about some of the components of intelligence, there is little agreement about a precise definition.

26. The answer is *D*. Using the IQ formula (IQ = MA/CA X 100), 10/8 X 100 = 1.25 X 100 = 125.

27. The answer is *A*. Reliability implies that the scores would be the same if the test was repeated. A test that is standardized is administered the same way to all who take the test. An objective test has agreed-upon right and

wrong answers.

28. The answer is *B*. Reliability means the scores are similar when taken on more than one occasion; validity means the test measures what it is supposed to measure.

29. The answer is D. Tacit intelligence refers to practical knowledge that is not typically taught in school.

30. The answer is *C*. Although the environment is also widely recognized as an important factor in intelligence, the question asked about the research conducted specifically with twins and adopted children.

31. The answer is *D*. According to the text, the correlation between IQ and these variables is about as high as between people's heights and weights.

32. The answer is *C*. The text does not cite evidence that people are more selective in their marriage partners.

33. The answer is *D*. The authors of *The Bell Curve* suggest intelligence cannot be modified and that intellectual differences are widening the gap between the "haves" and the "have-nots" in our society.

34. The answer is *D*. Terman's study has exploded some myths about intellectually gifted people. According to the research, they were considered more honest and trustworthy, enjoyed higher incomes, and had lower rates of alcoholism and criminal convictions when compared with their peers of average IQ.

35. The answer is *B*. Functional fixedness is a mental set in which there is difficulty in thinking of new uses for familiar objects.

Answers to True-False Questions

1. T	6. T
2. F	7. F
3. T	8. T
4. F	9. F
5. F	10. F

Part IV The Life Span

Chapter 9   Developmental Psychology

Learning Objectives

1. Describe the interplay of nature and nurture in development, and discuss the role maturation plays in development. (p. 320)

2. Identify imprinting, and describe the importance of critical periods. (p. 321)

3. Explain the impact of early social deprivation on development. (p. 323)

4. Explain the role of individual variation in development. (p. 324)

5. Identify the characteristics common to stage theories of development. (p. 326)

6. Identify and discuss Kohlberg's three levels of moral reasoning: premoral, conventional, and principled. (p. 328)

7. Compare and contrast Gilligan's and Kohlberg's theories of moral development. (p. 329)

8. Describe Erikson's stage theory of personality development, and list the stages of personality development. (p. 330)

9. Differentiate between the developmental stages termed the "neonatal period" and "infancy." (p. 333)

10. Identify the cognitive, emotional, and social aspects of development during infancy. (p. 333)

11. Identify the cognitive, emotional, and social aspects of development during early childhood. (p. 337)

12. Identify the cognitive, emotional, and social aspects of development during middle childhood. (p. 338)

13. Explain the changes that occur in physical development during puberty, including primary and secondary sex characteristics, menarche, the adolescent growth spurt, and physical changes in the brain. (p. 340)

14. Identify the characteristics of the formal operational stage, and discuss the characteristics of adolescent egocentrism. (p. 342)

15. Discuss the research results on adolescent social and emotional development. (p. 343)

16. Identify the physical and cognitive aspects of development in adulthood. (p. 345)

17. Discuss emotional and social development in adulthood. (p. 346)

18. Contrast Erikson's and Levinson's views of adult personality development. (p. 347)

19. Define *climacteric* and discuss how it affects men and women. (p. 350)

20. Explain the controversies associated with the stage theories of adulthood. (p. 351)

21. Discuss the biological and psychological changes that are involved in aging, and identify the factors associated with happy aging and longevity. (p. 352)

22. Identify and explain the stages of dying identified by Kübler-Ross. (p. 353)

23. (From the Application section) Identify the following: secure and insecure attachment, Baumrind's discipline styles, the two-way street of parenting, and common discipline mistakes. (p. 356)

24. (From the Application section) Discuss the results of research on sociocultural factors in parenting and the research regarding day care, divorce, and parenting. (p. 358)

Chapter Overview

Psychologists differ on the issue of how much our development is biologically determined (nature) or is shaped by the learning environment (nurture). Today, most psychologists believe that nature and nurture combine to influence our actions, thoughts, and feelings.

Research on imprinting in some animals shows that experiences during critical periods of early development can have long-lasting effects on behavior. Research conducted by the Harlows on the effects of early deprivation in monkeys showed the lasting effects of early social deprivation. Opinions are divided regarding the effects of abnormal early experiences in humans.

Stage theorists believe that all children pass through the same qualitatively different stages in the same order. For example, Piaget identified four stages of cognitive development from infancy to adulthood. According to Piaget, the process of assimilation adds new information to existing concepts, or schemas, which results in quantitative changes in a child's cognitions. The process of changing schemas in qualitative ways to incorporate new experiences is called accommodation. Piaget's four stages include (1) the sensorimotor stage (birth to 2 years), during which an infant conceptualizes the world in terms of schemas that incorporate sensory information and motor activities; (2) the preoperational stage (2 to 7 years), during which children can think in mental images, but exhibit egocentric thinking; (3) the concrete operational stage (7 to 11 years), during which children increase their ability to reason logically; and (4) the formal operational stage (11 years on), during which an individual uses full adult logic and can understand abstract concepts.

Kohlberg's theory of moral development is concerned with the logical process of arriving at answers to moral dilemmas. Kohlberg's theory proposes the following levels of moral development: (1) the premoral level, when the child has no sense of morality as adults understand the term; (2) the conventional level, when a child's moral view is based on what others will think of him or her; and (3) the principled level, when individuals judge right and wrong according to ethical principles rather than by the consequences of the actions.

Gilligan suggests that females progress through three stages of moral development: (1) morality as individual survival, (2) morality as self-sacrifice, and (3) morality as equality.

Erikson's theory of personality development suggests that individuals experience eight stages or crises, the outcomes of which will partly determine the future course of personality development. The development of the child proceeds through the following periods: (1) the neonatal period, the first two weeks of life marking the transition from the womb to independent life; (2) infancy, a time of rapid change in physical, perceptual, cognitive, linguistic, social, and emotional development; (3) early childhood, a period of great improvements in the coordination of small and large muscle groups; and (4) middle childhood, during which physical growth is slowed, but important cognitive changes occur, such as the ability to conserve and decenter.

Adolescence is the development period from the onset of puberty until the beginning of adulthood. The production of sex hormones in puberty triggers biological changes known as the primary sex characteristics. Menarche, the first menstrual period, occurs in American females at about 12 years and 6 months; males produce sperm about two years later. Within each sex, there is wide variation in the age at which puberty begins. Secondary sex characteristics appear in both sexes during puberty. The adolescent growth spurt lasts for slightly more than a year in early adolescence. In late adolescence, weight gain is common due to a decline in the basal metabolism rate. For both sexes different parts of the body grow at different rates, weight and physique change in irregular ways, and many adolescents experience skin problems. According to Piaget, the formal operational stage, which is characterized by the ability to use abstract concepts, occurs in some individuals by about age 11. Peers replace the family as the most important influence on the adolescent. Adolescent emotions are characterized by an increase in parent-child conflict, more mood changes, and an increase in risky behavior.

Adulthood is not a single phase of life. Challenges involving love, work, and play continue throughout adulthood. Psychologists disagree about whether the changes in adulthood are the result of programmed stages of biological development or are reactions to significant life events, such as starting a job, retiring, marriage, the birth of children, and so on.

Intelligence appears stable throughout adulthood in healthy adults. Some relatively positive personality changes that occur for many people during adulthood include becoming more insightful, dependable, and candid.

Erikson's developmental theory refers to early adulthood as the stage of intimacy vs. isolation. It is a time during which many individuals enter committed loving relationships. Erikson calls middle adulthood the stage of generativity vs. stagnation, the goal of which is to find meaning in work and family lives.

The period from the late 60s and beyond is referred to by Erikson as the stage of integrity vs. despair. According to Erikson, older adults who see meaning in their lives continue to live a satisfying existence.

Psychological variables associated with happy aging are staying engaged in life's activities, not believing the myths about old age, and avoiding smoking and excessive drinking. Older adults tend to be less frightened by death than younger adults. Studies by Elisabeth Kübler-Ross suggest that people who learn of their impending death tend to pass through five distinct stages: denial, anger, bargaining, depression, and acceptance.

Human infants who are securely attached enjoy physical contact with parents and move out quickly to explore; insecurely attached infants, however, cling excessively and are extremely upset by separation from parents. According to Baumrind, the three types of parental discipline styles are authoritarian, permissive, and authoritative. Children and parents are affected by each other's behavior. Research suggests that daycare children do not differ from those raised by others in their own homes in terms of physical health, emotional or intellectual development, or attachment.

Key Terms Exercise

For each of the following exercises, match the key terms on the left with the correct definitions on the right. Page references to the text follow the terms so that you may refer to the text for any items you answer incorrectly or do not understand completely. You may check your responses immediately by referring to the answers that follow each exercise.

Nature, Nurture, and Maturation

_____ 1. development (p. 320)
_____ 2. maturation (p. 320)
_____ 3. imprinting (p. 322)
_____ 4. critical period (p. 323)
_____ 5. early experiences (p. 323)
_____ 6. stage (p. 326)

a. a time period in development that is qualitatively different from the periods that come before and after

b. the more-or-less predictable changes in behavior associated with increasing age

c. a biologically determined period during which certain forms of learning can take place most easily

d. a form of early learning that takes place in some animals

e. systematic physical growth of the body

f. experience occurring early in development, believed by some to have lasting effects

ANSWERS

1. b	4. c
2. e	5. f
3. d	6. a

Development in Infancy and Childhood (I)

_____ 1. neonatal period (p. 333)
_____ 2. sensorimotor stage (p. 334)
_____ 3. object permanence (p. 334)
_____ 4. attachments (p. 337)
_____ 5. separation anxiety (p. 337)

a. the first 2 weeks of life following birth
b. the psychological bonds between infants and caregivers
c. the period of cognitive development from birth to 2 years
d. the distress expressed by infants when they are separated from their caregivers
e. the understanding that objects continue to exist even after they are removed from view

ANSWERS
1. a   4. b
2. c   5. d
3. e

Development in Infancy and Childhood (II)

_____ 1. preoperational stage (p. 337)
_____ 2. egocentrism (p. 337)
_____ 3. animism (p. 337)
_____ 4. transductive reasoning (p. 337)
_____ 5. concrete operational stage (p. 339)
_____ 6. conservation (p. 339)

a. the period of cognitive development from ages 2 to 7
b. the belief that inanimate objects are alive
c. the period of cognitive development from ages 7 to 11
d. the concept that quantity does not change just because superficial features have changed
e. self-centered thinking, characteristic of preoperational children
f. errors in inferring cause-and-effect relationships

ANSWERS
1. a   4. f
2. e   5. c
3. b   6. d

Adolescence

_____ 1. adolescence (p. 340)
_____ 2. puberty (p. 340)
_____ 3. formal operational stage (p. 342)
_____ 4. adolescent egocentrism (p. 342)

a. characterized by the ability to use abstract concepts
b. characterized by the imaginary audience, the personal fable, hypocrisy, and pseudostupidity
c. the point at which the individual is first physically capable of sexual reproduction
d. the period from the onset of puberty until the beginning of adulthood

ANSWERS
1. d   3. a
2. c   4. b

Who Am I?

Match the psychologists on the left with their contributions to the field of psychology on the right. Page references to the text follow the names of the psychologists so that you may refer to the text for further review of these psychologists and their contributions. You may check your responses immediately by referring to the answers that follow each exercise.

_____ 1. Konrad Lorenz (p. 322)

_____ 2. Harry and Margaret Harlow (p. 323)

_____ 3. Jean Piaget (p. 327)

_____ 4. Lawrence Kohlberg (p. 328)

_____ 5. Carol Gilligan (p. 329)

_____ 6. Erik Erikson (p. 330)

_____ 7. Elisabeth Kübler-Ross (p. 353)

a. While studying geese, I observed imprinting.

b. My stage theory focuses on the development of moral reasoning, especially in boys.

c. My theory focuses on personality development and assumes that people pass through eight important stages.

d. Our studies of early social deprivation led to some surprising results.

e. I developed a theory explaining the stages that occur leading to the acceptance of death.

f. I studied children extensively and proposed an important theory of cognitive development.

g. My research showed that the moral development of girls is different from that of boys.

ANSWERS

1. a   5. g
2. d   6. c
3. f   7. e
4. b

Review At A Glance
(Answers to this section begin on page 169)

Preview: Development

The more-or-less predictable changes in behavior throughout our lives are described as the process of ___(1)___.

The field of psychology that focuses on development across the life span is ___(2)___ psychology.

Nature, Nurture, and Maturation: Molding or Unfolding?

Most contemporary psychologists believe that behavior and developmental changes are controlled both by biological factors, called ___(3)___, and the psychological environment, called ___(4)___.

The most important biological factor in development is the systematic physical growth of the body, including the nervous system; this process is called ___(5)___. Research conducted with infants on toilet training supports the importance of ___(6)___.

Early Experience and Critical Periods

Konrad Lorenz has observed that goslings will follow any moving object that they are exposed to after hatching. He called this behavior ___(7)___. Imprinting can occur only during a brief period of a bird's life, called the ___(8)___ _____.

Harry and Margaret Harlow's research with monkeys focused on the effects of early ___(9)___ deprivation. Infant monkeys were raised in complete ___(10)___ for the first few months of life and never lived with a ___(11)___. When the monkeys reached adulthood and were placed in cages with normal monkeys, the Harlows noticed that their behavior was distinctly ___(12)___. When the mother-deprived monkeys became mothers themselves, they ___(13)___ their own infants. Opinions among psychologists are divided regarding the effects of abnormal early experiences among ___(14)___.

Normal development is highly variable in two respects: (1) the differences ___(15)___ children in their development and (2) the differences ___(16)___ individual children in the rates at which they move from one developmental period to the next.

Stage Theories of Development

Psychologists who believe that behavior goes through a series of abrupt changes are called ___(17)___ theorists. They believe that the changes occurring from one stage to the next are ___(18)___ different, while changes that occur within each stage are ___(19)___ different. Stages are believed to be ___(20)___ programmed, and all children pass through the same stages in the same order. A well-known stage theory is Piaget's theory of ___(21)___ development.

The stage theories of Kohlberg and Gilligan focus on the development of ___(22)___ reasoning. According to Kohlberg, we pass through three major levels in the development of moral reasoning. The first level, in which children make moral judgments to obtain rewards and avoid punishment, is called the ___(23)___ level. At the second level, moral decisions are based on what others, particularly parents, will think of them; this level is referred to as the ___(24)___ level. At the third level, called the ___(25)___ level, decisions are based on ethical principles rather than the consequences. According to Kohlberg, ___(26)___ people reach a stage in which they reason mostly in principled ways. Gilligan has claimed that Kohlberg's theory does not always accurately describe the moral development in ___(27)___. According to Gilligan, female moral development centers on the needs of people rather than on ___(28)___. Gilligan's theory suggests that moral development progresses from morality as individual ___(29)___, to morality as ___(30)___-_____, and finally to morality as ___(31)___.

Erik Erikson's theory describes major turning points or ___(32)___ that all people experience. According to Erikson, the outcome of these crises will help determine future ___(33)___ development.

Development in Infancy and Childhood

We are all in a constant change throughout our lives; the change is called ___(34)___. The first two weeks of life are termed the ___(35)___ period. When stimulated on the cheek, the neonate engages in the ___(36)___ reflex. Apparently, neonates cannot see very well beyond about ___(37)___ inches from their eyes.

At 2 weeks of age, the baby is called an ___(38)___. Infancy is characterized by rapid ___(39)___ development and rapid change in all ___(40)___. According to Piaget, the infant is in the ___(41)___ stage. From about 2 weeks on, the infant begins to interact ___(42)___ with its environment. According to Piaget, later in the sensorimotor stage, the child understands that objects exist even when they are out of sight; this is called ___(43)___ _____.

By 9 months, infants begin to understand some nouns. By age 2, the infant can communicate in word combinations called ___(44)___ speech.

At 2 months of age, the infant engages in true social behavior—___(45)___ at his caregivers. The emotion of ___(46)___ appears around four months. Shyness around strangers and fear of separation from caregivers begins between ___(47)___ to _____ months. Infants between 6 and 9 months also show fear and avoidance of Gibson's ___(48)___ cliff. By 2 years, infants have formed strong ___(49)___ to parents or other caregivers.

In early childhood, from ages 2 to 7, the child's physical growth is less explosive. According to Piaget, the child has entered the ___(50)___ stage. At the age of 2, most children can think in ___(51)___ images. The preoperational child's thought is self-centered, or ___(52)___, and the young child believes inanimate objects are alive, a trait called ___(53)___. The preoperational child also makes errors in understanding cause-and-effect relationships, called ___(54)___ reasoning. The preoperational stage is also characterized by dramatic growth in ___(55)___.

The sequence of development in a child's play activities is: (1) playing alone, called ___(56)___ play; (2) playing near other children, called ___(57)___ play; and (3) playing with others, or ___(58)___ play. By the age of 2, most boys and girls have begun to act in ___(59)___-_____ ways.

The elementary school years occur while the child is in Piaget's ___(60)___ _____ stage. Children in this stage are able to use most adult concepts, with the exception of ___(61)___ concepts. They can order objects according to size and weight, called ___(62)___, and they understand that logical propositions can be reversed, called ___(63)___. Children in this stage also understand that the quantity of objects does not change if the shape or other superficial features have changed; this concept is called ___(64)___. Piaget has stated that conservation is possible when a child can think of more than one thing at a time, referred to as the ability to ___(65)___. Although ties to parents remain important, after age 7 friendships with ___(66)___ become more important to children. Friendship groups, called ___(67)___, also emerge during this stage.

Adolescent Development

Adolescence begins with the onset of ___(68)___. The hormones produced at puberty trigger a series of changes that lead to ___(69)___ and menstruation in females and to the production of ___(70)___ in males; these are called the ___(71)___. The first menstrual period, called ___(72)___, begins at about 12 years and 6 months in females. Sperm cell production in males begins about ___(73)___ years later. For males and females, the more obvious physical changes occurring during puberty, such as lowering of the voice in males and development of the breasts in females, are called ___(74)___. Around the onset of puberty, adolescents experience a rapid increase in height and weight that is referred to as the ___(75)___. Important changes also take place in the adolescent's brain, particularly in the ___(76)___ system.

At about age 11, some adolescents demonstrate an ability to use abstract concepts, which Piaget calls the ___(77)___ stage. Adolescents often possess a self-centered type of thinking which Elkind has termed ___(78)___. The primary characteristic of this type of thinking is that the adolescent feels that he or she is the focus of everyone's attention; this is termed the ___(79)___. Adolescents may also feel that their problems are unique, which Elkind calls the ___(80)___. Another characteristic of adolescent egocentrism involves criticizing others for actions and traits that they find acceptable in themselves, called ___(81)___. A final characteristic, involving oversimplified logic, is called ___(82)___.

Socially, the adolescent experiences a shift in orientation from parents to ___(83)___. Although most adolescents are relatively happy and well adjusted, three areas in which adolescents have greater problems are conflicts with ___(84)___, more dramatic shifts in ___(85)___, and increases in ___(86)___ behavior.

Adulthood

The body begins slow physical decline after ___(87)___ adulthood. Declines occur in the senses, especially ___(88)___, hearing and ___(89)___. Throughout adulthood, from the twenties to the seventies, small but steady increases occur in the knowledge of ___(90)___ and word ___(91)___. Research suggests that older adults perform as well as younger adults on tasks involving learning and ___(92)___ about concepts. Older adults show increased ability in solving problems requiring ___(93)___. Finally, older adults do less well than younger adults on tasks involving ___(94)___ reasoning, divergent thinking, cognitive tasks requiring speed, and some aspects of short-term memory. Some facets of personality change more across the adult life span than others.

Some psychologists believe that adulthood consists of a series of ___(95)___ of development. Stage theories of adulthood have been proposed by ___(96)___ and Levinson. These stages differ from the stages of child development in that (1) not every adult is believed to go through every stage, (2) the order of the stages can ___(97)___ for some individuals, and (3) the timing of the stages is not controlled by ___(98)___ maturation.

Erikson refers to early adulthood as the stage of ___(99)___ vs. ___(100)___. According to Levinson, early adulthood consists of three briefer stages: (1) creating an adult manner of working and living independently characterizes the ___(101)___ to early adulthood; (2) reevaluating one's start into adult life occurs in the

___(102)___ ___ ___; and (3) working hard toward one's goals characterizes the culmination of ___(103)___ ___.

Middle adulthood is characterized by shifting from a focus on who we are ___(104)___ to thinking about who we ___(105)___. Erikson believes that the challenges of middle adulthood are to find ___(106)___ in our activities. He calls this stage ___(107)___ ___ ___. Levinson describes four brief stages of middle adulthood. The first of these stages reaches a peak in the early forties and is sometimes a period of anguish; it is called the ___(108)___. A period of calm and stability follows, called entering ___(109)___. Another period of reassessment occurs for most individuals in the age 50 ___(110)___, followed by another stable period from about age 55 to 65, called the culmination of ___(111)___ ___.

The ___(112)___, which begins around age 45, is marked by a loss of the capacity to reproduce in women and by a decline in the reproductive capacity of men. In women, the end of menstruation is called the ___(113)___. According to Erikson, individuals in their late 60s and beyond are in the stage called ___(114)___ vs. ___(115)___.

Among the criticisms of the stage theories are: (1) the early studies tended to focus more on ___(116)___; (2) the theories need to take into account cultural ___(117)___ and historical changes; and (3) not all developmentalists view adulthood as a series of ___(118)___.

Aging is partly a biological process, but it involves many ___(119)___ aspects as well. The keys to happy aging are (1) staying ___(120)___ in life's activities, (2) ignoring ___(121)___ about old age, and (3) avoiding smoking and excessive ___(122)___. Research found that people rated as having a ___(123)___, dependable and ___(124)___ personality in childhood experienced greater longevity. Those who were rated as ___(125)___ in childhood tended to die at a younger age.

Death and Dying: The Final Stage

Elisabeth Kübler-Ross has developed a theory stating that people who learn of their impending death (and sometimes of the impending death of loved ones) pass through five distinct stages. In the first stage, the individual strongly resists the idea of death; this is called ___(126)___. In stage two, the reaction is ___(127)___. In stage three, the individual tries to prolong his or her life by ___(128)___. In stage four, the terminally ill person experiences a loss of hope characterized by ___(129)___. Finally, the depression lifts and there is an ___(130)___ of death.

Application of Psychology: Parenting

At 6 to 9 months, infants typically become closely attached to their caretakers and develop ___(131)___. By 18 to 24 months, toddlers prefer to be near their caregiver, but, if ___(132)___, the toddler is able to explore the world and play. Children who are ___(133)___ attached cling excessively to the caretaker and become upset when separated. Secure attachment is a result both of a child's inborn ___(134)___ and parental ___(135)___.

According to Baumrind, parental discipline styles are of three types: (1) the ___(136)___ parent provides strict rules with little discussion of the reasons for the rules; (2) the ___(137)___ parent gives the child few rules and rarely punishes misbehavior; and (3) the ___(138)___ parent is an authority figure to the child, but explains and discusses rules. Children of ___(139)___ parents are happier and better behaved.

According to Richard Bell and others, children affect their ___(140)___ behavior as much as parents affect their ___(141)___ behavior. According to O'Leary, the most common discipline mistakes made by ineffective parents are lax discipline, reinforcement of ___(142)___ behavior, verbosity, and ___(143)___.

Sociocultural factors are important in understanding differences in parenting. For example, collectivistic cultures are more likely to emphasize the well-being of the ___(144)___ and the larger culture, whereas ___(145)___ cultures place more emphasis on individual achievement.

Research suggests that there are generally no differences between children in ___(146)___ and children being raised by parents in their own home in terms of their physical health, emotional or intellectual development, or attachment. Furthermore, children whose parents divorce may experience ___(147)___, but usually the disruptions are for a relatively brief period of time.

Concept Checks

Fill in the missing components of the following concept boxes. The correct answers are located in the "Answers" section at the end of the chapter.

Developmental Theories

Theorist	Developmental Areas	Proposed Stages
Piaget	cognitive	
	moral	premoral, conventional, and principled reasoning
Gilligan	moral	
	social	eight stages or crises, the outcome of which will determine future personality development
Kübler-Ross	death and dying	

Developmental Concepts

Term	Definition
imprinting	
critical period	
	a term that applies to the infant in the first two weeks of life
cooperative play	
	occurring during puberty, ovulation and menstruation in females and the production of mature sperm in males
	development of the breasts and hips in females; growth of the testes, broadening shoulders, and so on in males; growth of pubic hair and body hair in both sexes
climacteric	

Extending the Chapter: Psychology, Societal Issues, and Human Diversity

These questions may be assigned to you. Whether or not they are assigned, they are designed to be challenging questions to encourage you to think independently about the material in the chapter. Many of the questions have no right or wrong answers.

I. From the "Applications of Psychology" section

1. Describe the advantages and disadvantages of each of Baumrind's discipline styles. Include both the child's perspective and the parent's perspective in your answer.

2. Describe examples of sociocultural factors in parenting that you have observed.

II. Psychology, Societal Issues, and Human Diversity

1. How much freedom should a parent have to discipline a child? How can society balance the right of a parent to discipline a child with the duty to protect the rights of the child?

2. What steps should our society take to minimize the difficulties associated with adolescence?

3. Given the increasing reliance on daycare centers, to what extent should our society increase the regulation of daycare center operations, employees, and so on?

4. Should researchers engage in efforts to expand the upper limits of the human life span? Why or why not?

5. (From the Human Diversity section of the text) Discuss the choices parents must make when they have a child who cannot hear.

Practice Quiz

The practice quiz consists of three sections: 1) Short Answer questions, 2) Multiple-choice questions, and 3) True-False questions. At the end of the chapter you will find suggested answers to the short answer questions, answers and explanations for the multiple-choice questions, and answers to the true-false questions.

Short Answer Questions

1. Describe the development of cognitive abilities during the preoperational stage.

_____

_____

_____

2. List and describe the characteristics of adolescent egocentrism.

_____

_____

_____

3. List and describe the stages we are likely to pass through when we learn of our impending death.

_____

_____

_____

Multiple-Choice Questions

1. The debate among psychologists regarding the relative contributions of environment and heredity to the developmental process is called
   a. the critical period.
   b. the nature-nurture controversy.
   c. the stage controversy.
   d. behaviorism.
   LO 1

2. Research on toilet training conducted with identical twins illustrates the importance of which developmental factor?
   a. maturation
   b. imprinting
   c. nurture
   d. genetics
   LO 1

3. Lorenz observed that after hatching, baby goslings will follow any moving object to which they are exposed. He called this behavior
   a. maturation.
   b. exprinting.
   c. imprinting.
   d. follow-the-leader.
   LO 2

4. Research conducted by the Harlows underscores the profound importance of
   a. imprinting.
   b. maturation.
   c. early experiences.
   d. all of the above.
   LO 3

5. With regard to variation in development, the text asserts that
   a. different children develop at different rates.
   b. children vary in their *own* rate of development from one period to the next.
   c. little variation exists between children beyond the age of seven.
   d. both *a* and *b* .
   LO 4

6. Each of the following is a belief of stage theorists *except*
   a. as children progress through the stages, the differences between children are qualitative.
   b. as children progress through the stages, the differences are quantitative.
   c. children pass through the same stages in the same order.
   d. stages are biologically programmed to unfold.
   LO 5

7. According to Kohlberg, at what level of moral development would a child most likely be concerned about pleasing his parents and teachers?
   a. the preconventional level
   b. the premoral level
   c. the conventional level
   d. the principled level
   LO 6

8. Individuals who function at the principled level of morality, according to Kohlberg, make moral decisions based on
   a. ethical principles.
   b. receiving rewards and avoiding punishments.
   c. what they think others will think of them.
   d. sacrificing their own needs to meet the needs of others.
   LO 6

9. According to Gilligan, a woman in the most advanced stage of moral development experiences morality as
   a. individual survival.
   b. self-sacrifice.
   c. inequality.
   d. equality .
   LO 7

10. Which theorist is most likely to suggest that important gender differences exist in moral development?
    a. Gilligan
    b. Kohlberg
    c. Piaget
    d. Erikson
    LO 7

11. The stage during which Erikson believes a child learns to meet the demands imposed by society is
    a. basic trust vs. mistrust.
    b. autonomy vs. shame and doubt.
    c. industry vs. inferiority.
    d. identity vs. role confusion.
    LO 8

12. A child who failed to learn multiplication and division in grade school did not successfully complete which of Erikson's stages of personality development?
    a. autonomy vs. shame and doubt
    b. integrity vs. despair
    c. industry vs. inferiority
    d. initiative vs. guilt
    LO 8

13. The neonatal period refers to the first
    a. 2 hours of life.
    b. 2 days of life.
    c. 2 weeks of life.
    d. 2 months of life.
    LO 9

14. What best distinguishes the infancy stage from other stages of development?
    a. Physical growth is most rapid in the first year.
    b. Cognitive growth is 5 times greater than in any other developmental stage.
    c. Emotions are fully developed before the next developmental stage.
    d. It is the only stage that has no emotional development.
    LO 9

15. Which of the following is *not* developed during the infancy period?
    a. object permanence
    b. telegraphic speech
    c. separation anxiety
    d. transductive reasoning
    LO 11

16. Which of the following is characteristic of the preoperational child?
    a. The child is egocentric.
    b. The child uses transductive reasoning.
    c. The child is capable of abstract thought.
    d. both *a* and *b*
    LO 11

17. Which of the following describes the correct developmental sequence of play?
    a. parallel play, solitary play, cooperative play
    b. solitary play, cooperative play, parallel play
    c. solitary play, parallel play, cooperative play
    d. cooperative play, solitary play, parallel play
    LO 11

18. Friendship groups or cliques begin to develop during which of the stages of cognitive development?
    a. preoperational
    b. concrete operational
    c. sensorimotor
    d. formal operational
    LO 12

19. The recognition that the volume of water remains the same whether it is in a short, wide beaker, or a long, narrow beaker is called
    a. reversibility.
    b. conservation.
    c. decentering.
    d. formal operations.
    LO 12

20. Which of the following is *not* a primary sex characteristic?
    a. ovulation in females
    b. lowering of the voice in males
    c. menstruation in females
    d. production of sperm in males
    LO 13

21. According to Piaget, the concepts of liberty and justice can be meaningfully understood by an adolescent who
    a. has achieved the concrete operational stage.
    b. has achieved the formal operational stage.
    c. comprehends object permanence.
    d. has achieved the preoperational stage.
    LO 15

22. Debbie, an adolescent, feels that she is the only person in the world who has ever had a crush on the boy who sits next to her or who ever had complexion problems. Which component of adolescent egocentrism is she experiencing?
    a. imaginary audience
    b. personal fable
    c. hypocrisy
    d. pseudostupidity
    LO 16

23. In which of the following areas do adolescents have more challenges when compared to younger and older individuals?
    a. parent-child conflicts
    b. mood changes
    c. risky behavior
    d. all of the above
       LO 15

24. Which of the following cognitive abilities improves throughout adulthood?
    a. fluid intelligence
    b. knowledge of facts and word meanings
    c. abstract problem solving
    d. divergent thinking
       LO 16

25. Compared to individuals in their 20s, individuals in their 70s showed declines in
    a. knowledge of word meanings.
    b. understanding mathematical concepts.
    c. solving life problems.
    d. fluid intelligence.
       LO 16

26. Adult personalities are likely to increase in each of the following traits except
    a. acceptance of life's hardships
    b. dependability
    c. agreeableness
    d. emotionality
       LO 17

27. Jerry, age 67, and Al, age 65, are acquaintances. Jerry feels his life is meaningful and enjoys his existence, but he has noticed that Al has lately withdrawn and sees his life as a bunch of unmet goals. These individuals illustrate which of Erikson's stages?
    a. basic trust vs. mistrust
    b. intimacy vs. isolation
    c. generativity vs. stagnation
    d. integrity vs. despair
       LO 17

28. Hank, age 47, has recently changed careers and has joined a health club. His behavior falls into which of Levinson's stages?
    a. entering middle adulthood
    b. midlife transition
    c. age 50 transition
    d. settling down
       LO 18

29. Each of the following is true regarding the climacteric except
    a. it eventually leads to menopause in women.
    b. it is characterized by a decline in the reproductive capacity of men.
    c. about half of women experience discomfort during menopause.
    d. there are widespread psychological and sexual effects in men.
       LO 19

30. Each of the following is a criticism of stage theories except
    a. failure to include women, especially in early studies.
    b. failure to research stage theories in many different cultures.
    c. some studies have failed to find predictable crises or stages.
    d. stage theories always view transitions from one stage to the next as involving dramatic changes.
       LO 20

31. In the Terman study, which personality factor was most associated with early death?
    a. conscientiousness
    b. cheerfulness
    c. dependability
    d. truthfulness
       LO 21

32. The final stage of Elisabeth Kübler-Ross's theory is labeled
    a. denial.
    b. bargaining.
    c. acceptance.
    d. depression.
       LO 22

33. According to Baumrind, the best behaved and happiest children have parents who use what style of parenting?
   a. authoritarian
   b. permissive
   c. authoritative
   d. disciplinarian
   LO 24

34. The two-way-street concept in childrearing suggests that
   a. both mothers *and* fathers need to accept responsibility for childrearing.
   b. parents need to be consistent in their childrearing approaches with *all* their children.
   c. children act as important influences on their siblings.
   d. children's behavior affects their parents' behavior just as parents' behavior affects their children's behavior.
   LO 24

35. According to research comparing children in daycare centers with children raised by mothers in their own homes, significant differences were found in the children's
   a. physical health.
   b. intellectual development.
   c. attachment.
   d. none of the above
   LO 24

True-False Questions

_____ 1. Researchers have observed imprinting in human infants.

_____ 2. Neonate is the term applied to the newborn during the first two weeks of life.

_____ 3. According to Piaget, object permanence is a significant accomplishment during the sensorimotor stage.

_____ 4. Animism and transductive reasoning are characteristics of the concrete operational stage.

_____ 5. Adolescents rarely engage in egocentric behavior, since most adolescents have achieved formal operational reasoning.

_____ 6. Early and middle adulthood is marked by improvements in crystallized intelligence.

_____ 7. According to Erikson, middle adulthood is the stage of integrity vs. despair.

_____ 8. The Terman study found that those who were rated as being cheerful children tended to die at earlier ages.

_____ 9. According to Baumrind, the authoritarian parent encourages independence by explaining rules, and rarely uses punishment.

_____ 10. According to O'Leary, common parental discipline mistakes include lax parenting, verbosity, and overreactivity.

ANSWERS SECTION

Concept Checks

Developmental Theories

Theorist	Developmental Areas	Proposed Stages
Piaget	cognitive	sensorimotor, preoperational, concrete operational, and formal operational
Kohlberg	moral	premoral, conventional, and principled reasoning
Gilligan	moral	morality as individual survival, morality as self-sacrifice, and morality as equality
Erikson	social	eight stages or crises, the outcome of which will determine future personality development
Kübler-Ross	death and dying	denial, anger, bargaining, depression, and acceptance

Developmental Concepts

Term	Definition
imprinting	a form of early learning that occurs in goslings and other animals; imprinting can occur only during a critical period
critical period	a biologically determined period in the life of some animals during which certain forms of learning can take place most easily
neonate	a term that applies to the infant in the first two weeks of life
cooperative play	characteristic of the end of Piaget's preoperational stage, this type of play involves cooperation between two or more children; this type of play occurs after the stages of solitary play and parallel play
primary sex characteristics	occurring during puberty, ovulation and menstruation in females and the production of mature sperm in males
secondary sex characteristics	development of the breasts and hips in females; growth of the testes, broadening shoulders, and so on in males; growth of pubic hair and body hair in both sexes
climacteric	period between about ages 45 and 60, characterized by a loss of capacity to reproduce in women and a decline of reproductive capacity in men

Sample Answers for Short Answer Questions

1. **Describe the development of cognitive abilities during the preoperational stage.**

   The preoperational stage begins around the age of 2 and lasts until the age of 7. The young child's thinking is characterized by egocentrism, in which the child views himself as the center of the universe. One example of egocentric thinking is animism, the belief that inanimate objects are alive. Another characteristic is transductive reasoning, that is, errors in thinking about cause-and-effect relationships. Toward the end of this stage, the child has begun to grasp logical operations and engages in fewer cause-and-effect errors.

2. **List and describe the characteristics of adolescent egocentrism.**

   Adolescent egocentrism is Elkind's concept for explaining some adolescent thought. It is characterized by the imaginary audience, in which the adolescent is always on stage; another characteristic is the personal fable, in which the adolescent believes that nobody can understand what he or she is going through; a third characteristic is excessive hypocrisy; and the fourth characteristic is pseudostupidity, or thinking about issues by using oversimplified logic.

3. **List and describe the stages we are likely to pass through when we learn of our impending death.**

   According to Elisabeth Kübler-Ross's theory, we can expect to go through five stages. These are: denial, in which we strongly resist the idea of death; anger, during which we lash out at those around us; bargaining, during which we often make deals with God; depression, during which we experience a loss of hope; and acceptance, during which we achieve a sense of peace.

Answers to Review At A Glance

1. development	24. conventional	47. 6/9
2. developmental	25. principled	48. visual
3. nature	26. few	49. attachments
4. nurture	27. girls	50. preoperational
5. maturation	28. abstractions	51. mental
6. maturation	29. survival	52. egocentric
7. imprinting	30. self-sacrifice	53. animism
8. critical period	31. equality	54. transductive
9. social	32. crises	55. language
10. isolation	33. personality	56. solitary
11. mother	34. development	57. parallel
12. abnormal	35. neonatal	58. cooperative
13. rejected	36. rooting	59. sex-typed
14. humans	37. 12	60. concrete operational
15. between	38. infant	61. abstract
16. within	39. physical	62. seriation
17. stage	40. senses	63. reversibility
18. qualitatively	41. sensorimotor	64. conservation
19. quantitatively	42. actively	65. decenter
20. biologically	43. object permanence	66. peers
21. cognitive	44. telegraphic	67. cliques
22. moral	45. smiling	68. puberty
23. premoral	46. anger	69. ovulation
70. sperm cells	72. menarche	74. secondary sex characteristics
71. primary sex characteristics	73. two	

75. adolescent growth spurt
76. limbic
77. formal operational
78. adolescent egocentrism
79. imaginary audience
80. personal fable
81. hypocrisy
82. pseudostupidity
83. peers
84. parents
85. moods
86. risky
87. early
88. vision
89. smell
90. facts
91. meanings
92. reasoning
93. wisdom
94. abstract
95. stages
96. Erikson
97. vary
98. biological
99. intimacy

100. isolation
101. entry
102. age 30 transition
103. early adulthood
104. becoming
105. are
106. meaning
107. generativity vs. stagnation
108. midlife transition
109. middle adulthood
110. transition
111. middle adulthood
112. climacteric
113. menopause
114. integrity
115. despair
116. men
117. differences
118. stages
119. psychological
120. engaged
121. myths
122. drinking
123. conscientious
124. truthful

125. cheerful
126. denial
127. anger
128. bargaining
129. depression
130. acceptance
131. stranger anxiety
132. securely attached
133. insecurely
134. temperament
135. behaviors
136. authoritarian
137. permissive
138. authoritative
139. authoritative
140. parents'
141. children's
142. inappropriate
143. overreactivity
144. family
145. individualistic
146. day care
147. emotional turmoil

Multiple-Choice Answers

1. The answer is *B*. Nature refers to biological factors, and nurture refers to environmental factors.
2. The answer is *A*. Maturational factors refer to the systematic physical growth of the body, including the nervous system. The experience of the twins suggests that, when it comes to potty training, a child isn't ready until he's ready.
3. The answer is *C*. According to Lorenz, imprinting is a special form of learning because it is highly constrained by biological factors. Goslings will imprint on the first noisy, moving object they see, and this generally occurs only during a brief window of time, called the critical period.
4. The answer is *C*. The Harlows conducted research with monkeys who were raised in isolation for the first few months of their lives. Later in the monkeys' lives, they exhibited gross abnormalities in their behavior.
5. The answer is *D*. Although many psychologists are engaged in trying to describe and understand the normal developmental changes that take place in childhood, it is important to realize that development is highly variable.
6. The answer is *B*. Stage theorists believe that the changes occurring from one stage to the next make children different "in kind" rather than merely "different" in amount."
7. The answer is *C*. According to Kohlberg, children at the conventional level are concerned with making moral decisions on the basis of what others, especially parents, will think of them. At the next level, called the principled level, actions come to be based on the ethical principles involved.
8. The answer is *A*. Alternative *B* is consistent with Kohlberg's premoral level, *C* refers to Kohlberg's conventional level, and *D* is borrowed from Gilligan's theory.
9. The answer is *D*. According to Gilligan, in this most advanced stage of morality, the woman views her own needs as equal to those of others.
10. The answer is A. Kohlberg has argued that Gilligan's approach overestimates sex differences in moral development.
11. The answer is *C*. According to Erikson, each stage presents a crisis or turning point, the outcome of which will determine future personality development. The challenge of the stage of industry vs. inferiority, which occurs

between the ages of 5 and 11, is to meet the demands imposed by school and home; if these demands are not met, the child will come to feel inferior to others.

12. The answer is *C*. Erikson's theory would suggest that feelings of inferiority regarding math skills (and potentially other skills) might be a consequence of this situation. On the other hand, mastering skills leads to a sense that effort leads to success.

13. The answer is *C*. During this period of time, the infant engages in a variety of reflexes, displays well-developed sensory abilities, and exhibits the following emotional states: surprise, happiness, discomfort, distress, and interest (and, of course, sleep!).

14. The answer is *A*. Although recent research has underscored the cognitive achievements of infancy, the most dramatic changes of infancy appear to be related to physical growth.

15. The answer is *D*. Transductive reasoning refers to errors in cause-and-effect reasoning that are commonly made by preoperational children. Before proceeding, be sure you can describe object permanence, telegraphic speech, and separation anxiety.

16. The answer is *D*. According to Piaget, another characteristic of the preoperational stage is animism (the belief that inanimate objects are alive). The child is not capable of abstract thought, according to Piaget, until the formal operational stage.

17. The answer is *C*. This sequence seems to parallel cognitive development. That is, children whose thinking is still highly egocentric might be expected to engage in solitary play. As egocentric thinking declines, cooperative play becomes possible.

18. The answer is *B*. These friendship groups occur in middle childhood, a time marked by the intellectual achievements of conservation, reversibility, and decentering.

19. The answer is *B*. Reversibility is the concrete operational concept that logical operations can be reversed. Decentering allows the concrete operational child to consider more than one feature of an object at a time. Formal operations is the last stage of Piaget's theory.

20. The answer is *B*. Primary sex characteristics indicate that the adolescent has the ability to reproduce; thus, ovulation and menstruation in females and the production of mature sperm cells in males are considered primary sex characteristics. The more obvious changes, such as development of the breasts and hips in females and the lowering of the voice in males, are considered secondary sex characteristics.

21. The answer is *B*. The formal operational stage is characterized by an ability to understand abstract concepts, such as liberty and justice.

22. The answer is *B*. The imaginary audience is characterized by the belief that others are watching the adolescent's every move; hence, any blunder will be noticed by everyone! Adolescent egocentrism is also characterized by excessive hypocrisy and by pseudostupidity, the use of oversimplified logic.

23. The answer is *D*. In spite of these problem areas, current research suggests that a majority of adolescents are relatively happy and well-adjusted.

24. The answer is *B*. Reasoning about everyday problems does not decline before about age 75. Slight declines occur in abstract problem solving, divergent thinking, and cognitive skills involving speed.

25. The answer is *D*. Fluid intelligence, introduced in the previous chapter, refers to the ability to learn or invent new strategies to solve a new problem. Short-term memory skills also decline during later adulthood.

26. The answer is *D*. As they become older, adults also tend to become less anxious, less socially outgoing, and less creative.

27. The answer is *D*. According to Erikson, the older adult who sees meaning in his or her life continues to live a satisfying existence, while the person who sees life as a series of unmet goals may come to experience despair.

28. The answer is *A*. According to Levinson, the entry into middle adulthood generally takes place from ages 45 to 50 and is occasionally marked by career and other dramatic changes such as divorce or geographical moves. For most, however, it is a period of calm and stability.

29. The answer is *D*. Although men produce fewer sperm cells and experience slight changes in the pattern of sexual arousal, the climacteric seems to have few psychological or sexual effects for men.

30. The answer is *D*. Stage theorists tend to view the transition between stages as being a gradual blending.

31. The answer is *B*. An explanation of this finding is that cheerful children were more likely to take risks and to smoke and drink as adults.

32. The answer is *C*. The sequence described by Kübler-Ross is denial, anger, bargaining, depression, and acceptance.

33. The answer is *C*. At first glance the words *authoritarian* and *authoritative* might seem similar, but there are important differences. According to Baumrind, authoritarian parents dole out strict rules and little discussion.

Authoritative parents, however, act as authority figures for their children, but encourage their children to voice their opinions as well. Permissive parents provide few rules and rarely punish misbehavior.

34. The answer is *D*. The concept is actually quite logical: The child's behavior influences the style of discipline used by the parents and vice versa.

35. The answer is *D*. Research has not found any significant differences in these characteristics between daycare children and children raised by parents at home.

Answers to True-False Questions

1. F
2. T
3. T
4. F
5. F

6. T
7. F
8. T
9. F
10. T

Chapter 10   Motivation and Emotion

Learning Objectives

1. Distinguish between motivation and emotion. (p. 368)

2. Describe the relationship between primary motives and homeostatic mechanisms. (p. 369)

3. Describe the biological and psychological regulation of hunger. (p. 369)

4. Discuss the biological and psychological regulation of thirst. (p. 373)

5. Define "psychological motive," and identify the following psychological motives: the need for novel stimulation, the need for affiliation, and the need for achievement. (p. 375)

6. Distinguish between optimal arousal theory and the Yerkes-Dodson law. (p. 375)

7. Explain Solomon's opponent-process theory of motivation. (p. 379)

8. Distinguish between intrinsic and extrinsic motivation. (p. 381)

9. Identify the components of Maslow's hierarchy of motives. (p. 383)

10. Define "emotion" and explain the components of Watson and Tellegen's emotional map. (p. 386)

11. Distinguish among the James-Lange theory, the Cannon-Bard theory, and the cognitive theory of emotion. (p. 388)

12. Explain the procedures used in lie detector tests and discuss the effectiveness of these tests. (p. 394)

13. Discuss the roles played by learning and by culture in emotions. (p. 394)

14. Describe the results of research into happiness. (p. 395)

15. Distinguish among the following theories of aggression: Freud's instinct theory, the frustration-aggression theory, and the social learning theory. (p. 398)

16. Discuss the issues surrounding recent increases in violent youth gangs. (p. 400)

17. (From the Application section) Discuss the American obsession with being thin, and identify methods suggested to eat more healthily. (p. 402)

Chapter Overview

Motivation refers to an internal state that activates behavior and gives direction to our thoughts. Emotions are positive or negative feelings usually accompanied by behavior and physiological arousal that generally occur in response to stimulus situations.

Primary motives are motives for things that are necessary for survival, such as food, water, and warmth. Homeostatic mechanisms in the body help to regulate biological imbalances and stimulate actions to restore the proper balance.

Hunger is a primary motive that is biologically regulated by three centers in the hypothalamus; one is referred to as the feeding system; another is called the satiety system. The third center both increases and decreases appetite by controlling blood sugar levels. Among humans, the cues that help regulate hunger on a daily basis are stomach contractions and blood sugar levels; body fat levels appear to be involved in the long-term regulation of hunger. Psychological factors, such as learning, emotions, and incentives, are also involved in the regulation of food intake.

Thirst is also regulated by the hypothalamus. The cues that help regulate drinking include mouth dryness, loss of water by cells, and reductions in blood volume. Psychological factors such as learning and incentives also help to regulate thirst.

Psychological motives are motives that are related to the individual's happiness and well-being, but not to survival. Among the important psychological motives are (1) seeking novel stimulation; (2) seeking an optimal level of arousal (the Yerkes-Dodson law states that if arousal is too low, performance will be inadequate, but if arousal is too high, it may disrupt performance); (3) the motive for affiliation, the preference to be with others; and (4) achievement motivation, the psychological need for success.

Richard Solomon has proposed the opponent-process theory to explain how we learn new motives. Motivation can also be characterized as either intrinsic, which refers to motives stimulated by the inherent nature of the activity, or extrinsic, those stimulated by external rewards. According to Maslow, motives are organized in a hierarchy, arranged from the most basic to the most personal and advanced.

Emotions are the experiences that give color, meaning, and intensity to our lives. Theories that attempt to explain emotions include the James-Lange theory, the Cannon-Bard theory, and cognitive theories. According to Schachter and Singer, the cognitive process involves interpreting stimuli from both the environment and the body. Most psychologists believe that many basic emotions are primarily inborn but that learning plays an important role in emotions.

Aggression is a complex phenomenon, and its origins are the subject of continuing controversy. Freud suggested that all people are born with potent aggressive instincts released through the process of catharsis, while other psychologists believe that aggression is a reaction to the blocking of important motives (the frustration-aggression theory). A third view, held by social learning theorists, explains aggression as learned behavior. Violent youth gangs represent a special challenge to our society. According to Staub, harsh and inadequate parenting, peer rejection of aggressive children, and our society's mixed messages about violence all contribute to the violence of youth gangs.

Although many people are dieting to try to lose weight at any given time, there are dangers to dieting. These include the risks of developing anorexia nervosa or bulimia, and the health risks associated with yo-yo dieting. The text recommends not dieting but eating differently, emphasizing exercise, and avoiding lapses in a healthy lifestyle.

Key Terms Exercise

For each of the following exercises, match the key terms on the left with the correct definitions on the right. Page references to the text follow the terms so that you may refer to the text for any items you answer incorrectly or do not understand completely. You may check your responses immediately by referring to the answers that follow each exercise.

Primary Motives

_____ 1. motivation (p. 368)
_____ 2. emotions (p. 369)
_____ 3. primary motives (p. 369)
_____ 4. homeostatic mechanisms (p. 369)
_____ 5. hypothalamus (p. 369)
_____ 6. incentives (p. 372)

a. motives for things that are necessary for survival
b. internal mechanisms that regulate bodily functions
c. external cues that activate motivation
d. an internal state that activates behavior and gives it direction
e. positive and negative feelings that are accompanied by physiological arousal
f. the area of the forebrain involved with motives, emotions, and the autonomic nervous system

ANSWERS

1. d   4. b
2. e   5. f
3. a   6. c

Psychological Motives (I)

_____ 1. psychological motives (p. 375)
_____ 2. novel stimulation (p. 375)
_____ 3. optimal level of arousal (p. 376)
_____ 4. Yerkes-Dodson law (p. 376)
_____ 5. motive for affiliation (p. 376)

a. new or changed experience
b. effective performance is more likely if the level of arousal is suitable for the activity
c. individuals will make an effort to increase or decrease the amount of their stimulation to reach a comfortable level of arousal
d. motives related to happiness and well-being, but not to survival
e. the general preference to be with other people

ANSWERS

1. d	4. b
2. a	5. e
3. c	

Psychological Motives (II)

_____ 1. achievement motivation (p. 378)
_____ 2. opponent-process theory of motivation (p. 379)
_____ 3. intrinsic motivation (p. 381)
_____ 4. extrinsic motivation (p. 381)
_____ 5. Maslow's hierarchy of motives (p. 383)
_____ 6. self-actualization (p. 383)

a. the inner drive of humans to use their potential to the fullest
b. motives stimulated by external rewards
c. the psychological need for success in competitive situations
d. a theory that states we learn new motives when feelings contrast and when they lose intensity
e. motives stimulated by the inherent nature of the activity
f. the view that human motives are organized from the most basic (biological) to the most advanced (self-actualization)

ANSWERS

1. c	4. b
2. d	5. f
3. e	6. a

Theories of Emotion and Aggression

_____ 1. James-Lange theory (p. 388)
_____ 2. Cannon-Bard theory (p. 391)
_____ 3. cognitive theory of emotion (p. 391)
_____ 4. Freud's instinct theory (p. 398)
_____ 5. frustration-aggression theory (p. 399)

a. states that emotional experience and physical arousal are simultaneous and mostly independent events
b. the view that humans have inborn aggressive instincts that must be released in some way
c. the theory that aggression is a natural reaction to the frustration of important motives
d. states that sensations from bodily reactions to stimuli produce the emotions we feel
e. emphasizes the cognitive interpretation of events in the outside world and stimuli from our bodies

ANSWERS

1. d	4. b
2. a	5. c
3. e	

Review At A Glance
(Answers to this section begin on page 187)

Definitions of Motivation and Emotion

Motivation refers to an ____(1)____ state that activates and gives direction to our thoughts. The positive or negative feelings in response to stimulus situations are called ____(2)____. Emotions are accompanied by ____(3)____ arousal. Motivation and emotion are closely linked in the following ways: (1) both motivation and emotion ____(4)____ behavior; (2) motives are often accompanied by emotions; and (3) emotions often have motivational properties of their own. Human motives for things that are necessary for survival are called ____(5)____ motives. The essential life elements in the body are regulated internally by ____(6)____ mechanisms.

The biological control center for hunger is the ____(7)____. Hunger is regulated in the hypothalamus by three systems: the one that initiates eating when food is needed, called the ____(8)____ system is located in the ____(9)____ hypothalamus. A second system, which signals the body to stop eating, is called the ____(10)____ system and is located in the ____(11)____ hypothalamus. Destruction of the ventromedial hypothalamus leads to a condition called ____(12)____. The paraventricular nucleus, also located in the hypothalamus, regulates appetite by controlling blood ____(13)____ levels. Two cues regulate hunger on a daily basis: ____(14)____ contractions and ____(15)____ sugar levels. The liver and the ____(16)____ send messages to the hypothalamus to help regulate eating. The islets of ____(17)____ secrete two hormones that help regulate hunger. A feeling of hunger is produced when ____(18)____ is secreted into the bloodstream; conversely, a person no longer feels hungry when ____(19)____ is injected into the bloodstream. Long-term maintenance of body weight is regulated by the hypothalamus as it monitors ____(20)____ levels. When leptin is detected by the hypothalamus, it reacts in three different ways: the ventromedial satiety center sends a message to ____(21)____ eating, the paraventricular nucleus regulates the blood ____(22)____ level, and the ventromedial hypothalamus activates the ____(23)____ nervous system. Scientists have hypothesized that each of us has a different ____(24)____ for body fat. It appears to be difficult to raise or lower body weight above or below the ____(25)____.

Psychological factors, such as learning and ____(26)____, also regulate food intake. People trying to limit their food intake may have trouble with external cues (such as the sight of a dessert) that activate motives; these are referred to as ____(27)____. Laboratory research with animals has shown that incentives can push weight above the natural ____(28)____.

The hypothalamus also contains two centers that control drinking: the ____(29)____ system and the ____(30)____ system. The hypothalamus uses three main cues in regulating drinking: mouth ____(31)____, cell ____(32)____ levels, and total ____(33)____. Psychological factors also play a role in the regulation of drinking.

Psychological Motives

Motives that are not directly related to biological survival are called ___(34)___ motives.

Most people are easily bored if there is little stimulation; we have an apparently inborn motive to seek ___(35)___ _____. Too much stimulation or too little stimulation makes us feel uncomfortable; individuals strive for an ___(36)___ level of arousal. In the brain, arousal is linked to the activity of the ___(37)___ _____. To achieve an effective performance, the level of arousal must be suitable for the activity, according to the ___(38)___-_____ law.

Another psychological motive is the preference to be with other people, called the motive for ___(39)___. Some psychologists believe that this motivation is an ___(40)___ need, while others believe it is a ___(41)___ motive. Researchers have found that ___(42)___ and everyday painful experiences increase our motive to affiliate.

The psychological motive to succeed is called ___(43)___ _____. According to research by Elliott and Church, key elements in achievement motivation among college students include establishing ___(44)___ goals, performance-___(45)___ goals, and performance-___(46)___ goals. In research conducted in a college course, these different types of achievement motivation were associated with different ___(47)___ at the end of the course. A factor that can lead people to achieve below their potential is fear of ___(48)___.

Richard Solomon's theory, which explains how people learn new motives, is called the ___(49)___-_____ theory of motivation. Two concepts that are important to Solomon's theory are: (1) every state of positive feeling is followed by a ___(50)___ negative feeling, and (2) any feeling that is experienced many times in succession loses some of its ___(51)___.

When people are motivated by the inherent nature of the activity or its natural consequences, the situation is referred to as ___(52)___ motivation. Motivation that is external to an activity is called ___(53)___ motivation. Although low frequency behaviors can be increased with extrinsic motivation, adding incentives to an activity that is already intrinsically motivated may ___(54)___ from the intrinsic motivation. Research suggests that ___(55)___ factors are important in understanding motivation.

Abraham Maslow's theory states that motives are arranged in a ___(56)___. If lower needs are not met, then ___(57)___ motives will generally not operate. According to Maslow, individuals are motivated to realize their full potential, a process he called ___(58)___-_____. Some research suggests that high levels of motivation to achieve financial success are ___(59)___ correlated with levels of self-actualization. Research also suggests that the ___(60)___ we want to achieve success are almost as important as the way we ___(61)___ success.

Emotions

According to Watson and Tellegen, most human emotions can be thought of as combinations of ___(62)___ and ___(63)___ emotions. This view suggests that fear and ___(64)___ are variations of the same emotion. Most definitions of emotion include the following four elements: (1) a ___(65)___ _____ that provokes the reaction; (2) a positively or negatively toned conscious experience—the ___(66)___; (3) a bodily state of ___(67)___ arousal; and (4) related ___(68)___ that accompanies emotions.

William James believed that emotional stimuli first produce ___(69)___ reactions; the sensations from these reactions then produce the emotions we feel. This theory today is called the ___(70)___-_____ theory of emotion. Walter Cannon's criticisms of the James-Lange theory included the following: (1) evidence from people whose ___(71)___ _____ has been severed; (2) the relatively slow response of the ___(72)___ organs to stress; (3) the similarity of ___(73)___ reactions to emotions and (4) when research participants are injected with epinephrine, the feedback to the brain is experienced as ___(74)___ rather than as emotion. According to Izard, the most important sensory feedback comes from the ___(75)___ muscles. Most experts believe that efferent feedback from facial muscles, other muscles, and from visceral organs all play a role in ___(76)___. There is also evidence that brain activity in the ___(77)___ cortex plays a role in experiencing emotions.

Conscious emotional experience and physiological arousal are two simultaneous events according to the ___(78)___-_____ theory of emotion.

A third theory of emotion emphasizes the ___(79)___ interpretation of events. Cognitive theorists hold that cognitive interpretation of emotions involves interpreting stimuli from both the ___(80)___ and the ___(81)___. According to Schachter and Singer's model of emotion, the autonomic arousal that accompanies all emotions is similar; our ___(82)___ _____ of the arousal is important.

A device used in a lie-detector test that measures sympathetic arousal in response to questions is called a ___(83)___. The procedure used in a lie-detector examination is called the ___(84)___ knowledge test. According to Lykken, results provided by lie detector examiners are not much more accurate than tossing a ___(85)___.

Cultural learning influences the ___(86)___ of emotions. Culture also has a great deal to do with the ___(87)___ of situations that create emotional reactions.

Research on personal happiness has indicated that more people in ___(88)___ countries report being happy than those in poorer countries. People who say they are happy compare themselves to others ___(89)___ often; happy people believe they can learn useful lessons from ___(90)___ events. Happiness is also linked to personality traits such as ___(91)___. To a large extent, happiness is due to ___(92)___ factors.

Aggression: Emotional and Motivational Aspects

Sigmund Freud believed that aggression is the result of potent aggressive ___(93)___. Freud believed that aggressive energy must be released in some way. This process is called ___(94)___.

The belief that aggression is a natural reaction to the frustration (blocking) of important motives is called the ___(95)___-_____ theory. Recent research suggests a link between high temperatures and ___(96)___ crime. By contrast, social learning theorists believe that people act aggressively in reaction to frustration only if they have ___(97)___ to do so. According to Staub, harsh and inadequate ___(98)___ creates children who act aggressively toward their classmates. These aggressive children are attracted to gangs, because gang membership creates a sense of ___(99)___ for them. Gangs encourage their members to hate and demean members of other gangs. The attraction to gang membership, combined with our society's mixed messages about ___(100)___ and the widespread availability of ___(101)___ weapons, creates an atmosphere where violence is likely to occur.

Application of Psychology: Should You Lose Weight? If So, How?

Our society generally values ___(102)___. More people think they are overweight than is actually the case. At any one time, 24 percent of men and ___(103)___ percent of women are on a diet. People in our society are ___(104)___ against persons who are overweight. Two dangerous eating disorders, particularly for women, are ___(105)___ _____ and _(106)_. When dieters establish a pattern of gaining and then losing weight, this is referred to as (107)_-_____ dieting. In the Framingham health study, repeated yo-yo dieting was associated with increased (108)____ _____. Among the suggestions from the text are: don't diet—eat ___(109)___, emphasize ___(110)___, and don't give up if you lapse in your healthy lifestyle.

Concept Checks

Fill in the missing components of the following concept boxes. The correct answers are located in the "Answers" section at the end of the chapter.

Psychological Motives

Type of Motivation	Explanation
incentives	
	motivation to seek new or changed experiences
optimal arousal	
	best performance occurs when the level of arousal is suitable for the activity
motive for affiliation	
	psychological need for success
	motivation stimulated by the inherent nature of an activity or by its natural consequence
	motivation stimulated by external rewards

Models of Motivation and Emotion

Proposed by	Basic Elements of Theory
	in the opponent-process theory, every state of positive feeling is followed by a negative feeling; any feeling experienced many times in succession loses some of its intensity
Maslow	
James-Lange	
	conscious emotional experience and physiological arousal occur simultaneously
Schachter and Singer	

Extending the Chapter: Psychology, Societal Issues, and Human Diversity

These questions may be assigned to you. Whether or not they are assigned, they are designed to be challenging questions to encourage you to think independently about the material in the chapter. Many of the questions have no right or wrong answers.

I.   From the "Applications of Psychology" section

1.   What do you feel can be done to modify our culture's current obsession with being thin?

2.   Based on the information provided in the text, what advice would you give to people who are trying to lose weight? Which approaches would you suggest they avoid?

II.   Psychology, Societal Issues, and Human Diversity

1.   Under what circumstances do you feel employers should be allowed to use polygraph machines on their employees?

2.   Imagine you are watching your favorite sports team. Suddenly, the opposing team scores and wins the contest. Explain your emotional reaction from the standpoint of:
     a.   the James-Lange theory of emotion
     b.   the Cannon-Bard theory of emotion
     c.   the cognitive theory of emotion
     d.   sociocultural influences on emotion

3.   (From the Human Diversity section of the text) Describe the challenges faced by first-generation college students.

Practice Quiz

The practice quiz consists of three sections: 1) Short answer questions, 2) Multiple-choice questions, and 3) True-False questions. At the end of the chapter you will find suggested answers to the short answer questions, answers and explanations for the multiple-choice questions, and answers to the true-false questions.

Short Answer Questions

1. Describe the role played by the hypothalamus in regulating hunger.

   _____

   _____

2. List and discuss the cues used by the hypothalamus in regulating thirst.

   _____

   _____

3. Contrast the following three views of aggression: Freud's instinct theory, frustration-aggression theory, and social learning theory.

   _____

   _____

Multiple-Choice Questions

1. An internal state or condition that activates and gives direction to our thoughts is called
   a. motivation.
   b. emotion.
   c. aggression.
   d. all of the above
   LO 1

2. Homeostatic mechanisms are involved in
   a. drinking.
   b. eating.
   c. maintaining body temperature.
   d. all of the above.
   LO 2

3. Each of the following is a primary motive *except*
   a. hunger.
   b. thirst.
   c. avoidance of pain.
   d. desire to be competent.
   LO 2

4. Hyperphagic rats are the result of
   a. surgically destroyed satiety centers in the hypothalamus.
   b. surgically destroyed feeding centers in the hypothalamus.
   c. artificially raised blood sugar levels.
   d. blood fat levels that have been lowered.
   LO 3

5. Each of the following is a cue that helps the hypothalamus regulate eating *except*
   a. stomach contractions.
   b. blood sugar levels.
   c. red blood cell levels.
   d. body fat levels.
   LO 3

6. According to the text, which of the following is a psychological factor in hunger?
   a. incentives
   b. learning
   c. anxiety
   d. all of the above
   LO 3

7. Each of the following is a cue in regulating drinking *except*
   a. mouth dryness.
   b. cell fluid levels.
   c. blood sugar levels.
   d. total blood volume.
   LO 4

8. What happens when cell fluid levels in the body decrease?
   a. Sodium salts draw water out of cells.
   b. The hypothalamus signals the pituitary gland to secrete ADH.
   c. The hypothalamus signals the cerebral cortex to initiate a search for liquids.
   d. all of the above
   LO 4

9. The general preference among humans to be with others is called the
   a. affiliation motive.
   b. need for achievement.
   c. need for self-actualization.
   d. group motive.
   LO 5

10. According to Elliot and Church, the key elements in achievement motivation include each of the following *except*
    a. mastery goals.
    b. achievement goals.
    c. performance-approach goals.
    d. performance-avoidance goals.
    LO 5

11. According to Schachter, when people are anxious, their need to affiliate with others
    a. increases.
    b. decreases.
    c. virtually disappears.
    d. is not changed.
    LO 5

12. High levels of fear of success were correlated with high
    a. extrinsic motivation.
    b. fear of failure.
    c. self-esteem.
    d. self-actualization.
    LO 5

13. An effective performance is more likely if the level of arousal is suitable for the activity, according to the
    a. optimal level of arousal.
    b. performance-arousal model.
    c. Yerkes-Dodson law.
    d. James-Lange theory of motivation.
    LO 6

14. Arousal is linked to what brain structures?
    a. the amygdala
    b. the reticular formation
    c. the sympathetic nervous system
    d. both *b* and *c*
    LO 6

15. According to Solomon's opponent-process theory of motivation,
    a. every positive feeling is followed by a negative feeling.
    b. every negative feeling is followed by a positive feeling.
    c. any feeling that is experienced many times in succession loses some of its intensity.
    d. all of the above
    LO 7

16. People who donate anonymously to charity are probably motivated by
    a. intrinsic motivation.
    b. extrinsic motivation.
    c. biological motivation.
    d. affective habituation.
    LO 8

17. If an individual is already intrinsically motivated to perform an activity, adding an extrinsic reward will probably
    a. sharply increase the intrinsic motivation.
    b. increase both the intrinsic and extrinsic motivation.
    c. decrease the intrinsic motivation.
    d. none of the above
    LO 8

18. In Maslow's hierarchy of needs, which needs must be met before all other needs?
    a. self-actualization
    b. safety
    c. self-esteem
    d. biological
    LO 9

19. According to Maslow, the highest motive people can experience is
    a. biological.
    b. intellectual.
    c. self-esteem.
    d. self-actualization.
    LO 9

20. According to the text, each of the following is a component of the definition of emotion *except*
    a. a stimulus situation that provokes the reaction.
    b. a positively or negatively toned conscious experience.
    c. physiological arousal.
    d. a deep-seated unconscious response.
    LO 10

21. According to Watson and Tellegen's emotional map, all human emotions can be thought of as different combinations of what?
    a. love and hate
    b. happiness and sadness
    c. positive and negative emotions
    d. arousal and experience
    LO 10

22. According to which theory of emotion does the thalamus simultaneously relay information to the cortex and the hypothalamus?
    a. the James-Lange theory of emotion
    b. the Cannon-Bard theory of emotion
    c. the cognitive theory of emotion
    d. the Freudian theory of emotion
    LO 11

23. "We feel sorry because we cry" is an explanation of emotion associated with
    a. the James-Lange theory of emotion.
    b. the Cannon-Bard theory of emotion.
    c. the cognitive theory of emotion.
    d. all of the above.
    LO 11

24. Which of the following theories emphasizes the interpretation both of incoming stimuli and bodily stimuli in explaining emotions?
    a. cognitive theory of emotion
    b. Cannon-Bard theory of emotion
    c. James-Lange theory of emotion
    d. Freud's theory of emotion
    LO 11

25. According to the text, lie-detector tests
    a. are an accurate measure of one's guilt or innocence.
    b. use physiological measures from the parasympathetic division of the autonomic nervous system.
    c. have strict licensing requirements for polygraph operators.
    d. are used by companies to screen potential employees.
    LO 12

26. Which of the following processes may influence the role of learning in our emotions?
    a. modeling
    b. reinforcement
    c. classical conditioning
    d. all of the above
    LO 13

27. By studying different cultures, psychologists have concluded that learning
    a. influences the development of basic emotions.
    b. does not affect the interpretation of emotions.
    c. has had no effect on how emotions are displayed.
    d. influences the expression of emotions.
    LO 13

28. Which of the following is true regarding the roles of learning and culture on emotions?
    a. Learning and culture play minimal roles, since all emotions are genetic.
    b. Cultural learning influences the expression of emotions.
    c. Learning affects our emotional reactions to various stimuli.
    d. both *b* and *c*
    LO 13

29. Research regarding personal happiness suggests that
   a. much of our happiness is due to genetic factors.
   b. social comparison leads to greater personal happiness.
   c. hobbies and/or deep religious faith lead to greater happiness.
   d. college students no longer relate more money to greater happiness.
   LO 14

30. Which explanation of aggression involves the process of catharsis?
   a. Freud's instinct theory
   b. the frustration-aggression hypothesis
   c. social learning theory
   d. the James-Lange theory
   LO 15

31. According to the frustration-aggression hypothesis, aggression is a natural reaction to
   a. frustration.
   b. pain.
   c. heat.
   d. all of the above.
   LO 15

32. Which of the following correctly summarizes the positions taken on televised violence?
   a. Both the social learning and Freudian positions favor televised aggression as an outlet for people.
   b. Neither the social learning nor the Freudian positions view televised aggression favorably.
   c. The social learning theorists oppose televised aggression, while the Freudians view it as catharsis.
   d. The social learning theorists favor televised aggression while the Freudians oppose it.
   LO 15

33. Staub's theory seeking to explain the increase in gang violence in the U.S. supports
   a. the frustration-aggression hypothesis.
   b. Freud's theory of aggression.
   c. social learning theory.
   d. both a and c.
   LO 16

34. According to the text, yo-yo dieting is
   a. a reasonable way to lose a lot of weight quickly.
   b. effective because it moves the body's metabolism rate up and down.
   c. self-defeating and leads to a slowed metabolic rate.
   d. linked to anorexia nervosa.
   LO 17

35. According to the text, regular exercise is advantageous when dieting because it
   a. can burn calories.
   b. helps the metabolism rate to fall while you are dieting.
   c. helps keep the metabolism rate from falling.
   d. both a and c.
   LO 17

True-False Questions

_____ 1. Food, water, and warmth are examples of primary motives.

_____ 2. Blood protein levels are an important cue in the regulation of hunger.

_____ 3. According to the optimal arousal theory, after we adjust to high levels of stimulation, we actively seek more stimulation.

_____ 4. According to Schachter, affiliation motivation increases when we are anxious.

_____ 5. The enjoyment a person gets from keeping a personal journal is an example of extrinsic motivation.

_____ 6. According to Maslow, most of us will become fully self-actualized during adulthood.

_____ 7. According to Izard, the most important feedback in the experience of emotions comes from the facial muscles.

_____ 8. Although the cognitive theory of emotions makes logical sense, there is little research to support this view.

_____ 9. Lie detector tests can accurately pinpoint lies when combined with the guilty knowledge test.

_____10. According to Freud, catharsis allows the release of instinctual aggressive energy.

ANSWERS SECTION

Concept Checks

Psychological Motives

Type of Motivation	Explanation
incentives	external cues that activate motivation
novel stimulation	motivation to seek new or changed experiences
optimal arousal	motivation caused by too much or too little stimulation
Yerkes-Dodson law	best performance occurs when the level of arousal is suitable for the activity
motive for affiliation	motivation to be with others and to have personal relationships
achievement motivation	psychological need for success
intrinsic motivation	motivation stimulated by the inherent nature of an activity or by its natural consequence
extrinsic motivation	motivation stimulated by external rewards

Models of Motivation and Emotion

Proposed by	Basic Elements of Theory
Solomon	in the opponent-process theory, every state of positive feeling is followed by a negative feeling; any feeling experienced many times in succession loses some of its intensity
Maslow	our motives are arranged in a hierarchy from the most basic to the most personal and advanced; when lower motives have been met, self-actualizing needs become important
James-Lange	emotional stimuli first produce bodily reactions; these reactions then produce the emotions we feel
Cannon-Bard	conscious emotional experience and physiological arousal occur simultaneously
Schachter and Singer	we interpret stimuli from the environment and we interpret our autonomic arousal

Answers to Review At A Glance

1. internal
2. emotions
3. physiological
4. activate
5. primary
6. homeostatic
7. hypothalamus
8. feeding
9. lateral
10. satiety
11. ventromedial
12. hyperphagia
13. sugar
14. stomach
15. blood
16. duodenum
17. Langerhans
18. insulin
19. glucagon
20. body fat
21. inhibit
22. sugar
23. sympathetic
24. set point
25. set point
26. emotions
27. incentives
28. set point
29. drink

30. stop drinking
31. dryness
32. fluid
33. blood volume
34. psychological
35. novel stimulation
36. optimal
37. reticular formation
38. Yerkes-Dodson
39. affiliation
40. inborn
41. learned
42. anxiety
43. achievement motivation
44. mastery
45. approach
46. avoidance
47. outcomes
48. success
49. opponent-process
50. contrasting
51. intensity
52. intrinsic
53. extrinsic
54. detract
55. sociocultural
56. hierarchy
57. higher
58. self-actualization

59. negatively
60. reasons
61. define
62. positive
63. negative
64. anger
65. stimulus situation
66. emotion
67. physiological
68. behavior
69. bodily
70. James-Lange
71. spinal column
72. visceral
73. physiological
74. arousal
75. facial
76. emotion
77. somatosensory
78. Cannon-Bard
79. cognitive
80. environment
81. body
82. cognitive interpretation
83. polygraph
84. guilty
85. coin
86. expression
87. interpretation

88. affluent
89. less
90. negative
91. extraversion
92. genetic
93. instincts
94. catharsis
95. frustration-aggression

96. violent
97. learned
98. parenting
99. belonging
100. violence
101. lethal
102. thinness
103. 40

104. prejudiced
105. anorexia nervosa
106. bulimia
107. yo-yo
108. heart disease
109. differently
110. exercise

Sample Answers to Short Answer Questions

1. **Describe the role played by the hypothalamus in regulating hunger.**

   The hypothalamus contains three areas that help to regulate hunger. The lateral hypothalamus initiates eating; it is referred to as the feeding system. The ventromedial hypothalamus signals the cessation of eating when sufficient food has been consumed; it is referred to as the satiety system. The third area is called the paraventricular nucleus. This area helps to control appetite by controlling the level of sugar in the blood. The hypothalamus relies on three basic cues to help it in the regulation of hunger; these are stomach contractions, blood sugar levels, and body fat levels.

2. **List and discuss the cues used by the hypothalamus in regulating thirst.**

   The hypothalamus uses three main cues in the regulation of thirst. The first and most obvious is mouth dryness. A second cue is a decrease in cell fluid levels. When cell fluid levels drop, the fluids begin to dehydrate the cells of the body. The third cue is a decrease in total blood volume. The kidneys react to this drop by signaling the hypothalamus.

3. **Contrast the following three views of aggression: Freud's instinct theory, frustration-aggression theory, and social learning theory.**

   According to Freud's theory, aggressive energy is instinctual and must be released in some way. The goal of society is to find socially acceptable ways to provide these cathartic experiences. Frustration-aggression theory states that aggression is a natural reaction to frustration. Therefore, in order to minimize aggression, society should seek to minimize frustration for its members. According to social learning theory, people are aggressive because they have learned to be aggressive. Modeling and positive reinforcement are two ways in which people become conditioned to use aggression. Social learning theorists argue that watching violent television or playing violent video games doesn't reduce aggression (as Freud's approach might suggest); instead, these activities actually increase aggression.

Multiple-Choice Answers

1. The answer is *A*. Emotions are positive or negative feelings in reaction to stimuli. Motivation and emotion are closely linked concepts; motives are often accompanied by emotions, and emotions typically have motivational properties of their own.
2. The answer is *D*. Homeostatic mechanisms refer to internal mechanisms that help to regulate many bodily functions. Among the functions that are regulated are eating, drinking, and maintaining body temperature.
3. The answer is *D*. Primary motives refer to biological needs; these needs must be met or else the organism will die. The desire to be competent is an important psychological need, but not a primary motive.
4. The answer is *A*. Although the rats don't eat more often daily, they eat much longer—the signal to stop eating apparently has been destroyed.
5. The answer is *C*. Stomach contractions and blood sugar levels help to regulate hunger on a daily basis; blood fat levels help to regulate hunger on a long-term basis.

6. The answer is *D*. Incentives are external cues that activate motivation. In the case of hunger, the smell or sight of a favorite food can start those neurons firing in your hypothalamus. Learning and emotions are other psychological factors that impact hunger.

7. The answer is *C*. In the same manner that the hypothalamus regulates eating with a feeding system and a satiety system, it likewise regulates drinking with "drink" and "stop drinking" systems.

8. The answers is *D*. A complex process, initiated largely by the cells of the hypothalamus, is set into motion when cell fluid levels decrease.

9. The answer is *A*. Explanations of the motive for affiliation once again raise the nature-nurture issue. Some psychologists believe that the need for affiliation is inborn, while others suggest that motive is learned.

10. The answer is *B*. Researchers found, in a college course, that different types of achievement motivation were associated with different outcomes of the course.

11. The answer is *A*. In Schachter's research, participants who were frightened about their well-being preferred to wait in a room with others.

12. The answer is *C*. Kumari's research was conducted on women.

13. The answer is *C*. The Yerkes-Dodson law suggests that if arousal is too low (to use the vernacular, if you're not psyched up enough), performance will be inadequate, but if arousal is too high, performance may become disrupted.

14. The answer is *D*. Although biological factors are involved in arousal, there is no biological need for a moderate or optimal level of arousal.

15. The answer is *D*. Solomon's theory helps to explain our learning of new and seemingly unusual motives, such as seeking out dangerous experiences or hanging around with people we no longer particularly enjoy.

16. The answer is *A*. Presumably, people who donate anonymously to a charity are motivated by the desire to do a good thing, but do not seek the recognition or attention that often comes with such donations. Therefore, their behavior seems to be an example of intrinsic motivation.

17. The answer is *C*. The basic idea is that if somebody already enjoys something (intrinsic motivation), don't risk diminishing that motivation with extrinsic rewards.

18. The answer is *D*. According to Maslow, if these basic needs are not met, other needs are not important.

19. The answer is *D*. According to Maslow's theory, our motives are organized in a hierarchy. The higher human motives, however, cannot operate until the more basic, lower needs, such as hunger, thirst, and safety, have been met. At the highest level, according to Maslow, we are dreaming our impossible dream and realizing our full potential.

20. The answer is *D*. Although unconscious factors may be a part of human emotion, the missing element in the description of emotion is the related behavior that usually accompanies emotions, such as trembling, running, and punching.

21. The answer is *C*. An implication of Watson and Tellegen's theory is that human emotions can be thought of as combinations of positive and negative emotions.

22. The answer is *B*. The James-Lange theory suggests that the hypothalamus first produces a bodily reaction, which is then interpreted as the emotion we experience. By contrast, the Cannon-Bard theory suggests that information is first processed in the thalamus, from which it is simultaneously sent both to the cortex and the hypothalamus. Thus, the emotional experience and the physiological arousal are two simultaneous and independent events.

23. The answer is *A*. According to the James-Lange theory, the bodily reaction occurs first and is then processed by the cortex to produce the conscious experience of emotion.

24. The answer is *A*. The cognitive theory emphasizes the cognitive interpretation of stimuli as the major influence in emotions.

25. The answer is *D*. In fact, polygraph tests are estimated to be wrong at least 5 percent of the time, measure sympathetic arousal, and are often conducted by operators who have historically not been well regulated.

26. The answer is *D*. Although most psychologists who study emotions would agree that basic human emotions are inborn, the study of individuals in different cultures, in different families, and under different circumstances also underscores the importance of learning in many of our emotions.

27. The answer is *D*. Evidence suggests that learning influences both the expression of emotions and the way we interpret situations.

28. The answer is *D*. Although basic emotions are inborn, culture and learning affect the expression of emotions and our reactions to various stimuli.

29. The answer is *A*. According to the text, people who are happy compare themselves *less* with others. The evidence for alternative *C* is inconclusive; and yes, college students still tend to see money as the road to happiness!

30. The answer is *A*. According to Freud, aggression is instinctual, and aggressive energy must be released. Catharsis refers to the process of releasing instinctual energy. Freud believed that societies should find nonviolent ways for its members to release this energy.

31. The answer is *D*. Whereas Freud viewed aggression as an inborn part of human nature, frustration-aggression advocates view aggression as a natural reaction to the blocking of important motives.

32. The answer is *C*. The position of the social learning theorists is that people will behave aggressively if they have learned to do so. Televised aggression, therefore, will increase violence. The Freudian position, on the other hand, suggests that watching televised aggression and experiencing violence vicariously lead to a good cathartic release.

33. The answer is *D*. Staub views the modeling of aggression in the home and the frustration of being rejected by others as contributing to the perpetuation of violent youth gangs.

34. The answer is *C*. Yo-yo dieting is not only self-defeating; it was found to be associated with increased heart disease.

35. The answer is *D*. The body tends to try to compensate for dieting by lowering the metabolic rate. Exercise, however, helps to keep the metabolic rate from falling while dieting.

Answers to True-False Questions

1. T   6. F

2. F   7. T

3. F   8. F

4. T   9. F

5. F   10. T

Chapter 11 Gender and Sexuality

Learning Objectives

1. Distinguish among the definitions of sex, gender, and sexual orientation. (p. 410)

2. Distinguish between gender identity and gender role. (p. 410)

3. Describe the results of research regarding gender similarities and gender differences. (p. 411)

4. Distinguish between the evolutionary and the social-role theories of gender differences. (p. 417)

5. Compare and contrast the psychoanalytic and social learning theories of gender identity. (p. 422)

6. Distinguish between a heterosexual and homosexual orientation, and describe the results of the University of Chicago survey regarding sexual practices. (p. 423)

7. Discuss the controversies regarding the admission of openly homosexual men and women into the military. (p. 425)

8. Compare the theories of Money and Bem regarding the origins of sexual orientation. (p. 427)

9. Identify the efforts of those who pioneered the scientific study of sexual behavior. (p. 430)

10. Identify the anatomic structures and functions of male and female sexual anatomy. (p. 431)

11.	Identify and describe the stages of the human sexual response cycle. (p. 433)

12.	Compare and contrast sexual motivation with other primary motives. (p. 435)

13.	Recognize the relationship between hormones and sexual behavior. (p. 437)

14.	Recognize the patterns of sexual behavior identified by the University of Chicago survey. (p. 437)

15.	Distinguish between transvestism and transsexualism. (p. 441)

16.	Identify the patterns of sexual behavior called fetishism, sexual sadism, sexual masochism, voyeurism, and exhibitionism. (p. 441)

17.	Distinguish between the different types of forced sexual behavior. (p. 442)

18.	Define sexual dysfunction, and identify common sexual dysfunctions. (p. 446)

19.	Identify behaviors that decrease the risk of cancers of the sexual anatomy. (p. 448)

20.	Identify sexually transmitted diseases, and understand the four general types of infectious agents that cause STDs. (p. 449)

21.	Recognize how AIDS is transmitted, discuss the extent of the AIDS epidemic, and identify ways to prevent the spread of AIDS. (p. 451)

22.	(From the Application section) Discuss the issues surrounding date rape. (p. 454)

Chapter Overview

Although a person's sex is defined by either male or female genitals, a person's gender is the psychological experience of one's sex. The subjective experience of being a male or female is referred to as gender identity. Gender identity develops early in childhood.

Although small cognitive differences exist between men and women in some areas, the differences tend to be small and there are far more gender similarities than differences. Researchers have found greater differences regarding emotional and social behavior. Gender differences have also been found in the brain. Two theories that have been advanced to explain gender differences are the evolutionary theory and the social-role theory.

Theories of gender identity have been proposed by Freud, who emphasized the process of identification, and by social learning theorists, who emphasize the role of society.

Controversy swirls around President Clinton's proposal to ban discrimination against homosexual men and women in the military. Theories on the origins of sexual orientation emphasize social learning and predisposing biological factors.

The scientific study of human sexuality, often mired in controversy, was advanced at the turn of the century by Krafft-Ebing and Ellis, by Kinsey's surveys of sexuality, Money's studies of sexual development and gender roles, and Master's and Johnson's research on the human sexual response cycle.

The sexual anatomy and functioning of men and women is discussed, and the major structures are presented.

The human sexual response cycle is characterized by four stages: the excitement phase, the plateau phase, the orgasmic phase, and the resolution phase. The sexual motive is similar to other primary motives in that it is subject to hypothalamic control, and it is affected by external stimuli, learning, and emotions. The sexual motive differs from other primary motives in that sex is not necessary for survival. Other differences relate to our motivation to both increase and decrease our sexual arousal, the role of deprivation, and the fact that, unlike other motives, sexual behavior decreases energy.

The University of Chicago survey of sexual behavior found that a common sexual pattern for Americans is serial monogamy. The survey also found that people in committed relationships have sex more often than single persons. The survey found few differences in sexual practice across different levels of education, religious affiliation, or ethnic group.

Atypical sexual behavior discussed in the chapter includes transvestism, transsexualism, fetishism, sexual sadism, voyeurism, and exhibitionism. The traumas of rape and child rape are discussed, as well as the difficulties raised by sexual harassment.

Although there are a variety of physical causes of sexual dysfunction, many sexual dysfunctions are caused by psychological factors. Dysfunctions are categorized as dysfunctions of desire, arousal, and orgasm.

Among health problems related to sexual anatomy are cancers of the sexual anatomy, and sexually transmitted diseases, such as syphilis, gonorrhea, chlamydia, and a fatal STD called AIDS.

Date rape is a common occurrence on college campuses. In many cases, date rape begins with a miscommunication. Differing beliefs and attitudes about sexuality, communication, and the use of alcohol and other drugs are important factors in understanding and preventing date rape.

Key Terms Exercise

For each of the following exercises, match the key terms on the left with the correct definitions on the right. Page references to the text follow the terms so that you may refer to the text for any items you answer incorrectly or do not understand completely. You may check your response immediately by referring to the answers that follow each exercise.

Sex, Gender, and Sexual Orientation

_____ 1. sex (p. 410)
_____ 2. gender (p. 410)
_____ 3. gender identity (p. 410)
_____ 4. gender role (p. 410)
_____ 5. sexual orientation (p. 410)
_____ 6. androgynous (p. 411)
_____ 7. evolutionary theory of gender differences (p. 418)
_____ 8. social-role theory of gender differences (p. 419)
_____ 9. heterosexual (p. 423)
_____ 10. homosexual (p. 423)

a. a person who has both typical masculine and feminine characteristics
b. the psychological experience of being a female or male
c. persons who are sexually attracted to members of the same sex
d. persons who are sexually attracted to members of the other sex
e. states that gender differences are based on genes that resulted from different evolutionary pressures on women and men
f. the distinction between men and women based on biological characteristics
g. the behaviors consistent with being male or female in a given culture
h. one's view of oneself as male or female
i. the preference for romantic and sexual partners of the same or different sex
j. states that opportunities and restrictions in women's and men's different social roles create psychological gender differences

ANSWERS

1. f	6. a
2. b	7. e
3. h	8. j
4. g	9. d
5. i	10. c

Biological and Psychological Aspects of Sexuality

_____ 1. uterus (p. 431)
_____ 2. ovaries (p. 432)
_____ 3. fallopian tubes (p. 432)
_____ 4. clitoris (p. 432)
_____ 5. testes (p. 432)
_____ 6. vas deferens (p. 433)
_____ 7. prostate gland (p. 433)
_____ 8. penis (p. 433)
_____ 9. excitement phase (p. 434)
_____ 10. plateau phase (p. 434)
_____ 11. orgasm (p. 434)

a. a pair of structures in the female reproductive system that produce estrogen, other hormones, and ova

b. a structure in the male reproductive system that produces hormones and sperm cells

c. responsible for the production of semen, which carries sperm cells

d. a muscular structure that carries the fetus during pregnancy

e. the tube that carries sperm from the epididymis toward the outside of the body

f. part of the male reproductive system; its three tubes fill with blood during sexual arousal

g. part of the female reproductive system; they help transport the ova from the ovaries to the uterus.

h. part of the sexual response cycle, characterized by high levels of arousal

i. part of the sexual response cycle, characterized by an initial increase in physiological arousal

j. part of the sexual response cycle, characterized by a reflexive peak of physiological pleasure and arousal

k. a structure at the upper part of the vagina that is highly responsive to sexual stimulation

ANSWERS

1. d	7. c
2. a	8. f
3. g	9. i
4. k	10. h
5. b	11. j
6. e	

Atypical and Abnormal Sexual Behavior/Sexual Dysfunction and Sexual Health

_____ 1. atypical sexual behavior (p. 441)
_____ 2. transvestism (p. 441)
_____ 3. transsexualism (p. 441)
_____ 4. rape trauma syndrome (p. 443)
_____ 5. pedophilia (p. 444)
_____ 6. sexual harassment (p. 444)
_____ 7. sexual dysfunction (p. 446)
_____ 8. sexually transmitted diseases (p. 449)

a. obtaining sexual pleasure by dressing in the clothes of the other sex

b. diseases caused by microorganisms that are spread through sexual contact

c. subjective physical and/or psychological disturbances in any phase of the sexual response cycle

d. unwanted sexual advances or touching, sexually suggestive comments, and any form of coercive sexual behavior

e. unusual sexual behavior

f. characterized by feelings of anxiety and fear, and disturbances in sleep, relationships, and daily functioning

g. adults who experience sexual pleasure primarily through sexual contact with children

h. a condition in which an individual feels trapped in the body of the wrong sex

ANSWERS

1. e	5. g
2. a	6. d
3. h	7. c
4. f	8. b

Review At A Glance
(Answers to this section begin on page 209)

Gender and Sexual Orientation

Although a person's sex is defined by either male or female genitals, a person's ___(1)___ is the psychological experience of one's sex. The subjective experience of being a male or female is ___(2)___. The behaviors that communicate the degree to which we are feminine or masculine refer to a person's ___(3)___. The behaviors in which we engage for sexual pleasure, as well as the related feelings and beliefs, are referred to as ___(4)___. The tendency to prefer romantic and sexual partners of the same or different sex is ___(5)___.

Gender ___(6)___ develops early in infancy. Recent views of gender roles have conceived them as being on a ___(7)___, with people displaying varying degrees of both masculinity and femininity. A person who has both female and male characteristics is referred to as ___(8)___. Androgynous people are more likely to adapt well to a variety of situations because of their greater ___(9)___.

Regarding gender differences in physical strength and skills, men on the average have greater ___(10)___-_____ strength, and can throw objects farther and with greater ___(11)___ than women. Generally, women and men are more similar in ___(12)___ ability than they are different. On average, women perform better in a range of ___(13)___ skills, verbal and ___(14)___ memory, perceptual speed and ___(15)___ motor skills, whereas men perform better in mathematics, ___(16)___, and social studies. Although most of these average differences are small, men on average score considerably higher on tests of ___(17)___ and mechanical reasoning. With regard to mathematical ability, the average gender difference is small, although scores at the highest end of the scale are more common for ___(18)___. The greater success of men in scientific and technological fields may be explained in part by ___(19)___ against women. Although women, on the average, receive higher grades in ___(20)___ courses at all levels, they attribute their success in math courses to hard work, whereas men tend to attribute their success to ___(21)___ ability.

Most gender differences in social and emotional functioning tend to be greater than the differences in ___(22)___ performance. Women tend to be ___(23)___, friendly and helpful, whereas men tend to be ___(24)___, dominant, and assertive. Women are more likely to be anxious, depressed, and have slightly low ___(25)___-____, whereas men are more likely to engage in ___(26)___ aggression and risky behavior, and are more likely to commit most kinds of ___(27)___.

Regarding mating and sexual behavior, men tend to prefer a mate who is younger and physically attractive and has good ___(28)___ skills. Women tend to prefer mates who are ___(29)___, have good character, and high ___(30)___ potential. Many studies indicate that men are far more willing to engage in ___(31)___ sex.

According to brain imaging studies, the cortex of men is about 10 per cent larger than those of women; the difference is due to a greater volume of myelinated ___(32)___. As adults, the relative size of the right cerebral hemisphere is larger in ___(33)___. The ___(34)___ reaches a larger size in the adult female. Research on brain activity of males and females during a rhyming activity showed that men tended to use language areas only in the ___(35)___ cerebral hemisphere, whereas females tend to use language areas in ___(36)___ cerebral hemispheres. This difference is consistent with the superior ___(37)___ skills of women.

As children grow older, the ___(38)___ increases more rapidly in males, whereas the ___(39)___ increases more rapidly in female children. The amygdala is associated with the expression of ___(40)___; the hippocampus plays a role in everyday ___(41)___ and in the inhibition of previously ___(42)___ behavior. Structural differences are also found in the ___(43)___. Biological differences in the brain may be the ___(44)___ of gender differences, but they may be the result of gender differences as well.

A theory of gender differences that emphasizes genes that resulted from differing evolutionary pressures on ancestral men and women is called the ___(45)___ theory of gender differences. According to this theory, gender differences have resulted from: (1) pressures associated with ___(46)___, (2) selection of dominance and ___(47)___, (3) pressures created by child ___(48)___, (4) pressures created by differences in parental ___(49)___, and (5) pressures in mate ___(50)___. Among the criticism of this approach are that it is dehumanizing, a self-serving attempt by males to ___(51)___ their behavior, and it implies a genetic lock into gender differences. Evolutionary theory can't be tested ___(52)___.

A theory that the opportunities and restrictions inherent in different social roles create psychological gender differences is called the ___(53)___-_____ theory of gender differences. According to this view, ___(54)___ differences created the initial gender-based division of labor in the past, but gender roles are maintained today by the way we are ___(55)___. In support of this theory, research by Steele suggests that expectations of gender differences can create gender differences in ___(56)___ performance. Some cross-cultural research on ___(57)___ supports social-role theory.

According to Freud, young children take on the manners and ways of the same-sexed parent through a process called ___(58)___. According to social learning theorists, children learn gender appropriate behavior through ___(59)___ and ___(60)___.

People who are attracted to members of the other sex are termed ___(61)___, whereas those who are attracted to the same sex are ___(62)___. People who are attracted both to members of the same sex and to members of the other sex are called ___(63)___. In a 1994 survey conducted by the University of Chicago, 2.8 percent of males and 1.4 percent of females identified themselves as homosexual or ___(64)___. Gays and lesbians tend to live in ___(65)___ cities.

Persecution and discrimination against gays and lesbians is widespread and has been known to reach extreme forms of ___(66)___. Acts of aggression perpetrated against gays and lesbians are called ___(67)___ _____.

President Clinton sparked controversy by seeking to ban discrimination against homosexual men and women in the ___(68)___ _____. A review of research has found no convincing evidence that gays and lesbians are poor ___(69)___ risks or are unfit for military service. According to Herek, it would be useful to conduct active campaigns against ___(70)___ and to protect gays and lesbians in the military against retaliation. Studies have found gays and lesbians to be at greater risk for depression, suicide, and ___(71)___ abuse.

According to Money, social learning plays a role in the development of homosexuality, along with predisposing biological factors such as ___(72)___ and exposure to prenatal ___(73)___. According to Bem, predisposing factors interact with atypical ___(74)___-_____ behavior in the development of homosexuality. Bem's theory is ___(75)___ and doesn't explain the fact that many gays and lesbians did not show atypical sex-typed behavior as children.

Biological and Psychological Aspects of Sexuality

A Viennese neurologist, Richard von Krafft-Ebing, extensively studied variations and ___(76)___ in human sexual behavior. Krafft-Ebing incorrectly concluded that ___(77)___ was the cause of sexual deviation. An English physician, Henry Havelock Ellis, studied the role of ___(78)___ and ___(79)___ influences in shaping human sexual behavior. Alfred Kinsey conducted large ___(80)___ that allowed him to describe the range of human sexual behavior. John Money studied sexual development and ___(81)_____. Masters and Johnson conducted groundbreaking research on the human ___(82)___ _____ cycle.

The pear-shaped structure that carries the fetus during pregnancy is the ___(83)___. The structures that produce estrogen and other hormones, as well as the ova, are called ___(84)___. The ova are transported to the uterus through the ___(85)___ _____. At the bottom of the uterus, connected to the vagina, is the ___(86)___. The female external genitals, collectively called the ___(87)___, consist of (1) a fleshy mound called the ___(88)___, (2) the outer lips of the vagina called ___(89)___ _____, (3) the inner lips of the vagina, called ___(90)___ _____, and (4) the structure at the upper part of the vagina highly responsive to sexual stimulation, called the ___(91)___.

In the male, hormones and sperm are produced by the ___(92)___. After mature sperm have been produced, they are held in the ___(93)___. The tube that carries sperm from the epididymis to the outside of the body is called the ___(94)___ _____. The sperm cells are carried in a fluid called ___(95)___; semen is produced by the ___(96)___ gland and held in the seminal vesicle. The external genitals of the male consist of a tubular structure called a penis and a loose skin structure that supports the testes, called the ___(97)___.

The sexual response cycle consists of four stages: (1) an initial increase of physiological arousal occurs in the ___(98)___ phase; (2) high levels of arousal take place in the ___(99)___ phase; (3) a peak of physical arousal and pleasure is reached in the ___(100)___ stage; and (4) the body's level of physical arousal rapidly declines in the ___(101)___ phase. The resolution phase is accompanied by a time during which the male is unresponsive to additional stimulation; this is called the ___(102)___ period.

The sexual motive contains important similarities to and differences from other primary motives. As with other motives (1) the ___(103)___ plays a key regulatory role; (2) sexual motivation is sensitive to ___(104)___ _____ stimuli; (3) our motives are powerfully shaped by ___(105)___; and (4) sexual motivation is greatly influenced by our ___(106)___. Unlike the other primary motives (1) the sexual motive is not necessary for ___(107)___ survival; (2) while we seek to decrease the arousal created by hunger, thirst, etc., we are motivated to both ___(108)___ and ___(109)___ our sexual arousal; (3) sexual motivation is less related to ___(110)___ than the other primary motives; and

(4) while other primary motives help to increase our energy, sexual behavior ___(111)___ our energy. Although hormones secreted from the endocrine system play a major role in regulating the sexual behavior of animals, the sexual behavior of humans is much less influenced by ___(112)___ factors.

The University of Chicago survey of sexual behavior found that a common sexual pattern for Americans is serial

___(113)___. The survey also found that people in committed relationships have sex ___(114)___ often than single persons. The survey found that, by far, the preferred sexual practice is ___(115)___. The survey found few differences in sexual practices across levels of ___(116)___, religious affiliation or ___(117)___ groups. According to the survey, most people who are having sex in ___(118)___ relationships report ___(119)___ levels of enjoyment.

Atypical and Abnormal Sexual Behavior

Sexual practices that are unusual are called ___(120)___ sexual behavior.

Individuals who obtain sexual pleasure by dressing in the clothes of the opposite sex are ___(121)___. Transvestites are almost always males. When an individual feels trapped in a body of the wrong sex, the condition is referred to as ___(122)___. In some cases, the person will undergo ___(123)___ injections and ___(124)___ surgery to change his or her sex organs.

Some individuals are primarily or exclusively aroused by specific objects; this practice is called ___(125)___. Receiving sexual pleasure by inflicting pain on others is called ___(126)___. A condition in which receiving pain is sexually exciting is called ___(127)___.

The practice of obtaining sexual pleasure by watching members of the opposite sex undress or engage in sexual activities is called ___(128)___. Voyeurs are generally not considered ___(129)___. Individuals who obtain sexual pleasure from exposing their genitals to others are ___(130)___.

When an individual forces another person to engage in a sexual act, it is called ___(131)___. In the U.S., twenty-two percent of adult women and 2 percent of adult men have been forced to do something ___(132)___ at least once since the age of 13. Many rape victims experience feelings of ___(133)___ and fear, as well as disturbances in ___(134)___, relationships, and daily functioning; these behaviors are labeled ___(135)___ syndrome. Theories of rape suggest that male rapists are driven by aggressive impulses or by the need to feel (136) and ___(137)___. Many communities provide assistance and support to rape victims through ___(138)___ centers.

Sexual contact with a child perpetuated by a family member is called ___(139)___. When a sexual assault on a child involves force or the threat of force, the assault is called ___(140)___. When non-forceful means are used, the abuse of children is called child ___(141)___. Many of the effects of child sexual abuse are believed to be long-term. Adults who experience sexual pleasure through contact with children are called ___(142)___. In the vast majority of cases, the molester or rapist is known and ___(143)___ by the child victim.

Unwanted sexual advances, touching, sexually suggestive comments, and any form of coercive behavior all constitute sexual ___(144)___. Sexual harassment occurs between persons with different amounts of ___(145)___, often in schools or in the workplace. In some cases, sexual harassment can provoke serious levels of anxiety and ___(146)___.

Sexual Dysfunction and Sexual Health

Disturbances that occur in any phase of the sexual response cycle are called sexual ___(147)___. Although there are a variety of physical causes of sexual dysfunction, many sexual dysfunctions are caused by ___(148)___ factors. Dysfunctions of sexual desire include (1) infrequent or nonexistent sexual desire, called ___(149)___ sexual desire and (2) fearful avoidance of sexual contact, called sexual ___(150)___. Dysfunctions of sexual arousal include, for females, female sexual ___(151)___ disorder, characterized by a lack of vaginal lubrication and minimal sexual excitement, involuntary contractions of the vagina, called ___(152)___, and pain during intercourse, called ___(153)___. Male sexual arousal disorders include ___(154)___ dysfunction. Orgasm dysfunctions include, for women, inhibited female orgasm, and for men, ___(155)___ ejaculation or retarded ejaculation. People who experience sexual dysfunctions often are ___(156)___ to discuss the problem, may believe they are the only ones with such problems and may believe there is nowhere to turn for help.

Among health problems related to sexual anatomy are ___(157)___ of the sexual anatomy, including, for women, the cervix, ___(158)___, ovaries, and breasts. A low-dose X ray that can be accurate at detecting breast cancer is called a ___(159)___. For men, cancers of the ___(160)___ and testicles are potential health problems.

Diseases that are caused by micro-organisms spread through sexual contact are called ___(161)___ _____ diseases. Caused by a spiral-shaped bacteria called a spirochete, ___(162)___ has been increasing in incidence in the United States. Primary syphilis is characterized by ___(163)___ sores. ___(164)___ syphilis is characterized by rashes, fever, headache, and nausea. During these first two stages, syphilis can be treated with ___(165)___. If untreated, syphilis develops into the ___(166)___ stage, which is characterized by numerous serious health problems. A second STD spread by bacterial infection is called ___(167)___. The most common STD is ___(168)___. An STD commonly referred to as "crabs" is ___(169)___ _____. An STD caused by the herpes simplex virus, genital herpes is treatable but not ___(170)___. Another viral infection, usually not painful, is genital ___(171)___.

A fatal STD caused by the human immunodeficiency virus (HIV) is ___(172)___. HIV is transmitted through blood, semen, and ___(173)___ fluids. HIV destroys ___(174)___ cells, which aid the body's immune response. According to statistics, the highest rates of HIV infection are in sub-Saharan Africa, ___(175)___, and South America and the Caribbean. In the U.S., the annual death rate has fallen due to drugs called ___(176)___ _____. ___(177)___ are more likely to be infected than ___(178)___, and the most common routes of infection differ from men and women. The risk of contracting HIV can be minimized by ___(179)___ from sex, by having an exclusive relationship with a partner who is free from HIV and by the consistent use of ___(180)___.

Application of Psychology: Date Rape

Date rape is a common occurrence on ___(181)_____. One estimate is that 33 percent of women have experienced date rape. In many cases, date rape begins with a ___(182)___ between the persons. One reason for the miscommunication is a difference in beliefs and ___(183)___ about sexuality. Another factor that is related to date rape is the use of ___(184)___. Guidelines for men include the following; (1) It is always rape when she says "___(185)___"; (2) if it is not clear that she has consented to sex, then she has ___(186)_____; and (3) if she is drunk or high, she cannot ___(187)___ to sex. Guidelines for women include: (1) communicate your wishes about sex ___(188)___ and early; (2) ___(189)___ and sexual situations are a dangerous combination; and (3) even ___(190)___ guys can commit rape. Many ___(191)___ exist, both on campus and off-campus, to assist victims of date rape.

Concept Checks

Fill in the missing components of the following concept boxes. The correct answers are located in the "Answers" section at the end of the chapter.

Gender Differences and Gender Identity

Name of Theory	Explanation
evolutionary theory of gender differences	
	opportunities and restrictions in social roles create psychological gender differences
psychoanalytic theory of gender identity	
social learning theory of gender identity	

Sexual Response Cycle

Stage	Description
excitement phase	
	high levels of arousal maintained for variable periods of time
orgasmic phase	
	rapid decline in physical arousal, and a return to the pre-arousal state; males experience a refractory period

Sexually Transmitted Diseases

Disease	Symptoms/Cures
	caused by a bacterium called a spirochete; progresses through three stages of infection; one early symptom is a sore called a chancre; secondary symptoms may include fever, nausea, headaches and, swollen glands; primary and secondary stages can usually be treated with antibiotics; tertiary stage can cause serious health problems and can be fatal
gonorrhea	
	the most common STD; it has vague symptoms that can be treated with antibiotics; it is difficult to treat and may be recurrent
	commonly called "crabs," this disease causes skin itching and may be treated with medicated shampoo
genital herpes	
	caused by a virus, they are not usually painful and not considered dangerous, but they are related to the development of other serious conditions; they may be removed by surgery or by freezing
	caused by HIV and transmitted through blood, semen, and vaginal fluids; a person may be infected with HIV for a long period of time before becoming ill; there is no cure

Extending the Chapter: Psychology, Societal Issues, and Human Diversity

These questions may be assigned to you. Whether or not they are assigned, they are designed to be challenging questions to encourage you to think independently about the material in the chapter. Many of the questions have no right or wrong answers.

I.   From the "Applications of Psychology" section

1.   Is the incidence of date rape increasing, or is it just being more widely reported? Discuss the reasons for your answer.

2.   What steps should high schools, colleges, and universities take to prevent date rape?

II.   Psychology, Societal Issues, and Human Diversity

1.   Discuss the reasons for the continuing existence of widespread gender stereotypes, even among (presumably) intelligent college students.

2.   In the United States and elsewhere, gender relationships have increasingly been subject to public policy regulation. For example, laws exist to safeguard individuals against sexual discrimination and sexual harassment. To what extent should gender relations be regulated by public policy?

3.   To what extent should public schools be responsible for sex education? To what extent should sex education be left to parents? What about education about STDs?

4.   Consider the various ways sexual behavior is regulated by public policy: movie ratings, prostitution laws, laws prescribing acceptable and unacceptable sexual behavior between consenting adults, etc. Do you believe it is appropriate to devote so much public policy attention to sexual matters? Explain your answer.

Practice Quiz

The practice quiz consists of three sections: 1) Short answer questions, 2) Multiple-choice questions, and 3) True-False questions. At the end of the chapter you will find suggested answers to the short answer questions, answers and explanation for the multiple-choice questions, and answers to the true-false questions.

Short Answer Questions

1.   Compare and contrast sexual motivation with other human motives.

_____

_____

_____

2.   List and describe examples of atypical and abnormal sexual behavior.

_____

_____

_____

3.   List and describe examples of sexual dysfunction discussed in the text.

_____

_____

_____

Multiple-Choice Questions

1.   Which of the following is most directly related to the gender to whom a person is attracted romantically and sexually?
  a. sex
  b. gender
  c. gender role
  d. sexual orientation
     LO 1

2.   The behaviors consistent with being male or female in a given culture defines
  a. gender.
  b. gender identity.
  c. gender role.
  d. sex.
     LO 2

3.   The view of oneself as being male or female is
  a. gender.
  b. gender identity.
  c. gender role.
  d. sex.
     LO 2

4.   On the average, women score higher than men on tests of
  a. language skills.
  b. math.
  c. science.
  d. aggression.
     LO 3

5.   Which of the following is true regarding gender differences found in the brain?
  a. The amygdala is larger in the brains of adult men than adult women.
  b. The hippocampus is larger in the brains of adult women than adult adult men.
  c. The corpus callosum reaches a larger size in the brains of adult women.
  d. all of the above
     LO 3

6.   When presented with a rhyming task, males showed increased activity only in the left hemisphere, whereas females showed increased activity
  a. only in the right hemisphere.
  b. in both the left and right hemispheres.
  c. only in the corpus callosum.
  d. in the cerebellum.
     LO 3

7.   Which of the following theories is most likely to emphasize Darwin's theory of selection?
  a. social-role theory
  b. psychoanalytic theory
  c. evolutionary theory
  d. social learning theory
     LO 4

8.   The process of reinforcing appropriate gender roles is central to gender development according to which theory?
  a. psychoanalytic
  b. social learning
  c. humanistic
  d. evolutionary
     LO 5

9.   In psychoanalytic theory, what is the process through which gender identity develops?
  a. identification
  b. defense mechanisms
  c. reaction formation
  d. catharsis
     LO 5

10. According to the 1994 University of Chicago survey, individuals with a homosexual orientation are
  a. more common than other studies have found.
  b. less common than other studies have found.
  c. more likely to be found living in small towns.
  d. likely to exhibit a narrow range of gender roles.
     LO 6

11. Which of the following best reflects the view of researchers regarding admitting homosexual men and women into the military?
    a. Homosexuals should be admitted, but they should be in separate units.
    b. Homosexuals should not be admitted, because the morale of the military would suffer.
    c. Homosexuals should be admitted, and programs should be initiated to reduce prejudice and stereotyping.
    d. The present policy of not directly addressing the issue has worked for centuries and should continue.
    LO 7

12. According to Money, individuals develop a homosexual orientation as a result of
    a. social learning.
    b. biological factors.
    c. learned gender roles.
    d. both *a* and *b* .
    LO 8

13. One explanation in Daryl Bem's theory of homosexuality is that children with atypical sex-typed behavior find children of the same sex to be
    a. upsetting and later emotionally arousing.
    b. attractive even before puberty.
    c. easier to be with and more understanding.
    d. more valued than the opposite sex.
    LO 8

14. In the mid-1950s, large-scale sexual surveys were conducted by
    a. Masters and Johnson.
    b. Alfred Kinsey.
    c. John Money.
    d. Albert Ellis,
    LO 9

15. The idea that psychological problems could affect sexual functioning was first proposed by
    a. Freud.
    b. Ellis.
    c. Masters.
    d. Kinsey.
    LO 9

16. Estrogen, ova (eggs), and other hormones are produced by the
    a. uterus.
    b. fallopian tubes.
    c. cervix.
    d. ovaries.
    LO 10

17. Sperm cells are produced by the
    a. prostate gland.
    b. scrotum.
    c. testes.
    d. vas deference.
    LO 10

18. Which of the following describe the correct sequence of the human sexual response cycle?
    a. excitement, plateau, resolution, orgasm
    b. plateau, excitement, resolution, orgasm
    c. excitement, plateau, orgasm, resolution
    d. plateau, excitement, orgasm, resolution
    LO 11

19. During the sexual response cycle, the refractory period is experienced by
    a. males in the excitement phase.
    b. females in the excitement phase.
    c. males in the resolution phase.
    d. females in the resolution phase.
    LO 11

20. Each of these factors represents a difference between the sexual motive and other primary motives *except*
    a. sexual behavior decreases one's energy.
    b. sexual motivation is not necessary for individual survival.
    c. sexual motivation is less related to deprivation than are other primary motives.
    d. the hypothalamus seems unrelated to the sexual motive.
    LO 12

21. How does the hormonal control of human sexual behavior compare with the hormonal control of other animals?
    a. Humans are more influenced by hormonal factors.
    b. Humans are less influenced by hormonal factors.
    c. Humans and animals are equally influenced by hormonal factors.
    d. Hormonal factors play no role in human sexual behavior.
    LO 13

22. The results of the University of Chicago sex survey supported the notion of widespread
    a. serial monogamy.
    b. sexual promiscuity among those in relationships.
    c. differences in sexual behavior among different ethnic groups.
    d. dissatisfaction with sex among those in committed relationships.
    LO 14

23. The feeling that one is trapped in a body of the opposite sex is called
    a. transvestism.
    b. transsexualism.
    c. fetishism.
    d. exhibitionism.
    LO 15

24. Individuals who obtain sexual pleasure by watching members of the opposite sex undress or engage in sexual behaviors are called
    a. exhibitionists.
    b. sadists.
    c. voyeurs.
    d. pedophiles.
    LO 16

25. What is the common theme in sadism and masochism?
    a. using children for sexual pleasure
    b. suffering for sexual pleasure
    c. using inanimate objects for sexual pleasure
    d. watching sexual acts performed by others for sexual pleasure
    LO 16

26. Which of the following behaviors or feelings are likely of children who have been sexually victimized?
    a. acting out sexually
    b. feeling stigmatized
    c. feeling personally betrayed
    d. all of the above
    LO 17

27. Which of the following is a characteristic of sexual harassment?
    a. It consists of unwanted sexual advances.
    b. It consists of sexually suggestive comments.
    c. It occurs between persons with different perceived amounts of power.
    d. all of the above
    LO 17

28. A nearly complete fearful avoidance of sexual contact with others is called
    a. inhibited sexual desire.
    b. sexual aversion disorder.
    c. dyspareunia.
    d. vaginismus.
    LO 18

29. Which of the following is a female sexual dysfunction?
    a. dyspareunia
    b. premature ejaculation
    c. erectile dysfunction
    d. all of the above
    LO 18

30. Which of the following is (are) common beliefs about sexual dysfunctions?
    a. They are often embarrassing to discuss.
    b. People experiencing sexual dysfunctions may believe they are psychologically abnormal.
    c. People often believe they have nowhere to turn for help.
    d. all of the above
    LO 18

31. The text recommends which of the following to assist in the early detection of cancers of the sexual anatomy?
    a. sexual abstinence
    b. sexual moderation
    c. frequent self-examination
    d. engaging in safe sex
    LO 19

32. During which stage(s) of syphilis is it usually curable with antibiotics?
    a. primary
    b. secondary
    c. tertiary
    d. both *a* and *b*
    LO 20

33. The most common sexually transmitted disease is
    a. gonorrhea.
    b. syphilis.
    c. genital herpes.
    d. chlamydia.
    LO 20

34. A person with HIV is diagnosed as having AIDS when he or she
    a. is first infected with HIV.
    b. experiences one of several specific infectious diseases.
    c. loses a specific number of T-Helper blood cells.
    d. both *b* and *c*
    LO 21

35. Which of the following demonstrates the relationship between alcohol and date rape?
    a. A person who is drunk cannot give consent to sex.
    b. Alcohol lowers inhibitions and increases the likelihood of the use of force.
    c. Drinking alcohol allows people to attribute their behavior to the effects of alcohol.
    d. all of the above
    LO 22

True-False Questions

_____ 1. Gender differences in cognitive performance tend to be greater than differences in social and emotional functioning.

_____ 2. Researchers have found that the corpus callosum tends to be larger in the adult male than in the adult female.

_____ 3. The brain area called the amygdala is larger in males than in females.

_____ 4. Research results have conclusively supported the social-role theory of gender differences.

_____ 5. According to John Money, biological factors are an insignificant factor in the development of homosexuality.

_____ 6. In the female, the ovaries are involved in the production of estrogen and other hormones, as well as ova.

_____ 7. In the male, the prostate gland produces both hormones and reproductive cells.

_____ 8. Males experience a refractory period during the resolution phase of the sexual response cycle.

_____ 9. The most commonly contracted STD is syphilis.

_____10. Genital herpes is treatable, but not curable.

ANSWERS SECTION

Concept Checks

Gender Differences and Gender Identity

Name of theory	Explanation
evolutionary theory of gender differences	gender differences are based on genes that resulted from different evolutionary pressures on women and men
social-role theory of gender differences	opportunities and restrictions in social roles create psychological gender differences
psychoanalytic theory of gender identity	Freudian theory that emphasizes the process of identification with the same-sex parent and the desire for approval of the other-sex parent
social learning theory of gender identity	Bandura's theory that emphasizes learning through reinforcement and punishment of gender behaviors

Sexual Response Cycle

Stage	Description
excitement phase	increased level of arousal; blood flow increase to penis; vagina becomes lubricated
plateau phase	high levels of arousal maintained for variable periods of time
orgasmic phase	orgasm reflex occurs, characterized by peaking physical arousal and pleasure
resolution phase	rapid decline in physical arousal, and a return to the pre-arousal state; males experience a refractory period

Sexually Transmitted Diseases

Disease	Symptoms/Cures
syphilis	caused by a bacterium called a spirochete; progresses through three stages of infection; one early symptom is a sore called a chancre; secondary symptoms may include fever, nausea, headaches, and swollen glands, primary and secondary stages can usually be treated with antibiotics; tertiary stage can cause serious health problems and can be fatal
gonorrhea	caused by a bacterium; symptoms involve discharge from genital area; if left untreated, it can lead to serious health complications; it is usually cured with antibiotics
chlamydia	the most common STD; it has vague symptoms that can be treated with antibiotics; it is difficult to treat and may be recurrent
pubic lice	commonly called "crabs," this disease causes skin itching and may be treated with medicated shampoo
genital herpes	causes small painful lesions in the genital area; the lesions are highly contagious; herpes is treatable, but not curable
genital warts	caused by a virus, they are not usually painful and not considered dangerous, but they are related to the development of other serious conditions; they may be removed by surgery or by freezing
AIDS	caused by HIV and transmitted through blood, semen, and vaginal fluids; a person may be infected with HIV for a long period of time before becoming ill; there is no cure for AIDS

Answers to Review At A Glance

1. gender
2. gender identity
3. gender role
4. sexuality
5. sexual orientation
6. identity
7. continuum
8. androgynous
9. flexibility
10. upper-body
11. accuracy
12. cognitive
13. language
14. spatial
15. fine
16. science
17. spatial
18. men
19. prejudice
20. math
21. intellectual
22. cognitive
23. nurturing
24. competitive
25. self-esteem
26. physical
27. crimes
28. housekeeping
29. older
30. earning
31. casual
32. axons
33. males
34. corpus callosum
35. left
36. both
37. language
38. amygdala
39. hippocampus
40. aggression
41. memory
42. punished
43. hypothalamus
44. cause
45. evolutionary
46. hunting
47. aggression
48. care
49. investment
50. selection
51. justify
52. directly
53. social-role
54. biological
55. socialized
56. cognitive
57. mate selection
58. identification
59. reinforcement
60. punishment

61. heterosexual
62. homosexual
63. bisexual
64. bisexual
65. larger
66. violence
67. gay-bashing
68. armed forces
69. security
70. prejudice
71. substance
72. genetics
73. hormones
74. sex-typed
75. speculative
76. deviations
77. masturbation
78. social
79. cultural
80. surveys
81. gender roles
82. sexual response
83. uterus
84. ovaries
85. fallopian tubes
86. cervix
87. vulva
88. mons
89. labia majora
90. labia minora
91. clitoris
92. testes
93. epididymis
94. vas deferens
95. semen
96. prostate
97. scrotum
98. excitement
99. plateau
100. orgasmic
101. resolution
102. refractory
103. hypothalamus
104. external

105. learning
106. emotions
107. individual
108. increase
109. decrease
110. deprivation
111. decreases
112. hormonal
113. monogamy
114. more
115. vaginal intercourse
116. education
117. ethnic
118. committed
119. high
120. atypical
121. transvestites
122. transsexualism
123. hormone
124. plastic
125. fetishism
126. sexual sadism
127. sexual masochism
128. voyeurism
129. dangerous
130. exhibitionists
131. rape
132. sexual
133. anxiety
134. sleep
135. rape trauma
136. powerful
137. dominating
138. rape crisis
139. incest
140. child rape
141. molestation
142. pedophiles
143. trusted
144. harassment
145. power
146. depression
147. dysfunctions
148. psychological

149. inhibited
150. aversion disorder
151. arousal
152. vaginismus
153. dyspareunia
154. erectile
155. premature
156. embarrassed
157. cancers
158. uterus
159. mammogram
160. prostate
161. sexually transmitted
162. syphilis
163. chancre
164. Secondary
165. antibiotics
166. tertiary
167. gonorrhea
168. chlamydia
169. pubic lice
170. curable
171. warts
172. AIDS
173. vaginal
174. T-helper
175. Asia
176. protease inhibitors
177. men
178. women
179. abstaining
180. condoms
181. college campuses
182. miscommunication
183. attitudes
184. alcohol
185. no
186. not consented
187. consent
188. clearly
189. alcohol
190. nice
191. resources

Sample Answers for Short Answer Questions

1. **Compare and contrast sexual motivation with other human motives.**

    As is the case with hunger and thirst, the sexual motive is influenced by the hypothalamus. Similar to hunger, external stimuli (incentives) can stimulate the sexual motive. Sexual motivation is also influence by learning experiences, in the same way that what we eat and drink is influenced by learning experiences. Sexual motivation is also influenced by emotions, as is the case with eating. Sexual motivation differs from the other motives in that it is not necessary for individual survival, humans are motivated to both increase and decrease the sexual motive (unlike the arousal created by hunger and thirst), sexual motivation is much less linked to deprivation than the other primary motives, and, unlike the other motives, sexual behavior leads to a decrease in energy.

2. **List and describe examples of atypical and abnormal sexual behavior.**

    Tranvestism refers to obtaining sexual pleasure by dressing in the clothes of the opposite sex; in transsexualism, the individual feels trapped in the body of the wrong sex; fetishism refers to being sexually aroused by specific objects; in sexual sadism the individual receives pleasure by inflicting pain on others; in sexual masochism, the individual receives pleasure by receiving pain; in voyeurism, the individual receives pleasure by watching others undress or engage in sexual acts; exhibitionists obtain sexual pleasure by exposing themselves to others.

3. **List and describe examples of sexual dysfunction discussed in the text.**

    The text describes three types of sexual dysfunction: dysfunctions of sexual desire, including inhibited sexual desire and sexual aversion disorder; dysfunctions of sexual arousal, including female sexual arousal disorder, vaginismus, dyspareunia, and in males, erectile dysfunction; a third category is orgasm dysfunctions, including inhibited female orgasm, and in males, premature ejaculation and retarded ejaculation.

Multiple-Choice Answers

1. The answer is *D*. Sexual orientation is defined by those with whom we have a sexual or romantic relationship.
2. The answer is *C*. Gender identity is one's view of oneself as being male or female, and gender is the psychological experience of being male or female.
3. The answer is *B*. Gender roles consist of those behaviors consistent with being a male or female in a given culture.
4. The answer is *A*. Keep in mind, however, that the differences between women's and men's averages scores usually are small and are characterized by considerable overlap.
5. The answer is *D*. Although gender differences in brain structure exist, there is uncertainty whether these are the *cause* of gender differences or the *result* of gender differences.
6. The answer is *B*. Researchers have also found the corpus callosum of females and the hippocampus to be larger in females, whereas the amygdala is larger in men.
7. The answer is *C*. Evolutionary theory states that gender differences are based on genes that resulted from different evolutionary pressures on ancestral men and women. This theory relies upon Darwin's ideas regarding natural selection.
8. The answer is *B*. The social learning approach suggests that gender roles are learned from society.
9. The answer is *A*. Defense mechanisms, reaction formation and catharsis are all important components of psychoanalytic theory, but, according to Freud, identification with the same-sexed parent is crucial in the development of gender identity.
10. The answer is *B*. This survey found lower levels than the Kinsey surveys many years ago. The study also found those with a homosexual orientation tend to live in larger urban areas.
11. The answer is *C*. Researchers suggest that when people with prejudices against each other work together, the prejudices diminish dramatically.

12. The answer is *D*. According to Money, biological factors predispose some people toward homosexuality. Research studies on twins, on prenatal development, and on the hypothalamus are consistent with Money's hypothesis.

13. The answer is *A*. According to Bem this occurs as "the exotic becomes erotic."

14. The answer is *B*. Kinsey's surveys demonstrated that such phenomena as masturbation, sexual fantasies, and homosexual contact were more common than had been previously thought.

15. The answer is *B*. Ellis was an English physician who also studied the role of cultural and social influences on sexual behavior. Ellis related psychological problems such as anxiety and depression to problems in sexual functioning.

16. The answer is *D*. The uterus carries the fetus during pregnancy; the fallopian tubes transport the ova to the uterus, and the cervix, located at the bottom of the uterus, connects the uterus to the vagina.

17. The answer is *C*. The prostate gland produces semen, the scrotum supports the testes, and the vas deferens is the tube that carries sperm toward the outside of the body.

18. The answer is *C*. If you need an acronym to remember the sequence, how about *E*very *P*erson *O*ught to *R*elax (EPOR).

19. The answer is *C*. During the refractory period, males are unresponsive to further sexual stimulation.

20. The answer is *D*. The sexual motive resembles the other primary motives with respect to hypothalamic control, the role of external stimuli, and the roles played by learning and emotions.

21. The answer is *B*. Although humans are far less influenced by hormonal factors than other animals, a strong relationship does exist between hormonal factors and human sexuality.

22. The answer is *A*. Serial monogamy refers to a pattern of monogamy while in a relationship, but having different partners as we move from one relationship to the next.

23. The answer is *B*. Transvestism refers to those who derive sexual pleasure by dressing in the clothes of the opposite sex. Fetishism refers to those who are aroused by specific physical objects, and exhibitionism refers to those who obtain sexual pleasure by exposing themselves to others.

24. The answer is *C*. Exhibitionists obtain sexual pleasure by exposing their genitals to others. Sexual sadists receive pleasure by inflicting pain on others. Pedophiles obtain pleasure from sexual contact with children.

25. The answer is *B*. Whereas sadism refers to receiving sexual pleasure by inflicting pain on others, sexual masochism refers to receiving sexual gratification by receiving pain.

26. The answer is *D*. In addition, children who have been sexually victimized are likely to feel powerless and a lack of control.

27. The answer is *D*. Although there are laws that attempt to protect people from sexual harassment, most instances of harassment probably still go unreported.

28. The answer is *B*. Inhibited sexual desire refers to infrequent desire for sexual contact. Dyspareunia refers to painful intercourse for women, and vaginismus refers to involuntary contractions of the vaginal wall that make it too narrow to allow sexual intercourse.

29. The answer is *A*. Premature ejaculation and erectile dysfunction are male sexual dysfunctions.

30. The answer is *D*. Our society is still generally reluctant to discuss sexual matters openly, especially sexual dysfunctions. However, as the text suggests, help for these dysfunctions is widely available.

31. The answer is *C*. The importance of self-examinations reminds us that ultimately we are responsible for our own health and well-being.

32. The answer is *D*. The tertiary stage is also characterized by numerous serious health complications.

33. The answer is *D*. Recent research suggests that as many as 20 percent of college students may be infected with chlamydia.

34. The answer is *D*. Most people who are infected with HIV go several years before they become ill with AIDS.

35. The answer is *D*. All of these issues argue for the cautious use of alcohol, especially while dating.

Answers to True-False Questions

1. F 6. T

2. F 7. F

3. T 8. T

4. F 9. F

5. F 10. T

Chapter 12   Personality Theories and Assessment

Learning Objectives

1. Define the term personality. (p. 462)

2. Compare Allport's trait theory with the five-factor trait theory. (p. 462)

3. Describe the results of efforts to validate personality trait theory. (p. 464)

4. Distinguish among Freud's concepts of conscious mind, the preconscious mind, and the unconscious mind as part of his psychoanalytic theory. (p. 466)

5. Distinguish among the id, ego, and superego in Freud's psychoanalytic theory. (p. 468)

6. Distinguish among the processes Freud referred to as displacement, sublimation, and identification. (p. 469)

7. List and describe Freud's five psychosexual stages of development. (p. 470)

8. Discuss Jung's criticisms of Freud's theory; distinguish between extroversion and introversion and between personal unconscious and the collective unconscious. (p. 472)

9. Discuss the roles of inferiority feelings, social interest, and goals in Adler's personality theory. (p. 473)

10. Explain the role of anxious insecurity in the personality theory of Horney; describe Horney's criticisms of Freud's view of women. (p. 474)

11. Discuss Bandura's social learning theory, including the roles of cognition in personality development. (p. 476)

12. Discuss the alternative explanations to trait theories called situationism and interactionism. (p. 478)

13. Identify the basic concepts of humanistic theory, including inner-directedness and subjectivity. (p. 480)

14. Distinguish between the self and the ideal self, and understand the importance of congruence and conditions of worth in Rogers' personality theory. (p. 480)

15. Identify the characteristics of a self-actualized person according to Maslow. (p. 482)

16. Compare and contrast humanistic, psychoanalytic, and social learning theories of personality. (p. 483)

17. Discuss the ways in which interviews and observational methods are used to assess personality. (p. 488)

18. Discuss the uses of projective personality tests and distinguish between the TAT and the Rorschach Inkblot Test. (p. 488)

19. Discuss the use of objective tests such as the *MMPI-2*. (p. 489)

20. Discuss the usefulness and accuracy of personality tests. (p. 490)

21. (From the Application section) Describe the role of situational influences in everyday life. (p. 492)

Chapter Overview

Personality is the sum total of the typical ways of acting, thinking, and feeling that makes each person unique. Some psychologists believe that personality can be described in terms of traits. Traits are relatively enduring and consistent ways of behaving. There is now consensus that five traits are useful in describing personality; these are neuroticism, extroversion, openness, agreeableness, and conscientiousness. One influential theory of personality, psychoanalytic theory, was developed in the late nineteenth century by Sigmund Freud. Freud's theory distinguished three levels of conscious awareness—the conscious mind, the preconscious mind, and the unconscious mind. According to Freud, the mind is composed of the following three parts: (1) the id, which operates on the pleasure principle and seeks to obtain immediate pleasure and to avoid pain; (2) the ego, which operates on the reality principle and seeks safe and realistic ways of satisfying the id; and (3) the superego, which opposes the id by imposing moral restrictions and striving for perfection. Freud suggested that when the ego cannot find ways to satisfy the id, it seeks a substitute. The process of substituting a more acceptable goal is called displacement; the displacement of a socially desirable goal is termed sublimation. Another process that allows individuals to operate in society without friction is called identification; we tend to model our actions after individuals who are successful in gaining satisfactions from life.

Freud's theory also distinguishes five stages in the development of personality: the oral stage, the anal stage, the phallic stage, the latency stage, and the genital stage. According to Freud, events that happen as the individual passes through these stages can be critical in the formation of personality.

Alfred Adler and Carl Jung were two associates of Freud. They both developed influential personality theories of their own. Jung differed with Freud over his emphasis on sexual motivation. Jung believed that the unconscious mind contains positive and even spiritual motives. He also felt that we each possess both a personal unconscious and a collective unconscious. Adler felt that the primary struggle in personality development was the effort to overcome feelings of inferiority in social relationships and to develop feelings of superiority. Karen Horney was another influential revisionist of Freudian psychoanalysis. She felt that anxious insecurity, which stems from inadequate childrearing experiences, is the source of all personality conflicts. Horney also rejected Freud's notion of penis envy, claiming that important female issues revolved around the power and privilege of males in society.

Other personality theorists, the social learning theorists, emphasize classical conditioning, operant conditioning, and modeling in the development of personality. Albert Bandura, a prominent social learning theorist, believes that social learning is determined by the actions of behavior on the environment, and vice versa. Bandura also believes that behavior is self-regulated by our internalized cognitive standards for self-reward and limited by our perception of our own self-efficacy. Some psychologists believe that situations determine behavior; this is known as situationism. Social learning theorists have suggested a compromise termed interactionism, which says that behavior is influenced by a combination of personality traits and the situation.

Members of a third group of personality theorists, humanistic theorists, believe that humans possess an inner-directedness that pushes them to grow. To the humanist, reality is subjective. The concept of "self" is central to the personality theory of Carl Rogers and other humanists. Our self-concept is our subjective perception of who we are and what we are like. Rogers distinguished between the self (the person I think I am) and the ideal self (the person I wish I were). Problems result when there are major discrepancies between the self and the ideal self, or when a person's self-concept is not congruent with the way he or she actually acts, thinks, and feels.

Personality assessment is the use of psychological methods to learn about a person's personality. The most widely used method is the interview. Personality is also assessed by observing the person's behavior in a natural or simulated situation. Rating scales are used to help make observational methods more objective. The second most widely used method of personality assessment is the projective test, which psychoanalysts believe reveals the motives and conflicts of the unconscious mind. Objective personality tests, such as the MMPI-2, consist of questions that measure different aspects of personality. Objective personality tests are generally better at assessing personality than projective techniques, but all personality tests are only partly accurate.

Key Terms Exercise

For each of the following exercises, match the key terms on the left with the correct definitions on the right. Page references to the text follow the terms so that you may refer to the text for any items you answer incorrectly or do not understand completely. You may check your responses immediately by referring to the answers that follow each exercise.

Personality/Psychoanalytic Theory (I)

_____ 1. personality (p. 462)
_____ 2. traits (p. 462)
_____ 3. psychoanalytic theory (p. 466)
_____ 4. unconscious mind (p. 468)
_____ 5. repression (p. 468)
_____ 6. id (p. 468)
_____ 7. pleasure principle (p. 468)

a. the theory of personality developed by Sigmund Freud
b. the sum total of ways of acting, thinking, and feeling that make each person unique
c. the part of the mind of which we are never directly aware
d. pushing unpleasant information into unconsciousness
e. the attempt of the id to seek immediate pleasure
f. the inborn part of the unconscious mind
g. enduring patterns of behavior that are consistent across situations

ANSWERS

1. b	5. d
2. g	6. f
3. a	7. e
4. c	

Psychoanalytic Theory (II)

_____ 1. primary process thinking (p. 468)
_____ 2. ego (p. 469)
_____ 3. reality principle (p. 469)
_____ 4. superego (p. 469)
_____ 5. ego ideal (p. 469)
_____ 6. displacement (p. 469)

a. the part of the mind that enforces strict moral restrictions
b. formation by the id of wish-fulfilling mental images
c. substitution of an acceptable goal for an unacceptable goal of the id
d. the ego's attempt to find realistic ways to meet the needs of the id
e. the standard of perfect conduct of the superego
f. the part of the mind that uses the reality principle to satisfy the id

ANSWERS

1. b.	4. a
2. f	5. e
3. d	6. c

Psychoanalytic Theory (III)

_____ 1. sublimation (p. 469)
_____ 2. identification (p. 469)
_____ 3. psychosexual stages (p. 470)
_____ 4. Oedipus complex (p. 471)
_____ 5. Electra complex (p. 471)
_____ 6. feelings of inferiority (p. 473)

a. unconscious childhood conflict for boys
b. unconscious childhood conflict for girls
c. developmental periods in Freud's theory
d. the process of modeling one's actions after others
e. substitution of a socially desirable goal for one that is socially harmful
f. according to Adler, the feelings that result from children being less powerful than adults

ANSWERS

1. e	4. a
2. d	5. b
3. c	6. f

Social Learning Theory

_____ 1. social learning theory (p. 476)
_____ 2. reciprocal determination (p. 476)
_____ 3. self-efficacy (p. 477)
_____ 4. self-regulation (p. 478)
_____ 5. situationism (p. 478)
_____ 6. person X situation interactionism (p. 478)

a. the perception of being capable of achieving one's goals
b. the view that the individual and the social learning environment continually influence each other
c. the view that behavior is influenced by characteristics of both the person and the situation
d. the theory that our personalities are formed through learning from others
e. the process of cognitively reinforcing and punishing ourselves, depending on our personal standards
f. the view that behavior is consistent only if situations remain consistent

ANSWERS

1. d	4. e
2. b	5. f
3. a	6. c

Humanistic Theory

_____ 1. humanistic theory (p. 480)
_____ 2. inner-directedness (p. 480)
_____ 3. subjective reality (p. 480)
_____ 4. self-concept (p. 480)
_____ 5. conditions of worth (p. 481)
_____ 6. symbolization (p. 481)
_____ 7. self-actualization (p. 482)
_____ 8. projective test (p. 488)

a. an internal force that leads people to grow and improve
b. the third force in psychology
c. the human drive to use our potential to the fullest
d. our subjective perceptions of who we are
e. representation of experience, thought, or feelings in mental symbols
f. a test that uses ambiguous stimuli to reveal the client's personality
g. standards that are used by others or ourselves in judging our worth
h. each individual's unique perception of reality

ANSWERS

1. b	5. g
2. a	6. e
3. h	7. c
4. d	8. f

Who Am I?

Match the psychologists on the left with their contributions to the field of psychology on the right. Page references to the text follow the names of the psychologists so that you may refer to the text for further review of these psychologists and their contributions. You may check your responses immediately by referring to the answers that follow each exercise.

_____ 1. Gordon Allport (p. 462)
_____ 2. Sigmund Freud (p. 466)
_____ 3. Carl Jung (p. 472)
_____ 4. Alfred Adler (p. 473)
_____ 5. Karen Horney (p. 474)
_____ 6. Albert Bandura (p. 476)
_____ 7. Carl Rogers (p. 480)
_____ 8. Abraham Maslow (p. 482)

a. The personal unconscious and the collective unconscious are important to my theory.
b. I developed psychoanalytic theory.
c. I am a cognitive behaviorist and a leader in social learning theory.
d. My theory emphasizes overcoming feelings of inferiority, developing social interest, and achieving goals.
e. The concept of "self" is central to my personality theory.
f. I described the process of self-actualization.
g. I believe that personality traits are either cardinal, central, or secondary.
h. It was my belief that anxious insecurity is the source of all personality conflicts.

ANSWERS

1. g	5. h
2. b	6. c
3. a	7. e
4. d	8. f

Review At A Glance
(Answers to this section begin on page 230)

Definition of Personality/Trait Theory: Describing the Consistencies of Personality

Personality is the sum total of all the ways of acting, thinking, and feeling that are ___(1)___ for a person and make that person ___(2)___ from all others.

Psychologists refer to relatively enduring and consistent ways of behaving as ___(3)___. Trait theories of personality are more concerned with ___(4)___ traits than with ___(5)___ their origins.

According to Gordon Allport, the most important traits are those that relate to our ___(6)___. Allport called the traits that dominate a person's life ___(7)___ traits. He felt that few people possess these traits. Allport labeled those traits that influence much of our behavior ___(8)___ traits. The traits that are specific to a situation are ___(9)___ traits.

There is considerable agreement among trait theorists that there are ___(10)___ basic personality traits. Research studies have supported the validity of the ___(11)___ and the neuroticism dimensions.

Psychoanalytic Theory: Sigmund Freud

While working with patients experiencing conversion disorders, Freud became convinced that all such cases were caused by unexpressed ___(12)___ motives.

Freud believed that conscious awareness exists on three levels. The portion of the mind of which an individual is presently aware is the ___(13)___ mind. Memories that are not presently conscious but that can be easily brought into consciousness are found in the ___(14)___ mind. The storehouse for primitive instinctual motives and repressed memories and emotions is the ___(15)___ mind.

Freud also divided the mind in a different, but related, way. He viewed the mind as being composed of the ___(16)___, the ___(17)___, and the ___(18)___. At birth, the mind has only one part, the ___(19)___. The id is composed of two sets of instincts: the ___(20)___ instincts, which Freud termed ___(21)___, and the ___(22)___ instinct. The two most important motives of the life instinct are ___(23)___ and ___(24)___ motives. According to Freud, the id functions entirely at the ___(25)___ level. The id operates according to the ___(26)___ principle and attempts to satisfy its needs by using wish-fulfilling mental images, a process Freud called ___(27)___ _____ thinking. As we grow, we develop a second part of the mind, called the ___(28)___. The ego helps us to deal with the world through the ___(29)___ principle. The ego can be thought of as the ___(30)___ of the personality.

The only part of the mind containing a sense of morality is the ___(31)___. The superego is created mainly by ___(32)___. Parental punishment creates the moral inhibitions called ___(33)___, whereas parental rewards establish a standard of conduct called the ___(34)___ _____.

Sometimes the ego must settle for a substitute for the goals of the id. This process is called ___(35)___. A form of displacement in which a socially desirable goal is substituted for a socially harmful goal is called ___(36)___. The process of thinking, acting, and feeling like individuals who are successful in gaining satisfactions from life is called ___(37)___.

Freud believed that our personalities are formed as we pass through a series of developmental stages from infancy to adulthood. Stressful events experienced during a stage can leave the personality ___(38)___ at that stage. According to Freud, the developmental stages result from a shifting of energy from one ___(39)___ zone to another. Since these stages represent a release of sexual energy, they are called ___(40)___ stages. The first stage, from birth to 1 year, is called the ___(41)___ stage. Fixations here may lead to overeating and drinking, and the person is called an ___(42)___ _____ personality. If oral pleasures are frustrated, the infant may grow to be an ___(43)___ _____ _____ personality.

The second stage of development, from 1 to 3 years, is called the ___(44)___ stage. Fixations at this stage may lead to a personality that is either stingy and compulsive, called ___(45)___ _____, or cruel and disorderly, called ___(46)___ _____.

From ages 3 to 6, children are in the ___(47)___ stage, in which the genitals become the primary source of pleasure. During this stage, boys develop a sexual attraction to their mothers, referred to as the ___(48)___ _____. Boys also develop a fear of their fathers, called ___(49)___ _____. Girls develop desires for their fathers, called the ___(50)_____. The desire of young girls to possess a penis is called ___(51)_____. According to Freud, failure to resolve the phallic stage results in a ___(52)___ personality, characterized by egocentric ___(53)__, impulsiveness, and a lack of genuine feeling for ___(54)___.

From ages 6 to 11, children enter the ___(55)___ stage, during which sexual interest is relatively inactive. From age 11 through adulthood, the individual is in the ___(56)___ stage, in which sexual and romantic interest is directed toward one's peers. Most modern revisions of psychoanalysis agree that Freud overemphasized ___(57)_____ motivation and ___(58)___.

Carl Jung believed that people have a pair of opposite personality traits—a desire to be open and friendly, called ___(59)___, and a desire to be shy and focus attention on ourselves, called ___(60)___. He also felt that the unconscious contained two elements: motives that have been repressed because they are threatening, called the ___(61)___ unconscious, and an unconscious mind with which all humans are born, called the ___(62)_____ unconscious.

According to Alfred Adler, the task of personality development is to overcome feelings of ___(63)___. Later in his career, Adler felt that all humans are born with ___(64)_____ and that people's lives are governed by ___(65)___.

Another influential revisionist of Freudian psychoanalysis is Karen Horney. She believed that anxious ___(66)___, which stems from inadequate ___(67)___ experiences, is the source of all personality conflicts. Horney rejected the importance Freud placed on ___(68)_____.

Social Learning Theory: Albert Bandura

According to social learning theorists, personality is ___(69)___ from other members of society. Albert Bandura is a leading social learning theorist. Although he is a behaviorist, he emphasizes the importance of ___(70)___ in personality and believes that people play an ___(71)___ role in determining their actions. Bandura has observed that the individual and the social learning environment continually influence each other; that is, they are ___(72)_____ _____. According to Bandura, the perception of being able to achieve one's goals is called ___(73)___-_____. Bandura believes that we cognitively reinforce or punish ourselves, depending on whether or not our behavior has met our personal standards; this process is called ___(74)___-_____.

Some psychologists believe that behavior is determined by the situations people find themselves in rather than by the traits inside the person; this approach is called ___(75)___. A compromise view, called ___(76)_____ _____ _____, suggests that behavior is influenced both by the characteristics of the person as well as by the situation. According to Mischel and Shoda, the only way to fully describe personality is by using ___(77)_____ statements. Two important factors in understanding interactionism are: (1) evidence exists that people select situations that are consistent with their ___(78)_____; and (2) according to Bem, some people are influenced more than others by ___(79)___.

Humanistic Theory: Maslow and Rogers

Humanistic psychology is often referred to as the ___(80)___ _____. Humanists believe that all people possess an internal force that leads them to grow and improve. This force is called ___(81)___-_____. To the humanist, reality is ___(82)___.

According to Rogers, our selective perception of who we are is called our ___(83)___-_____. Carl Rogers distinguishes between the person one thinks he is, called the ___(84)___, and the person one wishes to be, called the ___(85)___ _____. Discrepancies between the self and the ideal self can be ___(86)___. An obscure view of ourselves may arise when our self-concept is not ___(87)___ with the way we actually are. According to Rogers, when a person denies feelings that are incongruent with her self-concept, she fails to ___(88)___ her experience. The process of denying awareness to certain feelings begins when parents ___(89)___ some behaviors but ___(90)___ others. This creates standards that Rogers calls ___(91)___ _____ _____. We often deny these feelings that are ___(92)___ with our internalized conditions of worth.

According to Abraham Maslow, the ultimate in completed growth is ___(93)___-_____. Among the characteristics of self-actualized people are the following: they (1) have reached a high level of ___(94)___ development and are usually committed to some ___(95)___ or task; (2) are open and ___(96)___, and have the courage to act on their convictions; they are not particularly interested in fads and ___(97)___; enjoy positive and caring friendships but enjoy privacy and ___(98)___; (3) have an ___(99)___, positive view of life; and (4) find life challenging and fresh. Although many of us may occasionally have a ___(100)___ experience, according to Maslow, these experiences are more common for self-actualizing individuals.

Humanistic psychology, psychoanalysis, and social learning theory all differ in their views of the basic ___(101)___ of human beings and society. Recently, there are signs that the major theories have begun to ___(102)___.

Personality Assessment: Taking a Measure of the Person

Psychologists use personality assessment techniques to develop a picture of their client's personality in a relatively brief amount of time. The most universally used method of personality assessment is the ___(103)___. Although widely used, interviews have limitations; they are inherently ___(104)___, and they are ___(105)___ situations. An alternative to the interview is to watch the person's behavior in a natural or simulated situation; this is called the ___(106)___ method. In an attempt to make observational methods more objective, a variety of ___(107)___ have been developed.

A personality test that uses ambiguous stimuli to reveal the contents of the client's unconscious mind is the ___(108)___ test. The individual is asked to make up a story about ambiguous pictures in the ___(109)___ _____ _____ (TAT); symmetrical inkblots are used in the ___(110)___ _____ _____.

An example of an objective personality test is the ___(111)___ _____ _____ _____ (MMPI-2).

Research with projective tests indicates they are generally not successful in predicting behavior. Although objective personality tests fare somewhat better, ___(112)___ is recommended in interpreting the results of personality tests.

Application of Psychology: Situational Influences on Personality in Everyday Life

Considerable research supports the importance of ___(113)___ in determining human behavior.

Concept Check

Fill in the missing components of the following concept box. The correct answers are located in the "Answers" section at the end of the chapter.

Major Theories of Personality

Theorist	Approach	Basic Components of Theory
Freud	psychoanalytic	emphasis on id, ego, superego; importance of displacement and identification; and five stages of personality development: oral, anal, phallic, latency, and genital
Jung	psychoanalytic	
	psychoanalytic	effort to overcome feelings of inferiority is primary emphasis
Horney		anxious insecurity is the source of all conflicts
Bandura	social learning	
Carl Rogers		importance is placed on self, self-concept, and ideal self
Maslow	humanistic	
	trait theory	cardinal, central, and secondary traits

Extending the Chapter: Psychology, Societal Issues, and Human Diversity

These questions may be assigned to you. Whether or not they are assigned, they are designed to be challenging questions to encourage you to think independently about the material in the chapter. Many of the questions have no right or wrong answers.

I.   From the "Applications of Psychology" section

1.   What are the implications of the power of situational influences in life?

2.   In the debate over traits vs. situationism, which side do you favor? Explain your answer.

II.   Psychology, Societal Issues, and Human Diversity

1.   Describe the challenges faced by psychologists as they integrate sociocultural factors into a general theory of personality.

2.   How would the psychoanalytic explanation for a selfish and aggressive personality differ from the explanation offered by the social learning perspective?

3.   If you were applying for a job and could choose to be evaluated by only one type of personality assessment, which would you choose? Why?

4.   Some people seem to be more prone to be involved in automobile accidents. If psychologists could devise a measure of personality to predict those at greater risk for an accident, should this measure be required of all drivers? Should those people whose score indicates they are at higher risk for accidents be denied licenses? Explain your answer.

5.   What steps should be taken to safeguard the results of personality tests in industrial, educational, and clinical settings? What implications do the use of computers have for the storage and transmission of these data?

Practice Quiz

The practice quiz consists of three sections: 1) Short Answer questions, 2) Multiple-choice questions, and 3) True-False questions. At the end of the chapter you will find suggested answers to the short answer questions, answers and explanation for the multiple-choice questions, and answers to the true-false questions.

Short Answer Questions

1.   List and describe the three parts of the mind as theorized by Freud.

_____

_____

2.   Distinguish between Bandura's concepts of self-efficacy and self-regulation.

_____

_____

_____

3. List and describe three different approaches to the assessment of personality.

_____

_____

_____

Multiple-Choice Questions

1. Which of the following helps define the term *personality?*
   a. characteristics that are typical for a person
   b. characteristics that make a person unique
   c. acting, thinking, and feeling
   d. all of the above
   LO 1

2. Allport calls the traits that influence and organize much of our behavior
   a. cardinal traits.
   b. central traits.
   c. secondary traits.
   d. source traits.
   LO 2

3. Each of the following is considered to be one of the "big five" personality traits *except*
   a. neuroticism.
   b. extraversion.
   c. conscientiousness.
   d. friendliness.
   LO 3

4. In a study conducted by Eysenck, a higher percentage of conditioned eyeblink responses were made by participants who scored high in
   a. extroversion.
   b. introversion.
   c. neuroticism.
   d. agreeableness.
   LO 3

5. According to Freud, primitive instinctual motives and repressed memories are stored in the
   a. conscious mind.
   b. preconscious mind.
   c. unconscious mind.
   d. superego.
   LO 4

6. According to Freud, information that you are not currently aware of that can be easily recalled into awareness resides in which part of the mind?
   a. preconscious
   b. conscious
   c. unconscious
   d. subconscious
   LO 4

7. The executive of the personality, which operates according to the reality principle, is the
   a. id.
   b. ego
   c. superego.
   d. none of the above
   LO 5

8. According to Freud, which part of the mind is dominated by the pleasure principle?
   a. the id
   b. the ego
   c. superego
   d. the superid
   LO 5

9. According to Freud, which part of the mind corresponds roughly to the conscience?
   a. the id
   b. the ego
   c. the superego
   d. the superid
   LO 5

10. All of the following are examples of sublimation *except*
    a. competing in contact sports.
    b. robbing a bank.
    c. painting nude portraits.
    d. competing in business.
    LO 6

11. To prevent itself from being overwhelmed by excessive demands from the id and superego, the ego relies on
    a. the Oedipus complex.
    b. defense mechanisms.
    c. the reality principle.
    d. the pleasure principle.
    LO 6

12. According to Freud, the Oedipus complex and the Electra complex develop during the
    a. oral stage.
    b. anal stage.
    c. phallic stage.
    d. genital stage.
    LO 7

13. According to Freud, lasting relationships revolving around sexual and romantic interests are possible during what stage?
    a. the oral stage
    b. the anal stage
    c. the phallic stage
    d. the genital stage
    LO 7

14. According to Jung, the unconscious mind with which all humans are born is called the
    a. preconscious.
    b. personal conscious.
    c. collective unconscious.
    d. none of the above
    LO 8

15. Most people intuitively understand that incest is wrong, even though they are not told this directly. Jung would explain that the incest taboo is part of the
    a. innate id.
    b. collective unconscious.
    c. collective superego.
    d. Electra complex.
    LO 8

16. According to Adler, to develop a healthy personality it is necessary to learn to express
    a. the social interest.
    b. the selfish interest.
    c. the superego.
    d. sexual and aggressive motives.
    LO 9

17. In Adler's theory of personality, human behavior is regulated by
    a. goals.
    b. feelings.
    c. defense mechanisms.
    d. selfish motives.
    LO 9

18. According to Karen Horney
    a. anxious insecurity is the source of all conflicts.
    b. self-actualization is a basic human motive.
    c. conflict is the inevitable result of the inborn motives of the id.
    d. we each possess both a personal unconscious and a collective unconscious.
    LO 10

19. To the social learning theorist, each of the following processes is important in the development of personality except
    a. classical conditioning.
    b. operant conditioning.
    c. modeling.
    d. feelings of inferiority.
    LO 11

20. According to Bandura, self-efficacy and self-regulation emphasize the importance of what determinant of behavior?
    a. learning
    b. traits
    c. situations
    d. cognitions
    LO 11

21. The mutual interaction between a person's behavior and his or her social learning environment is called
    a. reciprocal determination.
    b. self-efficacy.
    c. self-regulation.
    d. efficient regulation.
    LO 11

22. The view that behavior is influenced by characteristics of both the person and the situation is called
    a. situationism.
    b. interactionism.
    c. the trait approach.
    d. both *a* and *b*.
    LO 12

23. The humanistic view states that
    a. humans possess an inner-directedness.
    b. humans possess an objective view of reality.
    c. people should not frustrate themselves by continually trying to change and improve.
    d. personality is dominated by an active unconscious.
    LO 13

24. Rogers believes that differences between the self and the ideal self
    a. are uncomfortable.
    b. lead to incongruence.
    c. lead to unsymbolized feelings.
    d. all of the above
    LO 14

25. According to Maslow, all of the following are characteristics of a self-actualizing person *except*
    a. a high level of moral development.
    b. a romanticized view of people and life.
    c. a commitment to some cause or task.
    d. openness and honesty.
    LO 15

26. Each of the following is associated with Maslow *except*
    a. self-actualization.
    b. peak experiences.
    c. social learning.
    d. humanistic psychology.
    LO 15

27. Which approach to psychology is referred to as the "third force"?
    a. psychoanalysis
    b. social learning theory
    c. humanistic theory
    d. trait theory
    LO 16

28. Humanistic psychologists believe that people are born _____, whereas social learning theorists believe that people are born _____.
    a. good,;selfish
    b. selfish; good
    c. neutral; good
    d. good; neutral
    LO 16

29. Which of the following is a problem with the use of interviews as a method of personality assessment?
    a. They are subjective.
    b. They are artificial situations.
    c. They may bring out atypical behavior.
    d. All of the above.
    LO 17

30. Which method of personality assessment attempts to delve into unconscious areas?
    a. projective tests
    b. interviews
    c. objective tests
    d. none of the above
    LO 18

31. Which of the following is an example of a projective personality test?
    a. Thematic Apperception Test (TAT)
    b. Minnesota Multiphasic Personalty Inventory (MMPI-2)
    c. Rorschach inkblot test
    d. both *a* and *c*
    LO 18

32. Which of the following characterizes the *MMPI-2?*
    a. It consists of multiple-choice and fill-in questions.
    b. It is designed to reveal unconscious conflicts.
    c. It allows for objective interpretation of the results.
    d. The items are divided into 25 different scales.
    LO 19

33. Which objective personality test can be used to assess depression?
    a. MMPI-2
    b. TAT
    c. interview
    d. observation
    LO 19

34. Which of the following statements is correct?
    a. Projective tests are generally good predictors of behavior.
    b. Psychologists generally agree about the usefulness of personality tests.
    c. Objective personality tests are generally more effective than projective tests in distinguishing among groups with different traits.
    d. Projective tests are generally more effective than objective tests in distinguishing among groups with different traits.
    LO 20

35. Research conducted with participants who found a coin in a phone booth supports the notion that personality is strongly influenced by
    a. human altruism.
    b. situations.
    c. personal traits.
    d. the interaction of situations and personal characteristics.
    LO 21

True-False Questions

_____ 1. Trait theories are useful because they help to explain differences in personality.

_____ 2. The extroversion dimension of the five-factor model of personality has been experimentally validated.

_____ 3. According to Freud, the superego operates according to the pleasure principle.

_____ 4. Freud's theory indicates that all male children struggle with the Oedipus complex.

_____ 5. According to Jung, all humans are born with the collective unconscious.

_____ 6. Bandura believes that cognition plays a very small role in the development of our personality.

_____ 7. Humanistic theory emphasizes inner-directedness and subjective reality.

_____ 8. Maslow suggested that all human beings eventually become fully self-actualized.

_____ 9. Objective tests can provide valuable information about an individual's unconscious activity.

_____ 10. Projective tests are highly successful in predicting behavior.

ANSWERS SECTION

Concept Check

Major Theories of Personality

Theorist	Approach	Basic Components of Theory
Freud	psychoanalytic	emphasis on id, ego, superego; importance of displacement and identification; five stages of personality development are oral, anal, phallic, latency, and genital
Jung	psychoanalytic	emphasis on extroversion/introversion traits, personal unconscious, and collective unconscious
Adler	psychoanalytic	effort to overcome feelings of inferiority is primary emphasis; all humans are born with a social interest
Horney	psychoanalytic	anxious insecurity is the source of all conflicts
Bandura	social learning	personality is learned but reciprocally determined; emphasizes the role of cognition in personality development
Carl Rogers	humanistic	importance is placed on self, self-concept, and ideal self
Maslow	humanistic	self-actualization and peak experiences are primary components
Allport	trait theory	cardinal, central, and secondary traits

Answers to Review At A Glance

1. typical
2. different
3. traits
4. describing
5. explaining
6. values
7. cardinal
8. central
9. secondary
10. five
11. extroversion
12. sexual
13. conscious
14. preconscious
15. unconscious
16. id
17. ego

18. superego
19. id
20. life
21. libido
22. death
23. sexual
24. aggressive
25. unconscious
26. pleasure
27. primary process
28. ego
29. reality
30. executive
31. superego
32. parents
33. conscience
34. ego ideal

35. displacement
36. sublimation
37. identification
38. fixated
39. erogenous
40. psychosexual
41. oral
42. oral receptive
43. oral aggressive
44. anal
45. anal retentive
46. anal expulsive
47. phallic
48. Oedipus complex
49. castration anxiety
50. Electra complex
51. penis envy

52. phallic
53. selfishness
54. others
55. latency
56. genital
57. sexual
58. aggression
59. extroversion
60. introversion
61. personal
62. collective
63. inferiority
64. social interest
65. goals
66. insecurity
67. childrearing
68. penis envy
69. learned
70. cognition
71. active
72. reciprocally determined
73. self-efficacy

74. self-regulation
75. situationism
76. person × situation interactionism
77. if then
78. personal characteristics
79. situations
80. third force
81. inner-directedness
82. subjective
83. self-concept
84. self
85. ideal self
86. uncomfortable
87. congruent
88. symbolize
89. praise
90. punish
91. conditions of worth
92. inconsistent
93. self-actualization
94. moral

95. cause
96. honest
97. fashion
98. independence
99. accurate
100. peak
101. nature
102. merge
103. interview
104. subjective
105. artificial
106. observational
107. rating scales
108. projective
109. Thematic Apperception Test
110. Rorschach Inkblot Test
111. Minnesota Multiphasic Personality Inventory
112. caution
113. situations

Short Answer Questions

1.   **List and describe the three parts of the mind as theorized by Freud.**

According to Freud's theory of personality, the mind is composed of three parts. The id, according to Freud, is the inborn part of the mind. It engages in primary process thinking to satisfy its needs. The id is selfish, and it is dominated by the pleasure principle. The id wants to obtain immediate pleasure and to avoid pain regardless of the effect it has on others. The second part of the mind, the ego, is referred to as the executive of the personality. It operates on the reality principle. It holds the id in check until it finds a safe way to satisfy the demands of the id. The third part of the mind is the superego. The superego enforces moral restrictions as taught by parents and others. The superego opposes the desires of the id.

2.   **Distinguish between Bandura's concepts of self-efficacy and self-regulation.**

According to Bandura, our learned cognitions are the prime determinant of our behavior. When people perceive they are doing what is necessary to achieve their goals (both behaviorally and emotionally) they are demonstrating self-efficacy. We have all learned personal standards of behavior. When we cognitively reward or punish ourselves on the basis of these personal standards, then we are engaging in self-regulation.

3.   **List and describe three different approaches to the assessment of personality.**

One widely used method of assessing personality is the interview. This is a highly subjective method, and the person being interviewed may react to this situation with atypical behavior. Another method involves the use of projective tests, such as the Rorschach Inkblot Test and the TAT. These tests present ambiguous stimuli in an effort to reveal the client's unconscious mind. A third method uses objective personality tests, such as the MMPI-2. Although there are no right answers, the test is an objective test. Answers are compared with the answers of others with known personality characteristics who have taken the test.

Multiple-Choice Answers

1. The answer is *D*. Although it might appear contradictory on the surface, the definition focuses on characteristics that are typical for the person, yet make the individual different from others.

2. The answer is *B*. According to Allport, cardinal traits are those that dominate a person's life. Relatively few people possess cardinal traits. Secondary traits are those that are more specific but less important in an overall view of a person's personality.

3. The answer is *D*. A considerable degree of consensus exists among trait theorists that there are five basic personality traits.

4. The answer is *B*. Eysenck's hypothesis was that introverts have higher levels or cortical activity and that this cortical arousal facilitates classical conditioning.

5. The answer is *C*. According to Freud, the conscious mind contains our present awareness, but is actually just the "tip of the iceberg" of our mind. The preconscious mind, just below the surface, contains memories of which we are not currently conscious, but can easily be brought into our consciousness. The unconscious mind contains information that is not easily brought into consciousness.

6. The answer is *A*. The preconscious mind is the vast storehouse of easily accessible memories. The conscious mind is the portion of the mind of which we are presently aware. The unconscious mind is the storehouse of primitive instinctual motives and repressed memories.

7. The answer is *B*. According to Freud, the id is composed primarily of life instincts and death instincts. Life instincts consist largely of sexual and aggressive urges. The ego attempts to find realistic ways of satisfying the id's urges. The superego, the moral part of the mind, strives to attain a goal of perfection.

8. The answer is *A*. According to Freud, the id is the "selfish beast" of the mind, seeking immediate gratification and the avoidance of pain at any cost.

9. The answer is C. The superego develops as restrictions are placed on the actions of the id and ego, and punishment by parents helps to establish the conscience.

10. The answer is *B*. Sublimation is a form of displacement in which a socially desirable goal is substituted for a socially harmful goal.

11. The answer is *B*. An example of such a defense mechanism is displacement, the process of substituting a more acceptable goal.

12. The answer is *C*. According to Freud, the intense unconscious conflicts begin in the phallic stage, as the child feels an intense love for the opposite-sex parent.

13. The answer is D. According to Freud, mature love becomes possible after one's parents have been successfully ruled out as sex objects. Sublimation remains important as sexual and aggressive id motives are transformed into energy for marriage, occupations, and raising children.

14. The answer is C. According to Jung, the personal unconscious contains threatening motives, conflicts, and information that have been repressed, whereas the collective unconscious is the unconscious mind with which all humans are born.

15. The answer is B. According to Jung, the collective unconscious is the unconscious mind with which all humans are born.

16. The answer is *A*. According to Adler, the social interest is an inborn motive to establish loving, helpful relationships with other people.

17. The answer is *A*. Adler believed that in addition to the social interest, peoples' lives are motivated by their goals. These goals may or may not be realistic, but they nonetheless regulate our actions.

18. The answer is *A*. According to Horney, if parents are indifferent, harsh, or overprotective, the child will lose confidence in parental love and become anxiously insecure.

19 The answer is *D*. Social learning theorists hold that our personalities are formed primarily through interactions with other members of society. Thus, basic learning concepts, such as classical and operant conditioning and modeling, are the important forces in shaping personality.

20. The answer is *D*. According to Bandura, important determinants of personality are the cognitions both about ourselves and our relationships with others.

21. The answer is *A*. According to Bandura, reciprocal determination implies that we play an active role in our own lives.

22. The answer is *B*. As a counterpoint to the trait approach offered by Allport, situationism suggests behavior is consistent only as long as situations (especially those regarding other people) remain consistent. Interactionism represents a compromise view between the trait and situationism approaches.

23. The answer is *A*. Humanistic psychology, sometimes called the third force in psychology (the first two are psychoanalysis and behaviorism), suggests humans have the freedom to make choices. Inner-directedness is an internal force that pushes people to grow and to improve.

24. The answer is *D*. According to Rogers, the self is the person you believe yourself to be, whereas the ideal self is the person you wish to be. Rogers' theory suggests that slight differences between the self and ideal self are okay, although major discrepancies can lead to difficulties.

25. The answer is *B*. According to Maslow, self-actualizing people have an accurate rather than a romanticized view of life.

26. The answer is *C*. Maslow was a humanistic psychologist who emphasized the inner potential to grow and to use our potential to the fullest. The ultimate in completed growth is called self-actualization. Peak experiences are intensely moving, pleasurable experiences in which we feel a unity with the world. According to Maslow, self-actualized people often have peak experiences.

27. The answer is *C*. Humanistic theory burst on the psychological scene relatively late in psychology's history in the 1950s, after psychoanalysis and behaviorism were already established forces.

28. The answer is *D*. Humanistic psychologists believe that the inner-directedness with which we are born is basically a positive force. Social learning theorists, however, judge our slate to be clean (neutral) at birth; we can learn to be good or bad.

29. The answer is *D*. The interview is the most universally used, yet one of the most limited, methods for obtaining information about personality.

30. The answer is *A*. Projective tests ask the individual to interpret ambiguous stimuli. They assume the individual will project his or her unconscious needs into the interpretation of the stimuli.

31. The answer is *D*. Projective personality tests use ambiguous stimuli in an effort to get the client to project his or her unconscious mind. The *TAT* asks the client to make up a story about ambiguous pictures. The *Rorschach Inkblot Test* presents the client with a series of symmetrical inkblots. The *MMPI-2* is an example of an objective test.

32. The answer is *C*. The *MMPI-2* is an objective test—no effort is made by the test to consider what the respondent meant by each answer. Items on the test are presented as true–false questions and are divided into 10 scales, each measuring a different aspect of personality.

33. The answer is *A*. The only objective test listed among the choices is the *MMPI-2*.

34. The answer is *C*. Research suggests that projective tests are generally not successful in predicting behavior. The results suggest caution in the interpretation of personality tests.

35. The answer is *D*. The research cited in the Application section strongly supports the influence of person × situational factors in determining personality.

Answers to True-False Questions

1. F   6. F

2. T   7. T

3. F   8. F

4. T   9. F

5. T   10. F

Part VI   Health and Adjustment

Chapter 13   Stress and Health

Learning Objectives

1.   Define stress, and list its sources. (p. 500)

2.   Distinguish among the following types of conflict: approach-approach, avoidance-avoidance, approach-avoidance, and multiple approach avoidance. (p. 500)

3.   Discuss the relationship between life events and stress. (p. 503)

4.   Discuss our reactions to stress, and list and describe the stages of Selye's general adaptation syndrome; describe both healthy and unhealthy aspects of the general adaptation syndrome. (p. 506)

5.   Explain the relationship between stress, depression, and health. (p. 510)

6.   List and describe factors that influence reactions to stress. (p. 512)

7.   Identify the characteristics of the Type A personality, and describe the relationship between Type A personality and heart disease. (p. 515)

8.   Discuss the results of research regarding gender and ethnicity variables in our reactions to stress. (p. 516)

9.   List and describe three effective methods of coping with stress. (p. 519)

10. List and describe four ineffective methods of coping with stress. (p. 520)

11. Distinguish among the major defense mechanisms. (p. 521)

12. Describe how progressive relaxation training is used to treat a variety of health problems. (p. 523)

13. Discuss the ways in which improved eating habits, aerobic exercise, and medical compliance affect one's health. (p. 524)

14. Describe the role of safety management in promoting health. (p. 526)

15. Describe the relationship between health practices and mortality and discuss Rozein's concept of real age. (p. 529)

16. (From the Application section) Discuss the role health psychology can play in the prevention and management of AIDS. (p. 533)

Chapter Overview

Health psychology is a relatively new field in psychology; health psychologists attempt to prevent health problems by helping individuals cope with stress and by helping to promote healthy lifestyles. Stress is any event that strains or exceeds an individual's capacity to cope. Among the major sources of stress in our lives are frustration, the inability to satisfy a motive, and conflict, the result of two or more incompatible motives. Four types of conflict are (1) approach-approach conflict, (2) avoidance-avoidance conflict, (3) approach-avoidance conflict, and (4) multiple approach avoidance conflict. Pressure, an additional source of stress, arises from the threat of negative events. Another source of stress comes from the positive and the negative changes that occur in our lives. There is also growing evidence that environmental stresses, such as heat, cold, and air pollution, can be stressful. Reactions to stress are very similar whether the stress is physical or psychological. Selye has identified a consistent pattern of bodily responses to stress called the general adaptation syndrome. This syndrome consists of three stages: the alarm stage, the resistance stage, and the exhaustion stage. Stress affects our emotions, our immune system, our motivations, and our cognition.

Events are generally less stressful when we have had some prior experience with them, when they are predictable, when we have some control over them, and when we receive social support. The characteristics of individuals also affect their reactions to stress. Cognitive factors are important in our reaction to stress. Sensitizers and repressors react differently to stress.

Much research has been conducted on the Type A personality and its link to heart disease. Hostility seems to be the dangerous component of Type A behavior.

Our efforts to cope with stress can be either effective or ineffective. Effective methods of coping with stress include removing the source of stress, cognitive coping, and managing our reactions to stress. Ineffective coping strategies include withdrawal, aggression, self-medication, and the use of defense mechanisms.

A major goal of health psychology is to prevent health problems. Relaxation training is one technique used to achieve this goal. Health psychologists also seek to reduce health risks by helping individuals exercise properly, eat a healthy diet, and properly follow their medical treatments.

Some health psychologists seek to treat health problems. Psychologists have become involved with the AIDS epidemic through efforts to understand and control behavioral aspects of the transmission of AIDS and through efforts to slow the progress of the disease in those who are infected.

Key Terms Exercise

For each of the following exercises, match the key terms on the left with the correct definitions on the right. Page references to the text follow the terms so that you may refer to the text for any items you answer incorrectly or do not understand completely. You may check your responses immediately by referring to the answers that follow each exercise.

Stress: Challenges to Coping (I)

_____ 1. health psychology (p. 500)
_____ 2. stress (p. 500)
_____ 3. frustration (p. 500)
_____ 4. conflict (p. 500)

a.   any event that strains or exceeds an individual's ability to cope

b.   occurs when two or more motives cannot be satisfied because they interfere with each other

c.   the field within psychology that seeks to promote healthy lifestyles

d.   occurs when we are unable to satisfy a motive

ANSWERS
1. c   3. d
2. a   4. b

Stress: Challenges to Coping (II)

_____ 1. approach-approach conflict (p. 500)
_____ 2. avoidance-avoidance conflict (p. 501)
_____ 3. approach-avoidance conflict (p. 501)
_____ 4. multiple approach avoidance conflict (p. 502)
_____ 5. pressure (p. 503)
_____ 6. life events (p. 503)
_____ 7. general adaptation syndrome (GAS) (p. 507)

a.   when the individual must choose between two equally negative outcomes

b.   the changes in our lives that require readjustment and coping

c.   when the individual must choose between several alternatives all of which contain both positive and negative consequences

d.   conflict in which achieving a positive goal will produce a negative outcome as well

e.   when the individual must choose between two equally positive goals

f.   a pattern of responses used by the body to ward off stress

g.   the stress that arises from the threat of negative events

ANSWERS
1. e   5. g
2. a   6. b
3. d   7. f
4. c

_____ 1. social support (p. 513)
_____ 2. person variables (p. 515)
_____ 3. Type A personality (p. 515)
_____ 4. coping (p. 519)
_____ 5. defense mechanisms (p. 521)
_____ 6. progressive relaxation training (p. 523)

a. characteristics of a person that are relatively enduring
b. having somebody with whom we can talk, and from whom we can receive advice and reassurance
c. a personality characterized by intense competitiveness, hostility, and a sense of time urgency
d. a method of learning to deeply relax the muscles of the body
e. according to Freud, the ego's effort to discharge tension
f. efforts to deal with the source of stress or to control reactions to stress

ANSWERS
1. b   4. f
2. a   5. e
3. c   6. d

Review At A Glance
(Answers to this section are found on page 249.)

Stress: Challenges to Coping

The field that has emerged within psychology that seeks to promote healthy lifestyles is called ____(1)_____.

Any event that strains or exceeds an individual's capacity to cope is called ____(2)____. One major source of stress occurs when we are not able to satisfy a motive; this is called ____(3)____. Another source of stress occurs when two motives cannot be satisfied because they interfere with one another; this is referred to as ____(4)____. There are four major types of conflict: (1) when the individual must choose between two positive goals of approximately equal value, this is a(n) ____(5)____-_____ conflict; (2) when we must choose between two or more negative outcomes, this is referred to as a(n) ____(6)____-_____ conflict; (3) when obtaining a positive goal necessitates a negative outcome, this is called a(n) ____(7)____-_____ conflict; (4) when an individual must choose between alternatives that contain both positive and negative consequences, this is termed a(n) ____(8)____ _____-_____ conflict.

A third source of stress arises from the threat of negative events; this is called ____(9)____. Another type of stress comes from changes in our lives, both positive and negative; these are referred to as ____(10)_____. Negative life events such as the death of a family member, ____(11)____ disasters, witnessing violence, or being a victim of assault or terrorism are all important sources of ____(12)____. Lazarus has found that daily ____(13)____ of life can be sources of stress. Even ____(14)____ life events, such as marriage and job promotions can be sources of stress. Holmes and Rahe developed a scale that measures the amount of stress from life events in terms of ____(15)_____ _____. They found that Navy personnel who had experienced high levels of stress during the previous year were more likely to develop ____(16)____ problems. The scale, however, was developed using ____(17)_____ participants and may not apply equally well to ___(18)___. There is growing evidence that air temperature, air pollution, and other aspects of the ___(19)___ can be sources of stress.

Our reactions to stress are influenced by the following recent findings: (1) stress produces both ___(20)___ and ___(21)___ reactions; and (2) our reactions to stress are very similar whether the stress is ___(22)___ or ___(23)___.

Hans Selye has identified a pattern of bodily responses to stress called the ___(24)___ _____ _____. This syndrome consists of three stages: (1) the body begins to mobilize its resources in the ___(25)___ _____ stage, sometimes referred to as the ___(26)___-or-_____ reaction; (2) the body's resources are fully mobilized in the ___(27)___ stage; and (3) the individual's resources are depleted, and resistance to stress is lowered in the (28)___ stage. Although the GAS is helpful in dealing with emergencies and diseases, prolonged stress can lead to dangerous changes in the ___(29)___ system. Although stress can harm the functioning of the immune system, in some cases ___(30)___ _____ can restore immune system functioning. Many studies support the link between (31)___, impaired ___(32)___ system functioning, and poorer health.

The psychological reactions to stress include changes in emotions, ___(33)___, and cognitions.

Factors that Influence Reactions to Stress

Stress reactions are generally less severe when the individual has had some ___(34)___ _____ with the stress. The impact of stress is also affected by the ___(35)___ and ___(36)___ levels of those experiencing stress. Also, events are generally less stressful when they are ___(37)___, when we perceive that we have some degree of ___(38)___ over the stress, and when we have ___(39)___ _____ from friends and family members. One of the important benefits of social support appears to be having someone in whom to ___(40)___; social support can also help us to make ___(41)___ decisions. Personal characteristics, referred to as person ___(42)___, are also important in determining our responses to stress.

Individuals also differ in the ways they ___(43)___ about stressful events. The person with a Type A personality shows many of the following characteristics: highly ___(44)___, works ___(45)___, workaholic, speaks ___(46)___, perfectionistic and ___(47)___, and hostile or ___(48)___. An important Type A characteristic appears to be a particular kind of ___(49)___; individuals who react to frustration with ___(50)___ or ___(51)___ aggression seem to be at slightly higher risk for coronary heart disease. Type A behavior appears to be indirectly linked to heart disease through two major factors: high ___(52)___ _____ and ___(53)___.

There appear to be gender differences in reactions to stress; on average, ___(54)___ react with more distress than ___(55)___ to the same stressors. Research also suggests ___(56)___ provides more health benefits to men than to women. According to Taylor, women are more likely than men to react to stress with a ___(57)___-_-_ response. Members of minority race ethnic groups experience ___(58)___ stress than members of the majority culture.

Coping with Stress

Effective methods of coping with stress include removing the ___(59)___ of stress, ___(60)___ coping, and managing our ___(61)___ to stress. Psychological counseling involving all three methods has been successful in modifying ___(62)___ behavior. Ineffective coping strategies include ___(63)___, aggression, self-___(64)___ and the use of ___(65)___. According to Freud, the major defense mechanisms include (1) directing aggressive or sexual feelings toward someone safe, called ___(66)___, (2) converting impulses into sexually approved activities, called ___(67)___; (3) viewing one's own unacceptable desires as the desires of others, termed ___(68)___; (4) unconsciously transforming desires into the opposite desires, called ___(69)___; (5) returning to an infantile pattern of behavior, termed ___(70)___; (6) explaining away stressful events, called ___(71)___; (7) keeping stressful, unacceptable desires out of consciousness, called ___(72)___; (8) blocking from conscious awareness any information that is threatening, called ___(73)___; and (9) reducing the emotional nature of threatening events to cold logic, called ___(74)___.

Changing Health-Related Behavior Patterns

A major goal of health psychology is to ___(75)___ health problems by helping individuals modify behaviors that create health risks. One example involves teaching individuals to ___(76)___. Individuals are taught to deeply relax their large body muscles in a technique called ___(77)___ training. This technique has been found to be effective in treating ___(78)___, both tension and ___(79)___ headaches, asthma, and high blood pressure.

It is increasingly clear that diet plays an important role in our health, but most Americans do not eat a healthy diet. Although part of the reason is ___(80)___, psychologists have sometimes found difficulty in getting people to change their diets. Likewise, although the health benefits of regular exercise are well established, the majority of Americans do not get regular ___(81)___ exercise. Research suggests that the following factors can help individuals adhere to a regular exercise program; social ___(82)___, setting ___(83)___, finding an enjoyable type of exercise, and avoiding excessively ___(84)___ exercise. Other health psychologists help implement programs to help patients comply with their ___(85)___. Psychologists have developed and studied methods of reducing injuries and accidents, particularly at work and in ___(86)___.

Summing Up: How Beneficial Could Health Psychology Be?

In the future, health psychology may play an important role in fighting ___(87)___ disease, cancer, and ___(88)___. An important issue for the field of health psychology is this: How much impact can ___(89)___ factors have on our health? Research conducted on adults in Alameda County suggests that changes in lifestyle can produce dramatic improvements in ___(90)___ and ___(91)___. Rozein has used research data to devise a method of calculating a person's ___(92)___. Psychologists can help moderate health care costs by helping to ___(93)___ serious health problems and by providing effective psychological services.

Application of Psychology: The Prevention and Treatment of AIDS

AIDS is caused by the human ____(94)_____ virus (HIV). HIV infection leads to the destruction of immune cells called ____(95)___, thus rendering useless the important ____(96)____ of the immune system. The HIV virus is spread through ____(97)_____. The most common means of transmission is through ____(98)_____. Other modes of transmission include ____(99)____ drug use and transmission from an infected mother to her infant during birth. AIDS is much more common in some ____(100)____ groups. There is virtually no chance of acquiring AIDS if a person is not sexually active or is involved in a ____(101)____ sexual relationship with a partner who is not infected with HIV and does not use intravenous drugs. A study conducted by Kelly demonstrates the effectiveness of ____(102)____ for individuals engaging in high-risk sexual behaviors. Some research supports the benefits of (103)____exercise and stress-reduction therapy on the immune system.

Concept Checks

Fill in the missing components of the following concept boxes. The correct answers are located in the "Answers" section at the end of the chapter.

Sources of Stress

Name	Description
	inability to satisfy a motive
conflict	
	the threat of negative events
life events	

Stages in Selye's General Adaptation Syndrome

Stage	Description
alarm reaction	
resistance stage	
exhaustion stage	

Factors that Influence Reactions to Stress

Factor	Description
prior experience	
developmental factors	
predictability and control	
social support	
person variables	

Extending the Chapter: Psychology, Societal Issues, and Human Diversity

These questions may be assigned to you. Whether or not they are assigned, they are designed to be challenging questions to encourage you to think independently about the material in the chapter. Many of the questions have no right or wrong answers.

I.   From the "Application of Psychology" section

1.   Discuss the efforts of psychologists to aid in the prevention of AIDS.

2.   Describe the results of research by psychologists in helping HIV patients to better manage their disease.

II.   Psychology, Societal Issues, and Human Diversity

1.   Do you believe that members of our society experience more stress now than previous generations? Explain your answer.

2.   Has the rapid advancement of technology created new stressors for members of our society? Explain your answer.

3.   Given the fact that certain widely available foods are likely to contribute to heart disease, cancer, and other diseases, should these foods be more closely regulated? If known carcinogens are banned from public consumption, why should artery-clogging hamburgers be allowed? Where should our society draw the line on keeping its members healthy (and who should draw the line)?

4.   (From the Human Diversity section) Discuss health psychology challenges that are unique to women.

Practice Quiz

The practice quiz consists of three sections: 1) Short Answer questions, 2) Multiple-choice questions, and 3) True-False questions. At the end of the chapter you will find suggested answers to the short answer questions, answers and explanations for the multiple-choice questions, and answers to the true-false questions.

Short Answer Questions

1. List and explain the four major types of conflicts discussed in the text.

_____

_____

_____

2. Describe both effective and ineffective methods of coping with stress.

_____

_____

_____

3. Discuss the results of research on life events as a source of stress.

_____

_____

_____

Multiple-Choice Questions

1. A health psychologist would agree with all of the following *except*
   a. The functioning of the body is linked to psychological factors.
   b. Health psychologists seek to promote healthy lifestyles.
   c. Stress is less of a factor in health psychology than it was a few years ago.
   d. Our patterns of behavior have direct impact on our health.
   LO 1

2. Stress has been linked to
   a. heart disease.
   b. strokes.
   c. decreased immunity to infections.
   d. all of the above
   LO 1

3. A source of stress characterized by the inability to satisfy a motive is called
   a. conflict.
   b. life events.
   c. frustration.
   d. pressure.
   LO 1

4. Conflicts that require choosing the lesser of two evils are
   a. approach-approach conflicts.
   b. avoidance-avoidance conflicts.
   c. approach-avoidance conflicts.
   d. double-approach avoidance conflicts.
   LO 2

5. As Jennifer approaches the end of her senior year in college, she is excited about the prospects of graduating but scared about being on her own. Jennifer is experiencing
   a. an approach-avoidance conflict.
   b. an approach-approach conflict.
   c. an avoidance-avoidance conflict.
   d. the exhaustion stage of the general adaptation syndrome.
   LO 2

6. The Holmes and Rahe Social Readjustment Rating Scale explores the relationship between stressful life events and
   a. mental illness.
   b. physical illness.
   c. daily hassles.
   d. success in daily living.
   LO 3

7. In a study by Lazarus, participants recorded major life events, daily hassles, and daily positive events for a year. What was found to be the best predictor of both health and psychological well-being?
   a. daily hassles
   b. positive events
   c. major life events
   d. number of conflicts
   LO 3

8. In which stage of the general adaptation syndrome is resistance to stress lowered?
   a. the resistance stage
   b. the exhaustion stage
   c. the alarm stage
   d. the defensive stage
   LO 4

9. In which stage of the GAS are the body's resources fully mobilized and resistant to stress?
   a. alarm reaction
   b. resistance stage
   c. exhaustion stage
   d. any of the above
   LO 4

10. Research suggests that immune system functioning can be affected by
    a. stress.
    b. stress management.
    c. depression.
    d. all of the above.
    LO 5

11. Which of the following factors is known to depress immune system functioning?
    a. heavy alcohol consumption
    b. stress
    c. depression
    d. all of the above
    LO 5

12. In general, stress events are less stressful when they are
    a. predictable.
    b. unpredictable.
    c. controllable.
    d. both *a* and *c*.
    LO 6

13. With repeated exposures to stressful situations, a person's general stress level
    a. increases.
    b. disappears.
    c. decreases.
    d. remains constant.
    LO 6

14. Research on sharing negative feelings with others (getting it off your chest) found that participants
    a. had elevated blood pressure immediately after venting their feelings.
    b. reported feeling better immediately after venting their feelings.
    c. were less ill and visited the health center less often during the following six months.
    d. both *a* and *c*
    LO 6

15. Each of the following is true of social support *except*
    a. Individuals with social support react to stress with less depression and anxiety.
    b. The ability to confide in others is an important benefit of social support.
    c. There is little proven health benefit in sharing negative feelings with others.
    d. Social support can help us when we have to make stressful decisions.
    LO 6

16. According to the text, college students who procrastinate tend to experience
    a. lower levels of stress early in the semester.
    b. higher levels of stress early in the semester.
    c. lower levels of stress later in the semester.
    d. both *a* and *c*.
    LO 6

17. Which of the following components of Type A behavior has a strong negative effect on cardiac functioning?
    a. hostile/verbally aggressive
    b. hostile/suspicious
    c. highly competitive
    d. perfectionistic
    LO 7

18. Research on Type A behavior suggests that the link to heart disease may stem from
    a. high blood pressure.
    b. high cholesterol.
    c. poor dietary habits.
    d. both *a* and *b*.
    LO 7

19. Members of minority race-ethnic groups are likely to experience greater stress than members of the majority culture because
    a. they tend to have fewer advantages to shield them from stress.
    b. they experience stressful interactions with members of the majority culture.
    c. the acculturation of the children of immigrants into the new culture is stressful.
    d. all of the above
    LO 8

20. According to Taylor, those most likely to respond to stress with a tend-and-befriend response are
    a. children.
    b. clinical psychologists.
    c. men.
    d. women.
    LO 8

21. After being promoted to department head, Bill found the job to be uncomfortable and highly stressful. Ultimately, Bill resigned from the position and returned to his former job, where he reported being much happier. Which method of coping with stress did Bill use?
    a. managing stress reactions, an effective coping method
    b. withdrawal, an ineffective coping method
    c. removing stress, an effective coping method
    d. excessive use of defense mechanisms, an ineffective coping method
    LO 9

22. Each of the following is an effective method of coping with stress *except*
    a. removing stress.
    b. cognitive coping.
    c. defense mechanisms.
    d. managing stress reactions.
    LO 9

23. Jeff used a coping strategy that was ineffective because it distorted reality. What kind of strategy did he use?
    a. cognitive coping
    b. defense mechanism
    c. sensitization
    d. stress removal
    LO 10

24. Each of the following is considered to be an ineffective method of coping with stress *except*
    a. withdrawal.
    b. aggression.
    c. use of defense mechanisms.
    d. cognitive coping.
    LO 10

25. The process of blocking out of consciousness any upsetting thoughts is the defense mechanism called
    a. projection.
    b. reaction formation.
    c. denial.
    d. intellectualization.
    LO 11

26. When Ken called Barbie to ask her for a date, Barbie said, "I'm sorry, but I think I'm busy for the rest of my life!" Ken has decided that he is really relieved, because Barbie has lots of faults anyway. Which defense mechanism is he using?
    a. displacement
    b. repression
    c. rationalization
    d. suppression
    LO 11

27. Teaching a person to alternately tense the major muscles and then release that tension is used in
    a. progressive relaxation.
    b. aerobic exercise.
    c. behavioral inhibition.
    d. aversion therapy.
    LO 12

28. Which of the following has been successfully treated with progressive relaxation?
    a. insomnia
    b. tension and migraine headaches
    c. high blood pressure
    d. all of the above
    LO 12

29. Research suggests that when people are presented with accurate information concerning proper eating habits
    a. most people permanently change their eating habits.
    b. many people change their eating habits only briefly.
    c. few people change their eating habits.
    d. none of the above
    LO 13

30. According to psychologists, which of the following would be good advice for keeping a commitment to an exercise program?
    a. social support
    b. setting clear personal goals
    c. avoiding excessively strenuous exercise
    d. all of the above
    LO 13

31. Which of the following has (have) proven effective in increasing seat belt use?
    a. reminder signs
    b. signing pledge cards
    c. classroom instruction
    d. both *a* and *b*
    LO 14

32. In which of the following ways can psychologists help reduce health care costs?
    a. by helping to prevent serious problems
    b. by reducing recurrences of certain medical problems
    c. by increased use of clinical psychologists
    d. all of the above
    LO 15

33. The study of health practices in Alameda County suggested
    a. health psychologists can be effective at getting people to increase the number of positive health practices.
    b. a strong relationship between health practices and mortality.
    c. that stress and life-style practices can minimize the impact of infectious diseases.
    d. that sleeping and exercise were not strongly related to improving health.
    LO 15

34. AIDS impairs the body's immune system by destroying or disabling the immune cells called
    a. T-4 helper cells.
    b. B-cells.
    c. DNA.
    d. both *a* and *b*.
       LO 16

35. Health psychologists can lessen the negative impact of the AIDS epidemic by
    a. helping individuals change their high-risk behaviors.
    b. helping to cure those with the HIV infection by counseling.
    c. helping individuals with HIV to confront the reality of their disease.
    d. both *a* and *c*.
       LO 16

True-False Questions

_____ 1. The first stage of the general adaptation syndrome is called the resistance stage.

_____ 2. Stress reactions are generally more severe when the individual has prior experience with the stress.

_____ 3. According to Taylor, males are more likely than females to react to stress with the trend-and-befriend response.

_____ 4. The Type A personality dimension that increases one's risk for heart disease involves verbal and/or physical aggression.

_____ 5. According to the text, using defense mechanisms is an effective way to cope with stress.

_____ 6. Throwing temper tantrums or giving a friend the silent treatment are examples of the defense mechanism called regression.

_____ 7. Progressive relaxation training focuses primarily on the small muscle groups of the body.

_____ 8. The Alameda County study found a strong relationship between health practices and mortality.

_____ 9. According to Rozein, brushing and flossing one's teeth daily can improve longevity.

_____ 10. HIV attacks lymphocytes and T-4 Helper cells.

ANSWERS SECTION

Sources of Stress

Name	Description
frustration	inability to satisfy a motive
conflict	occurs when two motives cannot be satisfied because they interfere with each other
pressure	the threat of negative events
life events	negative life events, small daily hassles, and even positive life events

Stages in Selye's General Adaptation Syndrome

Stage	Description
alarm reaction	the body mobilizes its stored resources; sympathetic arousal occurs as the fight-or-flight reaction occurs
resistance stage	the body's resources are fully mobilized, and resistance to stress is high; any additional stress might overwhelm the body
exhaustion stage	individual's resources are exhausted, and resistance to stress is lowered

Factors that Influence Reactions to Stress

Factor	Description
prior experience	stress reactions are generally less severe when the individual has some prior experience with the stress
developmental factors	the impact of stress is different at different ages and levels of development
predictability and control	generally, events are less stressful when they are predictable and when the individual can exert some control over the stress
social support	the effects of stress are lessened when the individual has good quality social support
person variables	cognitive factors, emotional factors, and personality characteristics (Type A personality)

Answers to Review At A Glance

1. health psychology
2. stress
3. frustration
4. conflict
5. approach-approach
6. avoidance-avoidance
7. approach-avoidance
8. multiple approach avoidance
9. pressure
10. life events
11. natural
12. stress
13. hassles
14. positive
15. life change units
16. medical
17. male
18. women
19. environment
20. psychological
21. physiological
22. physical
23. psychological
24. general adaptation syndrome
25. alarm reaction
26. fight/flight
27. resistance
28. exhaustion
29. cardiac
30. stress management
31. depression
32. immune
33. motivations
34. prior experience

35. ages
36. developmental
37. predictable
38. control
39. social support
40. confide
41. stressful
42. variables
43. think
44. competitive
45. hurriedly
46. loudly
47. demanding
48. aggressive
49. hostility
50. verbal
51. physical
52. blood pressure
53. cholesterol
54. women
55. men
56. marriage
57. tend-and-befriend
58. more
59. source
60. cognitive
61. reactions
62. Type A
63. withdrawal
64. medication
65. defense mechanisms
66. displacement
67. sublimation
68. projection
69. reaction formation
70. regression

71. rationalization
72. repression
73. denial
74. intellectualization
75. prevent
76. relax
77. progressive relaxation
78. insomnia
79. migraine
80. ignorance
81. aerobic
82. support
83. personal goals
84. strenuous
85. doctor's orders
86. automobiles
87. heart
88. AIDS
89. psychological
90. health
91. longevity
92. real age
93. prevent
94. immune deficiency
95. lymphocytes
96. B-cells
97. bodily fluids
98. sexual intercourse
99. intravenous
100. sociocultural
101. monogamous
102. counseling
103. aerobic

Sample Answers for Short Answer Questions

1. **List and explain the four major types of conflicts discussed in the text.**

In approach-approach conflicts, the person must choose between two positive goals, such as two equally attractive job offers. In avoidance-avoidance conflicts, the individual must choose between two negative outcomes, such as an undesirable job and unemployment. Approach-avoidance conflicts cause stress because the same goal has both attractive and unattractive components. Finally, multiple approach avoidance conflicts involve several alternatives, each of which contains both positive and negative components.

2. **Describe both effective and ineffective methods of coping with stress.**

According to the text, effective methods of coping with stress involve removing the source of stress (example: quit a highly stressful job), cognitive coping (change the way you think about the stresses in your life), and managing your reactions to stress (for example, learning to relax). Ineffective methods of coping with stress include withdrawal, aggression, self-medicating, and using defense mechanisms to help discharge tension. While these ineffective methods may provide some comfort in the short run, they can lead to further problems in the long run.

3. **Discuss the results of research on life events as a source of stress.**

Life events create stress because they represent change and require adjustment and coping. Negative life events, such as the death of a family member or being the victim of an assault, lead to anxiety and depression for extended periods of time beyond the event. The daily hassles of life have also been studied, and have been found to be related to health and psychological well-being. Even positive life events can be stressful under some circumstances.

Multiple-Choice Answers

1. The answer is *C*. According to the text, stress is perhaps the key factor that must be understood if psychology is to improve our health and happiness.
2. The answer is *D*. Research has implicated stress in a wide variety of diseases and maladies in addition to those listed in the question.
3. The answer is *C*. Frustration refers to the inability to satisfy a motive, whereas conflict refers to a situation in which motives cannot be satisfied because they interfere with one another.
4. The answer is *B*. Situations in which we are faced with having to choose between two or more negative outcomes are called avoidance-avoidance conflicts.
5. The answer is *A*. Approach-approach conflict refers to situations in which the individual must choose between two positive goals; in avoidance-avoidance conflict, the individual must choose between two negative outcomes.
6. The answer is *B*. The scale was originally presented to Navy personnel. Holmes and Rahe found that those who reported higher levels of life stress were more likely to develop medical problems than participants reporting lower levels of life stress.
7. The answer is *A*. According to the text, daily hassles may be both a *cause* and a *result* of stress.
8. The answer is *B*. According to Selye, the body's resources begin to be mobilized in the stage called the alarm reaction. During the second stage, called the resistance stage, the body's resources are fully mobilized. In the final stage, the exhaustion stage, the individual's resources have become exhausted; thus, resistance to stress is lowered.
9. The answer is *B*. The resistance stage, the second in the GAS, fully mobilizes the body's resources but leaves it vulnerable to further stress.
10. The answer is *D*. The negative impact of stress on the immune system is most striking in those who become severely depressed under stress.
11. The answer is *D*. Although these factors can have an adverse impact on immune system functioning, stress management can actually restore immune system functioning in some cases.
12. The answer is *D*. Stressful events are less stressful both when they are predictable *and* when the individual can exert some control over the stress.
13. The answer is *C*. According to the text, prior exposure to stress may inoculate us to that specific stressor.
14. The answer is *D*. Although student participants felt sad and experienced a rise in blood pressure immediately after venting their feelings, the same students reported being less ill in the following six months. The research supports the value of getting it off your chest.
15. The answer is *C*. The study by Pennebaker and Beall described in the text suggests that there are positive health benefits in sharing negative feelings with others.
16. The answer is *A*. According to the text, procrastinators behave in ways that minimize stress until the moment

of truth the deadline. At that point, their earlier procrastination serves to concentrate the stress.

17. The answer is *A*. Although characteristics of the Type A personality include each of those listed in the question, research suggests that those who express their hostility with verbal or physical aggression are at risk for coronary heart disease.

18. The answer is *D*. One advanced theory to explain this suggests that people with Type A personalities react physiologically more to stress than do others.

19. The answer is *D*. Psychologists are increasingly turning their attention to ethnic and gender differences in response to stress.

20. The answer is *D*. Tend-and-befriend underscores the social nature of the response to stress.

21. The answer is *C*. Three effective methods for coping with stress are removing the source of stress, cognitive coping, and managing stress reactions. When Bill resigned his position, he removed the source of stress.

22. The answer is *C*. The use of defense mechanisms can be a harmless crutch, but is often an ineffective method for coping with stress.

23. The answer is *B*. According to the text, each of us uses defense mechanisms to some extent. The danger arises when we rely heavily on defense mechanism to cope with stress.

24. The answer is *D*. Cognitive coping, or changing how we think about stress, is considered to be an effective method for coping with stress.

25. The answer is *C*. Denial is commonly seen with individuals who have problems with health, drugs, and relationships.

26. The answer is *C*. Ken has successfully explained or justified to himself and others why he is relieved about Barbie. As the text suggests, the use of defense mechanisms, when used in moderation, can be relatively harmless. Problems begin when people rely too heavily on defense mechanisms.

27. The answer is *A*. Relaxation training has been found to be effective in helping to treat health problems from asthma to ulcers.

28. The answer is *D*. Progressive relaxation training teaches people to deeply relax their large body muscles.

29. The answer is *B*. Thus far, most research suggests that psychologists have been able to get people to change their unhealthy eating habits for only a limited period of time.

30. The answer is *D*. As is true with changing unhealthy eating habits, many people know about the importance of regular exercise, but adhering to behavioral changes seems to be difficult for many people.

31. The answer is *D*. Research helped to increase seat belt use, but even with successful outcomes, up to one-third of participants still did not buckle up.

32. The answer is *D*. Research has shown that providing psychological services can help reduce the cost of medical care.

33. The answer is *B*. The Alameda study, which isolated seven positive health practices, found that those who engaged in few of these practices tended to have higher death rates than those who engaged in most of the practices.

34. The answer is *D*. HIV invades the T-4 Helper cells, thereby disabling the B-cells from identifying and destroying hostile bacteria and viruses.

35. The answer is *D*. Although psychologists have had limited success thus far in helping people to change their high-risk behavior and in teaching skills to slow the progression of the disease, there is as yet no cure for AIDS.

Answers to True-False Questions

1. F	6. T
2. F	7. F
3. F	8. T
4. T	9. T
5. F	10. T

Chapter 14 Abnormal Behavior

Learning Objectives

1. Define abnormal behavior, and distinguish between the continuity hypothesis and the discontinuity hypothesis. (p. 540)

2. Describe the different ways abnormal behavior has been viewed throughout history, including supernatural theories, biological theories, and psychological theories. (p. 541)

3. Define insanity and describe its different legal meanings. (p. 543)

4. Distinguish among specific phobia, social phobia, and agoraphobia. (p. 545)

5. Distinguish between generalized anxiety disorder and panic anxiety disorder. (p. 546)

6. Discuss the causes and effects of post-traumatic stress disorder. (p. 548)

7. Define obsessive-compulsive disorders, and distinguish between obsessions and compulsions. (p. 549)

8. Identify the following somatoform disorders: somatization disorders, hypochondriasis, conversion disorders, and somatoform pain disorders. (p. 549)

9. Distinguish between depersonalization, dissociative amnesia, and dissociative fugue. (p. 551)

10. Define dissociative identity disorder and discuss the controversies surrounding its diagnosis. (p. 552)

11. Identify the characteristics of mood disorders, including major depression and bipolar disorder. (p. 555)

12. Discuss the importance of cognitive factors in depression. (p. 556)

13. Identify the three types of problems that characterize schizophrenia. (p. 560)

14. Distinguish among the following types of schizophrenia: paranoid schizophrenia, disorganized schizophrenia, catatonic schizophrenia, and undifferentiated schizophrenia. (p. 560)

15. Identify the characteristics of delusional disorder, and describe how it differs from schizophrenia. (p. 561)

16. Identify the characteristics of the personality disorders, including schizoid personality disorder and antisocial personality disorder. (p. 562)

17. (From the Application section) Discuss the civil liberty and psychological implications of homelessness and physician-assisted suicide. (p. 566)

Chapter Overview

Abnormal behavior includes actions, thoughts, and feelings that are harmful to the person and/or to others. Historically, the causes of abnormal behavior have been explained by supernatural theories, biological theories, and psychological theories. Contemporary psychologists view abnormal behavior as a natural phenomenon with both biological and psychological causes. The term *insanity* is a legal term with several different meanings.

Anxiety disorders, characterized by excessive anxiety, include the following: (1) phobias, which are intense and unrealistic fears; (2) general anxiety disorders, which are characterized by free-floating anxiety; (3) panic anxiety disorders, which involve attacks of intense anxiety; (4) post-traumatic stress disorders, a reaction to the stress of war, assault, or other trauma; and (5) obsessive-compulsive disorders, characterized by persistent, anxiety-provoking thoughts and by urges to repeatedly engage in a behavior.

Somatoform disorders are conditions in which the individual experiences symptoms of health problems that are psychological rather than physical in origin. One type of somatoform disorder is referred to as somatization disorder. This disorder involves multiple minor symptoms of illness that indirectly create a high risk of medical complications; hypochondriasis is characterized by excessive concern with health. Another type of somatoform disorder is the conversion disorder. This involves serious specific somatic symptoms without any physical cause; somatoform pain disorders involve pain without any physical cause.

In the various types of dissociative disorders, there is a change in memory, perception, or identity. For example, dissociative amnesia and dissociative fugue are characterized by memory loss that has psychological rather than physical causes. Individuals experiencing depersonalization feel that they or their surroundings have become distorted or unreal. Individuals who exhibit dissociative identity disorder (multiple personality) appear to possess more than one personality in the same body. The recent increase in the diagnosis of dissociative identity disorder has stirred controversy.

Affective disorders are disturbances of mood. The individual experiencing major depression is deeply unhappy and lethargic. In the condition known as bipolar disorder, periods of mania alternate irregularly with periods of severe depression.

Schizophrenia involves three major areas of abnormality: delusions and hallucinations, disorganized thinking, emotions and behavior, and reduced enjoyment and interests. The major types of schizophrenia include (1) paranoid schizophrenia, in which the individual holds false beliefs or delusions—usually of grandeur and persecution—that seriously distort reality; (2) disorganized schizophrenia, which is characterized by extreme withdrawal from normal human contact, fragmented delusions and hallucinations, and a shallow silliness of emotion; and (3) catatonic schizophrenia, which is marked by stupors during which the individual may remain in the same posture for long periods of time. Psychologists believe that schizophrenia may have biological causes such as deterioration of the cortex and abnormal prenatal development. Psychologists also view stress as a trigger for the disorder in those who are genetically predisposed to schizophrenia.

Personality disorders are thought to result from personalities that developed improperly during childhood rather than from breakdowns under stress. Schizoid personality disorders are characterized by a loss of interest in proper dress and social contact, a lack of emotion, and an inability to hold regular jobs. The antisocial personality frequently violates social rules and laws, is often violent, takes advantage of others, and feels little guilt about it.

Two important societal issues that have important implications for psychology are homelessness and physician-assisted suicide.

Key Terms Exercise

For each of the following exercises, match the key terms on the left with the correct definitions on the right. Page references to the text follow the terms so that you may refer to the text for any items you answer incorrectly or do not understand completely. You may check your responses immediately by referring to the answers that follow each exercise.

Anxiety Disorders

_____ 1. anxiety disorders (p. 545)
_____ 2. specific phobia (p. 545)
_____ 3. social phobia (p. 545)
_____ 4. agoraphobia (p. 546)
_____ 5. generalized anxiety disorder (p. 546)
_____ 6. panic anxiety disorder (p. 546)
_____ 7. obsessive-compulsive disorders (p. 549)

a. a phobic fear of leaving home or other familiar places
b. disorders involving anxiety-provoking thoughts and irresistible urges
c. an uneasy sense of general tension and apprehension for no apparent reason that is almost always present
d. psychological disorders that involve excessive levels of nervousness, tension, worry, and anxiety
e. an intense, irrational fear of one relatively specific thing
f. an anxiety pattern in which long periods of calm are broken by an attack of anxiety
g. a phobic fear of social interactions

ANSWERS
1. d   5. c
2. e   6. f
3. g   7. b
4. a

Somatoform Disorders/Dissociative Disorders

_____ 1. somatoform disorders (p. 549)
_____ 2. somatization disorders (p. 549)
_____ 3. hypochondriasis (p. 550)
_____ 4. conversion disorders (p. 550)
_____ 5. somatoform pain disorders (p. 551)
_____ 6. dissociative disorders (p. 551)

a. chronic symptoms of somatic illness that have no physical cause
b. disorders in which the individual experiences symptoms of physical health problems that have psychological causes
c. somatoform disorders characterized by serious somatic symptoms, such as blindness and deafness
d. characterized by excessive concerns about one's health
e. somatoform disorders characterized by a specific and chronic pain
f. conditions involving sudden cognitive changes, such as a sudden loss of memory or loss of one's identity

ANSWERS

1. b	4. c
2. a	5. e
3. d	6. f

Mood Disorders/Schizophrenia/Personality Disorders

_____ 1. mood disorders (p. 555)
_____ 2. major depression (p. 555)
_____ 3. bipolar disorder (p. 557)
_____ 4. schizophrenia (p. 559)
_____ 5. paranoid schizophrenia (p. 560)
_____ 6. disorganized schizophrenia (p. 561)
_____ 7. catatonic schizophrenia (p. 561)
_____ 8. delusional disorder (p. 561)
_____ 9. personality disorders (p. 562)
_____ 10. schizoid personality disorder (p. 562)
_____ 11. antisocial personality disorder (p. 562)

a. a psychological disorder involving cognitive and emotional disturbance and social withdrawal
b. an affective disorder characterized by episodes of deep unhappiness, loss of interest in life, and other symptoms
c. psychological disorders involving depression and/or abnormal elation
d. a condition characterized by periods of mania alternating with periods of severe depression
e. a type of schizophrenia characterized by shallow silliness, extreme social withdrawal, fragmented delusions, and hallucinations
f. a type of schizophrenia in which the individual spends long periods of time in an inactive, statue-like state
g. a type of schizophrenia characterized by false beliefs or delusions that seriously distort reality
h. a disorder characterized by delusions of grandeur and persecution that are more logical than those of paranoid schizophrenics and involve no hallucinations
i. a personality disorder characterized by smooth social skills and a lack of guilt about violating social rules and laws
j. psychological disorders believed to result from personalities that develop improperly in childhood
k. a personality disorder characterized by blunted emotions, little interest in social relationships, and social withdrawal

ANSWERS

1. c.	7. f
2. b	8. h
3. d	9. j
4. a	10. k
5. g	11. I
6. e	

Review At A Glance
(Answers to this section begin on page 267)

Abnormal Behavior

Actions, thoughts, and feelings that are harmful to the person and/or to others are called ___(1)___ behaviors. Approximately ___(2)___ percent of the people in the United States are considered seriously abnormal. This definition is ___(3)___ because (1) it is difficult to decide whether an individual's problems are ___(4)___ enough to be harmful, and (2) it is difficult to define what is ___(5)___.

The belief that abnormal behavior is just a more severe form of normal psychological problems is called the ___(6)___ hypothesis; the belief that abnormal behavior is entirely different from normal psychological problems is called the ___(7)___ hypothesis.

The oldest writings about behavior indicate that abnormal behavior was believed to be caused by ___(8)___ _____. In medieval Europe, abnormal behavior was treated by ___(9)___. Hippocrates believed that abnormal behavior resulted from an imbalance of the body's ___(10)___. Although inaccurate, Hippocrates' theory influenced other scientists to search for ___(11)___ causes of abnormal behavior.

In the 1800s, Krafft-Ebing's discovery of the relationship between paresis and syphilis contributed to the formation of the medical specialty of ___(12)___. Krafft-Ebing's discovery led to expectations that other forms of abnormal behavior also had ___(13)___ causes.

Pythagoras, a philosopher in ancient Greece, believed that abnormal behavior was caused by ___(14)___ factors. Although others throughout history have also advocated psychological factors, this approach did not become widely accepted until ___(15)___ theory was published. The contemporary view is that both ___(16)___ and ___(17)___ factors are involved in many psychological disorders.

The term ___(18)___ is a legal term. The term *insane* has three different legal meanings: (1) as a ___(19)___ defense in some states: not guilty by reason of insanity; (2) in hearings regarding ___(20)___ to stand trial; and (3) in hearings to determine involuntary ___(21)___ to mental institutions.

Anxiety Disorders

Ten to fifteen million Americans experience the disruptive levels of anxiety called ___(22)___ _____. An anxiety disorder characterized by intense, irrational fear is called a ___(23)___. The least disruptive phobias are called ___(24)___ phobias. A phobic fear of social interactions is called a ___(25)___ phobia. The most impairing of all the phobias involves a phobic fear of leaving familiar places; this is termed ___(26)___.

While phobias are linked to specific situations, free-floating anxiety is experienced by individuals with ___(27)___ anxiety disorder. People who experience this anxiety feel uncomfortable because of its almost ___(28)___ presence.

An anxiety in which the individual is seized by sharp anxiety attacks is called ___(29)___ ___ disorder. Many individuals experience an occasional ___(30)___ attack. While uncomfortable, they should not be a serious concern unless they are ___(31)___ or severe. According to current theory, some individuals experience panic attacks as a result of ___(32)___ conditioning.

Reactions that many soldiers experience as a result of stress of combat are called ___(33)___ ___ ___ ___ ___(PTSD). For women, the leading causes of PTSD are physical ___(34)___ , rape and sexual molestation, and witnessing ___(35)___ . The percentage of victims who develop PTSD depends in part on the type of ___(36)___ . About ___(37)___ percent of those who experience the sudden loss of a loved one develop PTSD, whereas 75% of women who are ___(38)___ victims experience PTSD. Researchers found more mental health problems among rape victims than among victims of ___(39)___ assault and other crimes.

Obsessive-compulsive disorders are two separate problems that often occur together. Anxiety-provoking thoughts that will not go away are called ___(40)___ , while irresistible urges to engage in irrational behaviors are termed ___(41)___ .

Disorders in which the individual experiences the symptoms of physical health problems that have psychological causes are called ___(42)___ disorders. There are four types of somatoform disorders:

1. Intensely and chronically uncomfortable conditions that involve many symptoms of bodily illness are called ___(43)___ disorders.

2. A mild form of somatization disorder marked by excessive concern for health is called ___(44)___ .

3. Dramatic somatoform disorders that involve serious symptoms, such as functional blindness and paralysis are ___(45)___ disorders. Some individuals with conversion disorders are not upset by their condition; this characteristic is known as ___(46)___ ___ ___ . Conversion disorders usually begin during periods of acute stress and generally provide some kind of ___(47)___ to the individual.

4. Finally, somatoform pain disorders are characterized by pain that has no ___(48)___ cause.

Dissociative Disorders

Conditions in which there are sudden cognitive changes, such as a sudden loss of memory or loss of one's identity, are called ___(49)___ disorders. A type of dissociative disorder in which the individual feels that his or her body has become distorted or unreal, or that the surroundings have become unreal, is called ___(50)___ . Experiences of depersonalization are common in ___(51)___ adults. A dissociative disorder in which there is a memory loss that is psychologically caused is called ___(52)___ ___ . A state of amnesia that is so complete that the individual cannot remember his or her previous life is a ___(53)___ ___ . The fugue episode may also involve a period of wandering. Individuals who shift abruptly from one personality to another are exhibiting dissociative ___(54)___ disorder (formerly called multiple personality). Some psychologists believe dissociative identity disorder is the result of childhood ___(55)___ ; other psychologists believe it is the result of social learning. According to the social learning theorists, the multiple personalities are taught to suggestible patients by their ___(56)___ .

Mood Disorders

The two primary types of mood disorders are ___(57)___ and ___(58)___ .

Extreme unhappiness and loss of interest in life are symptoms of ___(59)___ _____. In most cases, the individual experiences symptoms for a period of time and returns to normal; major depression is an ___(60)___ disorder. This disorder affects about 10 million Americans. Most cases of depression are mild; severe cases may require ___(61)___.

Aaron Beck and others emphasize the importance of ___(62)___ in emotional problems. According to Beck, ___(63)___ views of oneself are a critical component of depression. Many depressed people are troubled by ___(64)___ demands. Research by Lewinsohn has found that, under some circumstances, people who are depressed engage in ___(65)___ cognitive distortions than those who are not depressed..

Individuals who have periods of mania that alternate irregularly with periods of severe depression are experiencing ___(66)___ disorder. The portion of this experience characterized by euphoria and unrealistic optimism is called ___(67)___.

Schizophrenia and Delusional Disorder

Schizophrenia involves the following three characteristics: (1) delusions and ___(68)___ , (2) ___(69)___ thinking, emotions and behavior, and (3) reduced enjoyment and ___(70)___. According to the DSM-IV, there are three subtypes of schizophrenia: (1) ___(71)___ schizophrenia, characterized by false beliefs, delusions of grandeur, delusions of persecution, and hallucinations; (2) ___(72)___ schizophrenia, characterized by extreme withdrawal from normal human contact and a shallow silliness of emotion; and (3) ___(73)___ schizophrenia, an inactive, statue-like state, frequently broken by periods of agitation. A fourth category called ___(74)___ schizophrenia classifies those who don't fit into the other categories.

Paranoid delusions of grandeur and persecution characterize a rare disorder called ___(75)___ disorder. In this disorder, the delusions are less illogical and there are no hallucinations.

Personality Disorders

Although schizophrenia and other disorders are breakdowns in relatively normal personalities, the results of improperly developed personalities are called ___(76)___ _____. All personality disorders share these characteristics: (1) they begin ___(77)___ in life; (2) they are ___(78)___ to the person or to others; and (3) they are very ___(79)___ to treat. One example, ___(80)___ personality disorder, is characterized by extreme social withdrawal and a loss of interest in social conventions. Another personality disorder, in which the individual has smooth social skills but violates social rules and takes advantage of others without feeling guilty, is called ___(81)___ personality disorder. The primary harmfulness of this disorder is in the damage done to ___(82)___.

Other personality disorders, as listed in the DSM-IV, are (1) characterized by few friendships and strange ideas, called the ___(83)___ personality disorder; (2) suspiciousness, irritability, and coldness, called ___(84)___ _____ personality disorder; (3) self-centered and manipulating by exaggerating feelings, called the ___(85)___ personality disorder; (4) unrealistic sense of self-importance, requiring constant attention and praise, called the ___(86)___ personality disorder; (5) impulsive and unpredictable with unstable relationships, called the ___(87)___ personality disorder; (6) extremely shy and withdrawn and low self-esteem, called the ___(88)___ personality disorder; (7) passive dependence on others for support and low self-esteem, called the ___(89)___ personality disorder; and (8) perfectionistic, dominating, and excessively devoted to work, called the ___(90)___-_____ personality disorder.

Application of Psychology: Psychology and Civil Liberties

Research has found a high rate of serious psychological disorders among ___(91)___ people. Psychologists are divided on the issue of whether psychological treatment for homeless people with psychological disorders should be ___(92)___ or ___(93)___. Another issue with strong implications for civil liberties is ___(94)___-_____ suicide.

Concept Check

Fill in the missing components of the following concept box. The correct answers are located in the "Answers" section at the end of the chapter.

Major Disorders

Category	Description	Examples
anxiety disorders		
somatoform disorders		somatization, hypochondriasis, conversion disorder, and somatoform pain disorder
dissociative disorders		
	individual has disturbances of positive or negative moods	
schizophrenia		
	beginning early in life, these individuals are disturbing to themselves or others and are difficult to treat	

Extending the Chapter: Psychology, Societal Issues, and Human Diversity

These questions may be assigned to you. Whether or not they are assigned, they are designed to be challenging questions to encourage you to think independently about the material in the chapter. Many of the questions have no right or wrong answers.

I.   From the "Applications of Psychology" section

1.   What civil liberty questions are raised by homelessness and physician-assisted suicide?

2.   What is your opinion of the right of individuals to be homeless and to refuse psychological treatment? Explain your answer.

3.   What role should psychology play in physician-assisted suicide?

II. Psychology, Societal Issues, and Human Diversity

1. A friend who knows you're taking a psychology class says to you, "I think Jason is schizophrenic or something. Sometimes when I see him he's friendly and warm, but other times he's mean and nasty." How would you respond to your friend?

2. In some cultures, a person is considered good fortune to be able to communicate with a deceased member of one's family. Compare this to definitions of hallucinations and delusions in the text, and discuss the implications for diagnosis and treatment.

3. To what extent does our society view individuals as being responsible for their mental states? Provide evidence for your answer.

4. (From the Human Diversity section of the text) Discuss the roles played by ethnicity, race, and gender in depression and suicide.

Practice Quiz

The practice quiz consists of three sections: 1) Short answer questions, 2) Multiple-choice questions, and 3) True-False questions. At the end of the chapter you will find suggested answers to the short answer questions, answers and explanation for the multiple-choice questions, and answers to the true-false questions.

Short Answer Questions

1. List and describe the historical views of abnormal behavior.

_____

_____

_____

2. Describe the different legal meanings of the term insanity.

_____

_____

_____

3. List and describe the various types of anxiety disorders.

_____

_____

_____

Multiple-Choice Questions

1. In what ways are subjective judgments used to define abnormal behavior?
   a. deciding whether problems are severe enough to be harmful
   b. deciding what is harmful
   c. deciding if a pattern is unusual
   d. both *a* and *b*
   LO 1

2. A psychologist who uses terms such as insane, deviant, and mad in references to behavior probably advocates the _____ hypothesis.
   a. continuity
   b. discontinuity
   c. supernatural
   d. biological
   LO 1

3. Throughout history, the prevailing view of the cause of abnormal behavior was
   a. evil spirits.
   b. biological theories.
   c. psychological theories.
   d. sociocultural theories.
   LO 2

4. Treatment for the disorder known as paresis was important in advancing the _____ theory of abnormal behavior.
   a. supernatural
   b biological
   c. psychological
   d. interpersonal
   LO 2

5. Each of the following is a legitimate application of the term insanity *except*
   a. not guilty by reason of insanity.
   b. insanity due to genetic inheritance.
   c. incompetent to stand trial.
   d. involuntary commitment.
   LO 3

6. Liz is experiences great fear when she meets new people. She also avoids any situation where she might have to speak before a group of people. She might be experiencing
   a. agoraphobia.
   b. acrophobia.
   c. obsessive-compulsive disorder.
   d. social phobia.
   LO 4

7. Maria feels extremely uncomfortable walking outside of her home, even to check the mail or to pick up the morning newspaper. A psychologist might suggest she is experiencing
   a. agoraphobia.
   b. social phobia.
   c. obsessive-compulsive disorder.
   d. simple phobia.
   LO 4

8. Anxieties that occur due to irrational fears, usually of a specific event or object, are called
   a. compulsions.
   b. obsessions.
   c. conversions.
   d. phobias.
   LO 4

9. A usually mild, but relentless type of free-floating anxiety is experienced by those with
   a. panic anxiety disorder.
   b. phobic disorder.
   c. generalized anxiety disorder.
   d. agoraphobia.
   LO 5

10. A disorder in which long periods of calm are broken by sharp, intense periods of anxiety is called
    a. phobic disorder.
    b. simple anxiety.
    c. panic anxiety disorder.
    d. generalized anxiety disorder.
    LO 5

11. Post traumatic stress disorder has been linked to
    a. war veterans.
    b. rape victims.
    c. concentration camp survivors.
    d. all of the above.
       LO 6

12. Post traumatic stress disorder falls under the classification of _____ disorders.
    a. somatoform
    b. dissociative
    c. anxiety
    d. mood
       LO 6

13. Obsessions refer to
    a. thoughts.
    b. behaviors.
    c. psychotic behavior.
    d. insane behavior.
       LO 7

14. Each of the following is a compulsion *except*
    a. repeatedly washing one's hands.
    b. checking and rechecking the locks on doors.
    c. touching a spot on one's shoulder over and over.
    d. uncontrollable thoughts about somebody.
       LO 7

15. Individuals whose symptoms include chronic aches and pains, fever, fatigue, and anxiety are experiencing
    a. dissociative disorder.
    b. somatization disorder.
    c. conversion disorder.
    d. fugue disorder.
       LO 8

16. Each of the following is a type of somatoform disorder *except*
    a. somatization disorder.
    b. hypochondriasis.
    c. conversion disorder.
    d. obsessive-compulsive disorder.
       LO 8

17. Jim has begun to talk exclusively about the state of his health. Furthermore, he tries to see two or three doctors daily, although none can find anything wrong with him. He has also started wearing white gloves as a precaution against contact with germs. A psychologist might consider that Jim is experiencing
    a. hypochondriasis.
    b. somatization disorder.
    c. la belle indifference.
    d. none of the above.
       LO 8

18. La belle indifference is experienced by those suffering from
    a. hypochondriasis.
    b. somatization disorder.
    c. conversion disorder.
    d. somatoform pain disorder.
       LO 8

19. Individuals who suffer pain that has no physical cause are experiencing
    a. conversion disorder.
    b. somatoform pain disorder.
    c. obsessive pain disorder.
    d. agoraphobia.
       LO 8

20. Which of the following dissociative disorders involves an inability to remember one's previous life and involves wandering?
    a. dissociative amnesia.
    b. dissociative fugue.
    c. depersonalization.
    d. multiple personality.
       LO 9

21. The sensation of leaving one's body may occur to the individual who is experiencing
    a. depersonalization.
    b. psychogenic amnesia.
    c. psychogenic fugue.
    d. conversion disorder.
       LO 9

22. The movie *The Three Faces of Eve* focused on a type of disorder categorized as a
    a. depersonalization.
    b. neurotic disorder.
    c. somatization disorder.
    d. dissociative disorder.
       LO 10

23. According to the social learning view of dissociative identity disorders, multiple personalities are commonly taught to patients by
    a. parents and relatives.
    b. movies and video games.
    c. psychotherapists.
    d. the media.
       LO 10

24. Cindy, age 47, has begun experiencing deep unhappiness, frequent lethargy, and sleep problems. A psychologist might consider that she is experiencing
    a. bipolar disorder.
    b. a mood disorder.
    c. major depression.
    d. schizophrenia.
       LO 11

25. Severe major depression may be accompanied by
    a. bizarre beliefs.
    b. psychotic distortions of reality.
    c. conversion disorder.
    d. both *a* and *b*.
       LO 11

26. Which disorder involves periods of mania that alternate with periods of depression?
    a. bipolar disorder
    b. major depression
    c. schizophrenia
    d. somatization disorder
       LO 11

27. Which of the following has been identified as a cognitive factor in depression?
    a. perfectionistic beliefs
    b. repressive coping
    c. obsessive behavior
    d. both *a* and *b*
       LO 12

28. Each of the following is a characteristic of schizophrenia *except*
    a. delusions.
    b. blunted affect.
    c. disorganized thinking.
    d. alternating between two or more personalities.
       LO 13

29. Delusions of grandeur, delusions of persecution, and hallucinations characterize
    a. paranoid schizophrenia.
    b. disorganized schizophrenia.
    c. catatonic schizophrenia.
    d. undifferentiated schizophrenia.
       LO 14

30. A type of schizophrenia characterized by long periods in an inactive, statue-like state is called
    a. paranoid schizophrenia.
    b. disorganized schizophrenia.
    c. catatonic schizophrenia.
    d. undifferentiated schizophrenia.
       LO 14

31. Which of the following distinguishes delusional disorder from paranoid schizophrenia?
    a. Delusional disorder is not accompanied by hallucinations.
    b. The delusions in delusional disorder are not as illogical as in paranoid schizophrenia.
    c. Delusional disorders occur far more often than paranoid schizophrenia.
    d. both *a* and *b*
       LO 15

32. Which personality disorder is characterized by an unrealistic sense of self-importance and preoccupation with fantasies about future success?
    a. schizotypal
    b. histrionic
    c. narcissistic
    d. borderline
       LO 16

33. Which of the following characterizes the antisocial personality disorder?
    a. smooth social skills
    b. little interest in social contact
    c. lack of guilt about violating social customs
    d. both *a* and *c*
       LO 16

34. Studies of homeless people in large cities support the idea that the homeless
    a. for the most part are just individuals who are down on their luck.
    b. have high rates of chronic mental disorders.
    c. have high rates of substance abuse disorders.
    d. both *b* and *c*.
       LO 17

35. High rates of which of the following disorders have been reported among homeless adolescents?
    a. social phobia
    b. schizophrenia
    c. PTSD
    d. dissociative fugue
       LO 17

True-False Questions

_____ 1. Advocates of the continuity hypothesis favor the use of terms like insanity and mental illness.

_____ 2. The term insanity is a legal term.

_____ 3. Specific phobias are the most disruptive of the phobias.

_____ 4. In obsessive-compulsive disorder, the obsessions refer to anxiety-provoking thoughts.

_____ 5. La belle indifference is a characteristic of hypochondriasis.

_____ 6. Depersonalization is an extremely rare experience.

_____ 7. According to Beck, perfectionistic beliefs are an important factor in depression.

_____ 8. In bipolar disorder, periods of mania alternate with periods of depression.

_____ 9. Schizophrenia involves hallucinations, but rarely involves delusions.

_____ 10. Personality disorders usually begin in early adulthood.

ANSWERS SECTION

Concept Check

Major Disorders

Category	Description	Examples
anxiety disorders	the person suffering from anxiety is nervous, tense, and worried	phobias, generalized and panic anxiety disorders, PTSD, and obsessive-compulsive disorders
somatoform disorders	the individual experiences physical health problems that have psychological rather than physical causes	somatization, hypochondriasis, conversion disorder, and somatoform pain disorder
dissociative disorders	those suffering from a dissociative disorder may have sudden alterations in cognition, characterized by a change in memory, perception, or identity	dissociative amnesia and fugue, depersonalization, and dissociative identity disorder
mood disorders	individual has disturbances of positive or negative moods	major depression, bipolar disorder
schizophrenia	persons with schizophrenia experience delusions and hallucinations, disorganized thoughts, emotions and behavior, and reduced enjoyment and interests	paranoid, disorganized, catatonic, and undifferentiated schizophrenia
personality disorders	beginning early in life, these individuals are disturbing to themselves or others and are difficult to treat	schizoid, antisocial, schizotypal, paranoid, histrionic, narcissistic, borderline, avoidant, dependent, and obsessive-compulsive personality disorders

Answers to Review At A Glance

1. abnormal
2. 15
3. subjective
4. severe
5. harmful
6. continuity
7. discontinuity
8. evil spirits
9. exorcism
10. humors
11. natural
12. psychiatry
13. biological
14. psychological
15. Freud's
16. biological

17. psychological
18. insanity
19. legal
20. competence
21. commitment
22. anxiety disorders
23. phobia
24. specific
25. social
26. agoraphobia
27. generalized
28. continual
29. panic anxiety
30. anxiety
31. frequent
32. classical

33. post traumatic stress disorder
34. assault
35. violence
36. stress
37. 15
38. rape
39. aggravated
40. obsessions
41. compulsions
42. somatoform
43. somatization
44. hypochondriasis
45. conversion
46. la belle indifference
47. benefit

48. physical
49. dissociative
50. depersonalization
51. young
52. dissociative amnesia
53. dissociative fugue
54. identity
55. abuse
56. psychotherapists
57. depression
58. mania
59. major depression
60. episodic
61. hospitalization
62. cognition
63. negative
64. perfectionistic

65. fewer
66. bipolar
67. mania
68. hallucinations
69. disorganized
70. interests
71. paranoid
72. disorganized
73. catatonic
74. undifferentiated
75. delusional
76. personality disorders
77. early
78. disturbing
79. difficult
80. schizoid
81. antisocial

82. others
83. schizotypal
84. paranoid
85. histrionic
86. narcissistic
87. borderline
88. avoidant
89. dependent
90. obsessive-compulsive
91. homeless
92. mandatory
93. voluntary
94. physician-assisted

Sample Answers for Short Answer Questions

1. **List and describe the historical views of abnormal behavior.**

Ancient writings indicate that the earliest beliefs of abnormal behavior considered them to be caused by various evil spirits. Treatment generally involved prayer, although, at various times, it also included exorcism and the murder of those who were thought to be witches. This belief persisted until shortly before the American Revolution. A second approach, proposed by Hippocrates, was that biological disorders caused abnormal behavior. The work of Krafft-Ebing on paresis confirmed the influence of biological factors on mental disorders. Pythagoras, a philosopher in ancient Greece, held that psychological factors, including stress, were involved in abnormal behavior. Today, it is widely accepted that both biological and psychological factors are involved in psychological disorders.

2. **Describe the different legal meanings of the term insanity.**

The term insanity is actually a legal term. Its definition depends upon the context in which it is used. One application is "not guilty by reason of insanity," which means an individual is not legally responsible for a crime if found insane. A second application involves whether a person is competent to stand trial; that is, whether an individual can aid in his own defense. A third application pertains to involuntary commitment to a mental institution.

3. **List and describe the various types of anxiety disorders.**

One type of anxiety disorder is the category of phobias. These are intense and irrational fears. Three types of phobias are specific phobias, social phobias and agoraphobia. Another type of anxiety disorder is generalized anxiety disorder, characterized by free-floating anxiety. Panic anxiety disorder involves sharp and intense anxiety attacks. Post traumatic stress disorder involves anxiety and irritability, upsetting memories, dreams, and flashbacks in response to extremely stressful experiences. Obsessive-compulsive disorders involve anxiety-provoking thoughts called obsessions, and irresistible urges to engage in certain behaviors, referred to as compulsions.

Multiple-Choice Answers

1. The answer is *D*. The inherent subjectivity of judgments is a continual problem for psychologists who study abnormal behavior.
2. The answer is *B*. The discontinuity hypothesis views abnormal behavior as being fundamentally different from normal psychological problems, whereas the continuity hypothesis views abnormal behavior as being a severe form of normal psychological problems.
3. The answer is *A*. Consider an important implication of this question—the treatment and cures for those exhibiting abnormal behavior have been strongly influenced by the perceived causes of the abnormal behavior.
4. The answer is *B*. This now rare psychological disturbance was found to be an advanced stage of syphilis.
5. The answer is *B*. Remember that the term insanity is a legal rather than a psychological term.
6. The answer is *D*. Research suggests people with social phobia have unrealistically negative views of their social skills and attempt to avoid evaluation.
7. The answer is *A*. Agoraphobia is an intense fear of leaving one's home or other familiar places.
8. The answer is *D*. Specific phobias, social phobias and agoraphobia are all examples of phobias.
9. The answer is *C*. A person experiencing generalized anxiety disorder has a continual, gnawing sense of uneasiness, whereas the person with panic anxiety disorder usually has periods of calm that are broken by an explosive attack of anxiety.
10. The answer is *C*. While generalized anxiety disorder is characterized by free-floating anxiety that almost always seems to be present, panic anxiety disorder is characterized by a sharp and intense anxiety, although it is not continually present.
11. The answer is *D*. The upsetting recollections, combined with feelings of guilt, disgust, and terrible dreams are all components of PTSD.
12. The answer is *C*. PTSD is caused by extremely stressful experiences in which the person later experiences anxiety and irritability.
13. The answer is *A*. Whereas obsessions refer to thoughts, compulsions refer to behaviors.
14. The answer is *D*. Compulsions are irresistible urges to engage in behaviors, while obsessions refer to seemingly unstoppable thoughts. They usually go together to form obsessive-compulsive behavior.
15. The answer is *B*. The category of somatoform disorders contains (a) somatization disorder, (b) hypochondriasis, (c) conversion disorder, and (d) somatoform pain disorder.
16. The answer is *D*. In the question, the missing type of somatoform disorder is somatoform pain disorder.
17. The answer is *A*. The individual experiencing hypochondriasis is dominated by concerns about his or her health.
18. The answer is *C*. "The beautiful indifference" refers to the fact that, although individuals with conversion disorder appear to be suffering serious symptoms, such as paralysis or blindness, they often are not upset with their condition.
19. The answer is *B*. Somatoform pain often occurs in the person who is experiencing high levels of stress, and the condition may be beneficial to the individual in some way.
20. The answer is *B*. While dissociative amnesia involves a loss of memory, a dissociative fugue involves such a complete loss of memory that the individual cannot remember his or her identity or previous life. Often, during the fugue episode, the individual will take on a new personality.
21. The answer is *A*. During a depersonalization episode, the individual feels that he or she has become distorted or unreal in some way. The experience of leaving one's body is also a common experience in depersonalization.
22. The answer is *D*. *The Three Faces of Eve* was about dissociative identity disorder. Recall that the category of dissociative disorders consists of amnesia, fugue, depersonalization, and dissociative identity disorder. The common feature is that all involve a change in memory, perception, or identity.
23. The answer is *C*. According to this view, highly suggestible patients are influenced by their psychotherapist's subtle and not-so-subtle interpretations.
24. The answer is *C*. Major depression is a mood disorder characterized by deep unhappiness, frequent lethargy, and sleep problems.
25. The answer is *D*. Major depression is often relatively mild. Severe major depression, as described in the question, is less common but far more disabling.
26. The answer is *A*. Bipolar disorder, formerly known as manic-depressive behavior, is a type of mood disorder. Although the manic period can be enjoyable to the person in the short run, it can have disastrous consequences. When mania is recurrent, it alternates with severe depression.
27. The answer is *D*. In addition to the cognitive factors described in the question, research suggests that having a

positive opinion of oneself makes depression less likely following stressful life events.

28. The answer is *D*. One of the biggest misconceptions pertaining to the field of abnormal psychology continues to be the notion that people with schizophrenia have a split personality.

29. The answer is *A*. Although disorganized schizophrenia is also marked by hallucinations and delusions, the cognitive processes of the individual are extremely disorganized. Disorganized schizophrenia is also characterized by a shallow, silly affect. The person with catatonic schizophrenia spends long periods of time in a statue-like state often described as "waxy flexibility."

30. The answer is *C*. People experiencing catatonic schizophrenia exhibit a "waxy flexibility" while they are in this stuporous condition.

31. The answer is *D*. The delusions that accompany delusional disorder are more subtle and believable than those that accompany paranoid schizophrenia. Delusional disorders are also rare.

32. The answer is *C*. The schizotypal personality disorder is characterized by few friendships and strange ideas; the histrionic personality disorder is characterized by self-centered behavior and exaggerated emotional expression; the borderline personality disorder is characterized by impulsive, unpredictable behavior and an almost constant need to be with others.

33. The answer is *D*. In fact, many individuals with antisocial personality disorder have disarmingly smooth social skills.

34. The answer is *D*. Research conducted on homeless people living in New York and in Los Angeles has revealed that a majority have mental and/or substance abuse disorders.

35. The answer is *B*. High rates of alcohol and/or drug dependence are also reported among homeless people.

Answers to True-False Questions

1. F

6. F

2. T

7. T

3. F

8. T

4. T

9. F

5. F

10. F

Chapter 15   Therapies

Learning Objectives

1. Define psychotherapy, and describe the ways it is used to help people. (p. 572)

2. Identify the ethical standards for psychotherapy. (p. 572)

3. Discuss the characteristics of psychoanalysis, and identify the techniques of psychoanalytic psychotherapy. (p. 573)

4. Identify interpersonal psychotherapy, and describe its applications. (p. 576)

5. Compare and contrast client-centered psychotherapy and Gestalt psychotherapy. (p. 580)

6. Discuss techniques used by behavior therapists for reducing fear. (p. 583)

7. Identify the goals and techniques of social skills training and assertiveness training. (p. 584)

8. Describe the goals of cognitive therapy, and identify the maladaptive cognitions that, according to Beck, contribute to depression. (p. 588)

9. Identify the fundamental concepts of feminist psychotherapy. (p. 592)

10. Identify the advantages of both group therapy and family therapy. (p. 593)

11. Discuss the use of medical therapies, and distinguish among drug therapy, electroconvulsive therapy, and psychosurgery. (p. 594)

12. (From the Application section) Identify the guidelines for selecting a psychotherapist. (p. 599)

13. (From the Application section) Describe the research findings regarding the most effective form of psychotherapy, and identify ethnic and gender issues in seeking psychotherapy. (p. 599)

Chapter Overview

Psychotherapy is a form of therapy in which a trained professional uses methods based on psychological theories to help a person with psychological problems. One form of psychotherapy, founded by Sigmund Freud, is called psychoanalysis. Psychoanalysis tries to help the patient bring unconscious conflict into consciousness. The following techniques are used in psychoanalysis: (1) free association, which is used to relax the censorship of the ego; (2) dream interpretation, in which the symbols of the manifest content of dreams are interpreted to reveal their latent content; (3) resistance, which refers to any form of patient opposition to psychoanalysis; (4) transference, which refers to the development of a relatively intense relationship between patient and therapist during therapy; and (5) catharsis, the release of emotional energy related to unconscious conflicts. A new form of psychotherapy, derived from the psychoanalytic tradition is called interpersonal therapy. This type of therapy is used to treat depression by emphasizing the accurate identification of feelings, constructive communication, and improving social relationships.

Humanistic psychotherapists attempt to help the client seek more complete self-awareness to allow the client's inner-directed potential for growth to be realized. One type of humanistic psychotherapy is client-centered therapy. The goal of the client-centered therapist is to create an atmosphere that encourages clients to explore their unsymbolized feelings. Another humanistic approach, Gestalt psychotherapy, helps the individual achieve greater self-awareness by using directive techniques, such as questioning and challenging the client.

Another approach to psychotherapy is called behavior therapy. Behavior therapists help their clients to unlearn abnormal behavior and learn adaptive ways of thinking, feeling, and acting. Among the techniques used by behavior therapists are (1) systematic desensitization, a method of helping clients overcome fear; (2) social skills training, an approach that teaches new, adaptive skills using operant conditioning; and (3) assertiveness training, techniques to increase assertive rather than aggressive ways of expressing feelings.

Cognitive therapy assumes that faulty cognitions are the cause of abnormal behavior. Other models of therapy include feminist psychotherapy, which has evolved from the philosophical foundation of feminism. The basic principles of feminist psychotherapy are increasingly being integrated with other forms of therapy.

Group therapy, generally conducted with one or two therapists and four to eight clients, makes efficient use of therapists' time and provides an opportunity for clients to benefit from interactions with each other. Family therapy is a variation of group therapy that attempts to reestablish proper functioning within a family.

Medical therapies are designed to correct a physical condition that is believed to be the cause of a psychological disorder. Medical therapies include drug therapy, electroconvulsive therapy, and psychosurgery.

Professional mental health services are widely available. Many colleges and universities have student counseling or mental health centers. Referrals and board certification are guides in helping to select a professional. Important ethnic and gender inequalities exist in receiving psychological services in the United States.

Key Terms Exercise

For each of the following exercises, match the key terms on the left with the correct definitions on the right. Page references to the text follow the terms so that you may refer to the text for any items you answer incorrectly or do not understand completely. You may check your responses immediately by referring to the answers that follow each exercise.

Psychoanalysis

_____ 1. psychotherapy (p. 572)
_____ 2. psychoanalysis (p. 573)
_____ 3. free association (p. 574)
_____ 4. dream interpretation (p. 575)
_____ 5. resistance (p. 575)
_____ 6. transference (p. 575)
_____ 7. catharsis (p. 576)
_____ 8. interpersonal psychotherapy (p. 576)

a. occurs when a patient in psychoanalysis reacts to a therapist in ways that resemble the patient's reaction to other significant adults
b. the method of psychotherapy developed by Sigmund Freud
c. a variety of psychological methods used by a trained professional to help a patient with psychological problems
d. the release of emotional energy related to unconscious conflicts
e. focuses on the accurate identification and communication of feelings and the improvement of current social relationships
f. a Freudian method that attempts to reveal the latent content of dreams
g. a Freudian method that encourages the patient to talk about whatever comes to mind
h. patient opposition to psychoanalysis

ANSWERS

1. c	5. h
2. b	6. a
3. g	7. d
4. f	8. e

Humanistic Psychotherapy and Behavior Therapy

_____ 1. client-centered psychotherapy (p. 580)
_____ 2. reflection (p. 580)
_____ 3. Gestalt therapy (p. 581)
_____ 4. behavior therapy (p. 583)

a. psychotherapy based on social learning theory
b. a humanistic therapy that tries to create a safe environment for clients so they can discover feelings of which they are unaware
c. a humanistic theory in which the therapist takes an active role in helping the client become more aware of feelings
d. a technique in which the therapist reflects clients' emotions in order to help clients clarify their feelings

ANSWERS

1. b	3. c
2. d	4. a

Behavior Therapy Techniques

_____ 1. systematic desensitization (p. 583)
_____ 2. social skills training (p. 584)
_____ 3. assertiveness training (p. 585)
_____ 4. cognitive therapy (p. 588)

a. a behavior therapy method that teaches the client to overcome phobias by relaxing in response to increasingly threatening stimuli
b. a behavior therapy method that teaches individuals assertive ways of dealing with situations
c. an approach that teaches individuals new cognitions to eliminate abnormal behavior
d. using operant conditioning techniques to teach social skills

ANSWERS
1. a
2. d
3. b
4. c

Other Models of Therapy

_____ 1. feminist psychotherapy (p. 592)
_____ 2. group therapy (p. 593)
_____ 3. family therapy (p. 593)
_____ 4. drug therapy (p. 595)
_____ 5. electroconvulsive therapy (p. 596)
_____ 6. psychosurgery (p. 596)

a. a medical therapy that induces controlled convulsive seizures to alleviate some mental disorders
b. a medical therapy that uses drugs to treat abnormal behavior
c. a medical therapy that involves operating on the brain to alleviate some mental disorders
d. an approach to psychotherapy that emphasizes an understanding of the roles of each family member
e. psychotherapy conducted in groups
f. an approach that encourages women to confront issues created by living in a sexist society as part of their psychotherapy

ANSWERS

1. f	4. b
2. e	5. a
3. d	6. c

Who Am I?

Match the psychologists on the left with their contributions to the field of psychology on the right. Page references to the text follow the names of the psychologists so that you may refer to the text for further review of these psychologists and their contributions. You may check your responses immediately by referring to the answers that follow each exercise.

_____ 1. Sigmund Freud (p. 573)
_____ 2. Carl Rogers (p. 580)
_____ 3. Fredrick Perls (p. 581)
_____ 4. Joseph Wolpe (p. 583)
_____ 5. Aaron Beck (p. 588)

a. Gestalt therapy
b. psychoanalysis
c. client-centered therapy
d. cognitive therapy
e. systematic desensitization

ANSWERS
1. b   4. e
2. c   5. d
3. a

Review At A Glance
(Answers to this section begin on page 285)

Psychoanalysis

A trained professional uses psychological methods to help a person with psychological problems in the process called ___(1)___. The following ethical guidelines must be followed by psychotherapists: (1) the goals of treatment must be considered with the ___(2)___; (2) the choices for alternative treatments should be carefully considered; (3) the therapist must treat only the problems that he or she is ___(3)___ to treat; (4) the ___(4)___ of the treatment must be evaluated in some way; (5) the rules and laws regarding ___(5)___ must be fully explained to the client; (6) the therapist must not ___(6)___ the client in sexual or other ways; (7) the therapist must treat clients with dignity and respect differences among people.

Psychoanalysts feel that abnormal behavior is the result of ___(7)___ conflicts among the id, ego, and superego. According to Freud, problems can be solved only when unconscious conflicts are brought into ___(8)___ . This can occur only when the ego's guard is temporarily ___(9)___. The job of the psychoanalyst is to (1) relax the censorship of the ___(10)___ and (2) ___(11)___ the revelations of the unconscious mind.

Freud's primary tool of therapy was to encourage the individual to talk about whatever came to mind, a technique called ___(12)___ _____. The glimpse of the unconscious revealed during free association must be ___(13)___ to the patient by the psychoanalyst. Freud believed that another window to the unconscious was provided by ___(14)___ _____. Psychoanalysts believe that the manifest content of dreams symbolically masks the true or ___(15)___ content of dreams.

Freud also placed significance on any patient opposition to psychoanalysis, a process he called ___(16)___. Intense relationships often develop between therapist and patient. The patient often reacts to the therapist in ways that resemble how he or she would react to other authority figures. Freud called this process ___(17)___. Releasing emotional energy related to unconscious conflicts is called ___(18)___.

A new form of psychotherapy, derived from the psychoanalytic tradition, is called ___(19)___ psychotherapy. Interpersonal psychotherapy emphasizes the accurate identification of ___(20)___, constructive ___(21)___, and improving social ___(22)___. Studies have found interpersonal therapy to be effective in treating ___(23)___.

Humanistic Psychotherapy

Humanists view full self-awareness as necessary for the complete realization of our inner-directed potential; according to humanists, therapy is "growth in ___(24)___."

The therapy approach associated with Carl Rogers is called ___(25)___-_____ psychotherapy. According to Rogers, growth in awareness comes when the client feels safe enough to explore ___(26)___ _____. Rogers believes that therapists must be ___(27)___, able to accept their clients ___(28)___, and able to share their clients' emotions, a process called ___(29)___. The closest thing to a technique in client-centered therapy is the process of ___(30)___. Client-centered therapists strictly avoid giving ___(31)___ to clients.

Fredrick Perls developed a type of humanistic therapy called ___(32)___ therapy. In this type of therapy, the therapist takes a more active role to help the client increase his or her ___(33)___-_____. Gestalt therapists often deal with their clients in a challenging manner, a technique Perls called a ___(34)___ _____.

Behavior Therapy

The approach to psychotherapy based on social learning theory is called ___(35)___ therapy. This approach views abnormal behavior as ___(36)___ behavior. The therapist, who plays the role of a teacher, helps the client to unlearn abnormal behavior and to learn more ___(37)___ ways to behave.

Several behavior therapy methods are used to treat phobias. One technique, developed by Joseph Wolpe, is called ___(38)___ _____. In this technique, the client is taught to relax using ___(39)___ _____ _____. During the next part of the procedure, called ___(40)___ _____, the therapist and client rank all aspects of the phobic stimulus, from least feared to most feared. The client is directed to ___(41)___ the weakest phobic stimulus, until it no longer causes fear. Then the client progresses to the next stimulus, and so on. When the graded exposure is conducted in real-life settings, it is called ___(42)___ graded exposure. This procedure can also be accomplished using computer-generated ___(43)___ _____ techniques.

A major emphasis of behavior therapy is on the teaching of new skills using methods derived from ___(44)___ _____. For example, people who have difficulties interacting with other people might benefit from ___(45)___ _____ training. One technique, in which the therapist and client act as if they are people in problematic situations, is called ___(46)___ _____. Using this technique, the therapist might take the role of the client and ___(47)___ appropriate behavior. The therapist also provides ___(48)___ _____ for the client by praising the adaptive aspects of the client's behavior.

A technique that is used to develop assertive rather than aggressive ways of dealing with others is called ___(49)___ training.

Cognitive Therapy

A new approach to therapy teaches individuals new cognitions—beliefs, expectations, and ways of thinking—to eliminate abnormal behavior. This approach is called ____(50)____ therapy. Cognitive therapists believe that behavior therapists can be more effective if they teach both more adaptive ____(51)____ and ____(52)____.

According to the cognitive therapy program developed by Aaron Beck, depression is caused by the following erroneous patterns of thinking: (1) basing one's thoughts on a detail taken out of context, called ____(53)____ _____; (2) reaching a general conclusion based on a few bits of evidence, called ____(54)____; (3) reaching a conclusion based on little or no logical evidence, called ____(55)____ _____; (4) blowing statements out of proportion or minimizing their importance, called ____(56)____ / _____; (5) reasoning that external events are directly related to one's behavior, called ____(57)____; and (6) thinking in all-or-nothing terms, called ____(58)____ thinking. Cognitive therapy has been shown to be effective in treating a variety of ____(59)____ disorders, the eating disorder called ____(60)____, and major ____(61)____.

Other Approaches and Models of Therapy

An approach to understanding and treating the psychological problems of women that evolved from feminism is called ____(62)____ psychotherapy. Its basic concepts include: (1) an equal relationship between client and therapist; (2) encouragement for women clients to see the ways in which society has limited their development; (3) encouragement to become aware of ____(63)____ as a result of living in a sexist society; (4) help in defining women in ways that are ____(64)____ of their roles as wife, mother, and daughter; (5) skills to increase women's sense of self-worth and ____(65)____-_____; (6) encouragement to develop ____(66)____ not traditionally encouraged in women. Increasingly, principles used in ____(67)____ psychotherapy are being integrated into other forms of psychotherapy.

Therapy conducted with groups, usually four to eight clients at a time, is called ____(68)____ _____. Some of the advantages of group therapy are (1) ____(69)____ from other group members; (2) learning that a person is not alone in his or her problems; (3) learning from the ____(70)____ of others; and (4) learning new ways to ____(71)____ with others.

Another form of group therapy is conducted with parents, children, and other family members living in the home; this approach is called ____(72)____ therapy. One approach to family therapy assumes that the psychological problems of the individual can be understood only by knowing the role of that individual in the ____(73)____ _____. This systems approach suggests that an individual's problems are often caused by problems within the ____(74)____, and that they may serve a ____(75)____ in the family system. The family therapist attempts to improve the functioning of the family system by (1) giving family members ____(76)____ into the workings of the family system; (2) increasing the amount of warmth and ____(77)____ among family members; (3) improving ____(78)____ among family members; and (4) helping family members establish a set of ____(79)____ for the family.

When a physical condition is believed to cause a psychological disorder, ____(80)____ _____ are used. The most widely used medical therapy is ____(81)____ therapy, which uses chemicals to treat abnormal behavior. A drug that has been successfully used in the treatment of schizophrenia is ____(82)____. Some drugs have serious side effects; others can lead to considerable weight gain. Modern psychiatric medications are designed to improve psychological functioning by influencing ____(83)____ in the brain. These medications often have side effects that result from their impact on ____(84)____ systems.

The use of electrical current to induce controlled convulsive seizures that help alleviate some mental disorders is called ____(85)____ (ECT). Although side effects such as ____(86)____ loss and ____(87)____ are relatively common, studies have shown that ECT is somewhat effective in treating ____(88)____.

The most controversial approach to medical therapy, operating on the brain to alleviate some mental disorders, is called ____(89)____. The most common type of psychosurgery, the ____(90)____, cuts the neural fibers that connect the frontal region of the cerebral cortex with the hypothalamus. The procedure is performed ____(91)____ today, and its use is still hotly debated. A more precise type of psychosurgery, occasionally performed on individuals with severe obsessive-compulsive disorder, is called a ____(92)____.

Application of Psychology: What to Do If You Think You Need Help

The following are important considerations in deciding whether to use professional mental health services. An important issue concerns the ____(93)____ surrounding seeking professional help. A second consideration is where to get help. Many colleges and universities have a student counseling or mental health center. Services are also provided by professionals in ____(94)____ practice. Referrals and board ____(95)____ are guides in helping to select a professional. Research by Smith and Glass has confirmed that various types of psychotherapy all produced positive treatment effects, although there was variation in the size of the effects. More recent studies have found fewer differences in the ____(96)____ of different psychotherapy methods. Research has also focused on identifying the most effective therapy for ____(97)____ disorders. There are important ____(98)____ and ____(99)____ inequities in terms of receiving psychological services in the United States.

Concept Check

Fill in the missing components of the following concept box. The correct answers are located in the "Answers" section at the end of the chapter.

Approaches to Therapy

Psychologists	Type of Therapy	Techniques
Freud	psychoanalysis	
Sullivan		accurate identification of feelings and improving social relationships
Rogers	humanistic (client-centered)	
	humanistic (Gestalt)	active involvement in client's conversations during sessions, feelings, and creating a "safe emergency"
Wolpe	systematic desensitization	
Ellis and Beck	cognitive therapy	

Extending the Chapter: Psychology, Societal Issues, and Human Diversity

These questions may be assigned to you. Whether or not they are assigned, they are designed to be challenging questions to encourage you to think independently about the material in the chapter. Many of the questions have no right or wrong answers.

I. From the Applications of Psychology section

1. If a friend asked you for advice on getting help from a mental health professional, what steps would you advise him to take?

2. Summarize the research regarding the most effective form of psychotherapy.

II. Psychology, Societal Issues, and Human Diversity

1. A client goes to a psychotherapist, seeking help for an incapacitating phobia toward almost all members of the opposite sex. Describe what the therapeutic approach might be like if the therapist is a
    a. psychoanalyst.
    b. interpersonal psychotherapist.
    c. behavior therapist.
    d. Gestalt therapist.
    e. cognitive therapist.

2. Although the use of psychosurgery has declined, advocates might argue that, through the continued use of these procedures and the evaluation of results, psychosurgery will become more and more successful. Although the early psychosurgery cases were not completely successful, the same could be said for the first heart transplants and other types of surgery. How would you respond to these comments?

3. In addition to fees and therapy techniques, what other information should therapists be required to disclose to clients at the start of a therapist-client relationship?

4. Which of the techniques discussed in this chapter make the most sense to you? Which make the least sense? Which raise ethical concerns? Explain your answer.

Practice Quiz

The practice quiz consists of three sections: 1) Short answer questions, 2) Multiple-choice questions, and 3) True-False questions. At the end of the chapter you will find suggested answers to the short answer questions, answers and explanation for the multiple choice questions, and answers to the true-false questions.

Short Answer Questions

1. Describe similarities and differences between psychoanalysis and humanistic psychotherapy.

_____

_____

_____

2. Describe the use of systematic desensitization in reducing phobias.

_____

_____

3. List and describe maladaptive cognitions that, according to cognitive therapists, contribute to depression.

_____

_____

Multiple Choice Questions

1. Each of the following is part of the definition of psychotherapy *except*
   a. trained professional.
   b. psychological methods.
   c. medical treatment methods.
   d. based on psychological theory.
   LO 1

2. Which type of psychotherapy views the process of helping others as a form of teaching?
   a. humanistic therapy
   b. behavior therapy
   c. psychoanalytic therapy
   d. client-centered therapy
   LO 1

3. According to the Association for Advancement of Behavior Therapy, each of the following is an ethical consideration in the use of psychotherapy *except*
   a. the goals of treatment.
   b. the fees (splitting the fees when necessary).
   c. the choice of treatment methods.
   d. client confidentiality.
   LO 2

4. Which of the following is a situation where it is appropriate for a therapist to breach confidentiality?
   a. spouse inquiry
   b. court order
   c. insurance company order
   d. relative asks a question
   LO 2

5. Ann's psychoanalytic therapist asks her to relax on a couch and talk about whatever comes to mind. The technique being used by her therapist is
   a. catharsis.
   b. resistance.
   c. free association.
   d. transference.
   LO 3

6. According to Freud, when the patient reacts to the therapist in ways that resemble how he or she would react to other authority figures, the process is called
   a. resistance.
   b. catharsis.
   c. free association.
   d. transference.
   LO 3

7. In psychoanalysis, the release of emotional energy related to unconscious conflicts is called
   a. resistance.
   b. catharsis.
   c. free association.
   d. transference.
   LO 3

8. A contemporary neo-Freudian form of psychotherapy that ignores unconscious motivation is called
   a. social skills training.
   b. systematic desensitization.
   c. interpersonal psychotherapy.
   d. Gestalt therapy.
   LO 4

9. Research suggests interpersonal psychotherapy is effective in treating
   a. schizophrenia.
   b. bipolar disorder.
   c. phobias.
   d. depression.
   LO 4

10. According to Rogers, the ability of the therapist to share the client's emotions is an important process called
    a. reflection.
    b. empathy.
    c. catharsis.
    d. transference.
    LO 5

11. The role of the client-centered therapist is to
    a. interpret the client's unconscious conflicts.
    b. create a safe atmosphere for clients to express feelings.
    c. confront and challenge the client and point out inconsistencies.
    d. help the client unlearn abnormal ways of behaving.
    LO 5

12. Which of the following techniques is a client-centered therapist most likely to use?
    a. analysis
    b. giving advice
    c. reflection
    d. graded exposure
    LO 5

13. The techniques used by Gestalt therapists include
    a. interpreting the client's unconscious conflicts.
    b. creating a safe atmosphere for clients to express feelings.
    c. confronting and challenging the client and pointing out inconsistencies.
    d. helping the client unlearn abnormal ways of behaving.
    LO 5

14. Systematic desensitization is often used to treat
    a. schizophrenia.
    b. phobias.
    c. bipolar disorder.
    d. depression.
    LO 6

15. Progressive relaxation and graded exposure are important steps in
    a. assertiveness training.
    b. systematic desensitization.
    c. Gestalt therapy.
    d. interpersonal psychotherapy.
    LO 6

16. Which of the following is *not* a behavior therapy technique?
    a. client-centered reflection
    b. assertiveness training
    c. systematic desensitization
    d. social skills training
    LO 6

17. Anna frequently feels that she is being used by others. She has been told by her friends that she is too passive. She might benefit from a behavior therapy approach called
    a. systematic desensitization.
    b. assertiveness training.
    c. personalization training.
    d. none of the above.
    LO 7

18. Behavior therapy teaches skills based on methods derived from
    a. classical conditioning.
    b. operant conditioning.
    c. information-processing theory.
    d. Both *a* and *b*.
    LO 7

19. Jason's friends believe he is overly sensitive and often blows things out of proportion. According to Aaron Beck, Jason engages in
    a. minimization.
    b. magnification.
    c. absolutistic thinking.
    d. personalization.
    LO 8

20. After Mike moved to college, the first two people he called to ask for a date forcefully told him "No!" Mike has concluded he will never have a date. According to Beck, Mike is engaging in
    a. selective abstraction.
    b. personalization.
    c. overgeneralization.
    d. none of the above.
    LO 8

21. With which disorders has cognitive therapy been shown to be effective?
    a. anxiety disorders
    b. bulimia
    c. major depression
    d. all of the above
    LO 8

22. Persuading clients to abandon their erroneous ways of thinking is a goal of
    a. Gestalt therapy.
    b. cognitive therapy.
    c. systematic desensitization.
    d. social skills training.
    LO 8

23. Which of the following is true regarding feminist psychotherapy?
    a. It is only for women.
    b. It fosters independence.
    c. It encourages traditional roles.
    d. It is not accepted by other psychotherapies.
    LO 9

24. Which of the following is a fundamental concept of feminist psychotherapy?
    a. an equal relationship between therapist and client
    b. an awareness of anger over living in a sexist society
    c. encouragement to consider the clients' needs as valid and worthy
    d. all of the above
    LO 9

25. Group therapists tend to follow which orientation?
    a. humanistic
    b. psychoanalytic
    c. behavioral
    d. any of the above
    LO 10

26. Each of the following is an advantage of group therapy *except*
    a. it allows people with complex problems to have the therapist's full attention.
    b. it can provide encouragement from other group members.
    c. it permits learning from the advice of others.
    d. members can learn new ways to interact with others.
    LO 10

27. Which of the following describes the position of the family systems view?
    a. Individual problems are often caused by problems within the family.
    b. An individual's problems may serve a function within the family system.
    c. Family problems are usually caused by too many rules and regulations within the family.
    d. both *a* and *b*
    LO 10

28. The drug Thorazine has been helpful to many individuals suffering from
    a. depression.
    b. schizrenia.
    c. obsessive-compulsive disorder.
    d. agoraphobia.
    LO 11

29. Electroconvulsive therapy is believed by most psychiatrists to be useful for patients who are
    a. schizophrenic.
    b. epileptic.
    c. bipolar.
    d. severely depressed.
    LO 11

30. A side effect of electroconvulsive therapy is
    a. memory loss.
    b. increased depression.
    c. increased tendency to have seizures.
    d. both *a* and *c*.
    LO 11

31. Prozac and other antidepressants help improve psychological functioning by influencing a neurotransmitter called
    a. melatonin.
    b. dopamine.
    c. endorphin.
    d. serotonin.
    LO 11

32. Board-certified psychologists
    a. are more competent than those who are not board-certified.
    b. are eclectic psychiatrists.
    c. are the only ones who accept health insurance.
    d. have met national standards for competency.
    LO 12

33. Which of the following would be good advice for someone considering a therapist?
    a. Eclectic therapists are best because they can provide the widest variety of services.
    b. Student counseling centers are usually staffed by students and recent graduates who don't have much experience.
    c. Anybody can call themselves a psychologist.
    d. Referrals can be a good guide in choosing a psychologist.
    LO 12

34. According to research conducted by Smith and Glass, which of the following types of therapy produced the smallest magnitude of treatment effect?
    a. Adlerian psychoanalysis
    b. cognitive therapy
    c. Gestalt therapy
    d. client-centered therapy
    LO 13

35. Research suggests inequities in receiving psychotherapy based on one's
    a. gender.
    b. ethnicity.
    c. race.
    d. all of the above.
    LO 13

True-False Questions

_____ 1. When an intelligent and caring friend attempts to help others with their emotional problems, the friend is engaging in psychotherapy.

_____ 2. Free association is an important tool in Freudian psychoanalysis.

_____ 3. Interpersonal psychotherapy has been shown to be effective in treating depression.

_____ 4. Reflection is an important process in Gestalt psychotherapy.

_____ 5. Behavior therapists assume abnormal behavior is learned.

_____ 6. Systematic desensitization is a behavior therapy technique used to treat phobias.

_____ 7. Feminist psychotherapy has been developed exclusively for women.

_____ 8. According to the family systems view, it is important to understand the individual in the context of the person's family.

_____ 9. Cingulotomies are performed to help relieve patients of phobic behavior.

_____ 10. According to research by Smith and Glass, psychoanalysis yielded the largest treatment effect.

ANSWERS SECTION

Concept Check

Approaches to Therapy

Psychologists	Type of Therapy	Techniques
Freud	psychoanalysis	free association, catharsis, interpretation of dreams, resistance, and transference
Sullivan	interpersonal psychology	accurate identification of feelings and improving social relationships
Rogers	humanistic (client-centered)	focus is on ability of clients to help themselves; the therapist tries to create an emotionally safe atmosphere; the therapist must show warmth, unconditional acceptance, and empathy
Perls	humanistic (Gestalt)	active involvement in client's conversations during sessions, feelings, and creating a "safe emergency"
Wolpe	systematic desensitization	a fear-reduction method that involves relaxation and graded exposure to condition a new response to the phobic stimulus
Ellis and Beck	cognitive therapy	faulty cognitions are seen as the cause of abnormal behavior; examples of erroneous patterns of thinking include selective abstraction, overgeneralization, arbitrary inference, magnification/minimization, personalization, and absolutistic thinking

Answers to Review At A Glance

1. psychotherapy
2. client
3. qualified
4. effectiveness
5. confidentiality
6. exploit
7. unconscious
8. consciousness
9. relaxed
10. ego
11. interpret
12. free association
13. interpreted
14. dream interpretation
15. latent
16. resistance
17. transference
18. catharsis
19. interpersonal
20. feelings
21. communication
22. relationships
23. depression
24. awareness
25. client-centered
26. hidden emotions
27. warm
28. unconditionally
29. empathy
30. reflection
31. advice
32. Gestalt
33. self-awareness
34. safe emergency
35. behavior
36. learned
37. adaptive
38. systematic desensitization
39. progressive relaxation training
40. graded exposure
41. imagine
42. in vivo
43. virtual reality
44. operant conditioning
45. social skills
46. role playing
47. model
48. positive reinforcement
49. assertiveness
50. cognitive
51. behaviors
52. cognitions
53. selective abstraction
54. overgeneralization
55. arbitrary inference
56. magnification/minimization
57. personalization
58. absolutistic
59. anxiety
60. bulimia
61. depression
62. feminist

63. anger	76. insight	89. psychosurgery
64. independent	77. intimacy	90. prefrontal lobotomy
65. self-esteem	78. communication	91. infrequently
66. skills	79. rules	92. cingulotomy
67. feminist	80. medical therapies	93. stigma
68. group therapy	81. drug	94. private
69. encouragement	82. Thorazine	95. certification
70. advice	83. neurotransmitters	96. effectiveness
71. interact	84. neural	97. specific
72. family	85. electroconvulsive therapy	98. ethnic
73. family system	86. memory	99. gender
74. family	87. confusion	
75. function	88. depression	

Sample Answers for Short Answer Questions

1. **Describe similarities and differences between psychoanalysis and humanistic psychotherapy.**

   Both approaches focus on bringing into consciousness feelings of which the individual is unaware. However, whereas Freudians focus on the inborn unconscious, Rogers' approach suggests we deny awareness to information and feelings that differ from our concepts of self and ideal self. The methods used by humanistic psychotherapists also differ widely from those used by psychoanalysts. Whereas psychoanalysis uses techniques such as free association, resistance, transference, and so on, client-centered psychotherapists emphasize reflection. Gestalt psychotherapists tend to use a more confrontational and challenging approach, a concept referred to by Perls as a "safe emergency."

2. **Describe the use of systematic desensitization in reducing phobias.**

   Systematic desensitization involves two steps: progressive relaxation training, a method of deeply relaxing the body; and graded exposure, in which the client is exposed to progressively more fearful situations while learning to master anxiety at each step.

3. **List and describe "maladaptive cognitions" that, according to cognitive therapists, contribute to depression.**

   Aaron Beck has suggested the following erroneous thinking patterns are involved in depression: selective abstraction, basing one's thinking on a small detail; overgeneralization, reaching a general conclusion based on a few bits of evidence; arbitrary inference, reaching a conclusion based on little or no logical evidence; magnification/minimization, blowing comments out of proportion or minimizing positive comments made by others; personalization, viewing external events as being directly related to you; and absolutistic thinking, viewing the world in extremes (good or bad), when a more moderate view is more rational.

Multiple-Choice Answers

1. The answer is *C*. The definition of psychotherapy technically does not include medical treatment methods such as medication or surgery.

2. The answer is *B*. In behavior therapy, an important assumption is that psychological problems are the result of unfortunate learning experiences. A goal of behavior therapy is to unlearn abnormal ways of behaving.

3. The answer is *B*. The issue of fees for providing psychological services is not addressed in the text. It is, however, of special interest to consumers of psychological services.

4. The answer is *B*. Under some circumstances, the courts can require psychotherapists to reveal confidential information.

5. The answer is *C*. At $100 or more per hour, why is it called *free* association? Catharsis refers to the release of pent-up emotional energy. Resistance occurs when patients express opposition to the process of psychoanalysis. In transference, the patient in psychoanalysis comes to regard the therapist in ways that resemble the patient's feelings toward other significant adults.

6. The answer is *D*. Transference is interpreted by the psychoanalyst to give the patient additional insight into his or her situation.

7. The answer is *B*. Catharsis is not really a technique of psychoanalysis; instead, this brief relief from psychic discomfort is considered a benefit of psychoanalysis.

8. The answer is *C*. Interpersonal therapy also differs from traditional psychoanalysis in that it minimizes discussion of the past and does not involve interpretation of the individual's relationship with the therapist.

9. The answer is *D*. Research suggests this approach is as effective as antidepressant medication, and with fewer side effects.

10. The answer is *B*. Empathy, genuine warmth, and unconditional positive regard are important in client-centered therapy in creating a safe atmosphere.

11. The answer is *B*. According to client-centered therapists, the emphasis is on the ability of clients to help themselves. The goal of the therapist is to create an atmosphere conducive to this process. This is considerably different from the goal of psychoanalysis (option *A* of the question), or Gestalt therapy (option *C*), or behavior therapy (option *D*).

12. The answer is *C*. Client-centered therapists steadfastly avoid giving advice to clients. They believe that clients can solve their own problems once the problems have entered awareness.

13. The answer is *C*. The goal of Gestalt therapy is to help the client achieve greater self-awareness. Unlike the client-centered approach, Gestalt therapy involves challenging and confronting the client.

14. The answer is *B*. Systematic desensitization uses progressive relaxation and graded exposure to help clients learn to extinguish a fear response to phobic stimuli.

15. The answer is *B*. Systematic desensitization is a process in which the client learns not to fear a formerly phobic stimulus. The procedure involves learning to relax in the presence of progressively more threatening stimuli. The technique was pioneered by Joseph Wolpe.

16. The answer is *A*. Reflection is a technique used in client-centered therapy in which the therapist attempts to reflect back the emotions being expressed by the client. The other approaches in the question are behavior therapy techniques.

17. The answer is *B*. Assertiveness training seeks to teach individuals how to more effectively express feelings to others and/or to deal with interpersonal problems. Role playing is often used in this situation.

18. The answer is *D*. The assumption of behavior therapy is that abnormal behavior has been learned. Therapy, then, focuses on learning new behaviors.

19. The answer is *B*. Magnification is the cognitive process of blowing things out of proportion.

20. The answer is *C*. Overgeneralization is the process of reaching a general conclusion based on a few specific bits of evidence.

21. The answer is *D*. In most studies, cognitive therapy was found to be superior to either the traditional psychoanalytic or humanistic approaches.

22. The answer is *B*. The assumption of cognitive therapy is that it is a person's maladaptive beliefs and expectations about situations, rather than the situations themselves, that cause abnormal behavior.

23. The answer is *B*. The principles of feminist psychotherapy are increasingly being integrated into other forms of psychotherapy.

24. The answer is *D*. In addition, feminist psychotherapy encourages women to view themselves as powerful and to define themselves independently of their roles as wives, mothers, and daughters.

25. The answer is *D*. Group therapists can follow any of these approaches to psychotherapy.
26. The answer is *A*. Individual therapy is generally more appropriate for those with complex problems.
27. The answer is *D*. The family therapist attempts to solve the problems of each family member by focusing on the functioning of the family as a whole.
28. The answer is *B*. Thorazine belongs to a class of drugs called the phenothiazines. The introduction of these drugs in the 1950s helped to revolutionize the treatment of schizophrenia.
29. The answer is *D*. Although ECT seems to be effective with severely depressed patients, nobody seems to know exactly why.
30. The answer is *A*. Temporary or permanent memory loss and confusion continue to be side effects of ECT.
31. The answer is *D*. Prozac belongs to a class of drugs known as SSRIs, or selective serotonin reuptake inhibitors.
32. The answer is *D*. According to the text, seeking a professional who is board certified may not guarantee the therapist will be competent, but it helps to reduce uncertainty in choosing a therapist.
33. The answer is *D*. Eclectic therapists are skilled in a variety of therapeutic techniques. This doesn't necessarily make them the best. Student counseling centers generally provide high-quality services to students at moderate cost. It is true that in many states virtually anybody can call themselves a counselor or therapist, but only licensed individuals can call themselves psychologists or psychiatrists.
34. The answer is *C*. According to the Smith and Glass study, systematic desensitization had the largest average effect. As a group, behavior therapy techniques also seemed to provide the largest average effect.
35. The answer is *D*. Research suggests that the quality of treatment and whether or not one is receiving necessary treatment depend to a large extent on one's ethnicity, gender, and race.

Answers to True-False Questions

1. F
2. T
3. T
4. F
5. T

6. T
7. F
8. T
9. F
10. F

Part VII The Social Context

Chapter 16   Social Psychology

Learning Objectives

1.   Define social psychology. (p. 606)

2.   Describe how groups can contribute to deindividuation, and identify the conditions under which a bystander will get involved. (p. 606)

3.   Distinguish between social loafing and social facilitation. (p. 608)

4.   Discuss the ways in which groupthink and polarization affect group problem solving. (p. 609)

5.   Define conformity, and identify the factors that increase group conformity. (p. 610)

6.   Describe social roles and social norms, and discuss Zimbardo's prison study. (p. 611)

7.   Define obedience, and discuss Milgram's research on obedience. (p. 613)

8.   Identify the three components of attitudes. (p. 616)

9.   Identify characteristics of the speaker, the message, and the listener that affect persuasion. (p. 617)

10.   Identify techniques used in persuasion. (p. 620)

11. Define cognitive dissonance, and discuss its impact on behavior and attitude change. (p. 621)

12. Discuss the relationship between prejudice and stereotypes, and describe how stereotypes affect our attributions about other people's behavior. (p. 622)

13. Distinguish among the explanations for prejudice, and identify some effective techniques for combating prejudice. (p. 623)

14. Identify the primacy effect, and discuss the impact of emotions on person perception. (p. 629)

15. Explain the attribution process, and describe the fundamental attribution error. (p. 630)

16. Identify the general factors that influence attraction, including proximity, similar and complementary characteristics, competence, physical attractiveness, mutual liking, and gender differences. (p. 630)

17. Identify the roles played by expectations and equity in maintaining relationships. (p. 634)

18 (From the Application section) Discuss the implications of the gender discrimination lawsuit filed against PriceWaterhouse. (p. 638)

Chapter Overview

Social psychology is the branch of psychology that studies individuals as they interact with others. One topic of interest to social psychologists is the influence that others have on individual behavior. Among the group processes discussed are deindividuation, social loafing, social facilitation, group polarization, and groupthink.

Social psychologists have also studied group phenomena such as our tendency to conform to group pressure, the importance of social roles in our lives, and our tendency to obey authority figures.

Attitudes are beliefs that predispose us to behave in certain ways. Attitudes are learned from direct experience and from others. The persuasiveness of messages is determined by the characteristics of the speaker (credibility, attractiveness, and intent), the message (fear appeals and two-sided arguments), and the listeners (intelligence, need for social approval, esteem, and audience size). People are persuaded by such techniques as the "foot-in-the-door" and by "low-balling."

Cognitive dissonance theory has been proposed to explain the process of attitude change. According to Festinger, when behavior and attitudes are inconsistent, attitudes often change to match the behavior rather than the other way around.

Prejudice is a negative attitude based on inaccurate generalizations about a group of people. The inaccurate generalization on which the prejudice is based is called a stereotype. Stereotypes are harmful, because they take away our ability to treat each member of a group as an individual and because they lead to faulty attributions.

Friendship and love are powerful social phenomena based on the process of person perception. The process of person perception is complicated by the ways in which we gather and use information about others. Different people will perceive the same individual differently because of differences in interpreting the individual's characteristics. Negative information is generally weighted more than positive information in person perception. First impressions, also known as the primacy effect, generally influence person perception more than information learned about the person at a later date. Prolonged exposure to the person, the passage of time, and knowledge about primacy effects all can reduce the effects of the primacy effect. Person perception is also influenced by the emotional state of the perceiver.

Social behavior is strongly influenced by the attribution process. The fundamental attribution error involves our tendency to underestimate the impact of situations on others while more easily seeing its impact on ourselves. Although many factors ensure that each individual's perception of an individual will be unique, there are some general factors that partly determine to whom we will be attracted: proximity, similar and complementary characteristics, competence, physical attractiveness, and mutual liking. The attribution process is also involved in the perception of others. One aspect of the attribution process is deciding if a person's behavior is caused by the situation (a situational attribution) or by a trait of the person (a dispositional attribution).

Two major factors that determine whether a relationship will last are the differences between what you expect to find in a relationship and what you actually find, and the degree to which the relationship is equitable.

According to Susan Fiske, there are three sources of gender-based job discrimination: (1) evaluations of job performance are influenced by gender stereotypes; (2) narrow expectations for behavior created by stereotypes lead to discrimination; and (3) faulty attributions based on gender stereotypes operate in the workplace.

Key Terms Exercise

For each of the following exercises, match the key terms on the left with the correct definitions on the right. Page references to the text follow the terms so that you may refer to the text for any items you answer incorrectly or do not understand completely. You may check your responses immediately by referring to the answers that follow each exercise.

Definition of Social Psychology/Groups and Social Influence

_____ 1. social psychology (p. 606)
_____ 2. deindividuation (p. 606)
_____ 3. diffusion of responsibility (p. 608)
_____ 4. social loafing (p. 608)
_____ 5. social facilitation (p. 608)

a. a process in which group membership leaves one feeling anonymous and unidentifiable
b. the effect of being in a group that reduces an individual's sense of personal responsibility
c. the branch of psychology that studies individuals as they interact with each other
d. the tendency for individuals to work less hard when they are members of a group
e. improved performance on individual projects that sometimes occurs for a member of a group

ANSWERS
1. c   4. d
2. a   5. e
3. b

Groups and Social Influence

_____ 1. polarization (p. 609)
_____ 2. groupthink (p. 609)
_____ 3. conformity (p. 610)
_____ 4. obedience (p. 613)

a.   yielding to group pressure even when no direct request to comply has been made
b.   doing what one is told by people in authority
c.   the tendency for group discussion to make beliefs and attitudes more extreme
d.   faulty group decision making that often occurs in tightly knit, cohesive groups

ANSWERS
1. c
2. d
3. a
4. b

Attitudes and Persuasion

_____ 1. attitudes (p. 616)
_____ 2. persuasion (p. 617)
_____ 3. sleeper effects (p. 617)
_____ 4. cognitive dissonance (p. 621)
_____ 5. prejudice (p. 622)
_____ 6. stereotype (p. 622)
_____ 7. attribution theory (p. 623)

a.   the process of changing another person's attitudes through arguments and related means
b.   beliefs that predispose us to act and feel in certain ways
c.   an inaccurate generalization upon which a prejudice is based
d.   a negative attitude based on inaccurate generalizations about a group of people
e.   the potential for low credibility speakers to gain credibility after a period of time
f.   the theory that people tend to look for explanations for their own behavior and that of others
g.   the discomfort that results from inconsistencies between attitudes and behavior

ANSWERS
1. b   5. d
2. a   6. c
3. e   7. f
4. g

Interpersonal Attraction: Friendship and Love

_____ 1. person perception (p. 628)
_____ 2. primacy effect (p. 629)
_____ 3. fundamental attribution error (p. 630)
_____ 4. attribution (p. 630)
_____ 5. situational attribution (p. 630)
_____ 6. dispositional attribution (p. 630)
_____ 7. equity theory (p. 635)

a. the theory that partners will be comfortable in a relationship only when the ratio between their perceived contributions and benefits is equal
b. the process of forming impressions of others
c. the tendency to weigh first impressions heavily in forming opinions about other people
d. the process of attributing behavior to some external cause
e. the process of making judgments about the causes of behavior
f. the process of attributing behavior to an internal motive or trait
g. the tendency to credit our successes to our own talents, but attributing our failures to difficult circumstances

ANSWERS

1. b   5. d
2. c   6. f
3. g   7. a
4. e

Review At A Glance
(Answers to this section may be found on page 304)

Definition of Social Psychology/Groups and Social Influence

The branch of psychology that studies individuals as they interact with others is called ___(1)___ psychology. The group process in which a person feels anonymous and unidentifiable is called ___(2)___. In this state, people are less aware of their own ___(3)___ and less concerned with what others think. According to Latané and Darley, bystanders who are considering helping out in an emergency use a ___(4)___ _____ with several steps. The first step is

___(5)___; the next step is ___(6)___ the situation as an emergency; the bystander must assume ___(7)___ for helping, must know how to help and, finally, must decide to help. ___(8)___ factors affect the second and third stages of the decision process. Groups can create a ___(9)___ of ___(10)___.

Working individually in the presence of others sometimes improves performance; this is called ___(11)___ _____. When group performance is measured, individuals often exert less effort than when individual effort is measured; this phenomenon is called ___(12)___ _____.

Research suggests that the presence of others improves performance on ___(13)___ tasks and impairs performance on ___(14)___ tasks. A widely cited explanation of this phenomenon is the ___(15)___ level of ___(16)___. According to Janis, faulty group decision making, especially in cohesive groups, is called ___(17)___. Three key factors related to groupthink are the process of ___(18)___, the ___(19)___ of the members of the group, and the ___(20)___ of the group.

We generally offer less ___(21)___ advice when we are alone with the person seeking advice; when groups discuss the same issues, however, they are likely to offer ___(22)___ advice. Group discussion of issues often pushes our opinions toward the extremes, a process called ___(23)___.

The size of the group affects the interactions among the group members. In smaller groups, members engage in ___(24)___ dialogues, whereas in larger groups members are more likely to engage in ___(25)___ monologues.

Under many circumstances, individuals yield to group pressure, even when no direct request to comply has been made; this is called ___(26)___. In a study of conformity conducted by Asch, participants conformed to the group at least part of the time in ___(27)___ percent of the cases. People conform to gain ___(28)___, avoid punishment or to gain ___(29)___.

Sherif's study involving autokinetic effects found that participants not only went along with others' judgments, but actually ___(30)___ their own judgments. The following factors affect group conformity: (1) ___(31)___ of the group, (2) ___(32)___ groups, (3) cultural factors, and (4) gender. Zimbardo's prisoner-guard study underscored the importance of ___(33)___ in our lives. Our behavior is also affected by the spoken and unspoken rules called social ___(34)___.

Stanley Milgram has conducted research on ___(35)___. Participants believed they were participating in a learning experiment and were asked to administer electric shocks to a learner when the learner made a mistake. Milgram found that ___(36)___ percent of the participants gave the highest possible shock. Further studies found that the percentage of obedient participants declined (1) when the victim was in the same room, (2) when the ___(37)___ of the experimenter was reduced, (3) when the experimenter gave instructions by ___(38)___, and (4) when the participant was in the presence of other ___(39)___ participants. Although groups can produce negative effects, they can also be ___(40)___.

Attitudes and Persuasion

Beliefs that predispose people to act and feel in certain ways are called ___(41)___. This definition has three important components: (1) ___(42)___, (2) feelings, and (3) ___(43)___ to behave. Attitudes are learned from our experiences (they often are ___(44)___ conditioned) and from others.

Logic may be one of the least important qualities in determining the ___(45)___ of a communication. The qualities of persuasive communication fall into three categories: characteristics of the ___(46)___, of the ___(47)___, and of the ___(48)___. Among the characteristics of the speaker, Aronson and Golden found that the speaker's ___(49)___ is important to the persuasiveness of the communication. The key is whether the speaker is a credible source of ___(50)___ about the specific argument. Although speakers who are low in credibility are ineffective at first, they often influence opinions after a period of time through ___(51)___.

When advertisers use glamorous celebrities to help sell their products, they are using another persuasive characteristic of the speaker- ___(52)___. The persuasiveness of attractive speakers is limited to relatively ___(53)___ issues.

When the speaker is obviously trying to change an opinion, he or she will be less persuasive. This characteristic is referred to as ___(54)___ and helps to explain the use of the ___(55)___ _____ testimonials in television commercials.

One characteristic of the message that influences persuasiveness is an appeal to ___(56)___. Listeners will respond favorably to a fear-inducing persuasive communication only if (1) the emotional appeal is ___(57)___, (2) the listeners believe the fearful outcome is likely to happen to them, and (3) the message offers a way to ___(58)___ the fearful outcome. Another factor that influences persuasiveness relates to presenting different ___(59)___ of an argument.

When speaking to an audience that agrees with your position, the message will be more persuasive if you do not present ___(60)___ _____ of the argument; however, it's generally better to give both sides of the argument if the audience is initially ___(61)___ to your position.

The way in which problems are ___(62)___ has a strong influence on how we solve these problems.

The following characteristics of listeners help to determine the persuasiveness of an argument. (1) Generally, less ___(63)___ people are easier to persuade; however, if the message is complex, more intelligent listeners are easier to persuade. (2) People with a high need for ___(64)___ _____ are generally easier to persuade. (3) People with low ___(65)___-_____ are sometimes easier to persuade. (4) People are easier to persuade when listening to the message in a ___(66)___; larger groups are easier to persuade than smaller groups; (5) recent studies have found no gender differences in ___(67)___. People who agree to a small request are more likely to agree to a second, larger request; this forms the basis for the ___(68)___-_____-_____-_____ technique. In a related approach, you are initially offered a reasonable deal, and, after accepting it, the deal is changed; this is called the ___(69)___-_____ technique. Sometimes, important differences exist between our attitudes and our ___(70)___. When behavior and attitudes are inconsistent, ___(71)___ often change to become more consistent with behavior. Cognitive dissonance theory, proposed by Festinger, states that inconsistencies between attitudes and behavior are ___(72)___; people will change their attitudes to reduce this discomfort. To demonstrate cognitive dissonance, Festinger asked participants to perform a boring ___(73)___-_____ task for an hour, and then to tell the next participant that the task was interesting. Half of the participants were paid $20 and half were paid $1. When participants were asked how interesting the task really was, the most positive attitudes were expressed by the group that experienced cognitive dissonance—those that were paid ___(74)___. Research suggests cognitive dissonance may explain changes in attitudes toward ___(75)___ issues.

A harmful attitude that is based on generalizations about a group of people is called ___(76)___. The inaccurate generalization on which the prejudice is based is called a ___(77)___. Stereotypes are harmful for three reasons: (1) they take away our ability to treat each member of a group as an individual; (2) they lead to narrow ___(78)___ for behavior; and (3) they lead to faulty ___(79)___. Attribution theory states that people tend to attribute all behavior to some ___(80)___. Social psychologists have proposed the following explanations for why prejudice occurs: (1) people compete for scarce resources, according to ___(81)___ _____ theory; (2) the world is divided into two groups, __(82)__ versus __(83)__, perpetuated partly because it bolsters the self-esteem of those with weak __(84)__-_____; and, (3) prejudice is __(85)__ from others. Among the techniques suggested for combating prejudice are these: (1) __(86)__ prejudice; (2) control __(87)__ responses; and (3) increase __(88)__ among prejudiced groups. In order for increased contact to be effective, several conditions must occur. The groups must be __(89)__ in status, members should view each other as __(90)__ of their respective groups, the tasks should be __(91)__, and the contact should be __(92)__.

Interpersonal Attraction: Friendship and Love

The process of forming impressions of others is called __(93)__ _____. People seem to go through a process of __(94)__ _____ to help calculate perceptions of others. Other things being equal, a person's __(95)__ qualities are weighted more heavily than their __(96)__ qualities.

The tendency to weigh first impressions heavily in forming opinions of other people is called the __(97)__ _____. The impact of the primacy effect is reduced by (1) prolonged __(98)__ to a person, (2) passage of __(99)__, and (3) __(100)__ of primacy effects.

The emotional state we are in also affects person perception. __(101)__ emotional states lead to greater attraction to others than negative emotions do.

The tendency to underestimate the impact of situations on others, while more easily seeing it in ourselves is called the __(102)__ _____ error. The process of making judgments about what causes people to behave as they do is called __(103)__. When an explanation for behavior is based on an external cause, it is called a __(104)__ attribution; when the explanation is based on an internal motive, it is called a __(105)__ attribution. We tend to attribute the behavior of others to __(106)__ causes. People who live in East Asian collectivistic cultures are less likely to make the __(107)__ _____ error than people who live in individualistic Western cultures.

There are several general determinants of interpersonal attraction. An important factor is __(108)__ or geographical closeness. We are attracted to those people who have __(109)__ values, interests, and attitudes. We are attracted to opposites, however, when those opposite characteristics __(110)__ our own characteristics. It's also more flattering and attractive to be liked by someone who holds __(111)__ views than by someone holding similar views.

With regard to competence, we are more attracted to __(112)__ than to incompetent people; however, we are less attracted to those who are seen as being too competent.

Concerning physical attractiveness, people tend to be attracted to physically __(113)__ people. In the early stages of attraction between dates, physical attractiveness seems to be the __(114)__ important factor. In a study in which men thought they were talking to beautiful women, the men talked in a more __(115)__ way. Furthermore, the men apparently induced the women to act in a more __(116)__ way.

People tend to choose mates who closely match themselves in __(117)__ _____. Physical beauty is a highly __(118)__ quality. As we get to like people better, we begin to think they are more beautiful. Liking somebody often leads to liking in return; this is the basis for __(119)__ _____.

Recent surveys suggest that both men and women tend to feel that being in love is necessary for marriage.

However, women tend to place more emphasis on their romantic partner's ___(120)___, character, and education; men place a greater emphasis on ___(121)_____. People tend to evaluate the same characteristics in others in the different ways.

Two factors are important in maintaining relationships. The first concerns the difference between expectations and ___(122)___ in relationships. One common source of unfilled expectations is the shift from passionate love to ___(123)___ love. Expectations can fail to match ___(124)___ because people change over time. A second factor in maintaining relationships is whether the partners in a relationship feel that the ratio of their perceived contributions and benefits is ___(125)___. This is called ___(126)_____. Although the benefits the two people receive from one another do not have to be equal, the ___(127)___ between the benefits and contributions must be equal. Also, the benefits and contributions each person receives are based on their ___(128)___. If either member of the relationship perceives the relationship to be inequitable, he or she will either try to restore ___(129)___ or leave the relationship.

Application of Psychology: Stereotypes and Discrimination in the Workplace

According to Susan Fiske, there are three sources of gender-based job discrimination: (1) evaluations of job performance are influenced by the ___(130)___ we hold regarding the two genders; (2) the narrow expectations for appropriate behavior encouraged by stereotypes can contribute to workplace ___(131)___; and (3) faulty attributions based on ___(132)_____ operate in the workplace. The courts have upheld lawsuits brought against employers who discriminate against employees based on ___(133)___ and on other stereotypes. Some studies suggest prejudicial stereotypes can have ___(134)___ effects in the workplace; these stereotypes usually make life difficult for those experiencing prejudice, but occasionally it helps them.

Concept Check

Fill in the missing components of the following concept box. The correct answers are located in the "Answers" section at the end of the chapter.

Classic Social Psychology Research

Psychologist	Social Psychology Area	Research Findings
Asch	conformity	
Zimbardo		Zimbardo's mock prison experiment had to be stopped after six days because participants lost the ability to differentiate between role playing and self
Milgram	obedience	
Festinger	cognitive dissonance	

Extending the Chapter: Psychology, Societal Issues, and Human Diversity

These questions may be assigned to you. Whether or not they are assigned, they are designed to be challenging questions to encourage you to think independently about the material in the chapter. Many of the questions have no right or wrong answers.

I.   From the "Applications of Psychology" section

1.   Summarize the three sources of gender-based job discrimination presented by Susan Fiske in testimony to the U.S. Supreme Court.

2.   Describe the paradoxical effects of prejudicial stereotypes in the workplace.

II.   Psychology, Societal Issues, and Human Diversity

1.   If you were an advertiser, how would you apply the research information on persuasion in order to influence the behavior of consumers?

2.   Describe some ways in which the Internet potentially will affect social relationships.

3.   How would you have reacted had you been a participant in the Milgram, Asch, or Zimbardo studies? If any of these studies were to be repeated today, would participants react differently? Explain your answer.

4.   Will our knowledge of interpersonal attraction ever reach a point at which we can accurately predict which individuals will like or love each other? Why or why not?

5.   In what ways does our society benefit from having members who conform and who are obedient? In what ways are conformity and obedience potentially dangerous to our society?

6.   (From the Human Diversity section) What can be done to minimize the stereotypes between able-bodied students and students with physical challenges?

Practice Quiz

The practice quiz consists of three sections: 1) Short answer questions, 2) Multiple-choice questions, and 3) True-False questions. At the end of the chapter you will find suggested answers to the short answer questions, answers and explanations for the multiple choice questions, and answers to the true-false questions.

Short Answer Questions

1.   Describe the dynamics that occur when groups engage in problem solving.

_____

_____

2.   List the characteristics of the speaker that influence the persuasiveness of a communication.

_____

_____

3. Distinguish between situational and dispositional attributions, and explain the fundamental attribution error.

_____

_____

Multiple-Choice Questions

1. Which of the following topics would be studied by a social psychologist?
   a. attractions to other people
   b. the influence of groups on individual behavior
   c. the formation of stereotypes and prejudices
   d. all of the above
   LO 1

2. The process in which group membership makes a person feel anonymous and unidentifiable is called
   a. deindividuation.
   b. social facilitation.
   c. social loafing.
   d. polarization.
   LO 2

3. Each of the following is part of Latané and Darley's decision tree *except*
   a. noticing that something is out of the ordinary.
   b. interpreting an event as an emergency.
   c. assuming responsibility.
   d. consulting with other bystanders.
   LO 2

4. According to Latané and Darley, the diffusion of responsibility created by groups affects what part of the decision tree?
   a. noticing that something is out of the ordinary
   b. assuming responsibility for helping
   c. interpreting the event as an emergency
   d. deciding whether or not the bystander knows how to help
   LO 2

5. According to Latané and others, how does the effort exerted by individual members of a group compare with the effort exerted by individuals acting alone?
   a. Individuals exert more effort when in a group than when alone.
   b. There are no significant differences.
   c. Individuals exert less effort when in a group than when alone.
   d. Approximately half work harder when in a group and half work harder when alone.
   LO 3

6. Which of the following is more likely to occur with easily accomplished tasks?
   a. groupthink
   b. social facilitation
   c. group polarization
   d. deindividuation
   LO 3

7. In a heated group discussion of politics, Carla is somewhat surprised to hear herself arguing for a more extreme position than she usually does. According to social psychologists, this is due to
   a. polarization.
   b. groupthink.
   c. social loafing.
   d. Both *a* and *c*.
   LO 4

8. Which of the following is a common result of group discussion?
   a. polarization
   b. taking more extreme positions
   c. suggestions involving riskier options
   d. all of the above
   LO 4

9. When compared with larger groups, discussion in smaller groups is more likely to be characterized by
   a. serial monologues.
   b. interactive dialogues.
   c. polarization.
   d. both *a* and *c*.
   LO 4

10. The study of conformity by Asch found that
    a. most participants refused to conform.
    b. most participants conformed at least part of the time.
    c. participants conformed both privately and outwardly.
    d. both *b* and *c*.
    LO 5

11. Many people will sacrifice their own beliefs rather than risk rejection by their peers. This is demonstrated by
    a. Zimbardo's prison study.
    b. Festinger's theory of cognitive dissonance.
    c. Asch's research on conformity.
    d. Ellis's theory of maladaptive cognitions.
    LO 5

12. Zimbardo's prison experiment has underscored
    a. the inherent aggressive potential of humans.
    b. the kindness of some individuals in spite of a hostile environment.
    c. the extent to which our behavior is influenced by social situations.
    d. all of the above.
    LO 6

13. The experiment performed by Zimbardo in which prisoners and guards conformed to the social roles was a _____ experiment.
    a. comparative.
    b. correlational.
    c. naturalistic.
    d. survey.
    LO 6

14. Milgram's studies demonstrated that people do what they are told when
    a. they are under the grip of polarization.
    b. they are unsure of themselves.
    c. asked by an authority figure.
    d. in stressful situations.
    LO 7

15. In Milgram's research on obedience, the willingness of participants to deliver shocks decreased when
    a. the prestige of the experimenter was reduced.
    b. the experimenter gave instructions by telephone.
    c. the participant was in the presence of other participants who refused to deliver shocks.
    d. all of the above
    LO 7

16. Each of the following is a component of the term attitude *except*
    a. beliefs.
    b. facts.
    c. feelings.
    d. dispositions to behave.
    LO 8

17. Sleeper effects refer to the persuasiveness of
    a. speakers who are low in credibility.
    b. speakers who are high in credibility.
    c. intelligent listeners.
    d. emotional appeals.
    LO 9

18. Which of the following approaches can make a fear-inducing communication more powerful?
    a. if the emotional appeal is strong
    b. if the listeners believe the feared outcome is likely to happen to them
    c. if the message offers a way to avoid the fearful outcome
    d. all of the above
    LO 9

19. Each of the following is true regarding characteristics of an audience and persuasiveness of a message *excep.t*
    a. more intelligent audiences are generally easier to persuade.
    b. audiences with a high need for approval are generally easier to persuade.
    c. bigger audiences generally are easier to persuade.
    d. audiences with moderate levels of self-esteem are easier to persuade than people with high self-esteem.
    LO 9

20. Jason is a salesperson who begins his sales presentation with a small, reasonable request. He is using
    a. cognitive dissonance.
    b. low-balling.
    c. the door-in-the-foot technique.
    d. the foot-in-the-door technique.
    LO 10

21. According to Festinger, cognitive dissonance is a phenomenon that
    a. we seek because it makes us comfortable.
    b. we seek to avoid because it makes us uncomfortable.
    c. occurs when attitudes and behavior are consistent with each other.
    d. relies on attribution theory.
    LO 11

22. According to Festinger and others, cognitive dissonance results in
    a. attitudes shifting to become more consistent with behavior.
    b. attitudes shifting to become less consistent with behavior.
    c. behavior shifting to become more consistent with attitudes.
    d. behavior shifting to become less consistent with attitudes .
    LO 11

23. Stereotypes influence our explanations of behavior, according to
    a. cognitive dissonance theory.
    b. attribution theory.
    c. attitudinal modification theory.
    d. dispositional modification theory.
    LO 12

24. Which of the following is a harmful effect of stereotypes?
    a. Stereotypes permit us to treat each member of a group as an individual.
    b. Stereotypes take away our ability to treat each member of a group as an individual.
    c. Stereotypes lead to faulty attributions.
    d. both *b* and *c*
    LO 12

25. In a classic study, Sherif and colleagues showed that prejudice can arise between randomly divided students. This study demonstrated the explanation for prejudice called
    a. unrealized conflict.
    b. groupthink.
    c. us versus them.
    d. deindividuation.
    LO 13

26. Increased contact between prejudiced groups is more effective if
    a. the groups are equal in status.
    b. the groups are engaged in cooperative tasks.
    c. the contact is informal.
    d. all of the above.
    LO 13

27. The expression "First impressions are lasting impressions" refers to which person perception variable?
    a. the primacy effect
    b. negative information
    c. individual differences in the evaluation of others
    d. emotional states
    LO 14

28. In the process of person perception, negative information
    a. tends to leave a stronger impression.
    b. tends to leave a weak impression.
    c. is outweighed by positive traits.
    d. is not as long-lasting as positive information.
    LO 14

29. Ron is a salesperson who just made a big sale. He tells another salesperson, "The reason I'm such a successful salesperson is that I'm cheery, friendly, kind, and loyal." Which type of attribution is Ron using?
    a. equitable attribution
    b. dispositional attribution
    c. situational attribution
    d. none of the above
    LO 15

30. Which of the following is a component of the fundamental attribution error?
    a. the tendency to underestimate the impact of situations on others' behavior
    b. the tendency to overestimate the impact of situations on others' behavior
    c. the tendency to attribute our own behavior to situations
    d. both *a* and *c*
       LO 15

31. Which of the following expressions best summarizes interpersonal attraction?
    a. "birds of a feather flock together"
    b. "opposites attract"
    c. both *a* and *b*
    d. none of the above
       LO 16

32. With regard to romantic attraction, women place more emphasis than men on each of the following factors *except*
    a. intelligence.
    b. character.
    c. physical attractiveness.
    d. education.
       LO 16

33. According to the text, many relationships move predictably from
    a. companionate to passionate.
    b. passionate to companionate.
    c. romantic to passionate.
    d. sublime to ridiculous.
       LO 17

34. Equity theory states that partners will be comfortable in their relationship when the ratio between their perceived contributions and benefits is
    a. balanced.
    b. uneven.
    c. similar.
    d. equal.
       LO 17

35. The evidence presented by psychologist Susan Fiske in the Ann Hopkins lawsuit against PriceWaterhouse suggested which of the following as a source of gender-based job discrimination?
    a. Job performance is influenced by stereotyped beliefs about the genders.
    b. Narrow expectations for behavior encouraged by gender stereotypes can contribute to workplace discrimination.
    c. Faulty attributions based on gender stereotypes operate in the workplace.
    d. all of the above
       LO 18

True-False Questions

_____1. The feeling of anonymity that can arise from being in a group is called deindividuation.

_____2. Groupthink refers to the improved decision making that occurs in groups when compared with individuals.

_____3. Milgram's studies on obedience showed that highly-educated participants were far less likely to obey.

_____4. Cognitive dissonance helps to explain shifts in attitude.

_____5. Social psychologists have found that us-versus-them prejudice bolsters the self-esteem of those with weak self-images.

_____ 6. Social psychologists believe that minimizing contact among members of prejudiced groups can help reduce prejudice.

_____ 7. Prolonged exposure and the passage of time can help reduce primacy effects.

_____ 8. According to the fundamental attribution error, we tend to underestimate the importance of situations on the behavior of others.

_____ 9. Residents of East Asian collectivistic cultures are far more likely to make the fundamental attribution error.

_____10. Relationships tend to shift over time from companionate to passionate love.

ANSWERS SECTION

Concept Check

Classic Social Psychology Research

Psychologist	Social Psychology Area	Research Findings
Asch	conformity	conformity to group pressure was widespread
Zimbardo	social roles	Zimbardo's mock prison experiment had to be stopped after six days because participants lost the ability to differentiate between role playing and self
Milgram	obedience	Milgram found that a majority of participants were willing to obediently shock another participant to the maximum 450-volt level
Festinger	cognitive dissonance	participants participated in a boring spool-stacking experiment; those who were paid the least expressed the most positive attitudes

Answers to Review At A Glance

1. social
2. deindividuation
3. behavior
4. decision tree
5. noticing
6. interpreting
7. responsibility
8. Social
9. diffusion
10. responsibility
11. social facilitation
12. social loafing
13. easy
14. difficult
15. optimal
16. arousal
17. groupthink
18. polarization
19. cohesiveness
20. size
21. risky
22. riskier
23. polarization
24. interactive
25. serial
26. conformity
27. 74
28. rewards
29. information
30. changed
31. size
32. unanimous
33. social roles
34. norms
35. obedience
36. 65
37. prestige
38. telephone
39. disobedient
40. advantageous
41. attitudes
42. beliefs
43. dispositions
44. classically
45. persuasiveness
46. speaker
47. listener
48. message
49. credibility
50. information
51. sleeper effects
52. attractiveness
53. unimportant
54. intent
55. hidden camera
56. fear
57. strong
58. avoid
59. sides
60. both sides
61. unfavorable
62. framed
63. intelligent
64. social approval
65. self-esteem
66. group
67. persuasibility
68. foot-in-the-door
69. low-ball
70. behavior
71. attitudes
72. uncomfortable
73. spool-stacking
74. $1
75. political
76. prejudice
77. stereotype
78. expectations
79. attributions
80. cause
81. realistic conflict
82. us
83. them
84. self-images
85. learned
86. recognize
87. automatic
88. contact
89. equal
90. typical
91. cooperative
92. informal
93. person perception
94. cognitive algebra
95. negative
96. positive
97. primacy effect
98. exposure
99. time
100. knowledge
101. Positive
102. fundamental attribution
103. attribution
104. situational
105. dispositional
106. dispositional
107. fundamental attribution
108. proximity
109. similar
110. complement
111. opposite
112. competent
113. beautiful
114. most
115. sociable
116. likable
117. physical attractiveness
118. subjective
119. mutual liking
120. intelligence
121. physical attractiveness
122. reality
123. companionate
124. reality
125. equal
126. equity theory
127. ratio
128. perceptions
129. equity
130. stereotypes
131. discrimination
132. gender stereotypes
133. gender
134. paradoxical

Sample Answers for Short Answer Questions

1. **Describe the dynamics that occur when groups engage in problem solving.**

   Group problem solving leads to a variety of phenomena. Social loafing refers to the tendency of group members to work less hard when the performance of the entire group is measured. There are instances when working in the presence of others can improve performance; this is referred to as social facilitation. Group discussions can lead to polarization, which refers to making our opinions on issues more extreme. Another group dynamic, more likely to occur in cohesive groups, is called groupthink; groupthink refers to the faulty decision making that may occur in groups.

2. **List the characteristics of the speaker that influence the persuasiveness of a communication.**

   An important factor in determining the persuasiveness of a communication is the perceived credibility of the speaker. Even low credibility speakers can sometimes be persuasive as the result of sleeper effects. Speakers who are attractive, popular, famous, and likable will be more persuasive. Speakers are less persuasive if their intent is to change your opinion, particularly if the speaker stands to gain by persuading you.

3. **Distinguish between situational and dispositional attributions and explain the fundamental attribution error.**

   Situational attributions refer to explanations for a person's behavior based on external causes (the situation), whereas dispositional attributions are explanations for behavior based on personal characteristics of the individual (he's shy, she's witty, and so on). The fundamental attribution error is the tendency to underestimate the impact of situations on other people, while overestimating the impact of situations when it comes to explaining our own behavior.

Multiple Choice Answers

1. The answer is *D*. Social psychology studies individuals as they interact with others; therefore, all the topics mentioned in the question, and many others, are studied by social psychologists.
2. The answer is *A*. Deindividuation has helped explain behavior as dramatic as lynching.
3. The answer is *D*. A fourth part of the bystander's decision tree, in addition to choices *A, B,* and *C* in the question, is deciding whether or not the bystander knows how to help.
4. The answer is *B*. The diffusion of responsibility within a group affects the part of the decision tree in which a bystander would be willing to accept responsibility.
5. The answer is *C*. This phenomenon has been given the descriptive term *social loafing*.
6. The answer is *B*. This finding is consistent with the optimal levels of arousal, which indicate that easier tasks are easier to do when people are aroused.
7. The answer is *A*. Polarization refers to the fact that group discussions often lead its participants to take more extreme positions. Groupthink, a related process, refers to the fact that group decision making is subject to distorted, polarized thinking.
8. The answer is *D*. Group discussions can change the opinions of individual members in subtle, but powerful ways.
9. The answer is *B*. Interactive dialogues refer to the process wherein group members communicate with each other in reciprocal and connected ways. Members of larger groups are more likely to engage in serial monologues, or speeches that present their views without necessarily responding to the views of other group members.
10. The answer is *B*. Although Asch's study found that the majority of participants conformed to the group, most of the conformity was outward. When participants were allowed to make their judgments in private, there was little evidence of group conformity.
11. The answer is *C*. Asch's research reminds us about the tendency to yield to group pressure, even in the absence

of a direct request to comply.

12. The answer is *C*. Zimbardo and his colleagues were surprised at the extent to which the participants assumed their roles. In a short time, many of the guards exhibited very aggressive behavior and many of the prisoners became despondent.

13. The answer is *C*. It is considered naturalistic because the researchers simulated a realistic environment. Consider how the results would differ had Zimbardo merely surveyed students regarding how they would react if they were placed in such a situation.

14. The answer is *C*. In the studies, Milgram, in his lab coat and with a stern demeanor, acted as the authority figure.

15. The answer is *D*. An additional factor that lowered participants' obedience was when the victim was in the same room as the participant.

16. The answer is *B*. According to the text, attitudes are beliefs that predispose one to act and feel in certain ways.

17. The answer is *A*. Research has suggested that even speakers who are low in credibility can come to influence opinion after a period of time. This has been referred to as the sleeper effect.

18. The answer is *D*. Emotional appeals can be highly persuasive if all of the elements mentioned in the question are present.

19. The answer is *A*. Research suggests that less intelligent people are generally easier to persuade, except when the message is complex and difficult to understand.

20. The answer is *D*. The low-ball technique involves starting with a low-priced offer; the price begins to work its way up as the salesperson changes the deal ("Oh, you want an *engine* with that car?"). In the foot-in-the-door technique, you initially respond favorably to a small, reasonable request, which somehow turns into a larger and larger request.

21. The answer is *B*. When our attitudes and behavior are inconsistent, we are motivated to reduce the resulting discomfort. One way to accomplish this involves changing our attitudes.

22. The answer is *A*. According to cognitive dissonance theory, when attitudes and behavior are inconsistent, it creates discomfort; this discomfort is reduced when attitudes are modified to become consistent with behavior.

23. The answer is *B*. Attribution theory also explains why attitudes shift to become consistent with behavior, but the focus here is on our need to explain everything that happens or to attribute events to some cause.

24. The answer is *D*. Stereotypes are inaccurate generalizations that serve as the basis for prejudice.

25. The answer is *C*. According to some psychologists, us-versus-them prejudice helps to strengthen the prejudiced individual's self-esteem.

26. The answer is *D*. Another important factor is the extent to which group members view each other as being typical of their respective groups.

27. The answer is *A*. The impact of the primacy effect can be reduced with prolonged exposure, the passage of time, or knowing about primacy effects.

28. The answer is *A*. In person perception, the bad generally outweighs the good.

29. The answer is *B*. Situational attributions explain behavior as based on some external (environmental) cause, whereas dispositional attributions explain behavior as based on personal characteristics of the person. If Ron had attributed his selling success to a superior product, he would be using a situational attribution.

30. The answer is *D*. The fundamental attribution error involves attributing others people's behavior to dispositional causes ("that's just how they are") while readily attributing our own behavior to situations.

31. The answer is *C*. This seemingly contradictory answer can be explained as follows: Although we are attracted to people who hold similar values and attitudes, we also are attracted to opposites when those opposite characteristics complement our own.

32. The answer is *C*. The emphasis on different factors in romantic relationships holds up across different generations in the United States and across other cultures as well.

33. The answer is *B*. Companionate love, while less intense than passionate love, is a blend of friendship, intimacy, commitment, and security.

34. The answer is *D*. According to equity theory, the actual perceived benefits people receive from each other do not have to be equal, but the *ratio* of these perceived benefits and contributions must be equal.

35. The answer is *D*. The lawsuit, brought successfully against PriceWaterhouse, was the first in which psychological testimony on gender stereotyping was introduced as evidence.

Answers to True-False Questions

1. T	6. F
2. F	7. T
3. F	8. T
4. T	9. F
5. T	10. F

Chapter 17 Psychology Applied to Business and Other Professions

Learning Objectives

1. Identify the role of industrial-organizational psychologists in the workplace. (p. 644)

2. Identify the types of measures that are commonly used for employee selection and evaluation. (p. 645)

3. Compare the validity of various job selection measures. (p. 649)

4. Discuss the challenges involved in the fair selection of female and ethnic minority employees. (p. 651)

5. Describe the relationship between job satisfaction, happiness, and productivity; identify the strategies that are designed to improve these factors. (p. 653)

6. Identify the traits of successful leaders, and describe the challenges to women and minorities as they pursue leadership positions. (p. 656)

7. Identify the goals of human factors engineering. (p. 657)

8. Discuss the contributions of health psychology to the workplace. (p. 658)

9. Describe the contributions of psychology to employee training, computer-assisted instruction, and advertising and marketing. (p. 659)

10. Identify the field of environmental psychology. (p. 661)

11. Discuss the role of environmental psychology in preventing the further destruction of our environment. (p. 664)

12. Identify the characteristics of defendants, plaintiffs, and jury members that affect conviction rates. (p. 668)

13. Discuss the importance of psychological factors in presenting evidence and in interrogating criminal suspects. (p. 671)

14. Identify the activities of educational psychologists. (p. 673)

15. Discuss the effects of mastery learning and intelligent tutoring systems on children's education. (p. 674)

16. Describe the goals of Project Follow Through, and identify its significance to education. (p. 675)

17. Discuss the importance of person × situation interaction in the classroom and describe the use of criterion-referenced testing in the classroom. (p. 675)

18. Identify the goals of mainstreaming. (p. 676)

Chapter Overview

Psychologists who work for businesses are known as industrial-organizational psychologists. They are frequently found in personnel departments and are involved in employee selection and training. Interviews play an important role in the evaluation of job applicants and in the assessment of current employees for possible promotion. Industrial-organizational psychologists have helped to educate managers about the nature and limitations of interviews. Intelligence tests frequently are used in the assessment and selection process. Tests that measure specific skills and abilities are also frequently used. Performance tests, which measure actual manual performance, are used to predict behavior on the job.

Techniques that are used to assess the performance of current employees include job performance ratings and checklists. Assessment centers are frequently used to evaluate applicants for management positions. Research has indicated that intellectual ability tests are the most valid method of evaluating applicants for complex jobs, but performance tests are more valid when the job is less complex. Psychologists have studied systematic gender biases in employee selection; such prejudice tends to exclude women from the most powerful occupational roles. Ethnic biases have likewise excluded members of minority groups from positions of power.

Psychologists have helped improve employee satisfaction, happiness, and productivity by improving supervisory style, managerial organization, and physical conditions. Techniques such as participative management and management by objectives have been promoted by industrial-organizational psychologists, as well as methods to reduce social loafing. Human factors engineering is a branch of industrial-organizational psychology whose goal is the design of more user-friendly machines and controls. Health psychologists have also worked with businesses to improve the health-related aspects of the work environment. Other psychologists have worked to improve the efficiency of training techniques, including the use of computer simulation.

In recent years, environmental psychologists have become involved in the effort to create environments where people can live and work more happily, healthfully, and productively. For example, environmental psychologists have helped design workspaces, and have helped evaluate alternative designs of college dormitories.

Environmental psychologists are working to change human behavior in order to solve environmental problems. Three areas of particular concern involve overpopulation, resource depletion, and pollution. Behavioral, cognitive, and humanistic approaches have been applied by environmental psychologists to increase pro-environmental awareness and behavior.

In recent years, psychologists have also begun to apply their methods to the practice of law in the courtroom. They have found that the characteristics of defendants and plaintiffs affect the likelihood of conviction and the harshness of the sentence. They have also found that certain types of jury members are more likely to vote for conviction and to recommend harsher sentences than other types. Psychological factors are involved in the effectiveness of courtroom evidence. Eyewitness testimony is the most convincing evidence, but eyewitnesses can and do make mistakes. Research has also determined that the order in which testimony is presented can make a difference in the outcome of a trial.

Psychologists serve the field of education in three ways: as professors who help train teachers, as consultants on testing programs, and as school psychologists employed by school systems. Mastery learning is an approach based on Benjamin Bloom's belief that children should progress from one learning task to the next only when they have fully mastered the previous one. Project Follow Through is a federally funded experiment to test new ways of educating economically disadvantaged children. An approach to testing called criterion-referenced testing is designed to determine if a child can meet the minimum criteria for a specific educational objective. Public Law 94–142, the mainstreaming law, established that every child has a right to public education, regardless of his or her disability. Its successor is called the Individuals with Disabilities Education Act.

Key Terms Exercise

For each of the following exercises, match the key terms on the left with the correct definitions on the right. Page references to the text follow the terms so that you may refer to the text for any items you answer incorrectly or do not understand completely. You may check your responses immediately by referring to the answers that follow each exercise.

Psychology and Work (I)

_____ 1 industrial-organizational psychologist (p. 644)

_____ 2. performance tests (p. 647)

_____ 3. job performance ratings (p. 648)

_____ 4. assessment centers (p. 649)

_____ 5. simulated management task (p. 649)

a. an evaluation method in which the candidate plays the role of a manager

b. tests that measure actual manual performance

c. a psychologist who studies organizations and seeks to improve the human benefits of business

d. assessment of an employee's skills and ability to perform simulated management tasks are conducted here

e. designed by industrial-organizational psychologists to transform a supervisor's rating of actual job performance into a numerical evaluation

ANSWERS

1. c   4. d
2. b   5. a
3. e

Psychology and Work (II)

_____ 1. in-basket exercise (p. 649)
_____ 2. structuring (p. 654)
_____ 3. participative management (p. 654)
_____ 4. management by objectives (p. 654)
_____ 5. human factors engineering (p. 657)

a. a management method in which employees are given specific tasks to accomplish but freedom in deciding how to accomplish the tasks
b. activities of managers that organize and direct the work of employees
c. the branch of industrial-organizational psychology interested in the design of machines to be operated by humans
d. a simulation in which the candidate is given a problem that might show up in a manager's in-basket
e. a management method that involves all employees in decision making

ANSWERS
1. d   4. a
2. b   5. c
3. e

Environmental Psychology and Psychology Applied to Education

_____ 1. environmental psychologist (p. 661)
_____ 2. educational psychology (p. 673)
_____ 3. school psychologists (p. 673)
_____ 4. mastery learning (p. 674)
_____ 5. intelligent tutoring systems (p. 674)
_____ 6. criterion-referenced testing (p. 676)
_____ 7. mainstreaming (p. 676)

a. the branch of psychology that deals with learning and educational testing
b. the practice of integrating children with special needs into regular classrooms
c. specialists who are employed by school systems
d. testing that determines if a child meets the minimum standards of a specific educational objective
e. the concept that children should never progress to the next learning task until they have mastered the more basic one
f. a psychologist who studies the effect of the physical environment on behavior and mental processes
g. a computerized, individualized tutoring system based on the mastery approach

ANSWERS
1. f   5. g
2. a   6. d
3. c   7. b
4. e

Review At A Glance

(Answers to this section may be found on page 324)

Psychology and Work: Employees and Managers Are People

A psychologist who studies organizations and seeks to improve the human benefits of work is an ___(1)___-_____ psychologist. Industrial-organizational psychologists are often found in ___(2)___ departments.

The traditional heart of the process of evaluating job applicants and assessing current employees for possible promotion is the ___(3)___. Unstructured interviews used in employment screening are not good predictors of future ___(4)___ _____. A somewhat more valid approach is the ___(5)___ interview.

Tests of general intelligence are frequently used to evaluate job candidates, especially for ___(6)___ jobs. Tests that measure the actual manual performance necessary for the job to be performed are called ___(7)___ tests.

The most widely used method of assessing current employees is the ___(8)___ _____ rating. These measurements rate employees on different ___(9)___ of job performance. In another approach, the supervisor checks those items that are characteristic of the employee; this approach uses a ___(10)___.

Candidates for management positions are often evaluated by a team of upper managers and outside psychological consultants in an evaluation technique that takes place at ___(11)___ _____. This approach evaluates candidates while they are carrying out ___(12)___ _____ tasks. A frequently used simulation presents the candidate with problems that might show up in the in-basket of the new management position. This simulation is called the ___(13)___-_____ exercise.

A summary of research on the validity of job selection measures indicates that tests of ___(14)___ _____ are the best predictors of job success. The least valid selection method is the unstructured ___(15)___. No validity at all was found for ___(16)___ tests and handwriting analyses. According to a model proposed by Schmidt and Hunter, intellectual ability has its greatest impact by influencing how well and how quickly the employee ___(17)___ the job. Tests of intellectual ability are best for selecting employees for complex jobs, whereas the best selection techniques for less complex jobs are ___(18)___ tests. Schmidt and Hunter have also found that employees who score high in ___(19)___ learn job knowledge more quickly and perform their jobs better.

According to research by Pratto and others, occupations that produce high financial rewards and/or power over others tend to be filled by ___(20)___ in the United States, whereas careers that involve helping others are mostly held by ___(21)___. According to Pratto, women are more likely to ___(22)___ jobs that help others. Also, women are less likely to be hired when they seek ___(23)___ jobs. Members of racial and ethnic minorities have also been victims of ___(24)___ in employee selection. Research suggests that ___(25)___ racial prejudice is declining, but prejudice remains a barrier to fair employment for members of some race-ethnic groups. Attention has focused on the role played by ___(26)___ _____ scores in excluding members of ethnic minority groups from some occupations. Some psychologists view the differences in average scores between whites and ethnic minority groups as the result of ___(27)___ _____ in the test. Other psychologists view the differences as a reflection of ___(28)___ in our society.

According to Wagner, the differences between ethnic groups in actual ___(29)___ _____ is smaller than the difference in intelligence scores. According to the text, when testing experienced employees, ethnic bias can be minimized by emphasizing tests of ___(30)___ _____ and skills.

The goals of psychologists working in business include improving the happiness and the job ___(31)___ of employees and improving their ___(32)___. Researchers have determined that job ___(33)___ is not usually related to how well employees perform. When employees are ___(34)___, however, they are more productive. Job satisfaction can improve organizational performance in the following ways: (1) reducing the rate at which employees quit, called ___(35)___; (2) reducing the rate at which employees fail to show up for work, called ___(36)___; (3) improving relations between labor and ___(37)___; (4) improving the ability of businesses to ___(38)___ good employees; and (5) improving the ___(39)___ of the business.

Managers have developed several strategies to improve job satisfaction, happiness, and productivity. The supervisory style of effective managers includes being considerate and ___(40)___; in addition, they spend time organizing and directing the work of their employees, called ___(41)___.

Another strategy to improve job satisfaction, happiness, and productivity focuses on managerial organization. For example, employees at every level are actively involved in decision making in the ___(42)___ _____ method. In another approach, employees are given specific goals, but are provided considerable freedom in how they meet those goals; this approach is called ___(43)___ _____ _____.

Another approach to improving job satisfaction and productivity focuses on understanding the influence of lighting, noise, and other ___(44)___ _____.

Three suggestions to reduce social loafing are (1) to provide ___(45)___ incentives not tied to the group, (2) emphasizing that each member's contributions are unique and ___(46)___, and (3) making the task ___(47)___ and discouraging social loafing in every group member. Studies of social loafing in different cultures have found it to be

___(48)___.

The influence of one group member on the others as they work toward shared goals defines ___(49)___. Psychologists have found that successful leaders share the following traits: drive, honesty, leadership ___(50)___, intelligence, and creativity. Leaders also have the ___(51)___ to adapt to different situations. Although women tend to be more ___(52)___ in the workplace, they tend to be undervalued in leadership positions. Minorities may experience difficulties attaining leadership positions because of ___(53)___ in the workplace. Women and minorities continue to experience the ___(54)___ _____ in American organizations.

People who are successful entrepreneurs engage in less ___(55)___-_____thinking, have excellent ___(56)___ skills, and tend to be ___(57)___ attractive.

A branch of industrial-organizational psychology whose goal is the design of machines that can be more easily and efficiently operated by human beings is called ___(58)___ _____ engineering. The design of controls and the organization of ___(59)___ periods are examples of areas studied by human factors engineers. A future direction of human factors engineering is the development of ways to more effectively cope with such human ___(60)___ as advancing age, illness, and paralysis.

Many American businesses have found that programs to improve employee health are not only good for employees, but lead to greater ___(61)___ and fewer ___(62)___ among employees.

Psychological principles have been used in developing various training methods for employees. Many training procedures currently make use of ___(63)___ ___. Psychologists have also contributed to the fields of ___(64)___ and ___(65)___.

Environmental Psychology

Psychologists who are involved in the field that strives to create environments where people can live and work more happily, healthfully, and productively are called ___(66)___ psychologists. For example, environmental psychologists have helped to evaluate the effectiveness of a popular type of office design called the ___(67)___ ___ format. Psychologists have also helped to evaluate the design of college dormitories. One study found that the architecture of college dormitories can influence ___(68)___ over long periods of time.

Environmental psychologists are working to change human behavior in order to solve environmental problems. Three areas of particular concern involve ___(69)___, resource depletion, and ___(70)___ and waste management. An approach to environmental problems that attempts to alter behaviors through the principles of learning is the ___(71)___ approach. The behavioral approach attempts to apply an ___(72)___ approach to real-world problems. Cognitive and humanistic approaches attempt to change environmentally relevant behavior by changing peoples' ___(73)___ or by appealing to their higher ___(74)___. Some psychologists have called for an ___(75)___ of the various approaches in order to have the most impact on environmental protection.

Psychology and Law: The Behavior of Juries and Witnesses

Psychologists and the legal profession have worked together for many years: in testimony at trials and in hearings to commit patients to mental hospitals. Recently, psychologists have turned their attention to the practice of law in the ___(76)___. Thus far, the most extensive psychological study has focused on the ___(77)___ ___.

Research findings on the characteristics of defendants suggest that justice is not ___(78)___. Juries tend to be influenced by characteristics of defendants such as ___(79)___, ___(80)___, and ___(81)___. In mock civil trials, younger and male plaintiffs were awarded ___(82)___ settlements than were older and female plaintiffs. Mock jurors also awarded larger settlements when the defendant was presented as being more ___(83)___ for the injury. Mock jurors also tended to award larger settlements when the defendant was a ___(84)___.

Certain types of jury members are more likely to vote for conviction and to recommend harsher sentences than others. Generally, juries are ___(85)___ to their own kind. There is also evidence that jurors who believe in the ___(86)___ ___ are more likely to convict than those who do not. The outcome of a trial can be affected by the ___(87)___ in which evidence is presented. Police also use psychological techniques in ___(88)___ criminal suspects.

Psychology and Education: Better Teaching and Testing

Although educational psychology is an old field, its current excitement stems from recent innovations that may enhance the education of children with ___(89)___ _____. Benjamin Bloom has proposed an educational concept, suggesting that children should never progress to a new learning task until they have fully mastered the more basic one. This approach, called ___(90)___ _____, is effective for slow-learning children and does not penalize ___(91)___ children. The use of computers to serve as individualized tutors for students is called the ___(92)___ tutoring system.

Each year in school, children from disadvantaged families learn about ___(93)___-_____ of what the average child learns. A program designed to help educate economically disadvantaged children was ___(94)___ _____ _____. The most successful Project Follow Through project used a teaching method that included ___(95)___.

The concepts relating to person × situation interaction also apply to the ___(96)___.

A new approach to testing, designed to determine if a child can meet the minimum standards of a specific educational objective, is called ___(97)___-_____ testing. These tests play an important role in ___(98)___ and ___(99)___ teaching methods.

During the 1970s, Public Law 94–142 established that every child has a ___(100)___ to public education, regardless of his or her special needs. Whenever possible, children with special needs must be integrated into regular classrooms; this practice is called ___(101)___.

Concept Checks

Fill in the missing components of the following concept boxes. The correct answers are located in the "Answers" section at the end of the chapter.

Techniques to Select and Evaluate Employees

Technique	Description
interviews	
	these are widely used in hiring decisions by the government, the military, and the private sector
performance tests	
	in this approach, supervisors rate employees on a number of different dimensions
assessment centers	

Areas of Applied Psychology

Area of Applied Psychology	Description	Examples of Problems/Solutions
human factors engineering		designing gauges for airline pilots to maximize efficiency and safety
environmental psychology		
psychology and the law		characteristics of defendants, plaintiffs, and juries, and studies of the order in which evidence is presented
educational psychology		

Extending the Chapter: Psychology, Societal Issues, and Human Diversity

These questions may be assigned to you. Whether or not they are assigned, they are designed to be challenging questions to encourage you to think independently about the material in the chapter. Many of the questions have no right or wrong answers.

Psychology, Societal Issues, and Human Diversity

1. Identify three environmental protection issues described in the text, and discuss the efforts of psychologists to address these problems.

2. Select a machine or piece of equipment with which you are familiar, and describe it from a human factors psychology standpoint. Discuss the reasons for its overall design, and consider the reasons for the shape, color, and the style (consider also buttons, dials, switches, and so on). What suggestions would you make to improve the design?

3. Consider all the ways in which public policy impacts the workplace in terms of hiring, working conditions, promotions, salary, harassment, firing, and so on. To what extent is the workplace over-regulated by public policy? To what extent is the workplace under-regulated?

4. How should public policy address the special needs of families where both parents work, or of single-parent families where the parent must work?

Practice Quiz

The practice quiz consists of three sections: 1) Short answer questions, 2) Multiple-choice questions, and 3) True-False questions. At the end of the chapter you will find suggested answers to the short answer questions, answers and explanations for the multiple choice questions, and answers to the true-false questions.

Short Answer Questions

1. List and briefly describe ways in which industrial-organizational psychologists contribute to the business world.

   _____

   _____

2. List and briefly describe ways in which psychologists contribute to the legal profession.

   _____

   _____

3. List and briefly describe some of the ways educational psychology has helped to improve education.

   _____

   _____

Multiple-Choice Questions

1. Which of the following statements regarding industrial-organizational psychologists is true?
   a. They seek ways to help businesses produce more goods and services.
   b. They seek to increase job satisfaction.
   c. They try to fit the right person to the right job.
   d. all of the above
   LO 1

2. Assessment centers often evaluate candidates for promotion while they are
   a. eating lunch.
   b. carrying out orders from their supervisors.
   c. performing simulated management tasks.
   d. none of the above
   LO 2

3. Which of the following is an example of a simulated management task?
   a. the in-basket exercise
   b. intelligence tests
   c. job performance ratings
   d. job performance checklists
   LO 2

4. A "big five" personality trait that is associated with good job performance is
   a. extroversion.
   b. conscientiousness.
   c. neuroticism.
   d. intelligence.
   LO 3

5. Researchers have concluded that the most valid predictors of later job performance and success in job-training programs are
   a. tests of intellectual ability.
   b. derived from interviews.
   c. performance tests.
   d. projective personality tests.
   LO 3

6. According to Pratto, women in the United States hold a majority of the jobs that involve
   a. power.
   b. prestige.
   c. helping others.
   d. high financial rewards.
   LO 4

7. Alerting employers to the possible biases in employee selection is the job of
   a. Public Law 94-142.
   b. human factors psychologists.
   c. assessment centers.
   d. industrial-organizational psychologists.
   LO 4

8. The process of actively involving employees at every level in decision making is called
   a. management by objectives.
   b. participative management.
   c. structuring.
   d. both *a* and *c*.
   LO 5

9. According to the text, all of the following strategies are used to improve both job satisfaction and productivity *except*
   a. raising employees' salaries.
   b. improving supervisory style.
   c. improving managerial organization.
   d. improving physical conditions.
   LO 5

10. Which of the following is characteristic of management of objectives?
    a. Employees are given specific goals to achieve.
    b. Employees are given freedom in how they achieve their goals.
    c. Meeting and exceeding objectives often leads to bonuses.
    d. all of the above
    LO 5

11. Each of the following is an advantage of having employees with high job satisfaction *except*
    a. reduced employee turnover.
    b. reduced absenteeism.
    c. improved productivity.
    d. improved labor-management relations.
    LO 5

12. Studies of the workplace indicate that women do more of each of the following *except*
    a. interact with subordinates.
    b. develop networks.
    c. share information and power.
    d. make hasty decisions.
    LO 6

13. Of the following traits, which seems to be the most important for successful leadership?
    a. flexibility
    b. controlling
    c. manipulative
    d. introverted
    LO 6

14. The goal of human factors engineering is
    a. to find people in an organization who can work compatibly on projects.
    b. to design machines that can be more easily and efficiently operated by people.
    c. to design consumer products and packaging so that people will be more likely to purchase them.
    d. all of the above
    LO 7

15. Compared to persons who exercise regularly, sedentary persons are at twice the risk for____
    a. cancer.
    b. the common cold.
    c. cardiovascular disease.
    d. flu.
    LO 8

16. Companies that make the health of their employees a priority find
    a. they can attract healthy employees who will incur fewer health-related costs.
    b. they can save money by keeping employees healthy.
    c. that facilities for aerobic workouts and healthy foods offered in the cafeterias are used only by a small group of workers.
    d. both *a* and *b*.
    LO 8

17. Computer simulation has been effectively used in training
    a. sailors to operate submarines.
    b. pilots to fly aircraft.
    c. physicians to practice medical diagnoses.
    d. all of the above.
    LO 9

18. Psychologists who work in marketing and advertising deal with
    a. package design.
    b. advertising effectiveness.
    c. surveys of consumer preference.
    d. all of the above.
    LO 9

19. Environmental psychologists might conduct research on which of the following?
    a. an office landscape format
    b. the design of college dormitories
    c. psychological reactions to different wall colors
    d. all of the above
    LO 10

20. Research on office space organized around the office landscape concept found that workers
    a. were more productive.
    b. were more cooperative.
    c. interacted with each other more frequently.
    d. all of the above
    LO 10

21. According to research on the design of dormitories, which configuration led to increased interaction with other residents and more time spent in the dorms?
    a. traditional single corridors
    b. alternating rooms with males and females
    c. TV rooms and lounges on each floor
    d. suite design
    LO 10

22. Asking people to pledge to change their environmentally relevant behavior is an example of what approach to environmental protection?
    a. behavioral
    b. humanistic
    c. cognitive
    d. psychoanalytic
    LO 11

23. According to the text, which of the following represents a threat to the environment?
    a. overpopulation
    b. resource depletion
    c. pollution
    d. all of the above
    LO 11

24. Juries are most likely to acquit defendants with which characteristics?
    a. physically attractive, high social status, and nonwhite
    b. physically attractive, low social status, and white
    c. physically attractive, high social status, and white
    d. physically unattractive, high social status, and nonwhite
    LO 12

25. Which type of jury member is more likely to vote for conviction?
    a. younger
    b. better educated
    c. lower social status
    d. more liberal
    LO 12

26. Research has shown that information that is presented in a courtroom is more potent when
    a. it is presented first.
    b. it is presented last.
    c. it is presented by a male attorney.
    d. it is presented by a female attorney.
    LO 13

27. Educational psychologists
    a. treat children who have severe emotional disturbances.
    b. help design educational programs.
    c. help design educational testing programs.
    d. both *b* and *c*.
    LO 14

28. Mainstreaming and mastery learning are innovations of
    a. organizational psychology.
    b. environmental psychology.
    c. educational psychology.
    d. human factors engineering.
    LO 14

29. The mastery learning approach
    a. is equally effective for all children, regardless of their ability.
    b. is particularly effective for bright children.
    c. is particularly effective for slow-learning children.
    d. works best with children of average ability.
    LO 15

30. Intelligent tutoring systems use
    a. highly intelligent, well-trained volunteers.
    b. computers programmed to serve as individual tutors.
    c. teachers and educational psychologists in after-school programs.
    d. parents trained to tutor children.
    LO 15

31. School children from disadvantaged families learn about _____ that of the average child.
    a. one-eighth
    b. one-third
    c. one-half
    d. two-thirds
    LO 16

32. The most successful Project Follow Through project
    a. designed challenging curriculum by using reading levels above the children's current level.
    b. used the threat of failure to motivate children.
    c. used practice methods to help students remember what they had learned.
    d. involved children from high-income and low-income families.
    LO 16

33. The goal of criterion-referenced testing is to
    a. measure whether a child can meet the minimum standards of an objective.
    b. help to compare children.
    c. help to determine a child's grade level.
    d. all of the above
    LO 17

34. According to research, anxious children perform better
    a. in structured classrooms.
    b. in unstructured classrooms.
    c. with less experienced teachers.
    d. with more experienced teachers.
    LO 17

35. Mainstreaming
    a. refers to integrating children with special needs into regular classrooms.
    b. was legislated by Public Law 94–142.
    c. requires children to be educated in the least restrictive environment.
    d. all of the above
    LO 18

True-False Questions

_____ 1. Research suggests that unstructured interviews are excellent predictors of future job performance.

_____ 2. According to Pratto, women and men are likely to seek different types of occupations.

_____ 3. According to Wagner, intelligence tests used for employee selection are biased against members of minority groups.

_____ 4. Job satisfaction is strongly related to job productivity.

_____ 5. Studies of social loafing indicate it is universal.

_____ 6. Research suggests the single corridor design concept of dorms is superior to the suite design.

_____ 7. In mock trials, older, female plaintiffs were awarded larger financial settlements than were younger, and male plaintiffs.

_____ 8. Research suggests the order in which evidence is presented can influence jury decisions.

_____ 9. Teachers using a mastery learning approach would not let children progress from one learning task to the next until they master the more basic task.

_____10. The behavioral approach to environmental protection focuses on changing cognitions and values regarding the environment.

ANSWERS SECTION

Concept Check

Techniques to Select and Evaluate Employees

Technique	Description
interviews	conversations in which the employee or applicant is asked about prior training and education, future goals, and so on; unstructured interviews used in employment screening are not good predictors of future job performance
intelligence tests	these are widely used in hiring decisions by the government, the military, and the private sector
performance tests	these are based on the assumption that the most valid way to evaluate applicants is while they are actually working; the Perdue Pegboard is an example
job performance ratings	in this approach, supervisors rate employees on a number of different dimensions
assessment centers	these are used to evaluate candidates as they carry out simulated management tasks, such as the in-basket exercise

Areas of Applied Psychology

Area of Applied Psychology	Description	Examples of Problems/Solutions
human factors engineering	design of machines to be operated by human beings	designing gauges for airline pilots to maximize efficiency and safety
environmental psychology	studies the effects of the physical environment on behavior and mental processes	designing offices and workspaces to maximize efficiency for employees
psychology and the law	psychological factors in trials, testimony in sanity hearings	characteristics of defendants, plaintiffs, and juries, and studies of the order in which evidence is presented
educational psychology	principles of learning, cognition, and so on to help improve education	mastery learning, intelligent tutoring systems, criterion-referenced testing, mainstreaming

Answers to Review At A Glance

1. industrial-organizational
2. personnel
3. interview
4. job performance
5. structured
6. complex
7. performance
8. job performance
9. dimensions
10. checklist
11. assessment centers
12. simulated management
13. in-basket
14. intellectual ability
15. interview
16. projective
17. learns
18. performance
19. conscientiousness
20. men
21. women
22. seek
23. powerful
24. prejudice
25. overt
26. intelligence test
27. cultural bias
28. prejudice
29. job performance
30. job knowledge
31. satisfaction
32. productivity
33. satisfaction
34. happy
35. turnover
36. absenteeism
37. management
38. recruit
39. reputation
40. communicative
41. structuring
42. participative management
43. management by objectives
44. physical conditions
45. individual
46. indispensable
47. easier
48. universal
49. leadership
50. motivation
51. flexibility
52. democratic
53. racism
54. glass ceiling
55. counter-factual
56. social
57. physically
58. human factors
59. rest
60. frailties
61. productivity
62. absences
63. computer simulation
64. advertising
65. marketing
66. environmental
67. office landscape
68. friendships
69. overpopulation
70. pollution
71. behavioral
72. experimental
73. attitudes
74. motives
75. integration
76. courtroom
77. criminal trial
78. equal
79. income
80. attractiveness
81. race
82. larger
83. responsible
84. corporation
85. kinder
86. death penalty
87. order
88. interrogating
89. special needs
90. mastery learning
91. brighter
92. intelligent
93. two-thirds
94. Project Follow Through
95. positive reinforcement
96. classroom
97. criterion-referenced
98. evaluating
99. improving
100. right
101. mainstreaming

Sample Answers for Short Answer Questions

1. **List and briefly describe ways in which industrial-organizational psychologists contribute to the business world.**

   Industrial-organizational psychologists develop and use psychological measurements to assist in employee selection and evaluation. Psychologists have pointed out the flaws in using interviews, have suggested ways to use intelligence tests as well as tests of specific abilities and skills, have helped employers develop job performance ratings, and have consulted on the development of assessment centers. I/O psychologists have helped research gender and ethnic biases in employee selection, have helped design programs to improve job satisfaction, happiness, and productivity for employees, and have studied the traits of effective leaders. I/O psychologists are also involved in human factors engineering, advise employers about health programs in the workplace, assist in the training of employees, and consult on marketing and advertising issues.

2. **List and briefly describe ways in which psychologists contribute to the legal profession**.

   Psychologists have for many years been called upon to testify regarding an individual's sanity or competency to stand trial. Increasingly, psychologists are called upon to advise attorneys in such matters as jury selection and in the preparation of arguments to judges and/or juries. Psychologists have also studied and advised about the techniques for interrogating criminal suspects.

3. **List and briefly describe some of the ways educational psychology has helped to improve education.**

   Educational psychology is one of the oldest areas of psychology. Psychologists have historically been involved in the development of intelligence tests and have studied learning and memory. More recently, educational psychologists have contributed to the field of education by developing the mastery learning approach and have helped apply computer technology to education with intelligent tutoring systems. Educational psychologists have consulted on special programs like Project Follow Through, have improved the effectiveness of testing by developing criterion-referenced testing, and have consulted on ways to improve the efficacy of mainstreaming.

Multiple Choice Answers

1. The answer is *D*. Inasmuch as many of us will spend a good portion of our waking hours at work, it seems logical that industrial-organizational psychologists can have a dramatic impact on our lives.
2. The answer is *C*. One type of simulation often used in assessment centers is the in-basket exercise.
3. The answer is *A*. In the in-basket exercise, the candidate is given a simulated problem that might well show up in the in-basket of a manager.
4. The answer is *B*. Research suggests that conscientious employees learn job knowledge more quickly and perform their jobs better.
5. The answer is *A*. Hunter and Hunter also found performance tests and assessment centers were valid measures but were less useful than tests of intellectual ability.
6. The answer is *C*. According to Pratto's research, women are more likely to seek these kinds of careers, and women are less likely to be hired when they apply for more powerful jobs.
7. The answer is *D*. In addition to dealing with issues regarding employee satisfaction, motivation, and training, industrial-organizational psychologists help employers select the best person for the job.
8. The answer is *B*. Structuring refers to those managers who spend much of their time organizing and directing the work of their employees; management by objectives involves setting specific goals for employees to achieve.
9. The answer is *A*. Much research suggests that raising employees' salaries leads to only temporary improvements in job satisfaction and productivity.
10. The answer is *D*. Management by objectives is often used with a participative management strategy.
11. The answer is *C*. An important point in this section of the text is that job satisfaction is *not* related to how productive employees are. The text speculates that productivity is influenced by many factors.
12. The answer is *D*. Research suggests that women tend to be more democratic in the workplace. In spite of their effectiveness, however, women tend to be undervalued in leadership positions.
13. The answer is *A*. Other traits deemed useful for leadership roles include drive, honesty, leadership motivation, intelligence, and creativity.
14. The answer is *B*. While choices *A* and *C* might also involve industrial-organizational psychologists, *B* is a specific goal of human factors engineering.
15. The answer is *C*. Additional benefits of healthy employees include fewer missed days at work, fewer health care claims, and increased productivity.
16. The answer is *D*. By keeping employees happy and healthy, businesses typically can reduce turnover costs and increase productivity and profitability.
17. The answer is *D*. There seems to be no end to the possible applications for training with the use of computer simulation.
18. The answer is *D*. To be effective and competitive in today's marketplace, businesses consult with psychologists and others in designing product names, packaging, advertising, distribution, etc.
19. The answer is *D*. Architects and interior designers have often made good use of the findings of environmental psychologists.

20. The answer is *C*. Interestingly, workers who functioned for six months in an office landscape environment report they were less satisfied with their surroundings.
21. The answer is *D*. The suite design involves four rooms clustered around a lounge and bathroom.
22. The answer is *C*. An example of a humanistic approach is the appeal to higher motives. The behavioral approach uses the principles of learning and emphasizes the analysis of data in an effort to change behavior. There is hope for an approach that will eventually integrate the behavioral, cognitive, and humanistic approaches to environmental protection.
23. The answer is *D*. An important challenge to psychology is to change attitudes and behavior regarding the threats to our environment.
24. The answer is *C*. These same factors also affect the harshness of the sentence; perhaps it is not yet possible for all people to receive equal justice in the court system.
25. The answer is *B*. These are additional characteristics of jurors that make them more likely to vote for conviction: they are white, older, of higher social status, are more conservative, and strongly believe that authority and law should be respected.
26. The answer is *B*. Traditionally, the prosecutor in a trial presents to the jury last.
27. The answer is *D*. Although educational psychologists might help to identify children who have severe emotional disturbances, intensive treatment is typically left to clinical psychologists and psychiatrists.
28. The answer is *C*. Both mastery learning and mainstreaming began with innovations in the field of educational psychology. Mastery learning is the concept that learners should progress to the next learning level only after mastering the more basic level. Mainstreaming is the practice of integrating learners with special needs into regular classrooms.
29. The answer is *C*. The mastery learning approach suggests that children should not progress from one learning task to the next until they have mastered the more basic task.
30. The answer is *B*. Computers offer infinite patience, and they free up teachers to engage in other activities in the classroom.
31. The answer is *D*. These findings help us understand that, for many students, the cycle of poverty begins at an early age.
32. The answer is *C*. Project Follow Through was designed to help educate economically disadvantaged children. The successful programs made use of positive reinforcement and designed curriculum around the skills needed for reading, in addition to using practice methods to help students remember what they learned.
33. The answer is *A*. Criterion-referenced tests are designed to determine if a child can meet the minimum standards of a specific educational objective.
34. The answer is *A*. Research results like these remind us of the importance of the person × situation interaction.
35. The answer is *D*. The guiding principle behind Public Law 94–142 is that every child has the right to a public education regardless of his or her special need.

Answers to True-False Questions

1. F   6. F

2. T   7. F

3. T   8. T

4. F   9. T

5. T   10. F